CRYPTOGRAPHIC LIBRARIES FOR DEVELOPERS

CRYPTOGRAPHIC LIBRARIES FOR DEVELOPERS

ED MOYLE

DIANA KELLEY

CHARLES RIVER MEDIA, INC.
Hingham, Massachusetts

Cover Design: Tyler Creative

CHARLES RIVER MEDIA, INC.
10 Downer Avenue
Hingham, Massachusetts 02043
781-740-0400
781-740-8816 (FAX)
info@charlesriver.com
www.charlesriver.com

This book is printed on acid-free paper.

Ed Moyle and Diana Kelley: *Cryptographic Libraries for Developers*
ISBN: 1-58450-409-9

Library of Congress Cataloging-in-Publication Data

Moyle, Ed, 1973-
Cryptographic libraries for developers / Ed Moyle and Diana Kelley.
p. cm.
Includes index.
ISBN 1-58450-409-9 (alk. paper)
1. Computer software—Development. 2. Cryptography. I. Kelley, Diana, 1965- II. Title.
QA76.76.D47M72 2005
005.1—dc22

2005026626

Printed in the United States of America
05 7 6 5 4 3 2 First Edition

CHARLES RIVER MEDIA titles are available for site license or bulk purchase by institutions, user groups, corporations, etc. For additional information, please contact the Special Sales Department at 781-740-0400.

Requests for replacement of a defective CD-ROM must be accompanied by the original disc, your mailing address, telephone number, date of purchase and purchase price. Please state the nature of the problem, and send the information to CHARLES RIVER MEDIA, INC., 10 Downer Avenue, Hingham, Massachusetts 02043. CRM's sole obligation to the purchaser is to replace the disc, based on defective materials or faulty workmanship, but not on the operation or functionality of the product.

Contents

Acknowledgments

A number of people were instrumental in making this book a reality: Lisa Phifer for her assistance in editing and helping to create this material; Alan Borack, Adam Shostack, Larry Labella, Adam Emmet, and Mike Phillips, who provided formative ideas or helpful suggestions that influenced the direction and tone of the book; and the development teams we've worked with over the years, who could not help but influence the material presented here.

1 Introduction

In This Chapter

- Why We Wrote This Book
- Intended Audience
- How to Read This Book

This is not a security book, and, despite the title, it's not a cryptography book either. This is a *development* book. Almost every application today uses cryptography in some fashion, including word processors, compression utilities, and enterprise "business" software. Who is writing all that cryptography? Cryptographers? No, their purview is math, not development. Information security specialists? Rarely. Application developers write cryptography; developers who yesterday might have written a GUI, and tomorrow might be writing database access routines. As developers, our craft is simple: write readable, maintainable, and elegant software that makes our users' lives simpler, or makes our business more efficient. Solid development requires an entirely different set of skills than is required by those who spend their lives steeped in the mathematics of cryptography.

While writing this book, numerous people hearing the title said things like, "Cryptography, huh? Wow, you must have a mind for math." This assertion makes no sense. Would someone make a statement like, "Driving, huh? Wow, you must have a mind for mechanical engineering." Of course not. So why should using cryptography require any skills other than those we already have; for example, adapting our application to make use of someone else's code in a readable, maintainable, and elegant way? It shouldn't and it doesn't. You don't have to have a mind for math to use cryptography any more than you have to have a mind for mechanical engineering to drive a car, or be Edison to turn on a light bulb.

1.1 WHY WE WROTE THIS BOOK

We wrote this book because developers have no free time. In the course of developing applications, the authors of this book have on multiple occasions been asked to write software that uses cryptography for one reason or another. The first few weeks of this assignment are always the same: use trial and error to find out how to implement the cryptography, find out how to call it, and so on. Couple this with the fact that the documentation may be out of date, that each library has its own terminology, and you have something on the order of a month's work invested before you can even begin to write the software. That month, in our opinion, would be better spent trying to meet other deadlines rather than researching how a given cryptographic library works and experimenting with how to get it up and running.

Don't get us wrong, plenty of security books describe in painstaking detail each of the libraries we're going to be delving into here. However, learning everything there is to know about a particular library is not what we're after. We're interested in three things in this book:

- Giving developers as much of that "first month" back as possible by helping them select a library and *immediately* (without trial and error) be able to use it.
- Not taking for granted that a developer knows about security in order to do their job; the majority of the security concepts we need to write security software are hopefully laid out in a way developers can understand.
- Helping developers find the *essential* information about the library they will use without being bogged down by things they only might occasionally use.

1.2 INTENDED AUDIENCE

We don't expect you to know anything about security, math, or cryptography. However, a number of caveats, terms, and design decisions do require some understanding of information security, but we've tried to provide enough background so a developer can find those concepts here. If you are already familiar with some aspects of information security, that's all the better, but it's certainly not essential. We do, however, expect you to be fluent in at least one programming language, preferably Java, C, or C++. The material is readily applied to other languages as well, but most of the example code is in C, C#, C++, managed C++, Java, or J# (depending on section and context), both in the book and on the companion CD-ROM. We're also assuming that you're familiar with the common libraries and APIs for the language you're working in. For example, we expect Windows programmers to know about the Platform SDK, C developers to know how to use the standard C library, and Java developers to know about the Java API. We assume that you're somewhat familiar with sockets programming in your platform/language of choice; for example, Berkeley sockets in C/C++, java.net.Socket in Java, and Winsock 2 on Windows.

ON THE CD

1.3 HOW TO READ THIS BOOK

This book is divided into two sections: the first is about requirements and application design, and the second is about development and implementation. By "requirements and design," we mean that the goal of the first half of this book is to help you understand how your application's security requirements affect application design, what combination of security strategies meets the requirements, and how to select a library based on those strategies. In the second half, as we move into the material targeted toward the "development" phase, we've included usage information on the various libraries—not complete usage information by any means, but targeted usage information about the kinds of tasks we will most likely employ. Our goal is to provide reference source code for commonly used features, and enough general reference information so you can approach the product's user documentation with confidence to understand little-used features.

Like all technical books, we figure you'll probably "bounce around" from chapter to chapter, and we've tried to write the book accordingly. Specifically, we've tried to include "Bare Minimum" sections in the first half of the book during the descriptions of the security material so (in case you are reading out of order) you can easily refer back to those sections and get a concise description of a concept. We also understand that developers have varying levels of familiarity with information security. Therefore, we've tried to satisfy two goals at once: provide enough information so a developer who is unfamiliar can benefit, and make it easy for a developer who is familiar to skip ahead. We've tried to keep the pace lively and interesting if you decide to read straight through, but in most cases, we assume that you will target in on the material that is of greatest interest to you and most relevant to your application.

2 Security Concepts Developer Overview

In This Chapter

- Data Mapping
- Targets
- Threats
- Countermeasures
- Summary
- Selected Resources

The goal of all software is utility; in other words, as developers, it is our job to provide functionality to users (or to other software) they would not otherwise have. Security-aware software is no different: our job is to meet the needs of the business, except in this case, the needs of the business also include security of the business information assets. As developers, we are used to thinking about the "happy path," that path of execution that our software will take where everything performs as expected and there are no errors. There are also times when we are called on to think about the exception cases or "worst-case scenarios" when developing applications. For example, we are used to using highly error-prone support libraries where everything we want our application to do could fail unexpectedly through no fault of our software. Even when we perform extremely simple tasks (e.g., opening a file, allocating memory, writing to the screen), we always have in the back of our mind the knowledge that the routine we're calling to do these tasks could fail and "sweep the rug out" from under our application. For example, if we're opening a file for reading, we always check the return value to verify that the file is in fact open before attempting to read from it. Although the "happy path" dictates that the file will be there and it will contain the information we expect, a number of things could go wrong, and we check for them: if the file doesn't exist, if we don't have permissions, if the right data isn't in the file, and so forth. We don't usually have to stop and think why we perform this error checking; most of the time, checking for error conditions is second nature. In addition, many of the errors we check for are extremely unlikely to happen; for example, how often does `malloc()` fail? Yet, we still check to make sure the memory is valid before we write to it. We know that "best practice" dictates that we dot our Is and cross our Ts. Therefore, by validating that everything is functioning correctly (such as by checking the return value from a function that seldom fails), we save ourselves potential frustration later in the development process. In quite a few respects, adding application *security controls* is almost exactly like checking for application errors. Just as we make sure that erroneous or unsafe conditions in the application logic are accounted for, we'll also be examining how to make sure that unsafe conditions in the security logic are accounted for in our software. Sometimes, the security "error conditions" we are checking for will be as remote as a call like `malloc()` failing, and sometimes they will be much more likely—like a file not being readable. However, just as good development practice calls for checking the underlying call anyway, good security practice calls for addressing even an unlikely to occur security issue where possible. In authoring application logic, if an issue or bug cannot be fixed, we would document that in a "readme" or other form of deployment checklist. In much the same way, we'll document any "open" security issues so implementers are apprised and can work around any remaining issues we cannot specifically address in our application's software. Of course, the more likely a security issue is to appear, based on the way our application is implemented or designed, greatly affects the degree of security or insecurity (*risk*) inherent in our application, just as the more likely an unaccounted for error condition is to appear greatly impacts the likelihood of a failure in application logic. As developers of security functionality, we must understand ahead of time the adversarial conditions (*threats*) our application will face. At its most abstract, a threat is the potential that something negative might happen to or around our application that will impact the operation of our application and/or the business it supports. A *threat agent* is the person, event, or circumstance that causes the negative consequence to become a reality; in other words, the vehicle by which a potential threat is made real. For example, if our application processes credit card transactions, one possible threat would be the likelihood that thieves could steal that information. In this case, the stolen credit card data is the threat, and the thieves would be the threat agent. It is useful for us as developers to spend some time thinking about the threats our application will be designed to mitigate (prevent) when it is live and operational in the real world. Further, it is helpful for us to spend some time thinking about the threats that are outside our scope and won't be directly prevented by the functionality in our application (but could happen anyway). By understanding the latent threats associated with the application, we can document any remaining potential security issues and work around them through other methods during the implementation phases or deployment phases of our software development process. Throughout the first few chapters of this book, we outline some useful ways that we as developers can catalog, quantify, and address the particular erroneous security conditions that can occur in the software we write. We begin by understanding what our application does, how an attacker might seek to gain leverage against our application, and then discuss functionality we can build that addresses those issues specifically. Much later in this book, we go into specific, practical examples of how to implement some of the controls using the most commonly available security tools.

This section attempts to perform the first of those tasks: how to set up a framework for thinking about the threats our application might face, and to briefly outline some of the ways those threats might be realized. By understanding what we want to prevent ahead of time, we will immediately see how the tools and concepts we introduce in subsequent sections can be valuable in addressing some of these points. By determining up front what is in scope and what is not, we can save ourselves some time down the road, since we can approach the application security question with a clearly defined model of what functionality is the application's job and what security functionality is not.

To some degree, most (if not all) developers will already be familiar with a large amount of the material in this section; in today's world, security is not a new concept to the developer population. However, we ask those developers who are already familiar with this material to bear with us: the goal of this section is to level set the developers who are not familiar, and to bring a few new techniques to the table. By the end of this section, developers should be acquainted with the terminology associated with the concepts we'll be discussing, and understand some ways they can start to catalogue their own application(s) to save time as they introduce this functionality.

In this section, we present the developer with a number of security problems they will undoubtedly come across in developing secure applications. The solutions to these problems will become more apparent as we move into some of the design and development strategies in subsequent sections, but for the time being, we just want to develop a standard nomenclature and general familiarity of the types of security challenges we might face, and how/why these challenges arise in the applications we write.

2.1 DATA MAPPING

The first part of building any application is understanding what it is supposed to do. We understand this both formally and informally when it comes to application functionality, but it is also true when it comes to application security. Typically, we would initiate any new development activity by understanding the requirements as a formal or informal list of functionality the application is expected to implement. In the first part of this section, we discuss some of the most likely application security requirements that our applications will need to incorporate. We approach that discussion by understanding first the *threats* inherent in our application, and, as a subset of that discussion, look at likely areas within our application that are tantalizing targets to an attacker. In both cases, the goal is to categorize the potential security problems latent in a generalized system. These threats might be things we are already familiar with, or may be completely new. In either case, to understand our security requirements, we'll need to identify the "problem spots" first so we can start to address them with the tools that will be introduced in subsequent chapters. To satisfy the objective of understanding the threats, we start by creating a "road map" of the likely weak points in our application; in other words, a list of the places where each type of threat could occur. We then decide which of the threats are easiest to address within the application itself, and which are easiest to address outside the application.

There are, of course, numerous ways to catalog application security requirements, some more formal than others, and some more effective than others. As with functional requirements gathering, there are hosts of published methodologies and numerous dedicated adherents to every method out there. Over the past few years, there have been quite a few different methodologies proposed for understanding an application's security landscape in a formalized way. The most common process developers might be familiar with is formalized *threat modeling*. It is not our goal to replace a formalized methodology a developer may be currently employing with something else; if that process works and works well, by all means, use it. However, for developers who are unfamiliar, we've attempted to distill a number of the common methodologies into some practical steps that lend value. Some details of the formal methodologies are provided in the references section of this chapter, and some resources and tools that can be used in employing a formal model. A formalized threat modeling methodology is useful, in no uncertain terms, as is a formalized development process, formalized business requirements gathering, formalized design procedures, and so forth. However, many times, the degree to which we can employ any formalized process comes down to time and buy-in. In other words, for a formalized methodology to work, we need other developers in our organization to follow it, and we need time to create and implement a process.

Understanding that a developer reading this book might not have implementation time for a formalized threat modeling process or buy-in from other persons in his or her organization for such a process, we've tried to distill some of the main concepts to techniques a developer can use that require neither. In other words, it has been our experience that developers can achieve a number of the benefits of a formalized approach by strategically condensing the steps of a formalized process to just those few that provide maximum value. One thing all formalized methods have in common is providing a useful starting point that facilitates understanding what the application does, how it does it, and what is in scope versus out of scope for the application's security logic. These are the goals of a "shortcut" process as well. Instead of going through a whole formalized process, we can create an informal and informational data reference model for our own consumption by cataloguing just three things:

- What data is stored by our application
- How data is processed in our application
- Where it resides in our application (either transiently or permanently)

Later, we will use this information to investigate attacks that our application might be subject to in combination with its environment and functionality. Starting with the data in our application and the "dynamics" what/how/where that information is handled is a useful way to approach the problem in creating a shortcut threat modeling process. It does not allow us to take for granted any aspect of the application's processing, and also forces us to itemize the application's inputs and outputs, pathways to its data, storage localities, and so forth. When we combine the data catalogue with the threat information we'll cover in subsequent sections, we'll be able to determine what countermeasures are the responsibility of the application and which are not. In other words, the functionality that we as developers need to write versus those things that are in someone else's scope (such as the person deploying the application, the user, or system architects).

Turning to the practical, in gathering the information required for the first step of our informal reference model, we want to stress that we are interested in function rather than form. As such, any notations we make can be of any form since they are primarily for our own use. They can be sophisticated interaction diagrams created just for this purpose, notes on top of existing design/deployment documentation, or just collections of documentation we have already that summarize the pertinent information. In other words, it is not the format of the output that is useful, it is the steps involved and the value of having such a list. As an example, Figure 2.1 demonstrates how we might superimpose data storage information over an existing design; in this case, a UML 2.0 deployment diagram, a fairly common artifact.

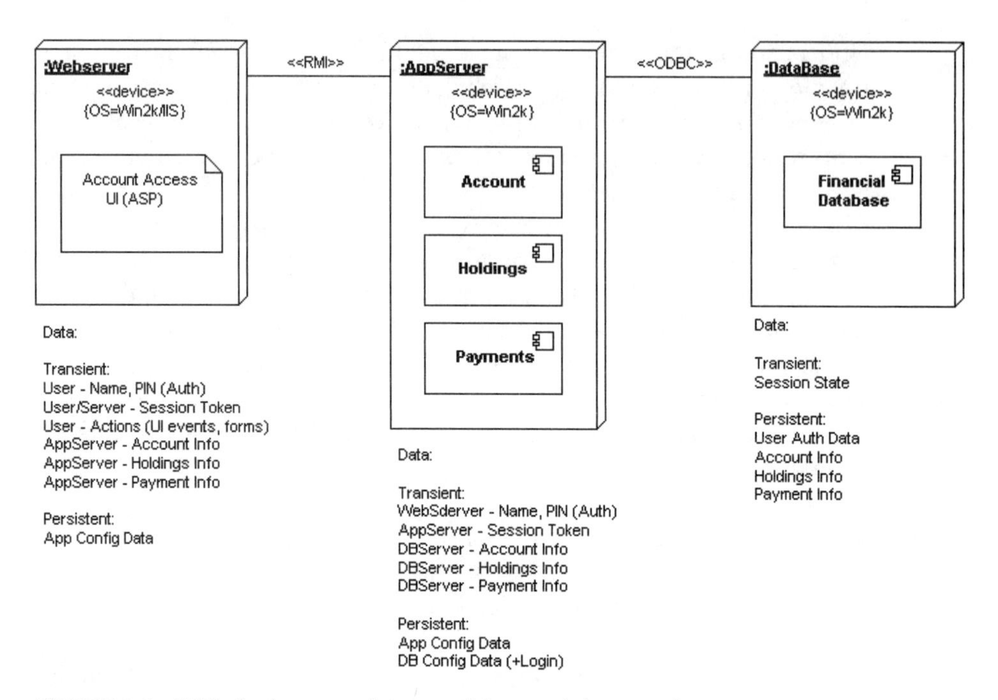

FIGURE 2.1 UML deployment diagram with stored data overlay.

Looking at the deployment diagram with our application's data on it, you'll notice a few things about the information we're recording. First, the application is very simple, involving only a few components and a very common architecture. In reality, there could be a number of interconnections with other systems, and there might be some additional research required to find out all the functionality and data associated with the application via all of the involved components. Additionally, we've put some information in about the source of the data in question—sometimes, a given piece of data might have a different source depending on the context. Where possible, we've attempted to note that. The usefulness of creating a map like this cannot be overstated. We'll see how all the threats we'll discuss tie back to this simple map, and how such a map allows us to easily locate application security functionality we might need to add to our application during the development phase. Later, when we've outlined the various tools at our disposal, we can come back to the data map and start to see how to apply the tools we'll talk about to solve likely threats to our application and the data. The most important thing is that we list all the data our application processes. Later, we will discriminate between data that is exchanged between components and pay particular attention to data transmissions. However, in this exercise, we just want to list all the data stored, sent, received, or processed no matter its significance.

2.2 TARGETS

In the mapping exercise, we did not discriminate between types of data. We took some simple steps to indicate which data was transient and which was persistent, but in general, we didn't make any delineations other than that. In our real-life applications, however, we know that some data we process will be of higher "value" than other data. By "value," we mean value from both an information security and application perspective. For example, if an application used by an online shoe retailer stores both credit card numbers (for payment processing) and user shoe size (for shopping convenience), obviously, the credit card numbers are of higher import than the shoe size in both respects. From an application perspective, they are of higher value, as they allow payment processing to take place, and from a security perspective, they are of higher value, as a loss can lead to significant bad press, required disclosure, and/or user attrition. For our purposes, we'll need to make note of the more "valuable" data since we'll want to pay special attention to where in our application we process it. Additionally, some areas of our application will be more vulnerable or at least more interesting to an attacker. These routines within the application can be at an application weak point (where it is easier for the application to be attacked), or a place where the application is doing something that is likely to be high-reward for an attacker. For example, the aforementioned component that processes credit card numbers will likely be more interesting to most attackers given the nature of the data it processes. Places in our application where components interact with each other (e.g., over a network) are more interesting to an attacker because they provide a potential opportunity for leverage against the application. These instances within the application have a higher likelihood of exploitation. Given their status as such, we will want to specifically address how we will prevent exploitation of these areas once our application is deployed.

2.2.1 Data

The first and primary target we will need to safeguard is our application's data, which we have now conveniently listed in an informal map. The data within our application is subject to different attacks depending on how and where it is located, the constraints it is under at the time, the manner in which it is being stored, and the duration within which it is being stored. In general, data can be in one of two states: in storage or in transit. However, for increased clarity, we can segregate "in storage" into persistent storage (*data at rest*) versus nonpersistent (*transient*) storage, given that different types of attacks apply depending on how the data is used. We'll briefly walk through what constitutes each classification in the next few subsections.

2.2.1.1 Data at Rest

Most of our applications will store data somewhere. Be it on a central server or on an end-user's hard drive, the application will likely need to save data from instance to instance. This data, stored by the application for processing at a later time, falls under the category of persistent storage, or "data at rest." Data at rest is data that is actively being saved by the application for a relatively long period of time. "Relatively long" is obviously subject to debate, but in general, we are referring to non-session data that is stored outside of a cache mechanism. This might be, for example, data stored within a database or on a local filesystem. We will want to make sure we enumerate all the data at rest present in our application's data map so we can look at how various threats might make it available to an undesired party. In fact, in the previous data map example, we segregated a section that contained only persistent data of this type.

2.2.1.2 Transient (Nonpersistent) Data

Sometimes, we don't need to store data for long periods. Alternatively, we might wish to maintain a "working copy" of application data in a place more readily accessible to a particular component within our application (e.g., a cache) to increase performance or to minimize expensive operations like database access. Anytime short-lived data is used in a nonpermanent way, the data is considered transient and is subject to different dynamics than if it were destined for long-term storage. Since this data is of a limited lifetime, the temptation is to have lower security requirements. Given that there are often reduced security goals in place for transient data, it is a likely place for attackers to attempt to gain leverage. In other words, if the ultimate goal of an individual is to gain access to our application's data, one of the places he or she might look to find that data is in the (potentially) less thoroughly defended caches and transient data stores such as temp files. Understanding that the potential is there for transient data to affect the security of our application, we'll want to make sure to include all the areas where our application uses transient data such as temporary files, caches, and the like during the preparation of our data map. While we might elect to have lower security requirements for transient data, it is unlikely that we will want to have no security requirements for it. In other words, we'll want to consider how to apply countermeasures in the same way as we would with longer term storage.

2.2.1.3 Data in Transit

Sometimes, we will want to send data between two different parts of our application. For example, in a Web-based application like the one in Figure 2.1, we'll likely want to exchange application data with middleware components, application servers, database repositories, and so forth. When we send data from point A to point B, the data is *in transit* during the actual sending process. By that, we mean that there is a communication channel between the data's source device and the destination device over which the data must traverse. When data is sent between two points, the data is subject to a different set of threats versus periods of time when it is not. As such, we will want to update our data map with any localities where data will be moved between two points.

In recalling the data map we created for our simple sample application in Figure 2.1, we had only entries for persistent and transient data and did not provide the details about the data transmissions across the various communication channels depicted. As developers of similar systems, given only that document, we could probably deduce the nature of what data flows over which channels. However, in practice, it is easier and more fruitful to construct informal notations indicating what data moves where—after all, data is subject to different attacks, and different countermeasures are more effective while the data is moving versus when it is stationary. Therefore, it is useful to specifically highlight the individual data items and the pathways they traverse. Again, the cataloguing and recording exercise is most valuable about creating the data map—as long as the results of the cataloguing exercise are recorded somewhere, the particular details of the format are irrelevant. For consistency, in Figure 2.2, we've used the same UML 2.0 deployment diagram, but we've updated it to reflect the position of data as it moves between systems rather than when it is stationary on any particular system.

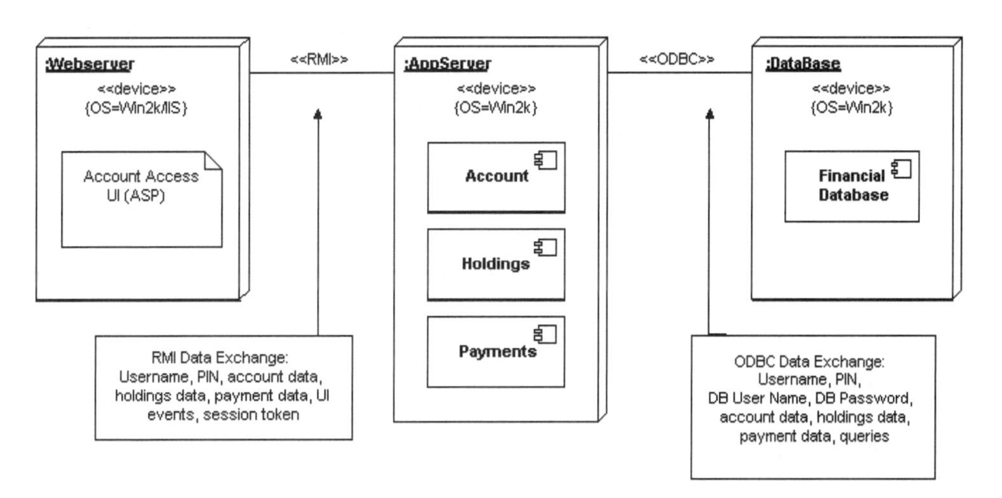

FIGURE 2.2 UML deployment diagram with data transfer overlay.

2.2.2 Application Functionality

We've spent some time discussing the data that our applications process in the context of a security landscape; ultimately, it is that data that can cause the most damage in the event of a compromise. It is also useful to discuss the possibility that our application's functionality, rather than its data, could be of interest to an attacker or unauthorized party, such as the capability to execute financial transactions, send queries to a database, and so on. For example, an ISP's "dialer" client application probably doesn't have much data an attacker would wish to harvest from it (with the possible exception of a potential stored password), but it does perform a service an attacker can make use of (i.e., dialing in to the Internet). Another example would be banking applications that have the capability to move money. In the event data from this application cannot be directly manipulated, quite a bit of nefarious profitability could potentially be had by making use of the functionality of the application (moving money) in creative and unexpected ways. Therefore, we need to consider the fact that our application's functionality might be the primary target of an attacker given certain circumstances.

Defending against such a possibility is more difficult than the defense of application data. We'll ultimately get to strategies that will help in these cases, but we will want to make sure we have on hand a list of the functionality that is built in to each of the logical components of our application for later analysis. In other words, we are going to want a "functionality map" in much a similar way as we have a "data map" when we get to the stage of introducing controls to the application. Fortunately for us, we almost never need to create new documentation for this purpose—in almost every case, some document somewhere will describe the functionality of the application in a way useful for our purposes in this respect. This can be something like a UML use case diagram, a business requirements document, a functional requirements document, or any other document that lists both the functional characteristics of a particular component and the input and output data we expect from a particular component. Since we want to keep our workload light, we'll just commandeer the existing documents that already describe the application's functionality for this purpose. We will use the application's "functionality map" in addition to the data map in later exercises for determining the possible attack vectors that our application is subject to, and possible countermeasures we can introduce to help mitigate those attacks.

2.2.3 Host Platforms

Last, but not least, our applications are likely to reside on a very tempting target in and of itself: a host operating system and platform. The underlying host is extremely versatile, containing processing, storage, and network resources that can be used by an attacker for a variety of ancillary purposes having nothing to do with our application. For example, if our application uses a database server with a large amount of filesystem storage space, an attacker might wish to make use of that space for illegal distribution of media files (music, movies) or pirated software. Alternatively, we might have a high-bandwidth connection to the Internet that would facilitate denial-of-service (DoS) attacks against other targets; an attacker might wish to leverage this connectivity for his or her own purposes. No matter what the reason, it is likely that the compromise and subsequent misuse of the computing components upon which our application resides is likely to have a detrimental effect on our application's functional goals. As such, we must recognize that the host itself is a viable target for attack. While we will not be specifically addressing targets of this type within the "mapping" exercise we have undertaken throughout this section, it is useful for us to remain cognizant of this potential as we move forward, particularly as we discuss countermeasures and hardening of the host.

2.2.4 The Bare Minimum: Targets

- Our application's data is likely to be the primary point of interest for attackers.
- Data at rest is data destined for long- or intermediate-term storage.
- Data in transit is data being sent between two points, such as between a user and our application or between two components within our application.
- Transient data is temporary or short-term data with a limited lifetime. Often, this data is used for caching purposes or for a single user session only.
- In some cases, an attacker might not be interested in the application's data, but might be interested in exploiting the functionality of the application.
- By creating a map of data at rest, transient data, and data exchanged between components, we can create a useful baseline for later introduction of countermeasures.
- Locating an existing design document that describes input, output, and functionality of individual components within our application adds value to the data map.
- The underlying platform of our application is a highly desired target, as it may have a high-performance connection to the Internet or accessible file storage. Even if none of these is available, just having a connection to the Internet can make the host a useful vehicle for DoS attacks against other targets.

2.3 THREATS

A *threat* is anything that affects the capability of our application to function within the "safe" operating boundaries (the "happy path") that we foresee during the design and authoring of our application. If the target (described previously) is "what" will be attacked, the threat is "how" it will be attacked. In other words, a threat is anything that compromises the privacy of the underlying data that our application processes (the *confidentiality* of our application), the error-free operation of our application or its data (the *integrity* of our application), or the ability of our users to use the application for its intended purpose (the *availability* of our application). Of course, there are limitless ways this can occur in the context of any application, but we're going to concentrate on a few broad classifications rather than delving into the near-infinite array of possible specific instances. Let's look at the broad threat categories in the order outlined earlier: attacks against confidentiality, integrity, and availability.

Some of the threats we'll discuss require an active participant for the threat to be realized; in other words, attackers who want to take advantage of and use our application design and implementation to perform tasks that are detrimental to our application or to the underlying business (or end users) our application supports. The mechanism within our application that an attacker might use, be it a design issue, an implementation issue, or an environmental issue, is referred to as the *attack vector* in this context. Sometimes, an attacker will not be required for detrimental effects to occur; these cases are less common, but are discussed here as well.

2.3.1 Eavesdropping

Eavesdropping in the physical world is a situation in which an unauthorized individual is able to gain access to information he or she should not have. Sometimes, eavesdropping can occur because the unauthorized person gains access to a location or resource that he or she should not (e.g., read our diary or listen to our phone calls). In other cases, the problem is caused as a result of us conducting a private conversation in a place or at a time when we don't have privacy (e.g., if there's a bug in our living room). In the digital world, the situation is analogous; if we conduct a digital conversation in a place or over a medium that is not private, or if an attacker gains access to a place or resource that allows him or her to violate our privacy, there is the potential for eavesdropping. In other words, all that needs to transpire is for an attacker to make observations of our application, or our application's data, that we did not anticipate. An example of eavesdropping would occur if our application needs to send data from point A to point B on a network, and an attacker is able to sit unnoticed on that network. In this case, unless we can ensure that the messages we send are somehow protected, the eavesdropper has full access to the conversation taking place. Alternatively, if an attacker were able to debug one of our application's processes and observe the memory space of our application during the act of modifying data, this would also be an example of eavesdropping.

Some types of eavesdropping are more difficult to prevent than others are. Of the two preceding examples, it is much easier to prevent an attacker from being able to read data that we submit over a network than it is to prevent someone with an appropriate type of an account (e.g., a system administrator) from using debugging tools to spy on our application while it's running. We'll want to enumerate ahead of time in developing a new application what we expect to be private and what we don't. We will also need to decide which users we trust with which data, and the contexts within which we trust them. We might decide, for example, that we trust the administrators of the machine we're running on; more specifically, we could decide that we expect the host operating system to enforce that only authorized personnel are able to access the administrator account. If that is the case, we'll outline ahead of time that it is acceptable for the administrative users of the machine (e.g., those individuals who can debug our application while it's running) to gain access to our data. This allows us to reduce the controls we build in to the application to enforce privacy to a corresponding degree.

During the process of delineating under what circumstances we will want to enforce the privacy of our application's data, we will obviously want to make use of the outline we created where we charted the location of the data during our application's operation. For example, if we expect that we will be storing the data on a database, we will include the database as a location where the data is stored in our data map, and any communication pathway our application shares with the database. We would then want to consider whether the exposure of the data at either of these two points indicates an "exposure" of our data. We would want to consider also any locality in which our data could become compromised: communication between front-end and application servers (if our application is n-tier), storage repositories on the local filesystem, and so on.

Defining ahead of time the places we anticipate eavesdropping could occur allows us to use tools to implement countermeasures or procedures to decrease the likelihood that this type of exposure can occur. In other words, in approaching the eavesdropping threat, we'll want to refer back to the map we created that delineates all the data our application processes, where it comes from and where it goes to for the purposes of making intelligent decisions about where it needs to be protected and where it does not. It should be explicitly stated that in this discussion, we are not just talking about "sensitive" data such as users' credit card information, their name and address, or social security number. This applies instead to *all* data used in our application. For example, if we write a log file that contains highly granular information about the type of error that occurred (e.g., a credit card transaction was unable to be authenticated), this information should be evaluated as well, along with any other data upon which our application relies: configuration files, data read in from the registry, any data a user will enter, and so on. Specifically evaluating and itemizing all of this material ahead of time may seem burdensome at first, but is really a time-saving measure in the long term. It will allow us to establish appropriate controls ahead of time with respect to the security of our application, and allow us to easily revisit the necessity of those controls (or the need for further controls) in subsequent revisions of the application.

2.3.1.1 The Bare Minimum: Eavesdropping

- Eavesdropping involves unauthorized individuals gaining access to data to which they are not authorized.
- Eavesdropping may occur on any data, stored either in a repository or being sent between two repositories.

2.3.2 Interception

Of course, if an attacker is able to view data private to our application as per eavesdropping, we will additionally need to consider the very real possibility that it would be more beneficial for the attacker to change that data instead of just viewing it. In addition to reviewing the data map to determine the scope of our application's need for privacy, we will want to consider data modification as well. The process whereby an attacker can gain access to our data and change it during the course of our application's operation is referred to as *interception.* Interception can take place anytime our application reads data from or writes data to a repository. Attackers will often look for places where they can manipulate the application's data processing for their own advantage; they might wish to intercept messages between components and subtly modify them for some purpose that is ultimately undesirable from our application's point of view. For example, if we are writing a trading application for a financial institution, attackers might want to change the amounts of the shares exchanged, or might wish to change the account into which those trades will be placed. On the surface, it would seem that if we solve the previous problem (preventing someone from viewing any data associated with our application), we would eliminate the problem of unauthorized data modification as well—after all, if they cannot see the data, how can they change it? This is sometimes (but not always) true; for example, if we implement controls that prevent disclosure of data within a database, that does not necessarily provide any assurance that someone cannot add values to the database or modify the values that are already stored there by going through another channel. We'll go through some of the different types of interception that can occur in the next few subsections, although they are all pretty much variations on the same theme.

2.3.2.1 Replay

The simplest case of interception is *replay*, in which a given communication, message, or transaction is recorded and sent verbatim at a time subsequent to the recorded operation. This is a useful concept to illustrate because it highlights why solving the privacy problem does not necessarily solve the interception problem. For example, attackers might not be able to read a particular piece of data *per se*, but by employing replay, they could cause a particular operation to be performed more than once. For example, if an attacker records a "log in" message of an authorized system user, he might attempt to replay it at a subsequent time under conditions more favorable (from a machine he controls, for example). Unless our applications specifically plan for this eventuality, an unauthorized party might be able to perform operations that are undesirable from the standpoint of our application. To prevent replay, there are a number of techniques we can use; for example, we can build into our applications a methodology to ensure that a particular message has a limited lifetime and thereby reduce the window during which replay may take place. There are a number of other strategies we can use as well, such as ensuring that a particular transaction is reliably placed in sequence within the context of a clearly demarked session, thereby ensuring that that message cannot be transmitted outside the context of that session. In subsequent sections, we'll talk more about how to use cryptographic techniques in combination with other techniques to ensure that our systems are as resistant to replay as possible. However, for the time being, it is useful for us to refer back to our data map, and in so doing pay particular attention to how our application's inter-component interaction would be impacted by a replayed message. Anything that stands out as "particularly dangerous" such as a replayed logon message is useful for us to note at this time.

2.3.2.2 Data Modification

In certain cases, an attacker may be able to inject or modify content into a communication stream. Additionally, in the case of a man-in-the-middle attack, an attacker can easily misrepresent data that was alleged to have originated from the other communicant in a dialogue. As was the case with eavesdropping, this can include the modification of user-related data (such as the account number to deposit funds into), or the modification of parameter data that our application requires for initialization or appropriate operation (such as changing a table name in a database call). In either case, modification of the data in question can have, at best, deleterious results on our software operation and, at worst, dire consequences for the functioning of our business/application as a whole. In preparation to build a defense against modification of the data upon which our application relies, it is fruitful to use the same "map" we created for charting the data we wish to keep private, and updating it for the data we wish to ensure is unmodified. By outlining ahead of time the data we need to preserve the integrity of (and correspondingly, the data for which modification is acceptable), we can determine when and where we need to apply mitigation concepts within our application design.

2.3.2.3 "Man in the Middle"

A "man in the middle" is an unauthorized party who is able to surreptitiously insert himself in the middle of an ongoing communication. In the best case, the two communicating parties will be aware of the presence of the intermediary, but in the worst case, neither the sender nor the receiver will be aware of the presence of the middle party. In practice, if two parties are communicating with each other, the man in the middle will pretend to be the opposite party to each of the participants in the communication. In the case of a client-server communication, for example, the man in the middle would pretend to be the server side of the communication to the client and the client side of the communication to the server. If this were to happen, both the client and the server in our hypothetical transaction would send their data unaware that there is a middle party in the session. This gives the man in the middle tremendous advantage, as he has access to the entirety of the communication contents, and the ability to modify the data during the discourse. In this instance, modification can mean the introduction of new data, the deletion of data from the stream, or deliberate tampering with the legitimate contents of the communication. It should be noted that a "man in the middle" is apropos both to data privacy and to interception of data, and implies a technique rather than a result. To develop countermeasures against this technique in subsequent sections, it is useful to examine the data map we created earlier for localities in which such an attack might be likely. In doing so, we'll need to keep in mind that an attacker might be motivated by changing the data (as described previously) or by eavesdropping on the data as it is transmitted.

2.3.2.4 The Bare Minimum: Interception

- Replay involves the verbatim iteration of a previous message sent between two communicating parties.
- Data modification can take place when an attacker is able to inject content into, remove content from, or modify a data stream.
- Man in the middle is a technique whereby an individual pretends to be the "end point" of a communication pathway to two or more different parties. The result is that all data passing between the parties is vectored through the attacker.
- A "map" of the data required for our application to function appropriately allows us to see ahead of time which data pathways require mitigation of interception attacks.

2.3.3 Software (Application) Attacks

So far, we've discussed attacks that can be performed externally to our applications that an attacker can use to gain access to data streams and data repositories used by our applications. However, it is also possible for an attacker to use our application software as a vehicle to gain access to those same data streams or repositories. For example, if our application can somehow be "tricked" into reading the data or modifying it on behalf of an attacker, the application itself would be the vehicle used to gain access to the privileged information or to make modifications to the data. Consider, for example, the case of a Web application that runs a number of server-side scripts to read data from and write data to a database. In that case, if an attacker were able to modify the application code (say, for example, a portion of the application code can be written to remotely by arbitrary users), an attacker could clearly modify the application in such a way as to gain access to the information contained in the database used by the application. Of course, in practice, these types of vulnerabilities are less straightforward than a simple example of this type; however, the principle remains the same. Sometimes, an application attack vector might be an issue with filesystem permissions (such as the simple example mentioned), or the attack vector might use flaws in the way in which C and C++ array (buffer) boundaries are handled to cause code written by the attacker to be executed. No matter how such attacks are performed, however, we as application developers need to be aware that such a possibility exists. Obviously, use of our application in such a negative manner is undesirable and something we want to avoid. In practice, it is not possible to completely bulletproof our applications against this kind of vulnerability, since our applications require access to the data, input, and other parameters to run. As such, ensuring totally that an attack like this cannot occur is not possible.

In many cases, bugs, logic errors, unexpected input, or other factors related to our application's code facilitate misuse of the application in this way. As anyone who has ever worked in or closely with QA knows, it is almost impossible to find all the bugs or unexpected behavior before releasing an application. As developers, we accept that there will be some bugs in the final release of our software. We do our best to find them during the development and testing cycles of our development process, but some always remain in the final cut. Couple that fact with the reality that very often, our development shops are not tasked with looking for security-related issues, and we can almost guarantee that some security issues will be present in any piece of software, commercial or otherwise. However, just because we don't know when or how an application attack will occur, does not mean that we can't design in some strategies ahead of time that will buy us some level of protection should an application attack occur. In other words, we can use some of the security tools we'll be covering to build in protections that provide a degree of safety for the eventuality that some attack vector will be present in our application. We'll discuss some of those measures in later sections; however, for now, just note that our applications can be misused in this way as one entry in our growing catalogue of challenges that our applications will face in the field.

2.3.3.1 The Bare Minimum: Application Attacks

- Application attacks use unanticipated aspects of our application code or application design to gain entry into the application.
- We cannot anticipate all areas in which such an attack may occur, so we will want to implement a number of generalized controls to minimize the impact of such an attack.

2.3.4 Accidental Information Disclosure

It is sometimes possible for our application to disclose sensitive or proprietary information through a confluence of events rather than by result of direct action from an attacker. This can occur, for example, if our application provides a significant level of user informational detail to administrators of the system, if an application server or a client machine with a large amount of cached data is lost or stolen, or in any other situation in which the underlying application data is transferred without direct action from an attacker. This situation is more likely to occur than is commonly realized. Therefore, we need to consider the situations in which equipment on which our application runs might be lost or stolen, that users or system administrators might walk away from the desktop they are using the application from, and a whole host of other events that might lead to application data being accidentally disclosed to the wrong party. Many of the protection measures we'll be discussing will mitigate the amount of damage done in the event this should occur. Insofar as preparation for adding the appropriate functionality in the right place, we'll want to use the same data map we created for analyzing the potential for eavesdropping in our application; however, this time we'll want to look for how that data might be compromised by accidental disclosure. For example, if we are storing information on a central server, that will be reflected in the data map. We'll want to consider the possibility of hardware theft or accidental non-secure disposal of hardware (such as fixed disks or backup tapes) containing any sensitive data, and use the tools at our disposal to limit the impact of such an occurrence.

2.3.4.1 The Bare Minimum: Accidental Disclosure

- Does not require the active participation of an attacker to occur.
- By charting where data (particularly sensitive data) resides, we can build in countermeasures to address accidental disclosure.

2.3.5 Forgery and Spoofing

Recalling our discussion about data in transit, we discussed situations in which an attacker might wish to modify data exchanged between different components in our application; for example, tampering with, replaying, or deleting from the data. However, it is useful to point out that an attacker can deliberately attempt to forge application artifacts that are not related to the application's data, but on which our application depends to maintain sessions or to authenticate individual components within the application. For example, a common mechanism used for maintaining session state in the context of HTTP is session cookies; if an attacker is able to *forge* a new artifact in exactly the format we expect our application to create, the application has no way of knowing (unless we build in a way) which artifact is real and which is false. If this were to occur, the forged artifact would cause the inauthentic session to be indistinguishable from the authentic session. In other words, *forgery*, much like counterfeit currency in the physical world, is the process whereby an attacker creates an artifact that looks enough like the "real thing" that our application does not perceive the difference.

It is particularly useful to examine this issue in the light of inter-host communication techniques such as RMI, SOAP, CORBA, and the like. For example, if we have two components that remotely execute objects or processes on other machines, an attacker might sit in the middle of the communication as we described earlier, and create forged messages that appear to be a valid request for a remote object or component. In this case, the attacker might also be able to control the parameters to the function/object unless we specifically implement measures to prevent this. Anytime our application accepts input from any source, particularly those transmitted between loosely coupled components, we should consider the very real possibility that that input could have been modified. Of course, depending on the input context, the amount of leverage an attacker is able to gain using this approach varies. Turning back to our map, we'll want to mark any locations where our applications require an artifact of this type; later in this book, we'll talk about ways we can make sure the artifacts created by our applications cannot be forged by anyone other than our application.

2.3.5.1 The Bare Minimum: Forgery/Spoofing

- Much like the modification of data in the middle of a communication stream, forgery/spoofing can be used by an attacker to create a counterfeit application artifact.
- Input values should be examined in the light of potential forgery to determine what effect such a forgery would have on our application processing.

2.3.6 Impersonation

Impersonation is when attackers attempt to trick our application into thinking they are someone authorized to use the system: either an administrator or a legitimate user of the application. This can be done in a straightforward manner such as by stealing a user's password, or by more roundabout means such as by forging an authentication credential that may be given to a user to maintain authentication state (such as an HTTP cookie or other authentication artifact). The possibility of impersonation is directly tied to the strength (or lack thereof) of the authentication methodology we build into our application and the corresponding defense of credentials we might issue. For example, if we build an authentication mechanism whereby a user logs in with a password over an undefended channel on a network (without any protection whatsoever), obviously the threat of impersonation is much higher than if we were to defend that password and the issued credential using a tool such as cryptographic protection of the communication channel. Authentication input values and credential output values should be present in the data map we created for our application (both of these artifacts are, after all, just data). To ensure that our passwords, credentials, and so forth are not stolen, we'll want to build in a mechanism to ensure that the authentication channel is confidential. Additionally, we'll want to make sure that the methodology we use has a reduced possibility of forgery or spoofed credentials.

2.3.6.1 The Bare Minimum: Impersonation

- Impersonation occurs when an attacker is able to "trick" our application into thinking he is a different user from the one our application expects him to be (if he is a user at all).
- Difficulty of impersonation is directly tied to the strength and level of protection surrounding the authentication methodology.
- Indicating how authentication is to be accomplished on our data map allows us to come back later and apply tools to the authentication mechanism and credentials to prevent impersonation (or at least make it more difficult to effect).

2.3.7 Denial of Service

Aside from directly attempting to "take over" our application, or to get it to perform undesirable tasks, an attacker might decide that it is sufficient to prevent authorized users from performing legitimate tasks. Known as *denial of service*, this type of attack attempts to burden an application to such a degree that it cannot perform its normal application processing. Alternatively, the attack might be designed to crash the application or otherwise render it inaccessible. These types of attacks we will find to be the most difficult to prevent as we author our application, especially with the tools we will be outlining throughout this book. However, it is useful to point out situations in which this attack can occur so we can implement alternative countermeasures.

2.3.7.1 The Bare Minimum: Denial of Service

- Attempts to limit or restrict normal application processing activity by overloading our application or otherwise rendering it inaccessible.
- Difficult to prevent, since it may leverage normal application functionality.
- It may be difficult to delineate between heavy use of a system and malicious attack.

2.4 COUNTERMEASURES

In a very real sense, this entire book is an exercise in making our application more difficult to attack; more specifically, we are interested in the creation of *countermeasures*, those controls and techniques that mitigate particular attacks against our applications. There are all sorts of countermeasures we can put in place to help mitigate various threats in our applications. However, in particular, we are interested in application-level countermeasures throughout this book; as developers, our purview is the application level. In other words, it is our job to make sure the application is as robust as possible through the tools and techniques we have at our disposal during the design and development phases. That is not to say that other aspects of the operation of a system are outside our scope—quite the contrary. There is much we can do at the application level, to mitigate attacks that might occur in other areas of system operation. We will be implementing those controls as well. This section provides an overview of the types of countermeasures we will be applying and where they will be applicable in our applications. These are all high-level, abstract techniques that will help mitigate the possibility of security issues arising in our applications. The majority of the countermeasures listed here are described in practical detail later in this book; others that are not in this book's scope are left up to you to implement in whatever way is familiar and comfortable.

2.4.1 Solid Development Practices

While there is much that we can build into our application to prevent misuse, there will always be certain situations that we cannot address completely in software. Primary among them is the jujitsu-like attacker technique of turning our own software against itself. Since our software must, in order to operate, have access to the same data we are trying to protect, anything that compromises the integrity of our software is problematic. Although we cannot completely address all of these issues in our software, the more solid and more controlled our development process is, the less likely that vulnerabilities will be introduced into the application. We understand this truism as it pertains to logic errors and other bugs, but it is equally true with security-related bugs. Additionally, the more controlled and inclusive the design process we use, the less likely that threats will slip by unaddressed through the design process. In other words, having a solid and robust development process can accelerate development in the long run, and can result in code that helps ensure that our defined security goals are met.

Obviously, it is not the goal of this book to provide a laundry list of "best practices" that a development shop can implement, or to provide guidance on ways to improve the maturity of a given development shop (there are numerous books on these topics already that you'll find references to at the end of this section). Additionally, it is a reality of the development world that we can't always work in an environment that we can reorganize or regiment as we see fit, and our commitment is to get deliverables out the door first and worry about process improvements after the immediate goals are met. In other words, if we are working in the context of a shop that for whatever reason does not have a high level of process maturity (perhaps we are working in a startup or a development team with very few members), the time to reinvent the software development process is *not* when there is a critical deliverable on the table. Therefore, while robust/mature software development processes can increase the security of applications over the long term, we'll probably want to make sure that we get there over time rather than sprinting there today. Therefore, while it is true that both maturity of process and use of secure coding techniques will help to provide additional security to our developed applications, we might have to accept that we are not there yet and seek to employ other means to help ensure our software's security rather than rearchitecting our development process.

2.4.1.1 The Bare Minimum: Development Practices

- Mature development practices can ensure that we do not overlook issues in application design or implementation that introduce security vulnerabilities.
- Application attacks can be reduced through the use of secure coding practices.
- Both secure coding and a mature software development environment are long-term endeavors that, while useful, may not be appropriate in the context of a critical deliverable.

2.4.2 Authorization

Authorization consists of assigning identity to the users of our application, ensuring the users are whom they claim to be, and that the appropriate users are authorized to perform particular functions. Technically, authorization is broken down into *authentication* (a particular user is who he claims to be) and *access control* (particular users only have access to the functionality they should). Since both topics apply at an application level, we as the developers of that application are responsible for ensuring both in our applications.

2.4.2.1 Authentication

Traditionally, authentication has been broken down into three *factors*:

- What you know
- What you have
- What you are

We're probably already familiar with each of these various factors in everyday practice. For example, "what you know" maps generically to passwords and PINs, "what you have" maps to access cards and dongles, and "what you are" maps to biometrics like fingerprint recognition or retinal scanning. The design goals of using these factors are relatively straightforward: we'll want to apply a suitably robust method of authentication to our application's logon methodology, safeguard the exchange of data required for authentication, and ensure that we appropriately tie an authentication event to a user context. We can accomplish these goals by employing at least one of the authentication factors in our application, and if our application requires a very robust authentication methodology, we can employ a combination of factors to increase the likelihood that the users of our system are, in fact, who they claim to be. We'll discuss that in just a minute.

2.4.2.2 Access Control

Once we know who a user is, we'll want to make sure he has access to only the functionality we want him to. This functionality the user does have access to (such as "read/write," "perform trading," or any other aspects of the application) is referred to as *entitlements*, and will likely vary from application to application. It is useful, from a programmatic standpoint, to enforce access control at the application layer (since our application is the entity that understands a particular action or functionality in the light of the business logic), and to perform the check in a locality that is somewhat protected from the user. For example, if we are writing a Web application, it would behoove us to perform application logic on the server side of an exchange rather than at the client side, since a client might have the ability to influence any logic performed on the client side of that connection (e.g., by disabling the scripting language we're using to perform the logic or by influencing the execution in a debugging environment).

2.4.2.3 Tokens, Entitlements, and Credentials

Once we have authenticated a user, we will likely want our application to maintain some awareness of the fact that the user has been authenticated; if we did not, we would have to ask the user to reenter his credentials each time he wants to perform a "restricted" transaction. This is true of access control decisions as well: once we have made an access control decision, we might wish to refrain from performing the same access control decision each time the user wants to perform the same functionality subsequently. Making these authorization decisions once and maintaining them throughout the application's "awareness" of the user's presence is useful in that it conserves system resources, eliminates the requirement for the user to have to reenter data, and can eliminate costly operations like trips to an authorization database.

Having established that maintenance of authorization state is a useful goal, one commonly used methodology for ensuring that this is the case is to bind a session to an authentication *credential*. The credential, simply put, is an artifact that indicates to our application that the user has already been authenticated. The exact method of binding the credential to the session will vary according to the nuances of the application, but as we move through the material, we will see certain strategies used repeatedly. In an HTTP context, for example, it will often behoove us to use the HTTP cookie header to store session context information including an authentication credential. This process can be thought of as analogous to file pointers in C: instead of using `fopen()` and `fclose()` each time we want to read some data from a file, we use `fopen()` once and maintain a pointer to our "file session." The underlying library maintains our position within the file, keeps the file open, and may maintain a lock on the file to keep other processes from accessing it at the same time (depending on what the other processes want to do with it, of course). We will want to ensure that the credentials we issue are resistant to counterfeit, tampering, and theft, so only an individual who has been successfully authenticated has access to an authentication token. The same can be done with access control decisions; we can assign to a user or to a user session a credential that includes entitlements as well, or we can bind the session to two artifacts—one that maintains authentication state and one that maintains access control decisions. The technical details of how to create such a credential are discussed in more detail later in this book, but for now, we just want to recognize that this kind of strategy exists.

2.4.2.4 The Bare Minimum: Authorization

- Authorization consists of both authentication and access control.
- Authentication is the process of ensuring that the users are who they claim to be, by determining what they know (e.g., a secret word or phrase we share with them), what they have in their possession (such as an access card), or personal characteristics.
- Access control is the process of mapping authenticated users to entitlements—things they have access to do within the application.
- We can issue credentials to users; we should attempt to make sure the credentials cannot be stolen or counterfeited.

2.4.3 Confidentiality and Integrity

Much of this book concerns itself with *confidentiality*; that is, the protection of the "private" (confidential) nature of data within our application. Implementing data privacy itself is not difficult, does not require much in the way of additional application logic, and when applied appropriately, will drastically improve the security of our application by making it much more difficult for an attacker to gain access to our application's data stores and communication pathways. At this time, we are looking at data privacy as a high-level control, so we will not delve into too much detail with respect to the implementation of those controls at this time. However, it is useful to delineate, in discussing privacy at a high level, that any methodology we implement in ensuring the privacy of data should maintain a level of privacy even if the data is divorced or separated from the application with which it is associated. If we build in a control that only ensures privacy if the application itself remains uncompromised, we run into difficulty in situations in which the application itself is compromised or when the data is sent to a locality not under the purview of the application (such as a filesystem, a database, or to a client).

Of equal import is ensuring that data is not modified in a manner not anticipated by our application. Errors or deliberate tampering (as discussed previously) can introduce application security and functional issues into our applications. Just as in the physical world, our applications will need to employ techniques that ensure *tamperproof* (it cannot be modified) data or *tamper-evident* (we know if tampering has been attempted) data. Fortunately, there are a number of strategies we can employ to make sure these goals are met within our applications. We'll be covering quite a few of these strategies within this book.

2.4.3.1 The Bare Minimum: Confidentiality and Integrity

- Data integrity allows us to ensure that data is not modified by parties either during transmission between two points or in storage.
- Data privacy consists of restricting access to application data to the application itself and/or the parties who have access to view that data.

2.5 SUMMARY

We've discussed within this section, at an extremely abstract level and in cursory fashion, the overall terminology and concepts we will need to arm ourselves with in venturing further into building secure applications. Hopefully, now that you have reached the end of this section, you have some idea of what is at risk in your applications, some of the common ways applications can be put at risk, and some of the high-level concepts you might employ to prevent some of these things from happening. Therefore, this is the end of the "abstract" portion of the discussion. Throughout the remainder of this book, we'll keep our attention and concentration focused squarely on the practical—"how to" approaches a developer can use to reach some of the goals we've highlighted here, both from an abstract perspective and a hands-on perspective.

2.6 SELECTED RESOURCES

Threat modeling:

Microsoft MSDN Threat Modeling page[1]: Provides useful links to the Microsoft threat modeling formal methodology, including numerous articles, tools, and off-site references.

Frank Swiderski and Window Snyder, *Threat Modeling*: Microsoft Press provides this thorough book on the Microsoft threat modeling process, its inception, and how to implement the process.

OCTAVE (Operationally Critical Threat, Asset, and Vulnerability Evaluation™) page at CERT[2]: A risk-based threat modeling approach for large and small enterprises.

Attack Trees (Schneier) description page[3]: A "no nonsense" approach from Bruce Schneier incorporating many of the benefits of a longer technique but with less overhead.

Software Development Life Cycle (SDLC) maturity:

Paulk, *et al, Capability Maturity Model, The Guidelines for Improving the Software Process.* Addison Wesley Professional: This book outlines the CMM (Capability Maturity Model™ for Software), providing case studies, technical information, and methodological descriptions.

Object Management Group's (OMG) UML™ (Unified Modeling Language™) resource page[4]: Provides a useful introduction to UML, links to the current UML (2.0) specification and prior iterations of the specification, and links to tools that assist in UML development.

Carnegie Mellon: Software Engineering Institute's (SEI) CMM (Capability Maturity Model™ for Software information page[5]: Provides informational resources about CMM, including links to the SW-CMM® technical reports.

2.7 ENDNOTES

1. *http://msdn.microsoft.com/security/securecode/threatmodeling/default.aspx*
2. *www.cert.org/octave/*
3. *www.schneier.com/paper-attacktrees-ddj-ft.html*
4. *www.uml.org/*
5. *www.sei.cmu.edu/cmm/*

3 Cryptographic Engineering

In This Chapter

- An Introduction to Cryptographic Primitives
- Common Techniques
- Cryptographic Libraries
- Secure Sockets
- Selected References
- Endnotes

3.1 AN INTRODUCTION TO CRYPTOGRAPHIC PRIMITIVES

Be it a bridge, an electronic device, or a grandiose archway, the process of engineering is always the same: we begin by understanding the "artifact" we wish to produce. Next, we break our goal into smaller "achievable" problems (ideally, ones we have solved in the past), and apply the appropriate tools at our disposal. This methodology is the cornerstone of all engineering activities, and applies equally to security engineering.

In this chapter, we examine some of the primary tools in our toolset that will assist us in writing software that solves security problems: the commonly occurring cryptographic primitives. *Primitives*, in general, are the smallest building blocks of something larger and more complicated. As developers, we are probably already familiar with the various data primitives occurring in the languages we use on a day-to-day basis (e.g., in C, we have int, char, long, etc.). In other words, in a programming language, the primitive data types are the smallest possible types we can put together to construct larger more complicated data types (such as structs, classes, and so on). The cryptographic primitives available to us as security engineers are analogous to those we find in the programming languages we work with on a daily basis: they are the smallest possible building blocks of cryptographic functionality upon which we will build larger and more complicated security functionality.

As we gain familiarity with the security primitives available to us, we start to see how they interrelate and can look at their use in various standard protocols. This will allow us to see how they fit into a bigger security picture and provide us with some useful prototypes for use in our applications. By the end of this chapter, developers should have a comfort level with the purpose of the various primitives they will use time and again in developing secure applications, and an understanding of the common implementations of those primitives in cryptographic libraries.

In this section, we are (purposefully) going to *breeze through* this material very rapidly. Our goal here is not to give an exhaustive overview of the implementations or to go in-depth into the mathematics involved; such an exercise extends far beyond what's required from a usage perspective and can prove very distracting to the individual who intends to use (not reinvent) cryptographic functionality. In other words, just as we don't have to understand the physics of radio waves to tune in a broadcast, we don't have to fully comprehend the intricate mathematics involved in using the cryptographic tools available to us. In this vein, we're also not going to delve into detailed specific usage instructions (this will come later). Each library we're going to cover has its own data structures, its own initialization routines, and its own unique "style," and bringing these particulars into the discussion at this point will muddy the waters rather than provide useful information.

This is not to discourage the industrious developer from delving deeper into the underlying science surrounding this topic. For those developers, we've included some references at the end of this chapter and on the companion CD-ROM that will hopefully allow them to explore the topic in more depth.

ON THE CD

That being said, let's take a moment to consider the present-day problem space. When it comes to writing applications, there are no universal truths (every application is different—just ask anyone in marketing). However, a few things are *usually* true, and they can give us some very important clues into what tools we might require—at least in the abstract. So, let's look at a "typical" application and some of the properties it might have.

Component Interaction

Very few developers in today's world have the luxury of creating monolithic applications. For the most part, we are writing a variety of components that interact with each other in a structured, formalized way. Over the years, we have referred to the componentization of applications in different ways (n-tier, application "layers," modular design, componentized functionality, etc.), but the principle is more or less the same—functionality A is somehow logically or physically separate from functionality B, and the two components interact with each other according to a set of well-defined rules or protocols. The mechanics of these interactions have changed over time (in keeping with enhancements in technology, changes in language popularity, etc.), but the principle in the abstract is the same.

The mechanisms used for inter-component interaction are extremely varied. Making the landscape more challenging, the typical application will use more than one component interaction methodology. For example, an application like the Apache Web server uses a number of inter-module/inter-component interaction methodologies: interprocess communication (via shared memory), structured network protocols (via HTTP), and more commonly occurring module communication such as shared objects, command-line arguments, child processes, and so forth. In the previous example, some of the interaction methodologies require tight coupling (the use of runtime linked libraries or shared objects), while others are loosely coupled (HTTP, shared memory). A number of the recent "trends" in application development are, at their core, strategies for decoupling application components from each other (e.g., CORBA, EJB, D/COM, Web services, etc.).

When it comes to communicating data between components, these components might need to communicate with each other over a (if not overtly hostile) less than trustworthy medium (such as the Internet, a corporate network, a telephone line, etc.). The medium might be faulty, unreliable, in open view of untrustworthy parties, and so forth. Of course, in keeping with the complex world in which our applications live, some of the communication mechanisms available for this interaction are more unsafe than others are, or we might not know for sure what the communication pathway between components will be with a high degree of certainty until implementation time. Therefore, taking it as a given that we will be dealing with modularized application components, and given that these components will need to interact with each other in some way, what hypothetical security challenges might we face? There are a few things we might say in the abstract, specifically:

- Data in transit from component A to component B might be stolen (by an unscrupulous party) or accidentally divulged (to nonhostile participants) while being transmitted across the insecure medium.
- Spurious individuals might pretend to be our components to gain information or access they are not rightfully allowed to access.
- Data could become corrupted (maliciously or otherwise) or be otherwise manipulated (such as by having data deleted or added) while in transit between components.
- One component might become overloaded with (legitimate or spurious) requests and thus be unable to handle new legitimate requests coming in.

And so on. Given these things, we'll need to somehow ensure that our components are as resilient to this type of misuse as possible. The issues listed here are all abstract threats; security professionals classify these, as discussed in the previous chapter, according to: *confidentiality* (preventing unauthorized data access), *integrity* (preventing undetected tampering or corruption of data), *availability* (making sure the resource continues to provide service), and *authorization* (ensuring that individuals can do what they are entitled to do and nothing else). In the components we write, we'll need tools and designs that increase our components' capability to ensure these three aspects of our data and resources are protected (confidentiality, integrity, and availability). This is particularly true when we're dealing with "weak points" (areas of vulnerability) within the application, such as when our components are communicating with each other.

Storage of Information

In addition to sending data and messages to each other, components usually need to store data or information about their individual state (e.g., logging/debug information or storage of data to a database). There are always exceptions, but most of the time, applications employ a number of standard storage mechanisms (files, databases, directories, etc.) for all the data items they want to "save for later." This is true both in the case of "persistent storage" (data we wish to keep for a long period of time) and "transient storage" (data such as temp files or cookies that are useful only for a very short time). Most of the time, we can only casually trust the information repositories available to us to safeguard our data (since they may be accessible to other parties or may not be adequately protected). In addition, we also may not trust the communication pathway we have with that repository. In other words, just as we don't inherently trust the communication pathways between components, we may also not trust the medium we use to communicate with our storage repository. For example, we may want to store information in a database, but we know that the database administrators have access to all the data items in that database (and might not need to know all the information we're storing there). In many cases, a database may be resident on a separate box for performance or architectural reasons. In those cases, the database might therefore be subject to the same kind of difficulties we enumerated when we discussed issues with the communication pathways. Since we can't trust that our data will be protected when we store it in these localities, it is imperative that we remain on the lookout for security problems anytime anything we store leaves the application boundary.

Interaction with Users

Most applications interact with a user in some way. Input from a user can be counted on to be highly error prone and "suspect" in a variety of ways. For example, rogue individuals may try to masquerade as authorized users of the system when instead they are criminals, terrorists, bored teenagers, or otherwise a "worker of iniquity." Alternatively, well-meaning users may intend to submit appropriate data, but due to "human error," they submit something that is outside the parameters of the expected input, or they may perform steps out of the appropriate order. Therefore, it is important that we take measures to safeguard another weak point: namely, any point in our application where we interact with a user of the system. Note that this does not only apply to application "front end" components; our application might also accept input from an administrator, command-line arguments, environment information, and so on. Any values that can be manipulated by a user or administrator of our application should immediately be viewed as suspect.

So, putting that all together, what can we say about the application "weak points" in the abstract? We've established that in most cases, we don't trust the medium over which our application's components need to communicate (this includes any medium we share with the user). We know that we might want to send private information over that medium or store data in a repository outside our control. We know we might need to ask the user for input (which could be provided in an incorrect format). In short, we'll need tools that either alone or in combination allow us to keep our information safe from eavesdroppers, and ensure that communications we have over any accessible medium are conducted with the parties we intend and not with others. For quite a few of these problems, judicious use of cryptography and cryptographic primitives (again, either alone or in combination) can provide some of our required building blocks.

It should be explicitly stated that cryptography is never an answer in and of itself. A useful way to think about this is in comparing cryptographic primitives with other more-familiar functional components like a hash table or linked list. For example, a hash table is a useful tool in implementing a larger system (such as a data storage repository), but we can't just say, "a hash table is the answer" because it isn't; it's just a tool within a larger context. It doesn't become useful until we consider the appropriateness of the tool for our particular application, tailor the tool's usage for our particular task (such as picking a hashing algorithm that makes sense for the data set that we're using), and build our application to make use of the tool (e.g., by designing a mechanism to put data in to—and get data out of—the hash table structure). Cryptography is the same; it's a tool that can be used to build other things, but any particular primitive needs to be analyzed for appropriateness in our application, a decision must be made as to how it will be used by our application, and we need to architect a mechanism for it to be incorporated into our overall software architecture.

Having said that, let's start to talk about the primitives themselves; in fact, most of what we are going to discuss are fairly straightforward concepts (ones that most developers are probably familiar with already). We're going to attempt to introduce the primitives in "ease of understanding" order; in other words, we're going to cover the concepts first that are most readily approachable, and build on each where appropriate to introduce the next.

3.1.1 Hashing Algorithms

Our first primitive is one with which almost every developer is probably already familiar at some level: *hashing* and *hash functions*. Believe it or not, a concept very similar to the hashing used to implement a hash table can be used in isolation as a cryptographic primitive or used in conjunction with other primitives to solve different challenges. We just put a stake in the ground and said that every developer already knows about hashing algorithms and how they work; trust us, even if you think you don't, you already do. All of us, at one point or another, have been called upon to write or use a hash table; it's one of the most commonly used data structures because of the efficiency of the searching that can be done within it. In most hash table implementations, we take an input value that we wish to store in the table, perform some operation on it to construct a small "representative" value (usually an integer), and then use this value as an index into the list associated with the data we want to store. This approach accelerates searches into the list when we wish to retrieve data at a later time. The high-level process we just went through might sound confusing, so let's go through it by example.

Say you have a list of four names: "Alice," "Steve," "Bill," and "Timmy." We could create a list of size 26 (one position for each letter of the alphabet), and use the first letter of the first name as a key into that list. In this case, "Bill" would be at position 2 since his name starts with "B" (because A=1, B=2, C=3… Z=26), and Alice would be at position 1 (since A=1). As long as we can ensure that every name in the list starts with a unique letter, the complexity of searches into this list is O(1), meaning that a "worst-case search" will take at most one iteration. However, as soon as we introduce another name with the same first letter (e.g., "Bob"), we have a "collision" (because they both map to position 2). In the case of collision, we usually implement a mechanism to store both values at the same position (this could be, for example, a linked list) to keep the list efficient (although in so doing it loses its worst-case-one property) and store all the values in the larger data set. If we can come up with an algorithm to ensure that every value we want to store maps to exactly a position in the list (with no collisions), we have a *perfect hashing algorithm*. As anybody knows who has implemented a hash table, perfect hash functions rarely exist except in certain specific data sets.

From a cryptographic point of view, the hashing concept is identical to the one described previously, in that we want to operate on the data to produce a (usually) smaller "representative" value from a large blob of data, but nonidentical in terms of the goal. In fact, hashing for cryptographic purposes is actually simpler than hashing as we are typically used to it. Specifically, when we hash data for optimizing searches, we start by producing a representative index that is useful as an index for data storage and retrieval. In addition, we usually want to optimize our hashing function according to the data we want to store to reduce possible collisions. When we produce cryptographic hash, we only care about making the "index"; it doesn't matter if the index makes an efficient identifier, we don't have to optimize the function for our data set, and so forth. The entire point of hashing in cryptography is simply to produce a *unique* (or as close as possible) small value for an input string. Said another way, the goal of a cryptographic hash is the unique value itself. Cryptographic hashing functions attempt to approach (as near as possible) a perfect hashing function for the data set that contains all possible input strings. This unique "index" value that is generated as a result of the hashing of an input string is usually referred to as a *message digest*, or a "hash."

For most purposes, there are some important properties a hash function should have; the first is low incidence of collision. In other words, our hash values should produce indices (digests) with an extremely remote chance of finding two or more different input values that map to the same index value. Having a low incidence of collision allows the message digest to be used in a manner similar to the way we use CRC (cyclical redundancy check) to ensure that a message hasn't been tampered with or corrupted. We can use the value as a type of secure "shorthand" for the complete message itself. For example, a usage scenario might involve a message being hashed and sent to another party. The receiver of the message can then hash the message again and check to see if the values match. If they do, the original string hasn't been modified unless the hash value was also modified.

An additional property for our hash functions to have is that they are "one way" or "trapdoor" functions; specifically, it should be designed so it is difficult to reconstruct the original message (or any part of) given only the hash. Like a one-way street or a trap door, it is "easier" to go one way than it is to go the other. Making the function difficult to reverse allows us to perform comparisons on sensitive values (such as passwords or social security numbers) without having to retain the value in a storage repository somewhere, and also facilitates comparison of messages without the fear that exposure of the hash value will compromise the original message.

3.1.1.1 The Bare Minimum: Hashing

- Hash functions produce a small fixed-length index value ("hash value" or "message digest") from an arbitrary input string.
- Hash functions are relatively easy to compute, but it is "very difficult" (effectively impossible given current technology) to determine the input string given only the hash value.
- The incidence of collision for a cryptographic hash function is extremely remote (difficult to find two strings that hash to the same value).
- A hash function can be used to detect data modification.

3.1.2 Data Encryption

In the abstract, if we want to send data from point A to point B in a private manner, we need tools to render the data "unreadable" in transit. There are numerous applications where this type of communication might prove beneficial. For example, generals might wish to send commands to troops over long distances without the enemy being able to intercept and read the communiqués, revolutionaries might wish to plot in secret without danger of being discovered, or a patron of an online merchant might wish to send his or her credit card number over the Internet to conduct a purchasing transaction. All these situations require that one individual be able to conduct discourse with another individual without fear that an eavesdropper can "listen in" on the conversation. There are a number of ways this can be done, and throughout the course of history, humans have involved themselves in a "trial and error" process of generating new and better ways to send secure messages and new and better ways for eavesdroppers to get access to those messages. A full discussion on the history of cryptography is outside the scope of this book, but suffice it to say that modern computing is the inheritor of a long tradition of incremental improvements in both these areas.

In authoring automated systems that wish to send data from point A to point B, we have at our disposal a number of tools that operate on arbitrary input data to transmute ordinary unencrypted text (*plaintext*) into meaningless gibberish that only our intended recipient can understand. *Encryption* (or *encipherment*) is the term used to refer to operate on the input string to produce the gibberish (*ciphertext*), and *decryption* (or *decipherment*) describes the reverse process of taking the gibberish and operating on it to change it back into the plaintext. As developers, we already know what algorithms are (an instructional "recipe"), so it should be intuitive when we say that the specific processes we'll use to encrypt are referred to as *encryption algorithms*, and the reverse as *decryption algorithms*; the term *cipher* is also used to describe these processes. These algorithms take an input string and operate on it in conjunction with a *key* to encrypt or decrypt the data. According to our requirements, we can either choose an algorithm where the encryption key and the decryption key are the same (*symmetric cryptography*), or we can choose from a different class of algorithms that use one key for encryption and another for decryption (*asymmetric cryptography*). We'll cover keys, symmetric cryptography, and asymmetric cryptography in more detail in the next few sections.

As users of cryptography, we will very often find it desirable to encrypt data in our applications; however, experience and history have taught some hard lessons about what works to keep data safe and what doesn't. In other words, there are an infinite number of ways to encrypt data, but only a few ways to encrypt it safely. Since our goal is to rapidly get up to speed to use the tools, we obviously don't want to waste time making an in-depth study of why particular strategies are safe and why others are not. The first and most important thing to keep in mind in using cryptography is to never, under any circumstances, write any new primitive ourselves. As developers, we usually like to understand thoroughly the tools we write; after all, debugging is so much easier when we can anticipate exactly what a particular instruction, subroutine, or function will do. We also like to tweak, optimize, and enhance. These two qualities usually help us to excel in creating efficient applications, but can be particularly dangerous when approaching cryptography from a "usage only" perspective. Keeping ourselves "usage focused" is sometimes a faith-based exercise in that we need to maintain a level of trust in what the mathematicians and scientists who have studied the topic in depth tell us with respect to some key points. For example, we might be tempted to write our own encryption algorithms because the ones in a given library are slower than what (we think) we could come up with on our own. Alternatively, we might be tempted to "tweak" the algorithms in our libraries so they run faster, compile faster, are optimized for particular hardware, or for some other reason.

Here's where the trust comes in: it's important that we avoid modifying the existing algorithms, creating new algorithms, or anything of the kind until and unless we can develop the cryptanalytic skills to ensure that the tweaks we make are robust. We're not going to even come close to covering those skills in this book. Going back to the radio or TV analogy: using a TV is easy, but building a TV from scratch (especially one with better resolution, more vibrant color, better sound, etc.) or "optimizing" an existing TV to have more features is almost certainly a doomed exercise until we understand the intricacies of what makes a TV work. This book instructs users how to "turn on the TV," not how to build, add features to, or upgrade grandma's old "black and white" to high-definition plasma. In other words, the hard truth is that cryptographic algorithms can and do become "broken" over time, numerous individuals look for attacks against cryptographic algorithms on a daily basis looking for anything from statistical weaknesses in the resultant ciphertext (i.e., does a particular byte or bit sequence appear at a greater frequency than others), to leaked key bits in the ciphertext, to mathematical attacks against the cipher itself. From both a practical and a security standpoint, we will never want to undertake the modification of an existing algorithm or the development of a new one. The security issues that can be introduced from doing so are enormous, and the practical aspects are so counterproductive as to be foolish. In other words, why spend weeks or months trying to "reinvent the wheel" when we're already under the gun to deliver a product having nothing to do with new ciphers?

There are a few reasons why we feel we need to say this explicitly: first, developing a new (or faster) cryptographic algorithm (whether it works or not) is almost certain to take longer than using the routines already invented. Second, unless we spend months or years researching the underlying principles of both cipher design and *cryptanalysis* (the study of breaking ciphers), our attempts to do this will almost always result in insecure software. The result of our attempts might *look* similar to the output of the supplied algorithms, but it won't be. Both of the authors of this book have, in the course of our careers, seen multiple instances of *production* software that uses insecure cryptography: one notable example involves thousands of machines, a bank, and an "encryption" algorithm that can be broken in minutes using a pencil and some paper. The developer who wrote this code thought his software was superior because of its speed, but didn't understand the security ramifications of his tinkering.

3.1.2.1 The Bare Minimum: Data Encryption

- Encryption algorithms are used in conjunction with keys to turn plaintext into ciphertext.
- Symmetric cryptography uses one key for encryption and decryption.
- Asymmetric cryptography uses different keys for encryption and decryption.
- Always use proven encryption and decryption algorithms—tweaking is insecure.

3.1.3 Keys

In some ways, much of the cryptographic functionality we're going to discuss is similar to the concept of a physical lock. And as we all know, locks and keys pretty much always go together; even a combination lock that does not have a physical key still has some type of key (a sequence rather than a physical artifact). When we stop to think about it, each of us has a large number of locks in our life: on our car, our house, the file cabinet at work, and so forth. Each of those locks is designed to do the same thing: allow a particular person (or group of people) to accomplish a particular task (e.g., start the car), or gain access to a particular place (e.g., get inside the filing cabinet) while keeping others from doing the same. Digital keys have the same function. Digital keys restrict access to data, resources, and application functionality, and prevent unauthorized individuals from gaining access to the artifacts they protect.

Let's review some properties of physical keys before we delve into digital ones. Specifically, we know the following about the keys we encounter every day:

- We need to protect keys when they are being used.
- We need to safely store keys when they are not being used.
- We sometimes need to replace keys.
- Keys vary in size and shape according to function (e.g., a car key looks different from a house key).

In the physical world, we always need to control access to our keys. Specifically, we need to make sure that the people we want to have access to them do, and the people we don't want to have access to them don't. If our keys govern access to a particular resource, we need to make sure we give the key only to persons we trust; as a corollary to this, we also know that we need to limit the opportunity for untrustworthy persons to steal, borrow, or make copies of the keys. There are all sorts of subtle variations on how, when, and to whom we distribute our keys. For example, we might own an apartment building and want the superintendent to have access to all apartments in a particular building, or we might be employed as an office manager and want to maintain a master key to all offices in a workplace just in case we have to fire somebody. Hand in hand with limiting access to the keys is having a place to safely store keys once they are distributed to the right (authorized) individuals. We usually put keys on a key ring and hang them somewhere where we can easily access them (and where we can be reasonably sure that no one else can get to them). We wouldn't want, for example, to tape the keys to our house to the front door, since passersby might notice the keys and use them inappropriately.

Since keys are something we want to keep secure, we run into trouble if a key loses its "safe" (i.e., "private" and "uncopied") property—if, for example, we lose our keys. Sometimes, if we lose our keys somewhere, we might not know where the key was lost, and the key is now "unsafe" because somebody we don't trust might pick it up and use it (or hold on to it to use it in the future). Other times, we might know exactly where the key is, but we know that it has been rendered "unsafe" or *compromised* for one reason or another (e.g., our ex-roommate has a copy). In these cases, the most common way to return to a state in which only authorized individuals have access to what we are trying to protect is to change the key. In most cases, we would have a locksmith come to change the locks, or purchase and install a new lock ourselves. In effect, we render the previous compromised key useless by making sure it no longer has practical value.

The properties of keys we outlined are equally true in the digital space. Before we get into the specifics of usage (how they're used, what they're used for, etc.), we can already intuit by analogy some of the most important properties associated with cryptographic keys. Specifically, we need to keep them safe, we need to make sure we are prepared to take some action if they become unsafe, we need to limit who has access to them, and so on. Without getting into specifics of what a digital key *is*, we've already touched on some of the more "advanced" issues associated with keys; for example, complexities of key distribution, key compromise, key changes, and (to a limited degree) key escrow (analogous to the building superintendent or the office manager). It is a true statement to say that dealing with *key management* (ensuring that keys remain safe, usable, and accessible) is where we will spend the largest portion of our time in developing secure applications. It is probably the most important topic we will cover, and is the place where the cryptographic libraries we'll be using offer the smallest "help" with respect to providing packaged solutions for us. In other words, the routines and primitives supplied to use within the libraries oftentimes help in generating keys, but we still need to pay attention to how we use those keys in our secure application and how they are handled outside of our application.

So, what is a cryptographic key? Simply defined, a cryptographic key is provided as input into an algorithm to render an arbitrary unencrypted buffer into an encrypted buffer, or vice versa. This is a patent oversimplification, of course, and is only true most of the time. However (fortunately for us), from a development point of view, we don't have to understand the miracle of mathematics that's going on under the hood in order to use keys in a powerful way. From our point of view, all we need to know is that a key is a buffer ("byte string"). Before continuing, let's qualify what we mean by that to prevent any confusion. We mean "byte string" here in its most literal sense: a contiguous string of bytes; another way to say this is that a key is an (usually) opaque buffer. Saying that a key is a "byte string" does not imply that the individual bits of the key are not important; quite the contrary. Every bit has significance, and (as we'll see in a minute) lessening the variability of individual bits in the key can have a tremendous impact on the security of our applications. Instead, we mean that the key is (most of the time) going to take the form of a buffer that we can usually view as opaque from a usage perspective. More specifically, a key will usually take the form of a byte string of a size that will be constant depending on the algorithm we are using. Sometimes, it might be one we can generate ourselves (with a few caveats), and other times it will be a byte string that we must have the library generate for us. Most of the challenge with cryptographic keys is associated with *how* we use them, *where* we use them, *who* we give them to, and *when* we use them. Fortunately for us, the "what" and the "why" (the "under the hood" questions) are safely out of scope from a usage perspective. There are a few notable exceptions and things to keep in mind in the "opaque buffer" premise, which we'll outline now.

From a usage perspective, it is useful to think of the key as an opaque buffer; however, in reality, each of the bits within the key has significance. One of the few things we do need to pay particular attention to is the fact that we need to do everything in our power to make sure the key is as difficult to guess as possible. There are a number of different types of keys that we're going to discuss, but this property is important no matter what type of key we apply it to. Since a key is a digital artifact, once the key value is known, just creating a copy of a key can entirely reproduce it. This could be done, for example, by antagonistic parties using a "trial and error" approach; in other words, there is nothing stopping someone from attempting to guess what the key might be by trying every possible value. This "guess every possible key and see what works" approach is referred to as a "*brute force*" attack or an "exhaustive search." We'll need to keep this in mind as we select our keys (since we want to make it as hard for attackers to do this as possible) and as we implement "key rotation" strategies (periodically changing the key to a new value). Obviously, the likelihood that someone can guess the key gets more remote the more we can increase the number of possible permutations the key can be. There are two ways we can do this: by increasing the number of possible characters the key can be, and by increasing the length of the key. Most of the time for our purposes, the key will be n number of bytes occupying the range of character values between 0 and 255 (the range of possible unsigned values in an 8-bit quantity), where n is the "key length" (or number of individual bytes comprising the string). Put another way, if we have a string of length 8 with each byte having a range of 0–255, this would be an 8-byte key—usually referred to as a 64-bit key (since each bit is part of the keyspace). Usually, key sizes are described by bit length (e.g., a 256-bit key), but it should be noted that key length is not always a reliable descriptor of strength without considering the algorithm with which it is used.

In addition to making sure we keep the key as difficult to guess as possible, we want to follow safe handling procedures. Again, the fact that the key is digital means that we need to make sure we limit the degree to which transient copies of it are made, and that unauthorized individuals are unable to get access to the value. This means that we'll want to be sure we protect the keys (both inside and outside the application boundary), we use the keys with care, we don't allow copies of the key to be indiscriminately bandied about, and so forth. Lastly, when creating keys, we'll want to review the properties of the keys that are relevant for the algorithm we choose, and follow any instructions/guidance given to us by the persons doing research in that area. Specifically, some algorithms might have known "weak values," guidelines for appropriate key lengths, particular instructions as to how the key can be used safely, and so forth. These are all criteria we should consider during the authorship of our software application design.

3.1.3.1 The Bare Minimum: Keys

- A key is a byte string where each of the bits (potentially) increases the strength of the key.
- The size and properties of the key will vary depending on the algorithm selections you make.
- Cryptographic keys must be protected by keeping distribution and exposure limited (both inside and outside the application).
- Applications should anticipate changing of the key (key rotation) over time.

3.1.4 Symmetric Encryption

Symmetric encryption will prove extraordinarily useful to us as we develop secure applications; in fact, we will find it applicable in almost every context where we wish to ensure data privacy. The purpose (if not the implementation) is extraordinarily simple to understand conceptually: take an arbitrary length (and arbitrary character) input string, and operate on it in combination with a key to "scramble" (more formally, *encrypt* or *encipher*) the string such that individuals without that particular key won't be able to reconstruct the original data. Later, we can take the *ciphertext* (encrypted string) and turn it back into *plaintext* (the original unencrypted string) by using the *same key* and operating on it with the decryption mode of the same algorithm.

There are a number of choices we can make in using symmetric cryptography. For example, we can select from dozens of algorithms and a number of modes in which those algorithms can operate. We'll make algorithm and mode choices based on a number of criteria, including, for example, performance, regulatory constraints, encumbrance (i.e., patent status), and so forth. Later in this book, we'll go into the details of the most common symmetric algorithms to give you the information you need to make a wise decision for particular types of tasks. There are two different classes of symmetric *ciphers* (algorithms) we can choose from based on whether we want to operate on data in chunks (blocks) or on a bit-by-bit basis.

3.1.4.1 Block Ciphers

The first class of symmetric algorithms we'll discuss form a general class of ciphers referred to as *block ciphers*. Block ciphers are so named because they manipulate data in "blocks," as discrete units of a given size. Block ciphers operate on a chunk of plaintext of a fixed input size and transform it into an encrypted output block of a fixed size (usually, the output block is the same size as the input block, although this can vary). Block ciphers don't inherently maintain state, so the encryption of each block is distinct and independent from the one before it (that is, before we add a "*mode of operation*" to it).

Block ciphers can operate in one of a few *modes*. The ones we'll discuss in this section are *ECB mode* and *CBC mode*, which are the most common (and probably the most useful) modes we'll come across. We'll talk about other modes in subsequent sections, as they might become relevant for backward compatibility with existing applications or for conformance to a particular protocol, but most of the time when we're creating new applications, these are the modes we'll consider first.

ECB Mode

ECB stands for "Electronic Code Book" and is basically just that: an electronic codebook. Imagine that you were going to come up with a book of codes in which every word in the English language had a "code word" that would be used when you wanted to have a secure communication with someone. For example, "paisley" might map to "zhibang," so when you said that to the person you were communicating with, he would look it up in his book and know what word you meant. ECB mode of a block cipher does exactly this: every "word" (block of n size where n is the "block size" of the cipher) transforms to exactly one encrypted word. Since the key tells you what book to use, if you select a different key, you completely change the codebook.

ECB mode can be useful for our purposes, but only in a few carefully selected situations. Since each block of the encrypted text will always map to the same value given a constant key, we have a big problem in that an attacker could make an intelligent guess about the data we are trying to protect when certain codes occur with greater frequency than others do. As an example, say we write an application to encrypt files in ECB mode and we use that application to encrypt a database file. Most database files are "sparse" files, and therefore have a huge incidence of nulls within them. An attacker might not be able to decrypt the file *per se*, but he could tell where the nulls are; by seeing a certain block of data appearing frequently throughout the file in encrypted form, he could assume that code refers to nulls. Since the attacker probably knows what database software we are using, he could make guesses about where the data is located in the database, how the tables are laid out, and so forth. This is obviously undesirable for most cases where we desire strong security. However, ECB does have the advantage that blocks can be encrypted and decrypted "out of order," meaning that if we were to encrypt a database file with it, we wouldn't have to decrypt the whole thing first to use it; we could only decrypt the blocks we intend to use at the time. For example, we could decrypt the

5th block in a sequence before we decrypted blocks 1 through 4. In other words, ECB mode does not require the sender or the receiver to maintain any state when exchanging a large quantity of data.

CBC Mode

Noting that there's an issue with ECB mode in that an attacker can make guesses about the contents of an encrypted message based on the frequency of "codes" appearing in certain messages, how can we modify the process such that he can't do this? One answer is CBC mode. CBC stands for *Cipher Block Chaining* and is designed to prevent exactly the problem we outlined earlier. CBC mode operates by making the output from each cipher iteration (each block that is to be encrypted) impacted by the one before it. In CBC mode, the first incidence of a block of nulls (or anything else for that matter) would encrypt to a different value than each subsequent incidence because of this inherent dependency. Since state is required to implement this dependency on previous blocks, an internal state must be artificially created "external" to the block cipher to get it to operate in this way. This is done by the incorporation of a *feedback register* into the encipherment process whereby previous encrypted blocks are stored for modification of subsequent operations. Why do we care about the feedback register (since after all, we don't have to know how the algorithm works to use it)? Unfortunately, this is one case where we have to care a little bit how the algorithm works, since the feedback register has to be populated before it can be used on the first block. That feedback register needs to be seeded before we can use it. This initial seeding is called an *Initialization Vector* (IV), and some of the libraries we will be using will require us or optionally allow us to supply a value for the IV in order to use CBC mode. Usually, "random" data can be used for the IV in these cases, and we'll need to hang on to the IV after we use it because the recipient will need to know it for the decryption of the data.

3.1.4.2 Stream Ciphers

As we've just seen, when using a block cipher, if we want to make sure the encryption of one block impacts the encryption of the following blocks, we use a feedback register to do so. This is because block ciphers don't inherently maintain an internal state; if we require "state"—for example, to chain blocks together—we have to add it (feedback register). Unlike block ciphers, stream ciphers *do* establish an internal state. Just like block ciphers, they operate on input to encrypt or decrypt data; however, stream ciphers operate on individual bits rather than on fixed-length blocks. In fact, a stream cipher in operation can be visualized as an incredibly complex finite state machine; as bits enter and leave the cipher, they (potentially) change the internal state and thus impact how the next bit entering the machine will be encrypted. For the most part, the "state" maintained by a stream cipher is concerned with generating an ongoing "stream" of bits (*keystream*) that will be used to encrypt the plaintext.

In general, stream ciphers are most useful for cases where we are working in the context of an unbuffered communication channel, where individual characters will be transmitted rather than larger chunks of data. Stream ciphers are most often used in network communication contexts (such as socket-based communication), where use of a block cipher would introduce inefficiencies into the application's data transport mechanism. Note that our selection of appropriate stream ciphers is much more limited than the selection of available block ciphers (there are many more block ciphers than stream ciphers).

3.1.4.3 The Bare Minimum: Symmetric Cryptography

- Symmetric cryptography (also called "secret key" encryption) refers to ciphers that use the same key for encryption and decryption.
- Symmetric ciphers allow us to encrypt data for the purposes of keeping our data private.
- Block ciphers work on fixed-size chunks of input data.
- Block cipher modes of operation can either work on each block independently (ECB mode) or chain blocks together (CBC mode).
- Stream ciphers don't need blocks (they operate on individual bits rather than on fixed-size "chunks"), but must maintain internal state.
- Cipher selection impacts performance and security.

3.1.5 Asymmetric Cryptography

While symmetric cryptography uses only one key for both encryption and decryption, asymmetric cryptography uses different keys for each of these operations (thus making it asymmetric with respect to key use). One key is used to encrypt a message, and a different (but related) key is used to decrypt that same message. Creative use of this concept allows us to solve a number of problems, both in the areas of privacy and authentication. In most asymmetric schemes, after the encryption and corresponding decryption keys are generated, one key is kept private and the other is made available to everyone with whom the holder of the secret key wishes to communicate. The withheld key is referred to as the *private key*, and the public key is referred to as the *public key* (sometimes, you'll hear the phrase "public key cryptosystems" used to refer to asymmetric cryptography). Only the private key can decrypt data encrypted with the public key, and/or only the public key can decrypt data encrypted by the private key.

Using the keys in this way allows a few things to happen. First, encrypted messages from a number of disparate senders intended for the holder of the private key can be generated without the need to share symmetric keys with any of the message senders (solving some particularly snarly key distribution problems historically associated with symmetric cryptography). This flexibility comes at a cost compared with symmetric cryptography, however: specifically, encrypting and decrypting data using asymmetric cryptography is a good deal slower than symmetric cryptography—we'll discuss some methods to get around this in the next chapter. Additionally, generation of keys is quite a bit more costly in terms of complexity and CPU cycles than symmetric cryptography is. Aside from these minor drawbacks, however, asymmetric cryptography does greatly reduce the complexity of key distribution (this feature in and of itself is "worth the price of admission"), but there is also an additional property that makes asymmetric cryptography even more useful. Namely, if the person holding the private key can encrypt a known value, individuals can decrypt that value and know with certainty that the party holding the private key encrypted it, thus authenticating by association the message sender (since only the person with the private key could have generated the message). Let's look in depth at how a few of these concepts work, since we will see them in use in almost every commercial cryptosystem on the market and in hundreds of open source and freeware tools.

Key distribution: While reading the section on symmetric cryptography, you might have noticed a few underlying difficulties associated with the process. For example, you might have asked yourself something along the lines of, "this is all well and good, but how do I get a key to the person I'm encrypting data for in the first place?" This is a challenging problem and one that numerous engineers and scientists have spent decades trying to solve. In fact, *key distribution* (getting the right keys to authorized parties) is probably the hardest challenge we'll encounter as we design our secure systems. One of the problems with symmetric cryptography is that in order to conduct secure communications, we have to share a key with everyone with whom we wish to communicate. For example, if we wish to communicate with person A, we need to share a key with him; if we want to communicate also with person B, we'll need a different key for her (unless we don't mind that A can read B's messages), and another one for person C, and so on. The situation gets more complex if the various parties involved want to communicate among themselves using a key that is not known to us. In fact, the key distribution problem associated with symmetric cryptography is so huge that it is almost impracticable to use it alone on any kind of large scale. One of the ways in which asymmetric cryptography can help us approach this problem is by reducing the number of keys we need to share among communicants. For example, since the user has a public key (one that anyone can use to encrypt data for them), individuals do not need to share keys on an individual basis. Rather, everyone and anyone can use the user's public key to encrypt data for which the user is the ultimate intended recipient. This reduces (although does not eliminate) many of the key distribution issues associated with the secure exchange of data.

Digital signature: Another challenge that asymmetric cryptography helps solve is the issue of authenticating the origin of a particular message. Using the techniques we've already discussed, we can implement a system that binds messages to a particular individual. Say, for example, we were to hash a message, and send a version of that hash encrypted with the private key of the originator along with a given message. In that case, the individual on the receiving end could decrypt the hash value (using the public key of the alleged sender), hash the message again, and ensure that both hashes match. Since only the sender has access to the private key associated with the public key we possess, this provides assurance that the originator of the message had access to that private key. Sometimes, this is referred to as *proof of possession*, which is just a fancy way of saying that the private key associated with the individual we know about has operated on the data in question; we are assuming that the public key we are using belongs to the individual we expect. This process is referred to as *signing*.

There are a few things we should note about asymmetric cryptography. First, it is slow. In fact, it is so incredibly slow to complete the encryption and decryption process that we want to exercise discretion about the size of data we encrypt, and we want to employ it as infrequently as possible in our application. Ideally, we want to be somewhat creative about how we go about employing asymmetric encryption to limit the intrinsic performance overhead. If, for example, we wanted to encrypt a file and send it to a recipient using asymmetric cryptography, encrypting the whole file with the asymmetric algorithm might take too long to be practical. So, instead (in keeping with being creative about usage), we might use symmetric cryptography (which is faster) and asymmetric cryptography together to reduce the overhead. One scheme might have us first generate a random symmetric key, then encrypt the data with that key using a symmetric algorithm, then encrypt the symmetric key with the receiver's public key, and finally send the whole package to our recipient in a formalized structure. In fact, this is the most common scenario for asymmetric encryption of files: Microsoft® EFS (Encrypted File System) employs a similar methodology, as does PGP (Pretty Good Privacy™), as do numerous other products on the market.

Asymmetric cryptography requires that we have the public key of the individual(s) with whom we wish to exchange data; this implies an effective mechanism for distributing the public keys of the parties who wish to converse. This is no small consideration for a few reasons: specifically, there may be a large number of individuals with whom we wish to communicate, or we may not share a trusted communication channel with these parties to exchange keys with them (meaning that someone could substitute a different public key other than our intended recipient's along the way). Moreover, the problem extends further: even if we had infinite space in which to store the keys of parties with whom we wish to converse and we could ensure that they are securely disseminated, using asymmetric cryptographic primitives alone without a larger context will only ensure secure communications with individuals of whom we have knowledge of ahead of time. If we encountered somebody new, we would not be able to use asymmetric cryptography until we could securely obtain his or her public key. This issue leads us to another strategy we see often employed in asymmetric cryptography; namely, the "trusted third party."

Trusted third party: If, for example, there was an individual whom we knew we could trust and with whom we knew we could conduct tamper-free discourse, we could ask him to tell us the public keys for any individuals he knows about. In this scenario, we wouldn't need to keep the communication channel private between our third party and us (since the keys we're asking for are already public), but we would need to make sure the channel is tamperproof. We could share our public key with this third party for distribution to others, and we could ask the third party for the public keys of others if we encounter new individuals. In other words, this third party would act as a sort of "public key broker," whose job it is to make sure he knows everybody's public keys and can be relied on to share the keys with us on an as-needed basis. One way this "third party" role is implemented in practice is to have the third party authenticate the individuals in question, put the public keys of the authenticated individuals into a common formalized structure (e.g., a *certificate*), and then use asymmetric cryptography to sign those keys (i.e., we have the third party—a trusted authority—sign the public keys of everyone). Now we only have to know the public keys of our trusted authority to employ asymmetric cryptography with a number of individuals. Whenever we encounter someone we don't know, we can ask the new party to send us his or her public key signed by the trusted third party, and we can verify the signature on those keys and in the process make sure the trusted third party has "signed off" that these public keys belong to the right individual. Such a scheme is typically referred to as a *Public Key Infrastructure*, or PKI. As the name implies, a PKI is the infrastructure put in place to ensure reliable distribution of public keys to all the parties who need to conduct secure communications. We'll go into more detail on some of the more common ways in which schemes like this are implemented further along in this book, but for now, we only need to know that such schemes exist and why they must, by necessity, operate the way they do.

3.1.5.1 The Bare Minimum: Asymmetric Cryptography

- Uses two different keys for encryption and decryption: a "public key" and a "private key."
- Can be combined with other cryptographic primitives to solve authentication and privacy problems, including data source authentication (signatures).
- Incredibly slow performance requires limited (or efficient) usage.
- Key generation is cumbersome and slow.
- A trusted third party (such as a PKI, "key broker," etc.) can be used to assist in reliable and safe key distribution.

3.2 COMMON TECHNIQUES

Having discussed the primitives we can use, we should probably take some time to discuss some of the common ways we'll use them repeatedly in our software. Sometimes, we'll need to come up with a unique and innovative strategy to perform a particular task, but this is the exception rather than the rule. More often than not, we'll want to use a standard structure, methodology, or technique when we encounter a given situation. We'll briefly run through some of these common high-level techniques and data structures here. The goal here is not to cover every technique in depth, but to give an idea of some of the most common ones so we know where to look when faced with a particular task (and so we're not intimidated when we drill down on these concepts later).

3.2.1 Common Data Structures

In general, as developers there are only exceptional circumstances where we want to create our own proprietary data structures and techniques. For example, most of the time, we are going to use the same sorting algorithms that have been studied in computer science since the 1960s; the algorithms are well known, well studied, and we're already familiar with exactly what their characteristics are and what they do. This keeps us from having to reinvent the wheel every time we're faced with a particular problem. In general, using standard techniques and methodologies cuts down on the amount of development work for us, makes our maintenance process easier, reduces the amount of documentation we have to write, reduces the amount of explanation we have to give to our clients about why we chose the implementation we did, and so forth. Use of standard structures and protocols is particularly important in a security context, as security professionals will tend to approach a new protocol or data structure with suspicion unless we can demonstrate exhaustive testing of our technique (which increases our testing and documentation workload even more). Therefore, we'll attempt to use data structures that already exist in every case we can to the extent that they are provided to us in an easy-to-use way. There may be times when we need to branch out, but for most platforms, techniques, and applications, there are standards-based mechanisms for doing just about anything we need to do with cryptography (e.g., manipulating or representing data). Since it is useful for us to have at least a passing familiarity with some of the standards as we "assemble our toolkit" (i.e., outline the broad categories of tasks we'll undertake), we'll run through some of the most important concepts quickly just to be acquainted. Later, when we need to start using them, we'll get into more of the details.

3.2.1.1 ASN.1, BER, and DER

Briefly, ASN.1 stands for *Abstract Syntax Notation One*, which details a methodology for creating self-describing *logical* structures formed of data primitives (integers, strings, etc.) and other constructed elements (which are themselves self-describing). BER and DER stand for *Basic Encoding Rules* and *Distinguished Encoding Rules*, respectively, and constitute a mechanism whereby ASN.1 logical structures can be translated into *concrete* encoded structures that we as developers will "allegedly" be familiar with and will be "supposedly" readily able to read and parse. Why the "allegedly" and the "supposedly"? Here's the "no holds barred" take on BER/DER: these structures are decidedly complex, very difficult to parse in practice, and implementations that parse them are often subject to error (to prove this, just do an Internet search for "ASN" and "vulnerability" and take note of the incredible number of results). This is not to say that we should never use ASN.1 (there are times when we won't be able to avoid it), but in so doing, we'll probably want to streamline our development by using a library rather than manipulating the structures ourselves. In general, since the libraries we'll be employing contain mechanisms for dealing with these structures without implementing a parser ourselves, we won't be interacting with these structures directly. After all, why introduce the extra headache of dealing with highly error-prone and difficult to debug code if we don't have to?

In understanding why we want to avoid manipulating these structures directly, let's examine their complexity in more detail. First and foremost, complexity is introduced because particular *bits* within these structures are ascribed specific meanings. Worse, the meanings are ascribed under difficult to anticipate circumstances; for example, depending on if bit #8 of a given byte is 1 or 0, there might be a particular significance; bit #7 might have an entirely different meaning, and so on. Some of the bits govern whether the rest of the byte contains length information of subsequent bytes or contains data. The complexity extends further in that particular *combinations* of bit sequences have particular meanings as well. Working with dynamic memory allocation for these structures is an error-prone and extremely difficult to debug process that can slow application development to a snail's pace.

Aside from making our development slower, it also makes our resultant software more susceptible to security issues unless we are extremely careful and test thoroughly. In particular, since using these structures entails parsing nested structures of dynamic length, we can anticipate a good deal of intricate and excruciating dynamic memory management as well as the pain of implementing the underlying parser. It's particularly embarrassing to make a mistake during these complicated memory management routines in a security module, and potentially introduce security vulnerabilities into the code. If we use a library instead of writing a parser, we can have a level of confidence that the code within that library has been tested and that updates to any discovered issues in the ASN.1 parsing routines will be accounted for without our involvement.

3.2.1.2 X.509 Public Key Certificates

Having gone through asymmetric (public key) cryptography in a cursory fashion, we know that if we have access to an individual's public key, we can encrypt messages that only he can read, and we can verify that messages originating from the key holder are trustworthy (or at least "semitrustworthy") by verifying any signatures that may be sent along with the message. We've also discussed mechanisms by which trusted third parties can assist with key distribution. Probably the most common way in which the "third-party trusted authority" model has been formalized is in the International Telecommunications Union's *X.509* digital certificates standard (X.509). At its simplest, X.509 is a mechanism whereby an entity's public key is associated to an X.500 *Distinguished Name* (DN). An X.500 DN is basically just a handy, efficient way of naming an entity uniquely among a much larger population of entities. X.509 gives us a way to bind an entity's name to a key, and to represent that entity's public key in a portable format (called a *certificate*). X.509 also ties into a larger body of work that allows us to efficiently look up those entities within a larger population. As you can probably tell, this is the most useful (or at least the most standardized) method we have for implementing the "trusted third party" approach we outlined earlier.

Let's talk a little about what certificates are, what they're used for, and how the process of obtaining one works in the abstract. An X.509 certificate is an encoded data structure; the structure contains information on the certificate lifetime, owner, and function (what it can be used for, when it expires, who issued it, who it belongs to, etc.). As these certificates are usually DER encoded, we'll want to avoid manipulating the structures directly in keeping with what we discussed previously. Fortunately for us, we almost never have to deal with certificates directly, as all of our target libraries contain interfaces for dealing with certificates. X.509 certificates are typically generated in the following way: a public/private key pair is generated, and the public key is placed inside a *Certificate Signing Request*, or CSR (a standardized request for obtaining a certificate that is sent to a *Certificate Authority*, or CA (the CA fills the role of the "trusted third party" described previously). The CA receives the certificate signing request and (ideally) authenticates the requestor in a robust and thorough way. The CA generates an X.509 certificate according to its rules of certificate issuance (*Certificate Policy*) and sends the completed certificate back to the requestor. During the issuance process, the CA may put constraints on the certificate, such as duration for which the certificate is valid, what the associated key can be used for (e.g., email, Web servers, signing, encryption, etc.), and so on. After the certificate has been issued, the CA will periodically update and publish revocation information (although this is not a requirement). Most CAs publish revocation in the form of a *Certificate Revocation List* (CRL), a list of certificates that have been revoked (certificates that have become invalid prior to their expiration). While CRLs are the most common method for checking revocation status, the CA may also implement a real-time revocation status query and response interface (e.g., via the *Online Certificate Status Protocol*—OCSP). As long as a certificate is not expired and does not appear on the CRL, the certificate is assumed valid (i.e., authorized by the signer) and the associated public key can be used with impunity by any party wishing to conduct secure discourse with the certificate holder.

In addition to the formalization of signatures, keys, and so on, certificates have a number of attributes they contain within the structure. In version 3 of X.509, certificates can contain a near-infinite number of extensible attributes that allow CAs and application authors to further extend the functionality of certificates. While the attributes will vary from CA to CA (and from usage to usage), the following are the ones we will be concerned with most often:

Serial Number: Every certificate has a serial number with which it can be easily located within the population of certificates issued by a given CA.

Subject: While the DN is the full name of the entity in the context of X.500, the CN (*Common Name*) is a "short name" that may or may not have a specific meaning depending on the application we are using the certificate for. For example, in the context of SSL authentication, the CN must match the DNS name of the Web site.

Issuer: The DN of the CA that issued the certificate.

Validity Period: The time interval during which the certificate is valid.

Key Usage, Basic Constraints, and Extended Key Usage: The allowed purpose(s) of the certificate and corresponding key; for example, if the certificate is for a CA, if it can only be used for certain purposes, etc.

CRL Distribution Points: The locality (usually a URL) of the CRL, if there is one.

3.2.1.3 PKCS #7, PKCS #11, and PKCS #12

RSA Security develops and maintains a number of PKCS or *Public Key Cryptography Standards* documents that lay out various standard methodologies, formats, APIs, and so on for low-level implementers of public key (asymmetric) encryption technologies. While these technologies are not formal standards *per se* (some have been submitted to formal standards bodies), RSA does attempt to facilitate the development of standards around them. Specifically, RSA retains final authority on each document, although input from reviewers is clearly influential. However, RSA's goal is to accelerate the development of formal standards, not to compete with such work. Thus, when a PKCS document is accepted as a base document for a formal standard, RSA relinquishes its "ownership" of the document, giving way to the open standards development process.

There are currently 13 PKCS documents (the number goes up to 15, but 2 have been incorporated into previous standards); of these, the ones we will come across most often are PKCS #12 and PKCS #7. PKCS #11 is another PKCS standard that will be discussed in more detail later as we start to discuss various hardware platforms, but is appropriate to introduce here.

PKCS #7

PKCS #7, "Cryptographic Message Syntax Standard," defines a structure whereby a message that has had public key cryptography applied to it can be represented in a portable and standardized way. Typically, we can avoid having to parse this structure directly, but it is useful to understand that most libraries will produce some output messages in this format. As outlined in RFC 2315, PKCS #7 is most often used to encode encrypted or signed mail messages such as those found in S/MIME.[2]

PKCS #11

PKCS #11, "Cryptographic Token Interface Standard," describes a high-level *application programming interface* (API) that we can use to interface with cryptographic hardware such as accelerators or key storage modules. We will discuss this API in more detail in subsequent chapters. Almost all of the key storage modules that we will encounter will have a PKCS #11 interface, thus making it very useful in dealing with these devices.

PKCS #12

PKCS #12 ("Personal Information Exchange Syntax Standard") defines a mechanism for exchanging personal information in a portable format; "personal information" in this context refers to information such as certificates, keys, and so forth. Again, it is not critical that we understand the intricacies of these structures at this point, only acknowledge that some of the libraries may produce output (and require input) in this format. An example use of PKCS #12 would be the importing or exporting of certificates and associated private keys from one Web browser to another (such as from Mozilla to Internet Explorer, for example).

3.2.1.4 The Bare Minimum: Common Data Structures

- ASN.1 is a language of logical description.
- DER and BER describe concrete structures based on ASN.1; DER and BER are difficult to implement correctly.
- X.509 certificates are formalized structures mapping an asymmetric key to an X.500 DN.
- PKCS #7 defines a formalized structure for cryptographic artifacts.
- PKCS #11 defines an API for interfacing with cryptographic modules.
- PKCS #12 defines a methodology for serializing keys, certificates, or other user information.

3.2.2 Password-Based Symmetric Key Derivation

Deriving an encryption key from a user password is something we may often require as we design and implement secure systems. Since this can be a very powerful tool for us, it pays to take some time to discuss the concept in depth and highlight it specifically as a useful tool that can be used in our application design. Additionally, since incorrect implementation of this concept is extremely dangerous to the security of the application, making sure that developers are forewarned about the potential dangers is particularly important before they undertake an implementation of it.

In our discussions of symmetric cryptography, we've highlighted that one of the main usability challenges deals with safely storing our secret keys. To put it another way, symmetric cryptography is our primary tool for ensuring data privacy, but the usage ironically requires as input a byte string that itself needs to be kept private. This quandary is compounded by the fact that one of the obstacles we may be trying to overcome is the relative insecurity of the storage repositories available to our application. Specifically, our applications may not completely trust the file-system on the host, and they may not trust the databases we can read from. We also can rule out hard coding keys somewhere in our application source code, since doing this presents security problems and complicates key rotation strategies. So, how can we store keys safely? One strategy is to use a hardware storage module, which are certain pieces of hardware that can be bought to assist in safely storing keys. However, they are expensive and time consuming to develop for—using such a device may also lock us into a particular vendor, may complicate deployment, or may just be overkill for the application we are trying to write. However, in addition to using a hardware module, there is another (free) key storage locality that may be available to us: a human user's memory.

In other words, one strategy we could investigate for storing keys is asking the user to remember them for us. We get a number of benefits from employing this approach, specifically:

- Users are used to remembering things to gain access to applications (e.g., passwords).
- The key is stored offline from the application, so an attacker needs to employ different and more creative strategies to get access to it.
- The user becomes responsible for keeping the key safe, not our application (harsh, but true).

There are three drawbacks to implementing this approach literally:

- As we covered earlier in this section (in discussing cryptographic keys), decreasing the possible values that can be in the key (such as by limiting it to printable or, worse yet, alphanumeric characters) has serious security ramifications.
- Users might pick a value that is easy for an attacker to guess if we ask them to come up with a string to use as a key.
- Asking a user to remember and type in many complex nonprintable characters would prove impossible without the user writing the password down somewhere.

To get around these problems, we might want to ask the user for a password and then use the password as input to another mechanism that will derive a robust cryptographic key from the password supplied (one that uses all of the bits available for the symmetric algorithm we're employing). Robust and strong methodologies for securely transmuting a password into a key are provided in the libraries we're investigating, and it behooves us to know about their existence for use in systems that we design and implement. A number of individuals argue that deriving a key from a password is a "bad idea," and they have a point: there are some issues with password-based key derivation. For example, it is quite a bit easier to guess a password than it is to guess a random string, so we will need to employ mechanisms for making sure that passwords we allow the user to supply are robust (e.g., we might want to ensure that passwords are of a particular length or contain both numbers and letters).

3.2.2.1 The Bare Minimum: Password-Based Key Derivation

- The need to store keys safely makes key storage by our applications difficult; our software can use a human user's memory for key storage.
- Passwords harvested from a user can be transformed into robust symmetric cryptographic keys.

- Using a robust derivation function based on standards (like those included in the libraries we'll be using) is much safer than implementing this functionality ourselves.
- Passwords used as input to these functions should be complex and difficult for other parties to guess.

3.2.3 Key Storage

The question of where to store keys when we can't use secure hardware storage and we can't ask a user is a huge challenge (as is anything having to do with key management). In fact, this is another area where we will spend most of our time and problem-solving abilities answering: specifically, where can we store our private keys, our secret keys, and anything else we don't want anybody else to have? For example, say we are writing an automated system (e.g., a server) that needs to start up without a user's intervention. In this case, we certainly can't ask a user for the key since there won't likely be one around every time we want to start up our application. If we work in a product company, trying to convince every customer that they need to purchase expensive key storage hardware in order to use our product is obviously not the most desirable solution. Therefore, we'll need to store at least one key somewhere. A number of people say that storing keys is dangerous and that keys should never be stored anywhere other than in a user's head in the form of a password or hardware (the number of people who say this is probably about the same number of people who say that password-based key derivation is completely unsafe and should be avoided). In the case of an automated system such as the hypothetical one just discussed, we'll need a secure locality wherein to store our keys. Most of the time, we'll need to purchase dedicated key storage hardware, build a secure key storage repository for ourselves in software, or (depending on the library we've chosen) use some of the built-in capabilities of our libraries to assist in doing these kinds of tasks.

3.2.3.1 Key Storage Locality: Hardware Security Modules (HSMs)

Arguably, the most secure place to store a key is a *Hardware Security Module* or HSM (also the most expensive option). Simply stated, HSMs are specialized hardware that attach to a system and perform various security services; one of the services that may be provided is a secure place to store keys. HSMs typically operate in one of two ways: they store the keys on the device and perform all cryptographic functions on the device, or they store the keys on the device and give those keys to the application on request. Obviously, keeping the keys on the device and not allowing them to be released to the operating system provides more security. However, there are disadvantages: since this kind of hardware device is more expensive, we're locked into the cryptographic functionality provided by the module, and we lose some flexibility (e.g., we become very tightly bound to the hardware vendor, etc.). On the other hand, if the device provides the key to us (leaving us to use the key in software cryptographic routines), we need to make sure we handle the key very carefully when it is in our possession. It is also arguable the degree to which storing the key on a hardware device is superior to implementing some sort of alternative key-storage strategy in software and storing an encrypted key artifact on the filesystem. Examples of HSM vendors and products would include SafeNet's Luna series (*www.safenet-inc.com,*) nCipher's nShield/netHSM, and Iteon's myHSM.

3.2.3.2 Key Storage Locality: The Filesystem

For some applications, the filesystem can be an appropriate place to store keys. It could be appropriate, but before we start writing our cryptographic keys all over the disk, there are a few things we should take into consideration first to make sure this is an appropriate strategy for our application. As with anything we do, we will first need to understand the threats we are trying to defend against within our application, and then we will make sure the approach we use does not violate that model. For example, if we wish to write an application whereby the system administrators for the system on which our application is writing cannot easily gain access to the cryptographic keys, we have a bigger challenge than if we don't need to defend against that possibility. Determination of when it is appropriate to employ filesystem key storage, specific access control mechanisms that we can use to safeguard the key during storage, and the like all need to be weighed in the context of the application that is being written. Therefore, it is difficult for a book like this one to give specific guidance on when (or when not) to do it. Once we've decided that it is appropriate to store the keys on the disk in some fashion, we now need to approach the problem of how to store them safely. In most instances, our libraries will supply a key protection strategy that we can leverage to apply a protected serialization or "wrapping" strategy to our keys before writing them to the filesystem. It is important to note that any type of cryptography we apply to the keys stored on the filesystem will itself require keys that we will need to store. While some have argued that wrapping keys before storage does not offer any additional security (since an attacker could potentially have access to anything we write on the filesystem), we'll outline a strategy later that combines the native access control features of our host operating systems with key wrapping strategies that can be applied to at least prevent an attacker from running "cat" on a key storage file and shattering our model.

3.2.3.3 Key Storage Locality: Smartcards

A *smartcard* is a small, portable, information processor (about the size of a credit card) that can implement some degree of tamper resistance and security functionality. One common use of smartcards is to store private keys and/or X.509 digital certificates containing the associated public key. Access to the private key may be protected on the card by means of a password or PIN. In situations where it is feasible to do so, we can use a design methodology whereby users are issued smartcards containing a public and private key, and these cards are used as the primary user key-storage mechanism. Note that such a scheme is likely not applicable for storage of machine-associated keys (such as might be required by a service or a daemon).

3.2.3.4 The Bare Minimum: Key Storage

- Specialized storage hardware (HSMs) can be used as a highly secure method for storing asymmetric or symmetric keys.
- The filesystem can provide a low-cost alternative to key storage hardware, but can only enforce protections to the extent that the underlying operating system security mechanisms are not circumvented.
- Smartcards can be used to store user-bound symmetric keys, user-bound asymmetric key pairs, and/or X.509 digital certificates.

3.3 CRYPTOGRAPHIC LIBRARIES

Now that we have some idea of how we might want to apply cryptography in our application, let's investigate how we might go about doing it and making it work. Since we're interested in "easy" rather than "exhaustive," we're going to start with the biggest shortcut we possibly can: rather than implement any of the underlying cryptography from scratch, we're going to rely on the many readily available implementations that already exist and are available to the developer. We're also going to take another shortcut; rather than selecting from the hundreds (if not thousands) of commercial and noncommercial cryptographic libraries that exist, we're going to select from the four most popular and readily obtained libraries. Each of these libraries has its own advantages and disadvantages, its own strengths and weaknesses, which we will attempt to highlight so developers can make an informed selection.

Our first task is to select a library that matches the appropriate context in which we are going to be doing our application development. Most importantly, we want to select a library that is platform and programming language appropriate. In addition, some libraries are better than others are for doing certain tasks, and we want to make sure we select one that will do what we need it to do. Lastly, we want to make sure there are no regulatory, usage, or support issues that would prevent the library we select from being appropriate for our application. Therefore, let's look at the most common libraries and highlight where each is the most useful. The libraries we're going to focus on are OpenSSL, Microsoft's Cryptographic API

(CAPI), Java's JCA (Java Cryptography Architecture), and RSA Security's BSAFE library. There may be some instances where we will need to employ other libraries outside those described here, but for the majority of applications and platforms, these four will suit our needs nicely.

3.3.1 OpenSSL

OpenSSL is a general-purpose open-source security library that provides both low-level and high-level cryptographic functionality to the developer. OpenSSL is based on the SSLeay project started by Eric Young in the 1990s, and retains in large part the API conceived in the 1990s. Although a great deal of functionality has been added to the library over the years, the library's API has demonstrated itself over time to be stable, flexible, and fairly easy to use. The combination of "free" and "easy to use" makes this library particularly attractive for a large number of projects.

3.3.1.1 Overview

OpenSSL is written predominantly in "C" and is primarily targeted toward Unix operating systems. That's not to say that we should discount the use of this library if we are using another platform such as Microsoft® Windows® or the like. As we'll demonstrate soon enough, the library is also suited to development in a Windows environment (although we'll need to go through a few extra steps to get everything up and running on that platform). In general, just about any platform we'll be interested in developing for can be supported by OpenSSL with a bit of tweaking. In addition to support for a large number of computing platforms, OpenSSL also incorporates "out of the box" support for a number of cryptographic hardware vendors (both HSM and accelerator vendors).

3.3.1.2 Advantages

It's difficult, from an advantage perspective, to beat "free"; open source supporters often discriminate between "free as in beer" and "free as in freedom," but for those of us writing commercial applications, the most appealing is "free" meaning "free of cost." After all, "free" is almost always guaranteed to work in any kind of cost justification to management. OpenSSL is released under a somewhat unusual "Apache-style" license that allows developers to use the functionality in commercial or noncommercial code without fee as long as a few provisions are met. Those provisions are spelled out in the license, but can basically be summed up as "attribution requirements." In short, the majority of what we need to do to stay compliant with the license is give attribution to the current (and previous) authors on the OpenSSL project—not difficult terms to meet. For the most part, we have more flexibility with OpenSSL than we do with any of the other libraries described in this book. OpenSSL is the only one of the libraries we are going to discuss that actually allows us to modify the source code if we so desire. In general, we probably won't want to do this, but it's nice to know we can if we need to (e.g., to integrate with legacy code that behaves in a nonstandard or unusual way).

The past few years have been particularly exciting for users of the OpenSSL library, as the developers have included transparent support for a large number of cryptographic accelerators and HSMs, support for a large number of new ciphers and standards, and there's even an upcoming FIPS 140-2 certification[3] (a standard required for cryptographic modules to be used in a U.S. government context, which we will discuss in more detail later).

3.3.1.3 Disadvantages

As with everything else in life, there's no magic bullet. Probably the biggest issue with OpenSSL is the lack of formalized support for the library. Some larger organizations require that any product they use be formally supported and controlled by a commercial entity. These enterprises want guarantees and SLAs that dictate how and when bugs will get fixed (ideally, within a short amount of time), that personnel will be on hand to patiently assist with install or usage problems, and (probably most importantly) that an underlying commercial entity can be relied upon to not go out of business and leave the organization stranded with "abandonware." OpenSSL has none of these things: no support, no guarantees about timeliness of bug fixes (although historically the library developers have always been on the "bug fixing" ball), and no fiscally solid organization with control of the project (some would argue that this is a good thing).

There are a few language and platform considerations to take into account when using OpenSSL as well. First, it is easiest to work with OpenSSL in C/C++ on a Unix platform. That's not to say there aren't other options available if we're using another platform or another language, only that the library is targeted toward that audience so developers using other platforms and languages have to adapt themselves by various degrees to the context in which the library was written. If, for example, we wanted to use OpenSSL within the context of Visual Basic, we'll need to employ one of a few encapsulation strategies to allow this to be readily accomplished (e.g., we could wrap the desired functionality in a COM object).

Last (but not least) on our list of disadvantages comes about for those working in the United States federal sector. Did you notice the key word "upcoming" in the recent mention of FIPS 140 certification? FIPS 140-2 stands for "Federal Information Processing Standard #140" and details a program whereby cryptographic modules must be certified by NIST (National Institute of Standards and Technology) before they can be used in U.S. government applications. The certification for OpenSSL is not here yet; as of the writing of this book, the FIPS 140-2 certification is still in the "Coordination" stage NIST Pre-Evaluation. So, for the time being at least, we're pretty much going to have to discount using OpenSSL if we're working in most government contexts.

3.3.2 RSA BSAFE

RSA Security (*www.rsa.com*) is a software vendor that bills itself as "the most trusted name in computer security," and for a long time held the patent to the RSA algorithm described in 1977 (December 14, 1977, US patent # 4,405,829) by Ron Rivest, Adi Shamir, and Len Adleman (hence the "R," "S," and "A"). The RSA algorithm is an asymmetric cipher, and is by far the most popular asymmetric algorithm in use in computer security today. Needless to say, until September 2000 when the patent expired[3], if one wanted to use the RSA algorithm in an application, one would need to pay RSA a tariff. During the years when the patent was active, probably the most straightforward way to license the algorithm from RSA was to use their BSAFE toolkit for cryptographic routines to be incorporated in the application. Sure, a developer always had the option of using another library or implementing the functionality him or herself, but the piper had to be paid either way. Needless to say, many organizations chose to just use BSAFE and avoid the added complexity. Given the history, there were (and still are) a number of applications written that use the RSA BSAFE toolkit to implement their cryptographic functionality.

3.3.2.1 Advantages

Just about anything you'd want to do with cryptography can be done in BSAFE. The toolkit provides functionality in Java and C, and is supported on a number of different platforms; specifically, Linux, Solaris, HP-UX, AIX, and 32-bit Windows. A number of hardware accelerators and HSM equipment have support for this toolkit, and the innate performance of the toolkit is noteworthy. The toolkit contains support for algorithms that are still encumbered by RSA patent, such as RC5. The toolkit is fully supported and manufactured by a commercial entity; as such, it is a good choice for an enterprise context where support and ownership by a company are desirable. For users in a government context, RSA BSAFE has undergone FIPS 140 approval (in later chapters, we'll go into exactly how to enable FIPS mode, and which algorithms to choose).

3.3.2.2 Disadvantages

The BSAFE toolkit must be licensed from RSA, and it is somewhat expensive to do so. The toolkit API in the C/C++ version of the library is somewhat more complex and difficult to use than some of the other libraries covered in this book, but this is certainly not an insurmountable obstacle. The functionality provided by BSAFE in

C is offered via a number of "low-level" APIs, and there are not many shortcuts for the developer.

3.3.3 Microsoft Windows Cryptographic API (CAPI)

Microsoft introduced the Cryptographic API (CAPI) into Windows NT® as a tool for third-party developers to use and as a building block for Microsoft developers to use in building security functionality within the operating system. Microsoft CAPI has been improved upon in subsequent iterations of the Win32 operating system (and SDKs). In today's programming environment, there are a number of ways to interface with CAPI (e.g., via a COM interface known as CAPICOM, through managed code by way of the .NET platform, and of course, directly by using the low-level SDK services offered). CAPI is built around a very flexible architecture whereby cryptographic implementations are abstracted from the developer—the developer writes to the high-level API, and Cryptographic Service Providers (CSPs) operate under the hood to do the actual work. This is a useful design in that new cryptography can be substituted rather transparently at a subsequent time.

3.3.3.1 Advantages

CAPI is lightweight (from a programmer's perspective), flexible, and easy to use. The modular design in particular provides a great deal of flexibility to the developer. For example, cryptographic accelerator hardware can typically be added to the system and leveraged by an application without recompiling the underlying source code—a huge plus. Additionally, CAPI supports a large number of interfaces (e.g., the managed code, C/C++, and COM interfaces we just mentioned) that give the developer tremendous language flexibility. All of the interfaces are easy to use, but the easiest of these (CAPICOM) is straightforward in the extreme.

CAPI is also free for use in any development context; if you're using the Microsoft Win32 platform, most of the required binary images are already loaded and installed on the system. There are no royalty payments required for using the functionality. Of particular interest to developers in the U.S. government markets is that FIPS-compliant applications can be written without incurring any licensing cost.

3.3.3.2 Disadvantages

The CAPI is supported only on Microsoft Windows platforms (excluding 16-bit Windows). If you're writing code that will ultimately be portable to other non-Microsoft platforms, this isn't your best bet since you'll have to rewrite to a different API on the other platforms. Aside from being locked into a Microsoft platform, a few counterintuitive usage aspects of the API must be taken into account (particularly with key management) depending on how high or low a level you'll be working with the API). We'll go into those more in subsequent chapters, but most of them are overcome with a bit of forethought and appropriate application design.

3.3.4 Java Cryptography Architecture and Java Cryptography Extensions (JCA/JCE)

JDK 1.1 included with it the first iteration of cryptographic functionality for Java called the JCA or *Java Cryptography Architecture*. Similar to CAPI, JCA implements a "provider-style" architecture to allow for (relatively) seamless and transparent replacement of one cryptographic provider with another, and to maximize the ability of third-party vendors to develop cryptographic service components for use by application developers. The Java™ JCA refers to the underlying implementation providers as "Cryptographic Service Providers" in the same way Microsoft CAPI does. The majority of the classes we will be using can be imported from `java.security` or `javax.crypto` to provide the majority of the cryptographic functionality we will need.

3.3.4.1 Advantages

Hands down, the JCA interface is the easiest of these libraries to use; in fact, the API is so powerful and flexible that one line of Java code can perform extremely complex operations (in a safe manner, no less). There are commercial third-party FIPS 140-2 certified providers available for those in the U.S. government sector, and other third-party modules that are optimized for speed, accelerator support, or HSM support. Additionally, the default provider is available free of charge from Sun for developers to use, and no royalties are required for distribution of products written on top of the JCA. Since Java is designed to be cross-platform, almost any OS and hardware architecture on which Java runs will allow cryptography to take place.

3.3.4.2 Disadvantages

This is Java only. There is no language independence, so if you're not writing a Java application, JCA is not an appropriate choice. From a performance standpoint, the JCA carries with it the same performance burden associated with Java's interpreted byte-code model; specifically, any performance deficit seen versus native code will also be present in the cryptographic routines. Additionally, the use of commercial third-party providers over and above the providers supplied by Sun may cause you to incur additional licensing costs.

3.3.5 The Bare Minimum: Cryptographic Libraries

While we don't have enough information yet to actually go about picking a library, the information in Table 3.1 is provided to showcase the relative strengths/weakness of the libraries at a high level. We'll go into much more detail later as we go through which library selections are appropriate for which types of applications.

TABLE 3.1 Overview

	OpenSSL	B/SAFE	CAPI	JCA
Support	–	+	+	+
U.S. Government Use (FIPS 140)	–[a]	+	+	+[b]
Language Independent	–	+	+	–
Platform Independent	+	+	–	+
Freely Available	+	–	+	+

[a] As stated, this is underway but not currently available.

[b] Available through third-party modules.

3.4 SECURE SOCKETS

Simply encrypting, signing, verifying, and hashing our data doesn't always offer us the full compliment of functionality we require in designing security-aware applications. These are only the primitives; in addition to putting the primitives together in new ways, we'll also want to draw on some of the common "prefabricated" ways in which those primitives have already been put together to provide powerful security. This section outlines some of the functionality that's ubiquitously available to us in our libraries, but provides much more functionality than what's available solely by working with primitives. We won't be delving too deeply into the technical aspects of SSL operation, since from our point of view, we can most of the time use them from a usage-oriented perspective alone. Note that there are hundreds, if not thousands, of secure communications methodologies in use in today's world; these technologies run the gamut from proprietary solutions to alternative non-SSL protocols that satisfy the same objectives. However, for the purposes of programmatic implementation of secure communications functionality, SSL/TLS is ubiquitously offered to the developer, whereas other methodologies require other packages that are not covered here. Therefore, we will be limiting our discussion to SSL and TLS.

Oftentimes, we will wish to conduct secure communications between two parties; there are numerous mechanisms that we could come up with for doing this in an automated fashion. However, in most cases, we'll want to use a standards-based approach that can be written and deployed quickly and easily. The *Secure Sockets Layer* (SSL) is the generic programmatic tool that we will use for accomplishing this. These sockets are usually implemented in a manner semitransparent to the application developer and have therefore become the standard for secured communications in most intranetworking situations, and the powerful functionality of creating a secure communications channel is available to us within the libraries with relative ease. Briefly, we'll go through an overview of SSL, what it is, and what's required to use the protocol. Note that a detailed explanation from an "under the hood" perspective is outside the scope of this book, as there are a number of publicly available documents that spell out the inner workings (including some really well-written books on the subject).

3.4.1 History and Overview

SSL was originally written by Netscape to solve a particular business problem: specifically, HTTP did not offer any inherent security, and there were numerous parties clamoring to use HTTP for commerce transactions, business transactions, and transmission of sensitive data. In response to this, SSL was created as a way to seamlessly provide private, authenticated, and secure capabilities to Web (HTTP) applications. While originally created to address HTTP transactions, SSL is also a convenient way to introduce security to other types of communication (e.g., POP3, FTP, SMTP, or any other TCP connection that requires security). Since its inception at Netscape, SSL has been turned over to the IETF (Internet Engineering Task Force), where it has undergone continued design in the form of TLS (Transport Layer Security). The current TLS 1.0 standard (sometimes referred to as SSL 3.1) is defined in RFC 2246 and provides a number of security improvements over and above the SSL 2 or 3 specifications. While at Netscape, SSL underwent some revision and has undergone further revision since the IETF handoff; further complicating the matter are similar but competing protocols (e.g., Microsoft PCT) that exist but are not universally implemented. For our purposes, we'll mostly be considering TLS 1 for implementation in new applications, although we'll review the other versions from an implementation perspective in the event we need to consider their usage for backward compatibility.

3.4.2 Ciphersuites

SSL/TLS follows an extremely flexible model whereby the party requesting an SSL connection (the client) and the party receiving the connection (the server) compare lists of supported ciphers and select one they both support (i.e., they select an algorithm that is contained in both the server and client's list of supported ciphersuites). The number of ciphersuites (combinations of ciphers) supported is enormous due to the fact that asymmetric algorithms, symmetric algorithms, and digest algorithms in combination form a ciphersuite, and individual instances of each of these primitives can be substituted within a ciphersuite. It should be noted that not all versions of the protocol and not all of the ciphersuites provide the same level of security; additionally, not all of the ciphersuites (and protocol versions) are supported by all Web servers with the same frequency. To work around this, we'll need to consider the ciphersuites that we intend to support in our applications carefully prior to deployment to ensure mutual support on both the client and the server.

3.4.3 Authentication

Authentication of a client or server in SSL and TLS is effected by possession of X.509 digital certificates signed by a CA recognized as trusted in addition to possession of the corresponding private key. SSL/TLS supports both mutually authenticated and server-authenticated models; this means that either the server can use a certificate as part of the transaction, or both the client and the server can. Let's look in more detail at these authentication models.

Server-only authentication: In this model, the server presents its X.509 digital certificate to clients that connect to the server. The clients are anonymous in that they do not have to authenticate themselves as part of the protocol.[4] Note that since we are using the server's certificate for the authentication criteria, clients must have foreknowledge of trusted CAs that issue server certificates. Also, note that the X.509 CN will contain the server's "DNS" name: in other words, the fully qualified domain name (FQDN) of the server that is being connected to.

Mutual authentication: In addition to the server certificate being used as per the previous model, the client must also supply a certificate for the connection to take place. This scenario is rarely deployed for most Web applications, but can be useful in a business-to-business or server-to-server context.

As indicated, for the vast majority of SSL/TLS sessions that are established, the server-only authentication model is used. However, in cases where we require programmatic secure connections between two parties, mutually authenticated SSL provides a robust, secure, and standards-based mechanism for accomplishing that goal.

3.4.4 Usage

All of the libraries we'll be using support SSL and TLS in an opaque manner. In almost all cases, the SSL API will mirror the socket API on that same platform; usage, therefore, will be familiar to developers who are accustomed to network programming. We will need to pay some attention to the ciphersuites that we support in our applications (to ensure that we pick both secure and well-supported ciphersuites), and we'll want to select versions of the protocol from a similar vantage point. We want to ensure robust cryptography, appropriate standards compliance where required, and the right authentication model for our needs.

3.4.5 Requirements for Use

To use SSL or TLS in our applications, we only need two things: network connectivity between the parties that need to communicate, and the installation of a digital certificate on the server and (optionally) the client depending on the authentication model we want to support. In general, any context where we can use standard TCP sockets, we can substitute SSL to add privacy, integrity, and some bit of authentication to the connection.

3.4.5.1 The Bare Minimum: Secure Sockets

- SSL/TLS provides near-transparent secure communications functionality to the developer.
- SSL/TLS servers and clients negotiate a combination of encryption primitives "bundled" together in ciphersuites in instantiating a secure channel.
- SSL/TLS operates in one of two authentication modes: server-authentication or mutual-authentication.
- Server authentication uses a server certificate that may include the FQDN of the server to be verified against the name of the expected server.
- Mutual authentication requires a client certificate issued by a CA that the Web server trusts.
- Establishment of a set of trusted CAs is required for SSL/TLS to operate.

3.6 SELECTED REFERENCES

Mathematics of cryptography:

Coutinho, S.C. ***The Mathematics of Ciphers: Number Theory and RSA Cryptography.*** A K Peters, Ltd. 1999: A useful book that lays the mathematical groundwork for understanding the RSA algorithm.

Menezes, Alfred J. *et al, Handbook of Applied Cryptography.* CRC Press, 1997: An extremely detailed book providing both a mathematical and practical framework for understanding cryptography at its lowest level.

Schneier, Bruce. *Applied Cryptography: Protocols, Algorithms, and Source Code in C.* John Wiley and Sons, Inc. 1996: A useful book describing the fundamental issues in cryptography as well as laying a mathematical framework for further investigation.

SSL and TLS: Rescorla, Eric. *SSL and TLS: Designing and Building Secure Systems.* Addison-Wesley, 2001: Detailed discussion of SSL and TLS from an implementation perspective. Describes all aspects of SSL operation in a high level of detail.

3.7 ENDNOTES

1. See also RFC #1422, "Privacy Enhancement for Internet Electronic Mail: Part II: Certificate-Based Key Management."
2. For more information as to the state of the FIPS 140 certification, details can be obtained from *http://oss-institute.org/fips-faq.html.*
3. Actually, RSA Security released the algorithm to the public domain a few weeks prior to the expiration of the patent.
4. Note that this is not to imply that the clients must stay anonymous; in fact, after the session has been established, other types of authentication may be used, or the server can request that the client reestablish the session over a mutually authenticated connection.

4 Basic Techniques (by Example)

In This Chapter

- Generating Keys
- Encrypting and Decrypting Data
- Signing and Verifying
- Basic Techniques Wrap-up
- Selected References
- Endnotes

Here's where the fun begins. In previous chapters, we laid out some of the common strategies we're likely to use to accomplish our goals, and talked about the tools and techniques at a 50,000-foot level. However, we still only introduced the concepts in the abstract; abstract knowledge of how to accomplish a task is important, but it's a far cry from actually understanding the principles in depth from an engineer's perspective. For example, if we were building a house, understanding that "building materials need to be affixed to each other in some way for the structure to stand" is very different from understanding how to use nails, a hammer, and glue. This chapter is designed to allow the developer to progress to the next level of understanding; specifically, that of practical understanding of the primitives and techniques already introduced. Progression to a more concrete level of understanding allows the developer to start applying those concepts to application design scenarios.

This section overviews strategies on how to accomplish the "basics" we covered in the previous chapter, the things we will be doing most often in the course of our development activities. We provide examples of how these basics are done, but the goal of this chapter is *not* to give the developer examples in every programming language that exists, or to give detailed how-to instructions on the cryptographic libraries (more details on how to use the libraries will come later). The goal of this chapter is to familiarize developers with the tasks they will need to perform time and again from a programmatic perspective; in other words, we've described at an abstract level most of the primitives and techniques the developer will use, but we haven't yet applied that knowledge. This chapter attempts to rectify that situation. It's not important that the developer understand every function call in the examples at this time (again, that will come later); the structures, signatures, conventions, and jargon vary with each library and in some cases are somewhat complex. The important part here is that developers understand the methodologies as they are applied and in the context of the techniques described in the previous chapter; in other words, they understand the functional steps at a high level. It should be noted that additional examples, advanced techniques, and a library-by-library breakdown of how to accomplish common (and some less common) tasks as well as detailed usage instructions (including how to install the libraries, how to use the APIs, etc.) will be covered in later chapters.

4.1 GENERATING KEYS

In almost every context, a key is required input before we can actually perform cryptography. Unless we are using only hash functions or a library where a key will be automatically generated for us in an "under the covers fashion," we will require a key to get any work done (to sign or encrypt data). Key generation procedures vary depending on the type of algorithm we'll be using, the library we're using, and depending on some other circumstances, we might need additional data in addition to a key (such as an IV). Let's examine these concepts in much more depth.

4.1.1 Symmetric Keys

Generating a symmetric key, in some respects, is one of the easiest things we'll be called upon to do. In our earlier (Chapter 3) discussion of symmetric encryption, we indicated that a symmetric key was little more than an opaque byte string for our purposes. While this is true, in real-world situations there are some practical considerations about the length and characteristics of the string we choose. Specifically, we want to meet our target goals for a robust key, which are ensuring that every *bit* of the key is as "unguessable" as possible, and the keys we generate meet the length requirements for the algorithm we're using.

Say, for example, that we want to use the recently standardized AES (*Advanced Encryption Standard*) algorithm to encrypt our data. AES is a block cipher and is a good choice for algorithm selection: it's strong, it's fast, and it's the current standard advocated by the U.S. government. As the recommended standard, no one can accuse us of not doing appropriate "due diligence" by choosing it. AES can use a variable-length[1] key, but for most purposes, we'll want to use either 128 bits or 256 bits. 128 bits is 16 bytes, so we want a 16-byte string as our key. Just about any string will work; from a practical (i.e., "getting it to work") perspective, even an arbitrary phrase like "The game's afoot" would be acceptable from the algorithm's point of view (not from a security point of view, though). The length of this string is 16 bytes excluding any terminating nulls, so this would be of appropriate length for use in AES. This is useful to illustrate the point that we're really dealing with a byte string, but there are a few reasons why something human-readable like a phrase or password would not be acceptable from a security point of view.

The primary reason why we don't want to use a phrase is for the reason we've outlined already: we want the key to be as difficult for someone to guess as possible—at a "bit" level. This means that because each bit contributes to the number of possible values the key can be, every *bit* of the key is important. Printable strings can be counted on to be in a certain value range; for example, the alphabetic, numeric, and punctuation symbols all fall between 32 and 126 on the ASCII chart. Since each byte is one of 256 possible values, we would lose more than half of the possible bits comprising the key by selecting a key in this range. This is actually worse than it sounds from a security perspective, because the complexity of the key increases exponentially as it gets more complex and longer. In other words, by selecting a less complex key, we reduce the encryption strength by orders of magnitude. Let's look at this in a way we might be more comfortable with; as developers, we're probably used to analyzing algorithms from a performance standpoint. Brute force attacks against a key are basically a "search algorithm," and as such can be analyzed the same way we would analyze any other searching algorithm's performance; after all, trying a key is a constant-time operation just the same way that comparing a string or integer is (although it takes somewhat longer than a string compare). Looking at a brute force attack in this way, "big-O" notation for this operation would be $O(n)$, meaning a worst-case search for the right key is n iterations, where n is the total keyspace. Filling in the n with the details of the key permutations, using all the bits of the keyspace makes a brute force operation of complexity $O(\text{characterset}^{\text{length}})$; if our character set is 256 and our key length is 16, our search algorithm's performance is $O(256^{16})$—a huge number. However, reducing the character complexity to 64—or $O(64^{16})$—exponentially reduces the length of the search. This would be a tremendous boon if we were trying to optimize the searching (the reason we usually do this exercise), but since we're trying to "unoptimize" it (make it harder for someone to perform a search and find it), the consequences of reducing the number of possible values are terrible.

In previous chapters, we discussed deriving a key from a password; this process would take a string like "The game's afoot" and turn it into a key that uses the full space of the symmetric key we wish to generate. This might be a good design choice for us to make in formulating symmetric keys as long as we have a user available to ask for the key. There might be times, however, where we will only need the key for a relatively small period of time. Alternatively, we might want to assign a unique key for a number of small things (such as an individual key used to encrypt a file). In cases such as this, it often behooves us to use an appropriately sized byte string of completely random data. True randomness is difficult (one could say impossible) to achieve on a computer, and we have to make sure that the random data we choose is as close to random as we can get. For example, the pseudorandom number generators we're typically used to using for other applications (e.g., the `rand()` function included in stdlib in C) are not sufficiently random for cryptographic purposes. In situations in which we wish to generate keys, we will most often need to leverage the internal random number generation capability of our libraries (where available), or build a robust random number generator ourselves if our libraries do not offer help in this capacity. An appropriate "take away" of this is that keys can (and often should) be comprised of completely random data. In short, there are four possible ingredients for generating symmetric keys: good random numbers, hardware key generators, user intervention, or a combination of the three.

4.1.1.1 The Bare Minimum: Symmetric Key Generation

- The strength of the cryptography depends on the complexity of the key.
- Robust random numbers make good symmetric keys.
- "Traditional" random number sources (e.g., C's `rand()` function) do not provide sufficiently strong randomness for cryptographic purposes.

4.1.2 Asymmetric Keys

Generating asymmetric keys is not much more difficult than generating symmetric ones from a user perspective; under the hood, the process is much more complex, but the complexity is hidden from us most of the time. In other words, the libraries we'll be using will do pretty much all the work for us. However, there are some ingredients we need to start the process. Basically, in all cases where we are going to generate asymmetric keys, we'll need cryptographically strong random number generation capability. This is universally true. With asymmetric keys, there are certain mathematical properties that the key pairs must have; that is, keys cannot take just any arbitrary value, but must be related to each other in very specific ways. The specifics of those mathematical properties are out of scope for our purposes, since in most cases they don't assist with usage (and since there are entire books on this subject already[2]). However, a cursory overview of the inputs required for key generation will help us to understand some of the steps we must take, why we need to take them, and why random numbers are so important. We'll endeavor to keep this short and relevant, as we're merely illustrating a point.

4.1.2.1 RSA

RSA key generation starts by selecting a large number with two known prime factors.[3] The important thing about this step is that the way to arrive at this number is to take two large prime numbers and multiply them together. This sounds easy enough on the surface, but the problem lies in the fact that these numbers form a key and therefore must be unique and different each time we do key generation (since we want our keys to be different every time). Let's be more specific: all the numbers (the two big prime ones, and the even bigger end-result one) have to be new and different every time we perform key generation. The fact that the numbers have to be "new and unique" forms the core of the requirement for random number generation, but to demonstrate the underlying causal relationship, let's take a few sentences to go into more detail how the key generation process works.

To generate a key for use with RSA, our implementation needs to feed into the key generation process two large prime numbers that are new and unique each time we go about generating a key. Selecting a prime number is usually done by judicious use of guessing and trial and error under the hood within the libraries; in other words, first they guess a huge number, and then they test it to see if it's prime. If it is, it gets used; if it isn't, the library will proceed to the next odd number—and so on until good numbers are chosen. The most important things to note about this process are the "guess" and "new and different" parts. To make the selections unique each time, the libraries will pick a random number starting position to begin guessing numbers. Stated in "reverse," the fact that the starting position for the guesswork needs to be unique means that we have to get the computer to give us a random starting position each time we generate a key.

There's one more thing we need to know about the key generation process for RSA to use the libraries appropriately. Some details of the algorithm aren't completely opaque during the key generation process in some of the libraries. Specifically, we are sometimes required to specify the "modulus bits" and the "public exponent" and supply them to the key generation process. For those of us who aren't mathematicians, the requirement to supply this kind of information might seem intimidating; however, this data isn't hard to come by, and with a little explanation makes perfect sense. The "modulus bits" can basically be translated as "key size." For RSA, the currently accepted "strong" key length is either 1024 or 2048 bits. We'll be given the option of supporting 512 bits for key generation in our libraries, but nowadays this is generally recognized as being of insufficient complexity for robust security practices and we should therefore avoid 512-bit RSA keys in new applications. "Public Exponent" is part of the public key and is usually 3, 17, or 65537. There are a number of competing recommendations for what this value should be, but for our purposes, we'll use 65537 when we are required to specify the value, since this value is recognized by the most standards documents as being robust (specifically, the International Telecommunications Union standard ITU-T X.509 Annex C, RFC 2313, and PKCS #1) [Schneier, 469].

4.1.2.2 DSA

DSA stands for *Digital Signature Algorithm* and is outlined in FIPS 186-2 ("Digital Signature Standard"). Unlike RSA, DSA provides only signature functionality and not encryption for privacy purposes. DSA uses randomness for two purposes: key generation and signing messages. At this time, we're only going to go into the randomness required for key generation, since that's the topic at hand. It should be noted that the key generation process for DSA is a bit more complicated than RSA, but fortunately, the libraries we'll use shield us almost completely from the underlying complexity of the algorithm. The only way this extra complexity impacts development usage is that there may be additional steps during the DSA key generation process. This additional step is typically generation of "DSA parameters" to initialize the key generation process; we won't go through the specifics of what the DSA parameters are since (unlike RSA) we don't need to understand them to use them.[4] We'll see this in action later. The generation of a DSA key requires random numbers in the same way RSA does, which is what we want to highlight here; basically, if you're going to generate an asymmetric key for any purpose, you'll need a random number source.

4.1.2.3 The Bare Minimum: Asymmetric Key Generation

- Asymmetric key generation produces a mathematically related key pair.
- Generating asymmetric keys requires a source of robust random numbers.
- RSA key generation may additionally require "public exponent" (usually one of a few small prime numbers) and "modulus bits" (basically, "key size in bits").

DSA key generation may require additional parameters and thus might require an additional step during usage; we are shielded from the mathematical details of DSA keys by the libraries' interface.

4.1.3 Random Number Generation

So, we've established that for every symmetric and asymmetric algorithm we're going to discuss, we're probably going to need robust random numbers. How do we get those numbers? How many do we need? What steps are required? Many times, we'll be authoring systems that require a large volume of random numbers. If, for example, we were going to write an application that uses a new random session key for each communication request—and will be used to process a large number of communication requests—we would need many new keys to be generated. Additionally, we might want to change the key with a certain frequency within each session, so we would need new randomness each time we want to do that. Two things help us out in the generation of random numbers: first, each of our libraries provides us with a *Cryptographically Strong Pseudo-Random Number Generator* (PRNG) that we can use. Sometimes, we can use this without any initialization, and sometimes we'll need to seed it first with some small "seed" randomness that will initialize the generator. This section will talk about when we need to seed the generator, why we need to seed it, how to seed it, and strategies of where to get the seed data.

4.1.3.1 Pseudo-Random Number Generators

First, trying to get a computer to produce a "random" value is extremely hard, to say the least. Without specialized hardware, "random" data really isn't random. This makes sense when we stop to think about it; after all, in the software that we write on a day-to-day basis, do "new" things that weren't authored into the code just "crop up" in a random or "organic" way? No. Everything that happens in our software happens because we put it there—no more and no less. Another way to say it is that everything a computer will do is knowable; the software on it moves from state to state according to the way it was written, and the underlying platform moves from state to state likewise. Therefore, there's nothing random about it.

That's not to say that there aren't things that are random that a computer can read. For example, the actions of a user are random. The amount a user nudges the mouse, for example, is effectively random (this can be debated from a philosophical perspective, of course, but for our purposes it is random). Alternatively, the rate at which the user presses the keys on the keyboard when typing is random. These events, points at which the user interacts with the system, do produce some random information, but for the most part, they are comparatively rare. Some platforms attempt to harvest and consolidate that random information and provide it to the developer or user in a handy way; for example, most Unix platforms provide a /dev/random file that can be read to produce random data. This device is basically a consolidation of what random information can be gathered (when it can be gathered) and provided as a handy convenience. However, not all platforms have such a feature, and sometimes there are limits to the amount of data we can extract from that source. Given these difficulties associated with obtaining random information, each of the libraries provides mechanisms to (at least) extend the random information we can provide to it as input. The initial random information that is supplied to the library to "extend" the random data sometimes needs to be *seeded* with information we extract from the system. The initial value we must supply is most often referred to as a *seed value*. Sometimes, the libraries will also do the work associated with gathering a seed value for us, and sometimes we will need to do the work ourselves. In either event, we need to at least be cognizant of the underlying necessity of random number generation, since this process is so important. Each of the libraries we've chosen includes at least one random number generator (some provide several). Each of these is different in implementation and usage, however, so it bears discussing the options of each, how they work, and our various usage options.

OpenSSL

The PRNG used by OpenSSL has changed (for the better) over time. Current versions of OpenSSL will attempt to use /dev/random or /dev/urandom on platforms under which this functionality exists (most Unix platforms, Linux, BSD, Macintosh OSX, etc.). On platforms where /dev/random and /dev/urandom do not exist (Microsoft Windows, Solaris 8 before certain patches, etc.), OpenSSL will attempt to use its default internal pseudo-random number generator unless a hardware random source has been indicated. When the internal random number generator is used, it must be seeded first; platforms with a functional /dev/random or /dev/urandom will attempt to "seed themselves" and thus do not require explicit seeding from us, whereas other platforms do require this.[5]

Important note about OpenSSL PRNG: *Versions of OpenSSL after 0.9.5 will not allow use of the random number generator to take place unless it has been properly seeded first. Lest we forget to seed the PRNG, we will get a "PRNG Not Seeded" error when we attempt to use functionality that requires a random source. This means that versions prior to 0.9.5 will use weak random numbers but will not warn us!*

When /dev/random does not exist, the OpenSSL PRNG uses SHA-1 to "stir" and stretch the seed data that we will add to set the initial PRNG state. As this would imply, the data we add to it is very important, because that is the initial source of randomness from which the entire internal state of the random number generator will be derived.

BSAFE

BSAFE provides us with a few choices of random number generators to use. We can use a "stirring" approach (in which we specify the algorithm we want to use from the choices of MD2, MD5, and SHA-1), we can generate random numbers according to ANSI X9.31, or we can generate random numbers according to ANSI X9.62 (for RSA key generation). We'll delve into which random number generation technique to use for which purpose when we get to more detailed usage instructions later in the book, but obviously we'll want to make some intelligent choices based on the context of the application we are writing and what we need the random numbers for. It is important to note that *all of these choices require seeding of the random number generator*; the BSAFE documentation tells us that if we neglect to seed the generator, a random pregenerated byte sequence (i.e., a known fixed value) will be used. Obviously, we want to avoid that highly insecure potentiality at all costs.

Microsoft CAPI

The Microsoft Cryptographic API leaves the matter of implementing a random number generator up to the particular CSP that's being used. While we have the option of requesting cryptographically strong random data from the CSP (and requesting that the CSP update its internal state with good random values supplied by us), we do not explicitly have to initialize the internal random state of the CSP prior to generating keys (or anything else, for that matter). This is a very useful feature in that it shields us from a very time-consuming task (seeding the random number generator). However, we should still remember what's going on underneath the hood, in case we are using a CSP that doesn't seed it with strong values (look for this explicitly in the documentation of any third-party CSP you're using), and in case we ever need to port our application to another platform. Note that the default CSPs will seed the generator if we do not explicitly do so; these default CSPs will use strong values for the seeding process should we elect to use the default instantiation functionality.

JCA/JCE

As with CAPI, the JCE attempts to randomize the internal state of the generator itself unless the developer explicitly seeds the generator. Given that Java is platform independent, obtaining useful seed values for seeding the random number generator is difficult in a client context, and even more difficult in a server context. Given the difficulty in this respect, it is fortunate that the generator attempts to randomize itself, because we would be hard-pressed to find strong random numbers if we had to without resorting to native code through the Java Native Interface, or JNI.

ON THE CD

(There's a demonstration of using JNI for this purpose on the companion CD-ROM in the /Examples/Chapter 4/JNI_Rand folder, but in most cases, the built-in seeding is an appropriate choice.) Early versions of the JCE had some issues with the seeding methodology of the random number generator, but most providers (since the seeding of the PRNG is provider dependent) nowadays use a robust methodology. Furthermore, since any additional values added by us do not overwrite but merely add to the internal state of the PRNG, we can't detract from the security of the random numbers through seeding, we can only add to it.

4.1.3.2 The Bare Minimum: Random Number Generators

- Each of the libraries has internal random number generation capability that we can use to stretch (i.e., gain many random bytes) an initial smaller random seed.
- Some libraries will automatically acquire an initial seed for the PRNG; some will require explicit initialization. Some libraries may or may not require seeding depending on the platform in use.

4.1.4 Gathering Random Seed Values

In at least one case (BSAFE), we must always randomize the PRNG before we use it, and there may be other cases in which we might wish to do so (e.g., OpenSSL[6] on a Windows or Solaris prior to the Solaris 8 12/02 distribution[7]). To do this effectively, there are a few strategies we should consider. First, if we are writing an application that can interact with the user, we can ask the user for assistance in helping us gather the entropy (randomness) in question. Note that we can do this without the user's knowledge that we are doing so in some cases. The primary mechanisms for gathering random seeds via a user are as follows:

- Asking the user to move the mouse randomly for a certain period of time.
- Asking the user to type random text.
- Obtaining randomness information from ancillary characteristics of the user's interaction with the application (e.g., the amount of time between keystrokes in an application where the user will be typing a sizable amount).

For applications in which direct interaction with the user is not possible (e.g., in a server context), we can also gather randomness information from the system on which the application runs. Note that this is less desirable than gathering the data from the user, as this data is likely to be more guessable than the "random mouse movement" strategy, for example. Probably the worst possible case for random seed generation is on a server (or other machine that is not actively used by anyone) where very little network or usage activity is going on. This is due to the fact the information sources we can query are very limited, and (depending on the circumstances) might be guessable by an attacker. A relatively robust strategy in a situation like this is to take a large amount of semipredictable information and use a hash function to "condense it" into a smaller value. Some of the data we might harvest for this purpose includes:

- Extremely granular "uptime" information such as tick count or uptime in milliseconds (note, however, that this data is not always as granular as advertised).
- Granular memory status information, such as the number of free bytes of virtual memory available or number of free bytes in the global heap.

- Network performance information, such as number of bytes received or sent on a given interface.
- Disk access information, such as bytes written to the paging file.
- Process information, such as number of running processes, handles to running processes, etc.
- Threading information, such as number of current threads and handles to current threads.

This type of data is trivial to obtain on a Windows system, and a little more difficult (although still doable) on a Unix platform (particularly because the APIs for obtaining this information will vary from platform to platform). Note, though, that this situation isn't as dire as it might appear, since it is not often that we'll need to gather this kind of data on a Unix system. As we stated earlier, most Unix platforms will have a usable/dev/random, and in cases where there is not such a feature (e.g., earlier versions of Solaris), the vendor has provided us with performance-gathering APIs we can use instead. Complete references, such as the recommended government standards for random number generation, the relevant RFCs on the subject, and numerous other sources of information have been provided both on the companion CD-ROM in the /References folder and at the end of this chapter.

ON THE CD

4.1.4.1 The Bare Minimum: Gathering Random Seed Values

- Interaction with the user provides a good opportunity to gather a good initial random seed.
- In cases where user input is not available, a large volume of unpredictable data can be gathered and condensed to form the initial seed.

4.1.5 Putting It All Together

So, now we have enough information to start generating keys. Let's briefly review what we've gone over so far, and look at how we might use these concepts in our application; in other words, let's take the concepts and build a "mini-application" that does those things.

4.1.5.1 Overview: The Goal

Let's write an application that generates symmetric keys and (ultimately) uses those random keys to encrypt files. Since we haven't talked about encryption in detail yet, we'll just create random symmetric keys and random asymmetric keys, and we can fill in the encryption part later.

Subsequent examples will vary, but for this example, we'll assume the following:

- We are using Microsoft Windows.
- We are using C++.

- We are using the OpenSSL library (to illustrate the generation of a random seed).
- The application will be a console application (to minimize extraneous code).

4.1.5.2 The Design

For the purposes of illustration, we'll generate both a symmetric key and an asymmetric key pair. Given what we've covered about random key generation, we know we'll need to cover the initialization and seeding of the random number generation mechanism. The following steps cover what we'll need to do at a high level:

1. Gather a random seed.
2. Seed the random number generator with the random seed.
3. Generate an asymmetric key.
4. Generate a (random) symmetric key.

Let's go through each step involved in depth.

Step 1: Gathering a Seed

To gather a seed, we'll draw upon the techniques outlined previously in this section; specifically, we'll assume that we can't ask the user to type text randomly and record the values and timing information from that exchange. Additionally, we'll assume that (since we're writing a console application) we can't leverage the native OpenSSL routine `RAND_event()`, which would gather entropy (randomness) information from Windows messages passed to our application. Therefore, we're left with gathering whatever information we can from the system. In doing so, we'll pay careful attention to RFC 1750, which points out the many problems associated with using high-resolution timers, so we'll want to include a large amount of other (semi-) unpredictable information from the system in addition to the timer information. Initially, when we gather the data, we will want to concatenate into a buffer of appropriate size. Once we assemble our buffer with this concatenated information, we can either pass it to the library directly or generate a digest of the data using a hash function, and use the hash instead (note that the hash and the full concatenated buffer will have the same amount of entropy). We'll gain access to the following to form the core of our randomness information (note that for space and clarity reasons, the sample code only includes a portion of this code).

- Global memory status information by calling the `GlobalMemoryStatus()` API function.
- High Resolution Timer information by calling `GetTickCount()`.
- Current Process Information by calling `GetCurrentProcess()` and `GetProcessTimes()`.

- Querying of the Windows NT HKEY_PERFORMANCE_FREQUENCY registry key.

Note that this code has been omitted from the sample due to its length and complexity. It is, however, provided on the companion CD-ROM for reference (contained in /Examples/Chapter 4/Win_Rand).

Please note that detailed usage information (including sample code) about how to access this value is available on the MSDN Web site (located at *http://msdn.microsoft.com/library/default.asp?url=/library/en-us/perfmon/base/displaying_object_instance_and_counter_names.asp*). Note also that this example (with the performance data included) is available on the companion CD-ROM in the / Examples/Chapter 4/Win_performance folder)

Step 2: Seeding the Generator

We'll seed the generator with the value that we obtained in Step 1 using the OpenSSL APIs. We'll then query the library to determine if sufficient randomness exists for us to proceed.

Steps 3–4: Generating Keys

Finally, we'll use the library APIs to generate the asymmetric (RSA) and symmetric (secret) keys our application needs. Note that we do not have to reseed the random number generator for each key we obtain, since the library will handle updating the internal state of the generator after each use without any explicit request from us.

All four steps, when put together, will accomplish the goals we outlined: random number generation and subsequent generation of keys.

4.1.5.3 Setting up the Environment

To follow these steps, first we'll need to set up our environment. It's not critical that you follow along with this example right now (although it is important that you step through the procedure). However, if you desire to do so, you'll need to set up your environment to compile OpenSSL code. This can be accomplished by completing the steps in Chapter 7 in the section entitled "Preparing the Environment." Alternatively, you can refer to the example on the companion CD-ROM (/Examples/Chapter 4/keygen), which contains a prepared Visual Studio project (including all project settings required for compilation).

4.1.5.4 The Result

The following code is reproduced here to demonstrate the steps we've outlined. When stepping through the code, take a moment to read the comments and quickly "breeze through" the function calls. We realize that the calls may seem unfamiliar at this point in the process, but what we really want the developer to get out of this is a "comfort level" with the steps (not with the API).

```
#include <iostream.h>
#include <windows.h>
#include "openssl/rand.h"
#include "openssl/rsa.h"

#define BUFFER_TOO_SHORT_EXCEPTION      -1
#define REQUIRED_RANDOM_BUFFER_LENGTH      64

void GetRandomSeed(unsigned char * randBuffer,
                   unsigned int length) {
    /*  We're going to need some values to seed the
        random number generator with.  We'll just use
        a few values to demonstrate the concept. */

    if(length < REQUIRED_RANDOM_BUFFER_LENGTH) {
        throw BUFFER_TOO_SHORT_EXCEPTION;
    }
    int offset = 0; //index into the randBuffer

    //tick count is the high-resolution uptime counter
    DWORD ticks = GetTickCount();
    memcpy(randBuffer+offset, &ticks, sizeof(DWORD));
    offset+=sizeof(DWORD);

    MEMORYSTATUS stat;
    GlobalMemoryStatus(&stat);
    //physical memory size never changes, so we'll just use
    //the values that do change
    memcpy(randBuffer+offset, &stat.dwMemoryLoad, sizeof(DWORD));
    offset+=sizeof(DWORD);
    memcpy(randBuffer+offset, &stat.dwAvailVirtual, sizeof(DWORD));
    offset+=sizeof(DWORD);
    memcpy(randBuffer+offset, &stat.dwAvailPhys, sizeof(DWORD));
    offset+=sizeof(DWORD);

    //for the example, let's use one more set of values.
    HANDLE myProcess = GetCurrentProcess();
    FILETIME startTime, exitTime, kernelTime, userTime;
    BOOL status = GetProcessTimes(myProcess, &startTime,
        &exitTime, &kernelTime, &userTime);
    memcpy(randBuffer+offset, &startTime.dwHighDateTime,
        sizeof(DWORD));
```

```
        offset+=sizeof(DWORD);
        memcpy(randBuffer+offset, &startTime.dwLowDateTime,
            sizeof(DWORD));
        offset+=sizeof(DWORD);
        //since this is an example, we are going to end here
        //for simplicity.  In real life, we'd want to fill
        //the entire buffer with the best random data we can find
    }

    void main() {
        unsigned char random[REQUIRED_RANDOM_BUFFER_LENGTH];
        GetRandomSeed(random, sizeof(random));
        RAND_seed(random, sizeof(random));
        //find out if the PRNG has enough randomness to operate
        //in our example, it DOESN'T, but putting enough in would
        //take up page after page of collection, so for example
        //purposes, this gets the point across.
        int status = RAND_status();

        //now, let's generate an asymmetric key
        //in the following call, the first parameter is the
        //size of the modulus or the "key size."  The
        //second parameter is the public exponent "e", which
        //is typically one of a few small values.  We'll use
        //3 here.  The third parameter is a function pointer
        //to a callback function or NULL if we want to block
        //until completion, and the last parameter are the
        //parameters to the callback function.
        RSA* context = RSA_generate_key(1024, //modulus size
            65537, //public exponent
            NULL, NULL);
        if(context == NULL) {
            //something went wrong.
            cerr << "An error occurred during the RSA key generation."
<< endl << flush;
            exit(-1);
        }

        //now let's get a random symmetric key
        unsigned char symmetricKey[128/8];//128 bit key
        status = RAND_bytes(symmetricKey, 128/8);
        if(!status) {
            cerr << "An error occurred obtaining the random key"
<< endl << flush;
        }
```

```
        RSA_free(context); //cleanup
        RAND_cleanup(); //cleanup
    }
```

4.1.5.5 The Bare Minimum: Issues and Lessons Learned

This example is relatively straightforward; in case it wasn't apparent from the comments, we did not implement a strong seeding of the random number generator in this example, as the space required to do so would be quite extensive (note that the accompanying CD-ROM does contain the more complete code). Let's walk through the steps involved here. With the inclusion of the ancillary library usage requirements, the steps we followed were:

1. Generate a random seed to prime the random number generator.
2. Seed the random number generator.
3. Query the random number generator to determine if sufficient randomness exists.
4. Use the library's API to generate the asymmetric key pair (specifying modulus size and public exponent).
5. Use the library's API to generate a random symmetric session key.
6. Free the resources required for the asymmetric key generation.
7. Free the resources required for the random number generator.

And that's that! In real life, we'd want to store our keys somewhere, and we'd want to use them for actual encryption or signing. However, this is all we have to do to generate complete and usable keys for encryption. Now that we have the keys, let's look at how we might go about using the keys to encrypt data.

4.2 ENCRYPTING AND DECRYPTING DATA

Encrypting data is something else we're likely to do frequently. We've talked about how to generate keys for our encryption algorithms, but what are the methodologies we need to employ to encrypt? What are the specifics of the usage? Let's delve into that now.

4.2.1 Selecting a Data Encryption Algorithm

There are many symmetric ciphers that can be used to encrypt data. In fact, there are probably dozens of known strong algorithms, and hundreds (if not thousands) of weak ones. In this section, we're going to talk about what criteria we use for selecting an algorithm (i.e., what algorithms are useful in what application contexts), and we'll actually go ahead and use some of them.

4.2.1.1 Block Ciphers

Block ciphers are particularly useful for bulk encryption of data in a storage context (e.g., the filesystem), in a "store and forward" context (e.g. email), and in a context where data buffering is to occur. In truth, providing we plan appropriately, block ciphers are useful in most any context where we need to encrypt large amounts of data. Most of the time, for "store and forward" applications (such as encryption of large or small data files), we will want to use a block cipher.

Algorithm Modes

Let's review the modes of operation under which block ciphers may operate; recalling the previous chapter, we've already discussed ECB and CBC mode. There are a number of other modes of operation, but let's limit our choices to the ones we've discussed. For the sake of completeness, we'll go through some of the other options available cursorily, but the situations in which we'll want to use some of the nonstandard choices are rare.

CBC: Cipher Block Chaining mode. Each block of ciphertext is linked to and dependent on the previous block. This is probably the most useful mode for the majority of our purposes, as it is easy to implement and offers good protection against certain kinds of attacks; in short, any time we can rely on the ciphertext to be read in sequence, CBC mode is a good choice.

ECB: Electronic Codebook mode. Each block is not linked to the previous block. This is useful for some situations (e.g., on-access encryption of sparse files) where we can't be assured in what order we will receive the encrypted data.[8]

CFB: Cipher Feedback mode. Each block of ciphertext is linked to the previous block using XOR. Using a methodology such as this allows for units smaller than a block to be encrypted (e.g., encrypting one byte at a time)—this allows a block cipher to function in a manner similar to a stream cipher. Use of this mode is rare in modern applications, but may be encountered in older applications for which we seek backward compatibility.

OFB: Output Feedback mode. Like CFB mode, blocks of ciphertext are obfuscated using XOR, but with a value that is not created from the previous ciphertext.[9] As with CFB, the goal of this is to provide stream cipher characteristics to a block cipher.

CTR: Counter mode. Counter mode uses (intuitively) the encrypted value of a "counter" (or other nonrepeating sequence) to generate a stream of characters that can be used as an ongoing stream of key material (a "keystream").[10] The goal of this is to turn a block cipher into a stream cipher[11], allowing us to encrypt individual bytes rather than fixed-length blocks.

Most of the time, we'll want to use CBC mode in cases where we're using a block cipher. CBC mode is almost universally supported for all the block ciphers in the libraries, and it prevents an attacker from deducing patterns in the plaintext. One disadvantage is loss of large amounts of data if errors occur (all the data after the error is lost), but most of the time, error-correction mechanisms ancillary to the cryptography will provide any necessary robustness (e.g., the innate error-correction of the filesystem, database, or socket library we're using). In the majority of the examples provided in this book dealing with block ciphers, we'll be targeting CBC mode for these reasons.

Initialization Vectors

A number of the block cipher modes of operation require an Initialization Vector, or IV; recalling our discussions in Chapter 3 about symmetric ciphers, an IV is required any time we need to "prime" (initialize) a register internal to the block cipher for the purpose of chaining encrypted blocks together. Sometimes, the libraries we're using will automatically generate an IV for us during the encryption process; other times, we will need to provide one explicitly. In general, use of a random value for the initialization vector is desirable. In cases where we do need to generate an IV, we'll want to instantiate, initialize, and seed a random number generator to obtain the value for the IV.

DES

DES is no longer a suitable choice from a security perspective; use of the algorithm in new applications is no longer defensible, and in most cases, we will want to remove support for the algorithm in legacy contexts as well. Published in 1993, the most recent version of the U.S. federal government document outlining the DES standard (FIPS 46-3) recommends the use of DES only in legacy applications, and NIST has subsequently (2004) proposed the complete deprecation of the standard in its entirety.[12] With the impending loss of standard status, it is understood that use of the algorithm should be avoided. This deprecation by NIST of the standard should be no surprise given the security issues inherent in its use. In January 1999, a collaborative effort succeeded in "breaking" a DES key in 22 hours and 15 minutes. Despite the issues, however, in the real world we can't always avoid the algorithm; for a long time, applications were developed that used DES (it was, after all, the standard), and we don't always have the luxury of replacing extant legacy systems. In other words, there are times when we will sometimes need to be compatible with those applications in the software we write. It bears saying, though, that unless we need to be backward compatible with an unmodifiable legacy application, we will want to avoid DES at all costs.

Triple-DES (3DES)

Triple-DES was recommended by NIST as a replacement for DES until the development on the AES in recent years. Triple-DES involves the encryption of the same data using DES three times using either two or three different keys. Unlike DES, Triple-DES does not have inherent security issues, and it is ubiquitously supported in all the libraries we'll cover. On the "con" side, repeating DES three times means a much greater decrease in performance compared to the improvement in security. While we won't favor Triple-DES in the creation of new applications (given that AES is a viable option), we're likely to encounter in it legacy contexts and in hardware contexts.

AES

AES has been recently approved by NIST after an extensive period of comment and study during which numerous algorithms were submitted for comparative analysis. Ultimately, the algorithm named "Rijndael" was selected by NIST for best overall performance in the various selection criteria and is the current AES standard. In most cases where we're going to do bulk encryption, we'll be using AES. There is a variety of reasons for this, not the least of which are:

- It is the NIST-approved and recommended algorithm for U.S. federal government use (FIPS 197).
- Given the fact that it is the current NIST recommended algorithm, it is appropriate for financial, banking, insurance, telecommunication, and health-care use (in other words, saying that "we use AES because it is the federal standard" is an extremely defensible position).[13]
- It provides extremely robust security given the speed.
- It is almost universally supported in current versions of our libraries and has support in newer cryptographic hardware.

Other Block Ciphers

There are many other block ciphers that we can use, as mentioned earlier. Most of the impetus to develop and use independently developed block ciphers came from the known weakness of DES and the poor performance characteristics of the workaround Triple-DES. With the adoption of the AES, the impetus for use of these other block ciphers has deteriorated, but we still might come across them in cases where we intend backward compatibility. For example, we may need to integrate our application with an application that was written prior to AES standardization and uses one of these "other" ciphers. We'll give an overview of some of the more commonly used algorithms (and hence algorithms we'll encounter in a legacy context), although given the standardization of NIST on AES, it isn't recommended that we use any of these for new applications.

Blowfish/Twofish: Bruce Schneier developed Blowfish and included the source code for it in his book *Applied Cryptography*. Twofish was also developed by Schneier and submitted to NIST for consideration in the AES competition, but was ultimately not chosen. For a period of a few years, Blowfish was used in some commercial products as an alternative to DES and Triple-DES.

CAST: CAST was (and is) used in applications developed by Entrust technologies; Entrust made CAST available for general use in 1997, and therefore we sometimes still see it in legacy applications. Although CAST is encumbered by patent (#5,511,123), Entrust has made CAST available on a royalty-free basis for any commercial or noncommercial purpose. It is unlikely that we'll encounter CAST in contexts outside of Entrust products, but some of the libraries we'll be using *do* provide support for CAST in case we need to be backwardly compatible with any of the Entrust products. Given the current ubiquity of AES, it is unlikely that we will select CAST for new application development.

IDEA: IDEA (International Data Encryption Algorithm) is a block cipher current encumbered by patents in the United States, Europe, and Japan (US Patent #5,214,703, European Patent #0482154, Japanese Patent #JP3225440B2).[14] The patent holder is Ascom-Tech AG (*www.ascom-tech.com*) and ETH (The Swiss Federal Institute of Technology).[15] There are some rare situations (particularly in European contexts) in which we might encounter this algorithm, an example being exchange of data between European and U.S. firms or in authoring software that will exchange encrypted data with applications that support only IDEA. Licensing must be arranged prior to using IDEA in an application; according to MediaCrypt (the holder of worldwide distribution rights to IDEA), royalty-free licenses may be obtained for developers of noncommercial software, while use within a commercial context is prohibited without first purchasing a valid license. Most of the time for new applications, we'll avoid using IDEA to reduce the complexity and cost associated with licensing.

Padding

One thing we might need to do, depending on the algorithm and library we're using, is pad the plaintext data (and be cognizant of padding schemes in processing ciphertext). Since block ciphers operate on fixed-sized blocks of data, there are often cases where we will have data that does not happen to cleanly fall along a block cipher's border. For example, we might be working with a block cipher that has a 16-byte (128-bit) block size (such as AES), and our data might not be a multiple of 16 bytes. Another example might be that we're working with a block cipher that has an 8-byte (64-bit) block size (such as DES or Triple-DES), and we have data that isn't a multiple of 8. This is usually handled by adding padding to the plaintext prior to the encryption to ensure that the input value is a multiple of the block size.

In creating new applications, we really don't have to worry too much about padding; all of our libraries will pad for us (sometimes we have to ask them to do so explicitly, but the functionality is always there). The difficulty arises, however, when we are called on to interface with legacy applications that use padding schemes that are unusual or nonstandard. Therefore, let's review some of the common approaches to the padding problem to ensure we know what's going on if we encounter a nonstandard padding situation in supporting legacy applications. There are, of course, almost limitless ways in which padding can be implemented. However, the majority of the time, we will see a few common strategies repeated over and over. If the padding scheme is not one of those listed here, observation of operations on the trailing bytes of a decrypted string in a debugger will eventually lead to the decipherment of the padding scheme in use. In other words, if we don't immediately recognize the padding scheme, we shouldn't panic, but we should instead start by investigating the encryption or decryption of the final bytes of a string to determine the padding scheme in use. Once we've determined what the padding scheme is, we can (if need be) re-create the right type of padding in our application. One word of caution, however: the process of reverse engineering a proprietary padding mechanism (although sometimes necessary) is a time-consuming endeavor. If we are making decisions about whether to replace an old component with a new one, this additional development overhead should be taken into account during the design process—it can often take days to find out what the old application is doing under the hood. The following are the most frequently occurring padding schemes that we'll see in practice:

Nulls: Oftentimes, messages will be padded with nulls (bytes of value "0x0"). This is most applicable in a context where we are encrypting C-style (null terminated) strings. Any extra nulls at the end of the string will just be ignored by string manipulation routines in C or C++ (since the C-style strings are terminated by at least one null anyway). This has limited usefulness in the context of binary (nonprintable) content due to ambiguity (i.e., how can we know if the terminating nulls are part of the data or part of the padding?). This scheme is sometimes seen with a "termination character" used to immediately precede the nulls, or with the last character set to the number of padding characters.

Constant characters: We'll encounter situations in which another nonnull constant character (e.g., space, tab, line feed, etc.) is used to pad the terminating block. This is somewhat rare, as it is ambiguous in both a printable and nonprintable character context.

PKCS5 padding[16]: By far, the most common padding scheme we will come across is PKCS5 padding; the ubiquity of the scheme is primarily because it is unambiguous (meaning padding characters can always be differentiated from data characters). In addition, the fact that there is a standard in place dictating its use adds to its ubiquity. The majority of the encryption libraries we'll be covering pad using this mechanism by default. The scheme proscribes padding applied to all data (even when the data falls along a block border); in other words, there is always padding applied. The padding character is the number (as an 8-bit quantity) of the amount of padding characters provided. For example, if four characters were required to pad to a full block, the padding character would be the value 4 as an 8-bit quantity repeated four times. By specifying that there is always padding, and by using the padding character to indicate the number of padding bytes, we are assured that there is no ambiguity between data and padding.

4.2.1.2 Stream Ciphers

For the most part, there is not the same wide variety of stream ciphers as block ciphers. Although a few stream ciphers exist and some of the block cipher modes of operation allow "stream cipher" characteristics to apply to traditional block ciphers, the most popular stream cipher by far is the RC4 algorithm. RC4 was RSA trade secret information prior to the disclosure of the specifics to the public on an Internet mailing list in 1994[17]. Public divulgence of the algorithm details nullifies its trade secret status, but the name "RC4" is still a registered trademark of RSA[18]. Therefore, while the algorithm details are not specifically encumbered, use of the name is. To get around this, numerous implementations using the same algorithm refer to their implementation as "ARCFOUR" rather than RC4 to avoid using the trademarked name (the underlying mechanics are identical).

RC4 is difficult to use properly. There are a number of caveats to keep in mind, and making sure our applications consider them all correctly can be difficult; the most important caveats from a usage perspective are:

- We *never* want to use the same key twice. We *can*, however, mix the key with a randomly generated IV each time we use the cipher, which alleviates some of the inherent security issues associated with key reuse.
- We want to throw away the first 256 bytes of the generated data to limit the applicability of attacks that exploit the nonrandom nature of the initial cipher output.

From our point of view, the internal mechanics of the RC4 algorithm is mostly a black box; we set the internal state of the algorithm by supplying a key as input, and as a result, we get an ongoing series of bits on the other side as output (the keystream). The bits that come to us as output are XORed with our input data to derive the encrypted output. Since a given key sets the internal state of the algorithm, we can expect the same keystream output if we later set the algorithm to the same internal state. The fact that the operation in use is XOR should give us some important clues into the caveats about RC4 we mentioned earlier; let's take a closer look at some of these aspects of XOR.

As developers, we're probably fairly acquainted with XOR and its properties: specifically, we know that in XORing two bits, the result is "false" if the two bits are not the same, and "true" if the two bits are the same. We also know that we can use XOR to "nullify itself" or "arrive back where we started" by XORing something by a constant value and XORing the result with the same constant. Let's look at that in more detail from a traditional development perspective. For example, if we have an unsigned byte representing the number "25" (binary 00011001) and we XOR it with a byte representing "50" (binary 00110010), we get "43" (00101011). Illustrated more graphically:

25—00011001

^ 50—00110010

= 43—00101011

Since every bit that is the same becomes zero and every bit that is different becomes 1, XORing this result (43) with "50" a second time gives us our original value of "25," like so:

50—00110010

^ 43—00101011

= 25—00011001

Extending this property, if we XOR two values with the same constant, XORing the result of both operations together will "nullify the constant" and yield the same value as an XOR of the two original values themselves. For example, if we take 25 and XOR it with 50, we get 43; if we take 29 and XOR it with 50, we get 47; if we take both results (43 and 47) and XOR them together, we get 4, which is the same value we would have obtained if we had XORed 25 and 29 in the first place. Expressed using bitwise operators, this would be (25^50)^(29^50)=25^29:

25—00011001

^ 50—00110010

= 43—00101011

29—00011101

^ 50—00110010

= 47—00101111

47—00101111

^ 43—00101011
= 4—00000100
25—00011001
^ 29—00011101
= 4—00000100

Keeping in mind that the internal state of RC4 is dependent on the key in use, we can readily see why we should never use the same key for more than one message. Specifically, if we use the same key for two different messages, those two message streams could be XORed together to produce the same result if the two plaintexts were XORed together just as we saw earlier. For the most part, if we can do this, we pretty much obviate the key. This is easiest to see if we know one of the plaintexts—in that case, it would be elementary to fill in the missing value: all we would have to do is line up the bits and "solve" for the missing piece based on the result and one of the inputs. In practice, we don't really have to know one plaintext for sure to remove the key from the two streams—it just makes the process easier.

This is just one of the reasons why RC4 is difficult to use correctly. The primary benefit of using a stream cipher over and above a block cipher rests in the stream cipher's capability to operate on smaller units of data than a block cipher. However, given that we will almost always find RC4 to be the predominant stream cipher available for use in today's world, and given that the use of RC4 comes with the caveats, development time is almost always reduced if we can use a block cipher instead. More often than not, architectural adjustments can allow us to substitute a block cipher and thus reduce the time required to develop, test, and debug our applications. For example, if we are writing an encrypted socket connection, we could choose to channel an unbuffered socket through RC4 according to the rules outlined previously, or we could "architect around" RC4 and introduce buffering to the socket to allow us to use a block cipher like AES. In this case, buffering would both reduce our development complexity and (depending on the underlying socket we intend to wrap) could actually improve the performance of our application.

4.2.1.3 Asymmetric Ciphers

The functionality provided by our libraries for asymmetric encryption functionality (both for signing and for privacy) is relatively straightforward. However, there are some aspects of engineering with asymmetric cryptography that we should take into account and are not (necessarily) handled for us by our libraries. The point of this is not to complicate the endeavor, so we'll limit the discussion to just those usage options that are under our direct control.

Performance Considerations

In general, we're fairly limited in the degree to which we need (or want) to control the operation of our asymmetric encryption algorithms. However, one aspect is incredibly important: performance considerations during encryption for privacy (e.g., nonsigning) operations. When creating a strategy whereby we will use asymmetric cryptography for privacy operations, we'll definitely want to reduce the amount of data involved in the encryption operation. This is usually done by encrypting our data with a symmetric key and then encrypting that symmetric key with our asymmetric one. In general, that's pretty much all we need to know to get started; the libraries will handle the rest of the heavy lifting for us.

4.2.1.4 The Bare Minimum: Selecting a Data Encryption Algorithm

- Block ciphers are useful and efficient for large volume (bulk) data encryption and decryption; AES is a good candidate given the security/performance ratio.
- A mode of operation must be selected when using a block cipher; CBC is a useful "general purpose" mode of operation for most circumstances.
- A stream cipher can be useful for unbuffered communication channels, but it is difficult to use properly.
- Asymmetric cryptography is much slower than symmetric cryptography; therefore, usage should be combined to get the best benefit from both methodologies.

4.2.2 Putting It All Together

So, now we've hopefully brought a bit more "concreteness" to the developer's understanding of the steps required for actual use of cryptography. The next step, therefore, is to move closer to a "usage level" understanding by looking at how to go about using this functionality in an application.

4.2.2.1 Overview: The Goal

In this situation, we'll design and build two applications that encrypt data. To make it a little more interesting (and to give a little more diversity), we'll use Java and CAPI for each of the two examples. The platform in the first case isn't important, since we won't be using any non-Java APIs or native (JNI) calls.[19] The platform in the second case will obviously be Microsoft on an Intel platform.

These two applications will each do different things to illustrate each of the points we've gone over in this section. Our first application will encrypt and subsequently decrypt data using the AES algorithm, and the second application will generate a random symmetric 3DES session key and wrap it using asymmetric cryptography—namely, RSA.

4.2.2.2 The Design

This example is relatively straightforward, so our design won't be anything particularly magnificent. We'll assume that we can use a version of the JDK that allows us to specify AES as our algorithm (versions prior to Java 2 Platform, Standard Edition (J2SE) 1.4.2 do not). We'll also be using the default provider supplied by Sun without installation of another provider; this provider is a little limited in some of its features, and we'll talk about installing new providers in detail in our discussion of the JCA in Chapter 9, but it is sufficient for our purposes here. Lastly, we'll be using the "enhanced" CSP from Microsoft in our second example, since this allows us to use Triple-DES. Other than that, all we're doing is taking some test data and encrypting it. The key generation functionality might be interesting for a developer to note, since it highlights some of the things we've seen in previous sections (e.g., using an arbitrary byte string as a key) and the incorporation of robust random number generation into our applications.

4.2.2.3 Preparing the Environment

Since this information is provided only for example purposes, if you're going to follow along and try this, you'll need to follow the detailed instructions laid out under the heading "Preparing the Environment" in both the chapters on CAPI and the JCA (Chapters 8 and 9, respectively) before this application will compile and run successfully. However, it should again be noted that to satisfy the goals of this section (specifically, gaining a "comfort level" with the process), compiling the examples and following along is not strictly necessary.

4.2.2.4 The Result

The following Java code, explained in more detail later in this section, encrypts some test data (specifically, a `java.lang.String` containing the value "Test Data") using a new random key created internal to the library. Note that we do not have to seed the random number generator before we use the key generation mechanism, since this is done automatically for us internal to the JCA library.

```
import java.security.*;
import javax.crypto.*;
import javax.crypto.spec.*;



public class Main {

    public static void main(String argv[]) throws Exception {
```

```
        String plainText = new String("Test Data.");

        //first, we get our symmetric (secret) keys
        KeyGenerator keyGen = KeyGenerator.getInstance("AES");
        keyGen.init(128);
        SecretKey secretKey = keyGen.generateKey();
        byte[] keyBytes = secretKey.getEncoded();
        SecretKeySpec keySpec = new SecretKeySpec(keyBytes,
                "AES");

        //now do the work
        Cipher aes = Cipher.getInstance("AES");
        aes.init(aes.ENCRYPT_MODE, keySpec);
        byte[] ciphertext = aes.doFinal(plainText.getBytes());

        System.out.println("AES operation completed");

    }
}
```

Now for the CAPI approach. Note that again, we do not have to explicitly specify random number generation for this, although random numbers are used internally by the library for key creation.

```
#include <windows.h>
#include <wincrypt.h> //required for crypto functions
#include <iostream.h>

void main() {

    //initialize null handles

    HCRYPTPROV providerHandle = 0;
    HCRYPTKEY asymmetricKeyHandle = 0;
    HCRYPTKEY symmetricKeyHandle = 0;
    //request a handle to a provider (impl & key storage)
    //first we'll attempt to use a context that already exists;
    //if there isn't one, then we'll attempt to generate one
    //using CRYPT_NEWKEYSET
    int status =
        CryptAcquireContext(&providerHandle, //provider handle
        "myContainer", //need to specify a container name
        MS_ENHANCED_PROV, //use the enhanced provider
        PROV_RSA_FULL, //provider type (RSA full)
        0); //no flags
```

```
        if(!status) { //no existing provider, need to create one
            status = CryptAcquireContext(&providerHandle,
                "myContainer",
                MS_ENHANCED_PROV,
                PROV_RSA_FULL,
                CRYPT_NEWKEYSET);
        }
        if (!status) { //there was no existing context and we can't
create one
            //we're in trouble.  Bomb out
            cerr << "An error has occurred during the container
creation." << endl << flush;
            exit(-1);
        }
        //generate a new wrapping key; this key will allow us to wrap
        //the second key we generate in the next call
        status = CryptGenKey(providerHandle, AT_KEYEXCHANGE,
            0, &asymmetricKeyHandle);

        //Generate a 3DES key.  Specify EXPORTABLE to allow it to be
wrapped
        status = CryptGenKey(providerHandle, CALG_3DES,
            CRYPT_EXPORTABLE, //default key, exportable
            &symmetricKeyHandle);

        unsigned long dataLen = 0;

        //we'll need to call CryptExportKey twice - first to find out
        //how big a structure we need, and the second time to do the
work
        int works = CryptExportKey(symmetricKeyHandle,
            asymmetricKeyHandle, SIMPLEBLOB, CRYPT_DESTROYKEY,
            NULL, //find out how big our structure needs to be
            &dataLen);
        //allocate memory for the structure
        unsigned char * blob = (unsigned char*)malloc(dataLen);
        works = CryptExportKey(symmetricKeyHandle,
            asymmetricKeyHandle, SIMPLEBLOB, CRYPT_DESTROYKEY,
            blob, &dataLen);
        //we're done for now - release the structure and free the
context
        free(blob);
        CryptReleaseContext(providerHandle, 0);
    }
```

You will notice that the second example is much longer and a bit more complicated than the first; this is due to both differences in the functionality illustrated (the second example is more complicated), and the manner in which we are calling the underlying APIs. At this point, a developer should not draw any conclusions about the relative ease of use associated with the different libraries merely on the basis of these examples.

4.2.2.5 The Bare Minimum: Issues and Lessons Learned

Here are the steps we went through to accomplish our goals, including the ancillary steps required to interact with the libraries.

Example 1:

1. Create the plaintext.
2. Obtain a reference to a key generator, specifying AES as our target algorithm.
3. Inform the `KeyGenerator` of the size key we wish to use; here we used the smallest of the three possible AES key sizes, 128 bits. Note that if the security policy of our organization or the security needs of our application demanded it, we could have chosen a larger key size during this call.
4. Generate the secret key.
5. Obtain a `KeySpec` (a representation of the key usable by the `Cipher` class).
6. Obtain a reference to a `Cipher`, specifying AES as our target algorithm.
7. Inform the `Cipher` of the key we wish to use for the encryption.
8. "Pull the trigger" on the encryption by calling `Cipher::doFinal()` on our test data to create the ciphertext.

Example 2:

1. Attempt to obtain a provider context; contexts are a bit tricky, so we won't go into much detail here. However, what we are doing is telling the operating system to "open our application's key container" (named "myContainer"); if that call fails (such as if our application does not yet have a key container), we try to create one in the second call using the flag CRYPT_NEWKEYSET. In both calls, we are specifying that the enhanced provider be used for the context we wish to acquire (there are other built-in providers, but the enhanced provider is required to use Triple-DES).
2. Generate a new "key exchange" RSA key (asymmetric key) to encrypt the symmetric key we are about to create. This key will be stored in the key container we just created.
3. Generate the new symmetric key, specifying Triple-DES (CALG_3DES) as our target algorithm.

4. Attempt to export the symmetric key, but specify a NULL target to get the library to tell us how big to make our structure.
5. Allocate memory for the key.
6. Export the key to the newly generated buffer by calling the same function again with the nonnull pointer value (the newly generated buffer).
7. Release the context and free resources.

4.3 SIGNING AND VERIFYING

Signing and digital signatures begins with creation of a message digest from the message we wish to sign; we will then apply the signing algorithm to the message digest, and ultimately the digest will be enciphered. However, before we go too far into that process, it should be mentioned that all the libraries that are under consideration provide layers of abstraction from the underlying process; this is particularly useful because it spares us from having to manipulate some of the structures to conform to the conventions of the relevant standards (PKCS #1) ourselves. The signing and verifying APIs are simple to use (as are the hashing algorithms), so let's look at the options we have when it comes to design and implementation of our application.

4.3.1 Selecting a Hashing Algorithm

We first must decide what hashing algorithm to use for generation of the message digest. For the most part, we'll only need to evaluate and consider two for our application: MD5 or SHA. There are, of course, others, but these two are the predominant choice for selection, because they are supported within all the libraries we'll be using and are readily accessible to us by those libraries.

4.3.1.1 Secure Hash Algorithm (SHA-1, SHA-256, SHA-384, and SHA-512)

In general, new applications should favor the use of SHA over MD5. SHA is NIST recognized and outlined in FIPS 180-2, so using one of these algorithms is pretty much the only choice for a U.S. government context standard (and also appropriately justifiable in a financial services or other regulated industry context). FIPS 180-2 specifies four algorithms within it: SHA-1, SHA-256, SHA-384, and SHA-512. SHA-1 produces a 20-byte digest value, meaning that the output value will be 20 bytes in total length; SHA-256, SHA-384, and SHA-512 are named for the size in bits of their output (meaning SHA-256 has a 256-bit or 32-byte digest size, SHA-384 has a 384-bit or 48-byte digest size, etc.). In general, the longer the output value, the less likely a collision is to occur, thus increasing the cryptographic strength of the algorithm. Since generating a message digest is by far the smallest portion of the digital signature process with respect to the corresponding performance hit, the security advantages offered by using a more robust hashing algorithm come at relatively little cost from an overall design perspective. SHA-1 is not recommended by NIST for new applications, and is slowly being phased out (with the goal of having the algorithm completely decommissioned by 2010). As such, where possible, we will avoid SHA-1 in favor of one of the more robust variants for new applications.

4.3.1.2 MD5

MD5, the successor to MD4, has some security issues, and therefore we will likely wish to avoid it in most "new application" contexts. However, we cannot rule out MD5 from our repertoire entirely, as we will almost certainly encounter legacy applications that use MD5 in some way. There are quite a few reasons why we would encounter the algorithm; specifically, before the weaknesses associated with MD5 were discovered, MD5 was thought to offer a slight performance improvement and a slight increase in storage efficiency due to its reduced digest size (16 bytes versus 20 bytes). A performance boost measured in milliseconds and a space savings of 4 bytes might not sound like much, but use of this algorithm was surprisingly prevalent in years past and is still in use in quite a few applications today. As we are extremely likely to encounter the algorithm in active use, it behooves us to familiarize ourselves with its existence and at least know how to generate an MD5 hash in our libraries when it is encountered.

4.3.1.3 The Bare Minimum: Selecting a Hashing Algorithm

- SHA-256, SHA-384, and SHA-512 make good security choices but are not available ubiquitously.
- SHA-1 is a good choice for situations in which the longer-digest SHA versions are unavailable.
- MD5, which in common use, has some security issues that make it less appealing for new application development.

4.3.2 Selecting a Signing Algorithm

Again, despite the fact that there are a number of asymmetric algorithms to select from, we're really only going to cover two in detail. We will, however, cover at least one other asymmetric algorithm in a cursory fashion later in this book when we start talking about key exchange, but in a signing context, we are likely to encounter only RSA and DSA. In general, RSA offers a number of advantages over DSA from a ubiquity, simplicity, performance, and flexibility standpoint. However, although NIST does recognize RSA for the purposes of digital signatures[20], typical federal FIPS-compliant implementations of digital signatures tend to use DSA rather than RSA. Therefore, we'll need to be familiar with DSA in the case of backward compatibility. In a government context, particular attention should be paid to the certification status of a particular toolkit and whether the FIPS certified mode includes

RSA functionality (some do, some do not). This point bears further clarification: in a government context, we *can* use RSA since it is NIST-approved, but we need to make sure that the FIPS mode of the cryptographic toolkit we are using incorporates RSA in its FIPS configuration. We'll need to explicitly check for this to meet our requirements under the regulation.

4.3.2.1 The Bare Minimum: Selecting a Signing Algorithm

- Unless we are in a U.S. government context, RSA is a good choice for new applications given the ease of working with the algorithm and the fact that it is implemented ubiquitously.
- If we are in the U.S. government, RSA is approved provided that RSA is listed as an "approved" algorithm for the module we are using; if not, DSA is the only choice.

4.3.3 Putting It All Together

So, understanding these things, let's incorporate the digital signature functionality into a sample application. We're primarily interested in the signing and verification aspects of the algorithms, so we'll go ahead and sign some data and then immediately verify it to see if the process worked. It should be pointed out that if this were a real-life application, we could do any number of things between signing and verifying, such as sending the signed data over a network, storing it to disk, and so forth before verifying it.

4.3.3.1 Overview: The Goal

As an illustration of the principles involved in signing, we'll create a sample application that exercises all of this functionality. Specifically, we'll use the BSAFE library to digitally sign and verify some data using RSA. We'll use RSA in combination with SHA-1 for generation of the message digest. In other words, we will set up a test application that uses SHA-1 to compute the hash and then signs the hash using the RSA algorithm.

4.3.3.2 The Design

Our application is relatively straightforward: first, we'll need to generate the asymmetric keys that will be used to do the signature. Then, we'll create a message digest of the text to be signed, and then we'll use the newly generated private key to apply the signature to the message digest[21]. As stated earlier, a real-life scenario would entail that we save the key pair somewhere for later use (since generating them is an expensive, time-consuming operation), but for the example, we can just get rid of them when we're done using them. Note that the RSA BSAFE library includes APIs in both C and Java, so we're going to be targeting the C API here (technically referred to as BSAFE Crypto-C).

4.3.3.3 Preparing the Environment

As we've stated in prefacing all the examples, we'll need to update the environment in order to compile and use the sample code. For detailed instructions on how to update the environment for BSAFE use in C, refer to the detailed setup instructions located in Chapter 10.

4.3.3.4 The Result

The following code demonstrates the use of BSAFE (Crypto-C) in the manner we've outlined. There are a few useful things to note about this example; specifically, there is a large amount of "boilerplate" code at the beginning of this example that is required by the RSA library. Since this boilerplate code is required to compile and run the sample, we've included it here, but we recommend that the developer skip over this and proceed directly to the functionality that illustrates the usage; you can get directly to it by skipping ahead to the example's `main()` function and following along.

```
    #include "bsafe.h"
    #include <stdlib.h>
    #include <memory.h>
    #include <string.h>

    #include <windows.h> //included so that wincrypt is error-free
    #include <wincrypt.h> //used to "cheat" during random seed
generation

    //define our algorithm choosers ahead of time. They could all be in
    //one chooser or broken up
    B_ALGORITHM_METHOD *SIGNVERIFY_SAMPLE_CHOOSER[] = {
        &AM_SHA,
        &AM_SHA_RANDOM,
        &AM_RSA_KEY_GEN,
        &AM_RSA_CRT_ENCRYPT,
        &AM_RSA_DECRYPT,
        (B_ALGORITHM_METHOD *)NULL_PTR };

    B_ALGORITHM_METHOD *RSA_KEYGEN_CHOOSER[] = {
        &AM_RSA_KEY_GEN,
        (B_ALGORITHM_METHOD *)NULL_PTR  };

    B_ALGORITHM_METHOD *RANDOM_CHOOSER[] = {
        &AM_SHA_RANDOM,
        (B_ALGORITHM_METHOD *)NULL_PTR };
```

```
//-----------BEGIN MEMORY HANDLING ROUTINES REQUIRED FOR BSAFE-----
void CALL_CONV T_memset (POINTER p, int c, unsigned int count)  {
    if (count != 0) {
        memset (p, c, count);
    }
}

void CALL_CONV T_memcpy (POINTER d, POINTER s, unsigned int count) {
    if (count != 0) {
        memcpy (d, s, count);
    }
}

void CALL_CONV T_memmove (POINTER d, POINTER s, unsigned int count) {
unsigned int i;

  if ((char *)d == (char *)s)
    return;
  else if ((char *)d > (char *)s) {
    for (i = count; i > 0; i--)
      ((char *)d)[i-1] = ((char *)s)[i-1];
  }
  else {
    for (i = 0; i < count; i++)
      ((char *)d)[i] = ((char *)s)[i];
  }
}

int CALL_CONV T_memcmp (POINTER s1, POINTER s2, unsigned int count) {
    if (count == 0) {
        return (0);
    } else {
        return (memcmp (s1, s2, count));
    }
}

POINTER CALL_CONV T_malloc (unsigned int size) {
  return ((POINTER)malloc (size == 0 ? 1 : size));
}

POINTER CALL_CONV T_realloc (POINTER p, unsigned int size) {
  POINTER result;
```

```
  if (p == NULL_PTR) {
    return (T_malloc (size));
  }

  if ((result = (POINTER)realloc (p, size == 0 ? 1 : size))
      == NULL_PTR) {
    free (p);
  }
  return (result);
}

void CALL_CONV T_free (POINTER p) {
    if (p != NULL_PTR) {
        free (p);
    }
}

unsigned int CALL_CONV T_strlen(char * p) {
    return strlen(p);
}

void CALL_CONV T_strcpy(char * dest, char * src) {
    strcpy(dest, src);
}

int CALL_CONV T_strcmp (char * a, char * b) {
  return (strcmp (a, b));
}
//-----------END MEMORY HANDLING ROUTINES REQUIRED FOR BSAFE-----


void main() {
    int status = 0;
    //set up the structures that we'll use to sign and verify.
    //these are all required B/SAFE types
    B_ALGORITHM_OBJ random          = (B_ALGORITHM_OBJ)NULL_PTR;
    B_ALGORITHM_OBJ sign            = (B_ALGORITHM_OBJ)NULL_PTR;
    B_ALGORITHM_OBJ verify          = (B_ALGORITHM_OBJ)NULL_PTR;
    B_KEY_OBJ publicKey             = (B_KEY_OBJ)NULL_PTR;
    B_KEY_OBJ privateKey            = (B_KEY_OBJ)NULL_PTR;
    B_ALGORITHM_OBJ keyGen          = (B_ALGORITHM_OBJ)NULL_PTR;
    A_RSA_KEY_GEN_PARAMS keyParams;
```

```
//create the algorithms and key data structures we'll need
status =        B_CreateAlgorithmObject(&random);
status =        B_CreateAlgorithmObject(&sign);
status =        B_CreateAlgorithmObject(&verify);
status =        B_CreateAlgorithmObject(&keyGen);
status =        B_CreateKeyObject(&publicKey);
status =        B_CreateKeyObject(&privateKey);

//now set the algorithms to the appropriate types
status =        B_SetAlgorithmInfo(sign,
                          AI_SHA1WithRSAEncryption, NULL_PTR);
status =        B_SetAlgorithmInfo(verify,
                          AI_SHA1WithRSAEncryption, NULL_PTR);
status =        B_SetAlgorithmInfo(random,
                          AI_SHA1Random,  NULL_PTR);

//set up our random source for key generation
status =        B_RandomInit (random, RANDOM_CHOOSER,
                          (A_SURRENDER_CTX*)NULL_PTR);
//seed it.  Note that we're going to cheat here to save a bit
//of space for the example.  Let's use a seed from CAPI
HCRYPTPROV  ctx;
CryptAcquireContext(&ctx, NULL, NULL, PROV_RSA_FULL, 0);
unsigned char randSeed[64];
CryptGenRandom(ctx, sizeof(randSeed), randSeed);
CryptReleaseContext(ctx, 0);
//done cheating, let's use our seed for the BSAFE random init

status =        B_RandomUpdate(random, randSeed,
                               sizeof(randSeed),
                               (A_SURRENDER_CTX *)NULL_PTR);

//initialization's done.  Now off to work.  First gen the RSA key
unsigned char f4Data[] = {0x01, 0x00, 0x01};
keyParams.modulusBits = 1024; //1024 bit key
keyParams.publicExponent.data   = f4Data;
keyParams.publicExponent.len    = sizeof(f4Data);
//this next bit would have been nice to have before when we
//were setting up our algorithms, but we needed to set
//the parameters for key generation first.
status =        B_SetAlgorithmInfo(keyGen,
                          AI_RSAKeyGen, (POINTER)&keyParams);
status =        B_GenerateInit(keyGen,
                          RSA_KEYGEN_CHOOSER,
```

```
                                (A_SURRENDER_CTX*)NULL_PTR);
    status =        B_GenerateKeypair(keyGen, publicKey, privateKey,
                                random, (A_SURRENDER_CTX*)NULL_PTR);

    //done generating the keys.  Now we can sign
    status =        B_SignInit(sign, privateKey,
                                  SIGNVERIFY_SAMPLE_CHOOSER,
                                    (A_SURRENDER_CTX *)NULL_PTR);
    const char * dataThatWeAreGoingToSign = "Data to sign.";
    status =        B_SignUpdate(sign, (unsigned char*)
                                  dataThatWeAreGoingToSign,
                                  strlen(dataThatWeAreGoingToSign)+1,
                                  (A_SURRENDER_CTX *)NULL_PTR);
    //our array wants bytes, but key size is bits so divide by 8
    unsigned char signature[(1024+8)/8];
    memset(signature, 0x0, sizeof(signature));
    unsigned int signatureLen = sizeof(signature);
    status =        B_SignFinal(sign, signature, &signatureLen,
                                  (1024+8)/8,
                                  (B_ALGORITHM_OBJ)NULL_PTR,
                                  (A_SURRENDER_CTX *)NULL_PTR);

    //signature created.  now we can verify that we can use the
    //public key to decrypt the hash and compare it
    status =        B_VerifyInit(verify, publicKey,
                                  SIGNVERIFY_SAMPLE_CHOOSER,
                                  (A_SURRENDER_CTX *)NULL_PTR);
    status =        B_VerifyUpdate(verify, (unsigned char*)
                                  dataThatWeAreGoingToSign,
                                  strlen(dataThatWeAreGoingToSign)+1,
                                  (A_SURRENDER_CTX *)NULL_PTR);
    status =        B_VerifyFinal(verify, signature,
                                  signatureLen,
                                  (B_ALGORITHM_OBJ)NULL_PTR,
                                   (A_SURRENDER_CTX *)NULL_PTR);

    //clean up
    B_DestroyAlgorithmObject(&random);
    B_DestroyAlgorithmObject(&sign);
    B_DestroyAlgorithmObject(&verify);
    B_DestroyAlgorithmObject(&keyGen);
    B_DestroyKeyObject(&publicKey);
    B_DestroyKeyObject(&privateKey);
}
```

4.3.3.5 The Bare Minimum: Issues and Lessons Learned

As you probably noticed, this example took *much* more space than the previous ones; it can be correctly stated that BSAFE (or, more specifically, the Crypto-C toolkit within BSAFE) by far requires more verbose code to use than other libraries. The same functionality could have been implemented in another library in far fewer lines. This should not be interpreted as a critique of BSAFE, though, since there is a great deal of control available to the developer allowing the developer to govern all aspects of key generation, signing, and so on. RSA has chosen to provide the developer with greater flexibility and control over the cryptographic functionality, although doing so does require a bit more software on our part.

As we've done with the other examples in this chapter, here are the highlights of the previous example, including those points required to interact with the library:

1. Create any algorithm choosers required by our sample.
2. Implement the memory handling routines required by BSAFE.
3. Declare and initialize any structures required.
4. Create the algorithm and key objects that will be required.
5. Further initialize the algorithm objects with the specific message digest and signing algorithms we intend to use.
6. Initialize (not seed) the random number generator.
7. Obtain a random seed for the random number generator (using CAPI to save some time).
8. Describe the parameters of the key type we wish to create.
9. Initialize the key generation process.
10. Generate the asymmetric keypair.
11. Initialize the signing process.
12. Load the data we wish to sign into the signing process (note that the signing process includes both hashing and the signature).
13. Sign the data (i.e., generate a signature) using the private key.
14. Initialize the verification process.
15. Load the data we wish to verify into the signing process.
16. Verify the data to ensure the signature is valid.
17. Destroy all algorithm and key objects and free resources.

4.4 BASIC TECHNIQUES WRAP-UP

In this section, we've gone through a few of the basic techniques that we'll use again and again; ideally, at this point, you will have an understanding of how to use the primitives, and how to select appropriate modes of operation and algorithms for your application. We've also presented those techniques in the context of actual usage with our libraries. If you didn't see the precise application of cryptography that you'll be using for your particular application, don't worry—we'll be covering much more ground in the chapters ahead, particularly in terms of strategies for application development, more specific information on library usage, and some important "gotchas" to avoid in development. However, this chapter should have provided you with at least some examples of the primitives that will be used in designing and implementing security software. As we'll see as we move forward, there are many ways we can fit these primitives together to form more complicated, automated, and robust functionality.

4.5 SELECTED REFERENCES

Random number generation:

Eastlake, Donald *et al. RFC 1750: Randomness Recommendations for Security*: Provides useful guidance on seed generation, including warnings against high-resolution timers currently used for this purpose.

Ernesto Guisado's RNG information page (*http://triumvir.org/articles/rng/*): A useful page with relevant advice as well as links to informational pages on the Internet concerning random number generation.

FIPS 186-2 (*http://csrc.nist.gov/publications/fips/fips186-2/fips186-2-change1.pdf*): Contains one of the three NIST-approved random number generators.

NIST Cryptographic Toolkit random number generation page (*http://csrc.nist.gov/CryptoToolkit/tkrng.html*): Includes information and referential links to NIST-approved random number generation techniques.

4.6 ENDNOTES

1. Note that while Rijndael (the underlying AES algorithm) has more flexibility with respect to key size, the standard delineated by NIST requires one of 128, 192, or 256 bits.
2. A particularly helpful guide to understanding the mathematics of the RSA algorithm is *The Mathematics of Ciphers: Number Theory and RSA Cryptography* by S.C. Coutinho.
3. For those who wish to pursue this topic further, some useful references are the Coutinho book already cited, or Schneier's *Applied Cryptography*.
4. For the interested reader, the "DSA parameters" (sometimes referred to as "PQG parameters") are the p, q, and g values used by the DSA

key-generation process. These numbers become part of the public key as a result of the key generation process.

5. *www.openssl.org/support/faq.html#USER1*
6. OpenSSL does provide some useful functionality to assist in gaining this type of information on the Windows platform; we'll go through those tools in detail in later chapters.
7. Actually, SUN has made available a patch that will install a /dev/random on Solaris 8, and patches for previous versions. This package is 112438-03 (current at the time of this writing) and 112439-02 (current at the time of this writing) for Sparc and x86, respectively. SUN has also made available the SUNWski package as part of the Easy Access CDs in previous platforms. Please refer to the SUN document entitled "Differing /dev/random support requirements within Solaris™ Operating Environments" located at *http://sunsolve.sun.com/search/document.do?assetkey=1-25-27606-1.*
8. *www.fact-index.com/b/bl/block_cipher_modes_of_operation.html*
9. *www.x5.net/faqs/crypto/q83.html*
10. *http://csrc.nist.gov/CryptoToolkit/modes/workshop1/papers/lipmaa-ctr.pdf*
11. *http://en.wikipedia.org/wiki/Block_cipher_modes_of_operation*
12. Docket # 040602169-4169-01, "Announcing Proposed Withdrawal of Federal Information Processing Standard (FIPS) for the Data Encryption Standard (DES) and Request for Comments"
13. An interesting and useful reference is the NIST AES homepage, located at *http://csrc.nist.gov/CryptoToolkit/aes/.*
14. MediaCrypt Web page (*www.mediacrypt.com/forcefs.asp?http://www.mediacrypt.com/_contents/20_support/206000_ord_ind.asp*)
15. MediaCrypt April 1, 2003, Press Release
16. Actually, this padding scheme is recommended by PKCS #5, RFC 2630 ("Cryptographic Message Syntax") and NIST (in NIST SP 800-38a, "Recommendation for Block Cipher Modes of Operation—Methods and Techniques").
17. *http://en.wikipedia.org/wiki/RC4_%28cipher%29*
18. USPTO serial number 74463805
19. In case you're curious, the environment in which the test was built, written, compiled, and run on is Solaris 9 on Sparc architecture.
20. *http://csrc.nist.gov/cryptval/dss.htm*
21. Note that a conceptually similar (although much "busier") example occurs in the BSAFE CRYPTO-C developer's handbook. We've chosen to use this example, as the BSAFE manual lacks any explanation regarding what these APIs might be used for; a situation we thought deserved clarification.

5 Implementation Choices

In This Chapter

- Library Selection
- Building Cryptographic Schemes
- Selecting Appropriate Primitives
- Integrating with Hardware
- Integrating with Standards
- Endnotes

So far, we've gone over some of the features we would look for in a cryptographic library, and we've covered some of the basic tools (such as the most common cryptographic primitives) those libraries provide. We've talked at a high level about which libraries might be useful for a particular purpose and some of the constraints of each (e.g., the JCE can only be called from Java or that the Microsoft CAPI only runs on Windows), but we have yet to drill down into the process for how we would choose a library. After all, we don't want to have to learn everything about a library's usage in order to pick one, and we don't want to pick one that we can't use because we have to be compliant with a particular industry standard or federal regulation. As such, this section is designed to assist in library selection. It outlines the "hard and fast" rules first (some of which we've covered in less detail in the overviews of the particular libraries), and then provides other information that might be apropos, such as support for particular hardware, support for particular algorithms, and how industry standards and/or regulation figures into the equation. Once we've decided what library we're going to use, we'll talk about cryptographic hardware and some of the mechanics of working with them. Finally, we'll talk a bit about what algorithms we'll use for a particular purpose, what situations are better for which algorithms, and some industry standards that might play a role in the selection of algorithms.

5.1 LIBRARY SELECTION

There is only one step to selecting a library: pick a library that does what we need, or pick a combination of libraries that do what we need. This statement sounds trite and obvious, but it bears saying, because it carries with it an important implication. The implied truth in the statement is that we *know* what we need. In other words, the implication is that we understand our application's requirements and the boundaries within which our application will operate. This is a truism: we need to understand what our application does before we can select a cryptographic library, select cryptographic protocols, make use of security protocols, or otherwise implement any security functionality whatsoever. Some of the selection criteria will be readily apparent, such as:

Programming language: We will need to use a library that is callable from whatever programming language we've decided to work in; for example, if our application will be written in Java, we need to use one of the libraries with a Java API.

Platform: We will need to use a library that supports the platform on which our application will run. This might include operating system, system architecture (e.g., Sparc, 64-bit Intel systems, Alpha, etc.). This will also include higher level environment considerations such as if we are writing an application that will be run inside the context of an application server or if we are writing a shell script.

Protocol support: Based on the needs of our application, does the library support the required security protocols we'll need to employ to perform the tasks our application demands?

These factors alone can sometimes allow us to "zero in" on a single target with respect to library selection. For example, if we're writing C or C++ code on a Unix box, we can immediately rule out two of the libraries; depending on which Unix platform we're working on, we'll have either two choices or just one choice. However, putting aside these extremely apparent selection criteria, we must also consider the less-apparent criteria, such as:

Regulatory: Are we working in a government (which will likely have its own rules about cryptographic implementations), or are we in a heavily regulated industry (such as health care or financial services) where industry or legal regulation may hold sway?

Policy: Does the organization that we're a part of have any specific security policy specifying what can or cannot be done. For example, do we have the requirement to support FIPS 140-2 or other standards in our use of cryptographic libraries?

Hardware support: Will we be using cryptographic hardware such as accelerators or HSM? If so, are we using particular hardware, and how will we be calling the library?

These secondary selection criteria are equally as restrictive as the first set. Ideally, we will know ahead of time what parameters our products will encounter when they are deployed (e.g., if hardware is in scope or out of scope). The ideal is seldom the reality, however: in some situations (particularly if we are developing a commercial product), we might now know what our potential client's regulatory environment might be, or whether our customers are willing to spend extra money for cryptographic hardware. In situations in which it is difficult to know these answers ahead of time, it will behoove us to pick the most "general" library we can, one that has the flexibility to incorporate these secondary factors if we desire. This section attempts to lay out the libraries with a high degree of specificity so we can make as intelligent a library choice as possible as early in the development phase as we can. At the end of the day, between the four extremely comprehensive libraries covered here, we should be extremely likely to find one that fits our usage. Let's begin the process by looking at platform criteria.

5.1.1 Platform Selection Criteria

Our platform is a combination of all the aspects of the environment within which our application will be running. As stated, this extends to more than just operating system or processor architecture, and can include any additional runtime context our application might be running in—such as a Web server, a scripting environment, a command shell, and so forth. The selection process for determining a compatible library with respect to this constraint is straightforward (it will become a little more complex when we add cryptographic hardware to the equation in the next step). Specifically, the following library-by-library breakdown of the libraries covered in this book illustrates the environments in which they will function:

OpenSSL (source distribution): Since OpenSSL is distributed as source, we literally can build the library for any machine that has a C compiler. OpenSSL is the most versatile of the libraries with respect to platform coverage.

Microsoft CAPI (Windows): Microsoft CAPI is only available on "recent" versions of Microsoft operating systems (>= Windows NT 4.0). In addition, the extent to which certain algorithms, functions, and structures are available depends on the version of Microsoft Windows we are using. If we require support for a particular algorithm, and we want to use CAPI, it pays to check ahead of time to determine which platforms support the functionality we need and ensure that we have a plan in place to address the other platforms.

Microsoft .NET (Windows + .NET framework support files): The .NET classes available through the .NET API require Microsoft Windows in addition to the .NET framework runtime (installed via the Microsoft .NET framework redistributable or via "Windows Update").

RSA BSAFE: The BSAFE library supports the Java virtual machine, Microsoft Windows (32 bit), Red-Hat Linux, and Solaris.[1] Other platforms may be available from RSA as well, but these are the ones listed as being actively supported for the most recent version of the product.

SUN Java JCA: Java virtual machine only; in other words, OS is not, strictly speaking, a factor, but our software does have to be written in Java to make use of the functionality.

Looking at this list, we can see that depending on the platform we are using, we can potentially eliminate some of the library possibilities from the list. In addition, coupled with language requirements, we can find ourselves even more constricted with respect to library selection:

OpenSSL: C/C++ or languages that allow C/C++ style calls via shared objects or .dlls (e.g., Perl, Python, Microsoft Visual Basic, C#, J#, etc.). Additionally, the library has a command-line interface to cryptographic functionality, making it suitable for shell scripting.

Microsoft CAPI: C/C++ or languages that allow C/C++ style calls via .dlls (e.g., ActivePerl, Microsoft Visual Basic, C#, J#, etc.).

Microsoft .NET: The .NET API allows for any language supporting the common language runtime to invoke the methods and properties of the security namespace (e.g., C/C++, Visual Basic, C#, J#, etc.).

RSA BSAFE: C/C++ (static libs). Additionally, the toolkit has a Java interface for use from the Java language.

SUN Java JCA: Java language only.

Figure 5.1 summarizes this information.

Library	Language Support	Platform
OpenSSL	Easiest in C/C++	Most platforms including Unix, Linux, Windows, OS X
Microsoft CAPI	CAPI in C/C++, .NET classes in Visual Basic, J#, C#, Managed C++, and scripting languages	Microsoft platforms only
RSA BSAFE	Easiest in Java and C/C++	Microsoft 32bit Windows, Red Hat Linux, Solaris
SUN Java JCA	Java only	Platfroms for which a JVM exists

FIGURE 5.1 Library overview.

Aside from the "yes or no" question of "Can we use the library?" it is also useful to take into account the convenience associated with doing so. For example, while it is *possible* to load and run the OpenSSL .dll from Visual Basic, "possible" is not the same as "easy." OpenSSL is most often used from C; a language like Visual Basic where we would have to pass all the right parameters to a dynamically loaded function without constants, easy access to structs, and difficult to use pointers would prove exceedingly challenging. The Microsoft .NET API, on the other hand, was designed with Visual Basic in mind, and therefore is extremely easy to call from the language.

5.1.2 HSM/Accelerator Support

If we have a requirement to use a cryptographic module with our application, we will find that the libraries targeted in this book allow us to support the most common hardware devices. Of course, that is not to say that every piece of hardware will support every library, but for the most part, the most common hardware will support these (the most common) libraries. For example, the following is the list of supported libraries as per the usage documentation of the nCipher nShield:

- PKCS#11 v. 2.01
- Microsoft CryptoAPI (Windows 2000)
- Java JCE/JCA
- Crypto Hardware Interface Library (CHIL)
- OpenSSL v. 0.9.6g
- nCipher nCore API Suite (C and Java)
- RSA BHAPI
- NSAPI

Putting aside NSAPI (since it's not a crypto library) and the nCipher proprietary APIs, we're left with "out of the box" support for the libraries covered in this book (RSA BHAPI support is provided via BSAFE), and PKCS #11, which is the "must implement" interface standard. The same is true of the SafeNET (formerly Rainbow) CryptoSwift and CryptoSwift 2. These products have "out of the box" support for the libraries we are covering here, and in most cases, one or two lines of code simply "turn on" the hardware features[2]. However, if we have a need to support a particular HSM or accelerator, we should check with both the library and the HSM/accelerator manufacturer to ensure the level of support. In other words, we'll only want to use a cryptographic module that supports the library we're using, either directly or via PKCS #11.

5.1.3 Performance Selection Criteria

In some cases, performance may also be a library selection criterion; although this is likely to be the exception rather than the rule; note that performance is also directly linked with the previous library selection criterion, "HSM/Accelerator support." As an example, we might be authoring a network server that accepts inbound connections over SSL, and so we would have a minimum performance "floor" we would be willing to tolerate. Alternatively, we might need to support a large number of concurrent connections within the server, and libraries with a large footprint might carry with them an unacceptable overhead. While all the libraries discussed in this book perform SSL, some do it more efficiently than others do. In particular, given the nature of the MSIL and Java bytecode, we can expect some performance degradation using these interfaces (with or without JIT enabled). However, it is more likely that expediency will outweigh performance in most cases, which leads us to our next factor.

5.1.4 Development Timeline

Some libraries are easier to work with than others are; this, of course, is a subjective assessment based on relative comfort with different coding styles and level of familiarity with the library. For example, if we are consummate C programmers, we might find it easier to work within the context of a C-only API. Alternatively, if we have a high level of familiarity with one of the APIs over and above others, we might find it much easier to work with the API with which we are most familiar. While these statements are both true, it is, however, much more likely that we are approaching the libraries without previous familiarity with any of the APIs. In that case, it is most likely that brevity of usage will lead to ease of use. In other words, the more code we have to write and the less automation provided by the library, the more challenging our usage of that library will be.

So, accepting that "brief" code (i.e., more automated code requiring fewer calls to use) is likely to be easier for most developers to learn and use, the .NET classes and the JCE are the easiest libraries from this perspective. From a functional perspective, for both SSL and cryptographic operations, they require the least amount of user-authored software and do their best to remove redundant calls through automation. The BSAFE C toolkits, SSL-C and Crypto-C, are the most verbose to use; but the Java BSAFE libraries (coming as they do with a Java JCE interface and a Java socket library) require about as much code to use as the non-BSAFE Java routines. Therefore, if we are looking to conserve development time, we will likely find the Java routines or the .NET classes to be the easiest to write to. Again, this is a matter of personal preference and will vary from developer to developer.

5.1.5 Regulatory and Policy Constraints

We might also need to maintain a certain level of regulatory compliance with respect to the tools we use. If we are working in the context of a U.S. government development shop (or authoring a product we intend to sell to the U.S. government), we will need to use a library that has been certified according to FIPS (Federal Information Processing Standard 140-2). Not all the libraries we'll be covering are FIPS certified. BSAFE supplies a specific FIPS version, CAPI is FIPS certified (when operated using specific algorithms), the JCE is not FIPS certified without the use of third-party add-on components, and OpenSSL is not FIPS certified (but is currently undergoing the certification process). The .NET API uses CAPI for certain algorithms, and CAPI is FIPS certified (although we have to be careful what algorithms we use).[3]

If we are working in a highly regulated private sector industry such as health care or financial services, it is very possible that the security organization of our firm has a policy in place with respect to the appropriate use of cryptography. That policy may specify that we use only modules that have been validated according to FIPS 140-2; alternatively, they may have a policy about which cryptographic libraries have been validated by the organization and are acceptable for use. If this is the case, we should ensure that the library we are using meets the standards as specified in the policy.

5.1.6 Price

As with everything in life, price is always a factor in our decision-making process. With two exceptions, all of the libraries we are covering are free from licensing fees of any kind unless we require support for an encumbered algorithm like IDEA (which we will have to pay for if we want to use). The two exceptions to this are BSAFE, which is a commercial product sold by RSA Security, Inc., and some of the add-on cryptographic providers that can be used to extend the functionality of the

JCE. The JCE in and of itself does not require a license fee, but if we want additional functionality that can only be supplied by third-party vendors, we will need to pay for the privilege. A full description of which vendors sell what additional JCE cryptography providers is covered in Chapter 9 where we discuss the JCE in depth.

5.2 BUILDING CRYPTOGRAPHIC SCHEMES

Once we've chosen a library, we'll then want to use that library to protect our data. We've already spent time discussing what the various primitives do, and how each solves a particular security challenge. However, in only very seldom cases will a cryptographic primitive in isolation do anything useful for us. We'll most likely want to apply the primitives in combination with each other to perform security functions. Realistically, we want to write our software as fast as possible, so we'll make use of any shortcut provided to us by the libraries as long as the usage of the library is easier than doing it ourselves. In some cases, it *is* just easier to write it ourselves—especially if we implement a few easy to use classes that abstract us away from using the cryptographic routines directly.

This section first describes some ways we can wrap some of the more difficult to use C APIs in a stateful C++ class. Following that, it outlines some of the ways we can put the primitives together to form more complex functionality. This material can be used either alone or in combination with the material in the next chapter detailing how to write security into the noncryptographic portions of our library (e.g., how to write buffers that zero themselves after use and how to write policy enforcement into symmetric key usage).

5.2.1 Wrapping Library Cryptographic Functionality

Before we get into the specifics of *what* to use the library for, it is useful to take some time out to talk about *how* to use it. Working on the premise that we posited earlier, that brevity of usage correlates to increased time savings, we can save ourselves a great deal of time by making it so our usage of the library is as concise as possible. More specifically, when using any of the C APIs (CAPI, Crypto-C, OpenSSL), it is a good idea to encapsulate the library calls into a single-purpose class that takes care of the various library initialization, library releasing, structure setup, string loading and unloading, mapping of algorithms to names, and so on. After we went to all this trouble to select a robust, practical library for our application, it seems a bit ironic that one of the first things we are discussing about usage is how to abstract ourselves away from the library API. After all, what's the point of learning how the library works if we're only going to call it directly once to completely encapsulate it? All of these questions are right on the money! The truth is, we *don't* want to have to remember the nuances of how to use the libraries. Ideally, we'll want to figure out how to use them once by reading through a reference, implement it in a way that's a snap to use, and forget it ever existed. Take, for example, the required usage steps to symmetrically encrypt data with RSA BSAFE Crypto-C. Recalling the "weighty" RSA example from the previous chapter, it should be clear that the usage of that library is anything but concise.

For example, looking at the sample code provided in Chapter 10 to encrypt a small `char *` buffer with AES, we find that the sample is 57 lines of code. That's not just 57 lines of fluffy familiar C code; those lines are filled with unfamiliar structs, multiline macros that we have to really concentrate to figure out how to use, and functions that we'll never see again outside the context of that one API. This is not to disparage the developers at RSA; in fact, they've done an excellent job and they've put together some really useful functionality for us to use, and quite consciously substituted complexity for advances in flexibility. However, the truth is that most of the time, we don't need the kind of flexibility the library provides; after all, we are usually interested in *basic usage* and not all-encompassing usage.

As an alternative to "sprinkling" BSAFE (or any other library's API) code throughout the entirety of the applications we write, we propose implementing an intermediate abstraction layer between our application and the library API for two reasons. First, if we ever need to change the library to a different one (e.g., if Microsoft decommissions CAPI, if we want to port to a new platform, or if the company we work for decides it wants to stop paying for BSAFE), we can do so without impacting the rest of our code. Second, so we can replace the 57 lines of confusing C code with an interface like:

```
//bind random key and IV
AESCipher aes;
//get data
Data plainText("This is the plaintext");
//encrypt
Data cipherText = aes.Encrypt(plainText);
```

Just a thin wrapper around Crypto-C allows us to do this. In fact, if we implement the wrapper correctly, we can cause it to conditionally compile in support for Crypto-C or compile in something else such as OpenSSL. This usage is much more "compact" than the default Crypto-C API; it handles allocation of library-specific structs on initialization, and releasing of those structs on deallocation. From a usage perspective, it is simplicity itself; we don't have to remember to free memory, we don't have to worry about obtaining a key, and we don't have to worry about seeding the random number generator. All these implementation details are contained inside the class so we (or a maintenance programmer) can safely "forget" that we have to call a number of routines after we are done encrypting the data. Obviously, we'll want to provide enhanced usage capability in the class to allow us to encrypt large or noncontiguous regions of memory; we'll also want to update it so we can get the key value for later serialization to a file or whatever other format we desire. The class definition (leaving out the private structures that are required for the actual implementation) would be as follows:

```
#ifndef SCAESCIPHER_H
#define SCAESCIPHER_H
#include "SCGlobal.h"
#include "SCData.h"
#include "SCSymmetricCipher.h"
class SCBASE_CALL AESCipher : public SymmetricCipher {
public:
    AESCipher();
    AESCipher(const Key & encryptWith,
        const Data * IV = 0);
    ~AESCipher();
    const Data& GetIV() const;
    const Key& GetKey() const;
    Data Encrypt(const Data& plainText) const;
    Data EncryptPart(const Data& part);
    Data EncryptDone();
    Data Decrypt(const Data& cipherText) const;
    Data DecryptPart(const Data& part);
    Data DecryptDone();
private:
    //removing private members for clarity
};

#endif
```

Ideally, we would want to implement similar interfaces along these lines for any of the library functionality we use. Adding a new class takes only a few moments longer than adding the library calls inline to our source, and reusing the functionality decreases our development time, since we do not have to consult the reference, and we do not have to debug as thoroughly (since we're calling the same class over and over again, we only have to debug it once).

Note that this is only a suggestion to the developer; developers can use whatever methodology they prefer with respect to their application. We're just sharing what saves us time; your mileage may vary. In the event that you desire to use this functionality in your applications, there is source code on the companion CD-ROM for a "quick and dirty" encryption library. Feel free to cut and paste from it

ON THE CD

or to compile and link against it; in exchange, we just ask that you let us know about any bugs you find so we can get them fixed and keep the toolkit maintained. The following classes are included in the /Examples/Chapter 5/Framework directory:

- AESCipher
- TripleDESCipher
- SHA1Digest
- MD5Digest
- RSASigner
- DSASigner
- RandomSource
- EncryptedOutputStream
- DecryptedInputStream

In addition to support classes for the preceding (such as interface classes, data structure classes, and the like), and including the enhanced functionality support structures described in the next chapter, we could add a tremendous amount of additional functionality to the library, such as an SSLSocket and an SSLServerSocket (currently not implemented). Any of these would be useful to add as we incorporate this type of functionality into software we write.

5.2.2 Tying Primitives Together

We've deliberately avoided talking about using multiple primitives in conjunction with each other until we've had a change to describe ways to make the functionality opaque. It is much more feasible to realistically add support for a number of different primitives in combination once we've reduced the usage down to only a few lines. If we started with the same 57 lines of BSAFE code and proceeded to add to it other primitives (such as RSA to encrypt the symmetric key for someone else), or to add data conversion routines (such as Base64 to make it readily printable), we would wind up with a wild mess of straight C code. Since we obviously don't want to write hundreds of lines of C code to perform basic tasks, we thought it would soften the discussion somewhat to lay out beforehand how we'll make the designs we come up with here approachable. Figure 5.2 is a chart of the cryptographic primitives we've discussed in the previous section; the top row and the left column contain the same values. The entries in the chart describe some ways the two primitives can be used together to solve different security challenges than what's solved by the primitive alone; if there is more than one way the two primitives are put together, we've listed both. If there is more than one way the primitives can be put together and one way is unsafe for us to implement directly or consists of antiquated usage, we've noted that as well with an asterisk.

	Symmetric Encryption	Asymmetric Encryption (Privacy)	Message Digests	Asymmetric Encryption (Authentication)	Random Numbers (PRNG)
Symmetric Encryption	N/A	**Enveloped data** (e.g. EFS, PGP/GPG)	Authentication "token" (encrypted hash value)	- Signed, encrypted data (e.g. PGP/GPG messages, S/MIME) - Secure Channels (e.g. SSL, SSH)	Key Generation
Asymmetric Encryption (Privacy)	**Enveloped data** (e.g. EFS, PGP/GPG)	N/A	Limited Use	Signed, Wrapped Keys	Key Generation
Message Digests	Authentication "token" (encrypted hash value)	Limited Use	N/A	**Signature** (X.509 certs, DSS, PGP/GPG, etc.)	**MAC**
Asymmetric Encryption (Authentication)	- Signed, encrypted data (e.g. PGP/GPG messages, S/MIME) - Secure Channels (e.g. SSL, SSH))	Signed, Wrapped Keys	**Signature** (X.509 certs, DSS, PGP/GPG, etc.)	N/A	- Key Generation - Signature (e.g. DSA)
Random Numbers (PRNG)	Key Generation	Key Generation	**MAC**	- Key Generation - Signature (e.g. DSA)	N/A

FIGURE 5.2 Primitive usage.

For quite a few of the strategies listed, we'll notice that the usage is deprecated, or that it is already implemented at some level in the libraries we're using. Believe us, that's a good thing. Not having to implement them saves us the work of calling the two things directly and saves us from having to worry about making sure we've done it right (e.g., not introducing new security vulnerabilities through incorrect usage). Sometimes, though, there are situations in which we can't avoid but implement it ourselves; for example, if we wanted to create a file format that is compatible with PGP/GPG (e.g., according to RFC 2440), we would probably need to implement that ourselves. We could look around and see what we might come up with, but we'd probably have to go ahead and write it ourselves. Alternatively, if we wanted to create a structure that's compatible with Microsoft EFS, we would need to write that as well. However, that's not to say that we couldn't write an application that performs the same methodology as either of these programs. We very well could; doing so would involve steps like the following:

1. Generation of a random key and random IV to use for the bulk data encryption.
2. Binding of the IV to the data (prepend, append, linear serialization, or through indicator/header text).
3. Bulk encryption of the file or text.

4. Encryption of the symmetric key with the public key of the recipient (and any other persons at this time).
5. Packing of the structure.
6. Destruction of the original file or text.

By performing these steps in order, we in effect accomplish almost exactly what these other products do. Our data is not packaged in the proprietary structure (or IETF draft standard structure as the case may be); instead, it's in our proprietary structure. However, the result is more or less the same; some of the libraries even provide us with routines to assist in doing this (see, for example, the OpenSSL EVP_SealInit() method described in Chapter 7), and some do not. All in all, where the functionality is provided, it's both easier and a "better bet" security-wise to use the inherent capabilities of the libraries rather than implementing anything directly ourselves. As we've said before, "why reinvent the wheel?"

5.2.3 Searching for Standards

For almost anything we want to do insofar as tying multiple cryptographic primitives together, chances are that it has already been addressed by a standard somewhere. Again, in general, it is safer to "toe the line" with respect to standards compliance in implementing cryptographic functionality. Oftentimes, there's a tool somewhere that implements the "task at hand," and there are often security vulnerabilities associated with performing operations the wrong way or in the wrong order. There are also practical reasons for following the standards as well; for example, if we want to exchange an encrypted file with a remote party, we'll probably want to compress the file under some circumstances. Since encrypted output has poor compression properties, we'll want to compress the file first, and then encrypt it only after compression has been completed. If we had gone looking for a standard mechanism rather than implementing a mechanism ourselves, we could have determined that ahead of time and adjusted our implementation appropriately. As an aside, if you want to see this in action, check out the utility class for encrypting a file on the companion CD-ROM; it's located in the `FileEncryptor` class and demonstrates exactly this usage.

ON THE CD

So, how do we locate the appropriate standard we can use in our applications? A good place to start is in the References section contained in this book. We've tried to put together lists of a number of different sources that you can use in a variety of situations. Of course, if what you need is not in the references, the IETF RFC database is another good place to look to get started. There are a number of standards documents in that repository detailing a variety of ways to approach the majority of problems we will encounter (some currently in use, some deprecated or superseded). In general, though, the libraries will have built-in functionality for doing just about anything our application needs.

5.3 SELECTING APPROPRIATE PRIMITIVES

Once we've established the library we're going to use, and once we've decided how we're going to use it, we'll have some options about what ciphers to use, which primitives we will support within our application, and so on. We've already discussed many of the ciphers we'll come across, but we thought it would be useful to include some industry-specific guidance (for those of us working in regulated entities), some guidance about strength and encumbrance (patent) status, relative strength information about some of the algorithms including what algorithms not to use, and some warnings about how we could use them inappropriately (according to generally accepted best practices).

5.3.1 Strength Considerations

A number of algorithms are weak today and have been weak since the advent of modern computing. Fortunately, these algorithms are not located in the libraries that contain the implementations we're using. There are, however, a number of algorithms we considered "strong" in the past, but have since proved far too weak to be relied on for day-to-day application. We've grouped these algorithms according to "broken" algorithms, and "algorithms on the watch list." In addition to algorithms that are just plain broken (and algorithms that are "up and coming broken"), a number of algorithms aren't necessarily problematic, but have been implemented in a number of weak ways for a variety of reasons in the libraries we're using (hence something we have to watch out for).

5.3.2 Broken Algorithms

This section is an overview of the algorithms that are in the "broken" state; note that this only includes broken algorithms that are actually *implemented* in the libraries we're discussing. These algorithms and modes, while supported by the libraries, should be avoided under most circumstances (most of the time, even for backward compatibility). For example, in the examples coming up in subsequent chapters, we've used AES and Triple-DES almost exclusively for block cipher encryption. This is by design, since there are only limited circumstances in which one of the two wouldn't be useful (such as embedded hardware where it is more difficult to implement a block cipher like AES than it is to implement a stream cipher like RC4). Since we aren't likely to encounter those limited circumstances in a day-to-day development context, we haven't used much of the other algorithms in the examples. Within the context of the libraries we're using, DES is the primary algorithm we'll need to refrain from implementing due to its broken status. DES has been broken in a very rapid period in recent public demonstrations. If we ever want to use DES for the purposes of backward compatibility, and we have to generate new keys, we'll want to use our source library's capability to check for "weak DES keys" (pretty much all of them by definition nowadays). DES has always had the capability of producing weak keys just through random happenstance; the likelihood of this happening was extremely remote, but since we have a function to explicitly check for them, why not do so? For example, the OpenSSL function `DES_is_weak_key()` provides DES key checking functionality; were we to want to use this function, we would want to call it after we've generated a DES key to ensure it is not one of the known DES weak keys.

5.3.3 Algorithms on the "Watch List"

There are a few algorithms whose status is indeterminate; they have known issues, but are implemented to a large degree throughout the libraries we'll be using. In most of these cases, they're in the process of being "phased out" of use in the industry across the board, but have remained in the libraries for one reason or another. The following are the algorithms on the "watch list" according to current research:

SHA-1: For a long time, SHA-1 was the only standard for message digests that was accepted by NIST for digital signatures. However, based on recent academic activity, it appears as if its lifetime is approaching its natural end.[4] All of the libraries retain implementations of SHA-1 due to its long-standing ubiquity. NIST has already published stronger replacement versions (e.g., SHA-256), but not all of the libraries we'll be using actually provide the updated capability.

MD5: MD5 has been on the decline for the past few years. However, a 2005 paper by Vlastimil Klima describing how to generate MD5 collisions on your laptop at home[5] is a warning about persisting usage of MD5. The algorithm is provided through all the libraries we will be covering. As such, as the libraries we're covering incorporate support for MD5, we'll want to avoid it for new application development and use it with caution in backward compatibility situations.

5.3.4 Problematic Key Lengths

For quite a long time, 512 bits was the standard length for an RSA key; at the time, it seemed like 512 would be impervious to attack for quite a long time into the future. However, slow but steady advances in computing, coupled with advances in the ability to factor programmatically have rendered 512-bit RSA keys insufficient for most applications. To make the matter even more complicated, most of the libraries we will be calling originated at a time when that smaller key length was still the case. Although they have been updated since they were written, some functions have maintained backward compatibility with previous versions of the API. We will find, for example, numerous instances where a 512-bit RSA key is the default unless we specify a larger value. For example, the `–genrsa` flag to the `openssl` command-line utility (a procedure that allows for command-line generation of a new RSA private key) uses 512 as a default value.[6] Additionally, the "ceiling" (highest) key size value within the Microsoft Base Cryptographic service provider (one "implementation" we can bind to in order to use CAPI) is 512 bits.[7] Obviously, we'll want to keep our eyes open when it comes time to use the RSA functionality to make sure we are using strong keys (in situations in which a default value can be used), rather than just "assuming" the library will generate a strong value for us.

5.3.5 "Export Grade" Cryptography

For a long time, the United States government considered it a crime to export cryptographic technologies. Companies that made software that incorporated cryptographic functionality (such as browser manufacturers, operating system manufacturers, Web server manufacturers) were not permitted to export the capability to encrypt in a strong way. They were, however, allowed to ship software that had "crippled" key lengths. This was primarily done so individuals residing overseas were able to conduct transactions that were "safe enough" from the casual observer, but were not, strictly speaking, strong cryptography. Since the versions of these browsers that supported shorter key lengths are still in operation today (legacy software never completely goes away), a number of them support an "export mode" that use symmetric encryption key lengths of 40 bits or less or 56 bits or less. In today's world, these keys offer little protection against an individual with the savvy and wherewithal to brute force the key (try all possible combinations). There are situations in which we will need to be aware of our intended usage and ensure that the mode we select for our cryptographic operations are *not* export grade encryption. For example, if we are using CAPI, we will need to connect to a cryptographically strong CSP rather than the "base CSP," since the base CSP uses the reduced key lengths. In today's world, there is often no longer any practical need for this reduced "export grade" encryption; we'll get into more detail in subsequent sections when we talk about export concerns, but for now, it's just important to recognize that export grade does exist, and we may encounter it in certain situations, particularly with respect to legacy software.

It is also useful to note that the changeover to allowing strong key lengths was not instantaneous. For a period of time, the BXA (United States Bureau of Export Administration) allowed financial institutions (banks, brokerage) *only* to conduct strong cryptographic communications with individuals residing outside the United States. This introduces an additional layer of complexity, as during that period of time, financial institutions were given the capability to obtain "global certificates" that allowed export-grade browsers in an SSL session to "step up" to strong encryption. Most of the support routines to handle this "stepping up" (sometimes called SGC, server gated cryptography) are still present in the libraries we'll be using. Of course, there is little or no need for a server to actually have a global certificate in today's world, but in any event, this is something we will need to keep our eyes open for, particularly in an SSL context.

5.3.6 Encumbered Algorithms

For the most part, the algorithms contained in the libraries are *unencumbered*, meaning that they are not covered by U.S. or international patent. There are a few exceptions to this, however. Since we probably don't want to pay someone a license fee to run our application, we are responsible for knowing what is covered by patent and what isn't, so we can make sure not to use it or explicitly compile out support for the encumbered algorithms if we are a commercial entity. As of now, both Diffie-Hellman and RSA (both previously encumbered by patent) are expired. However, a few algorithms are still encumbered; following is a list of algorithms we may encounter that are covered by patent as of 2005 (note that this does not include algorithms that are patented but are royalty free or have expired)[8]:

IDEA: Covered by U.S., European, and Japanese patent, this algorithm cannot be used for a commercial purpose without express licensing from its owner. Additionally, if we are authoring a noncommercial software project, we can't just use the algorithm blithely; even if we are not using it for commercial purposes, we still have to apply for and wait to receive usage permission from the patent owner.

RC5, RC6: Covered by U.S. patent, both RC5 and RC6 are patented by RSA Security, Inc. RC6 was made available royalty free for a period of time (which, according to RSA statements, has subsequently expired, so watch out)[9] during the AES finalization process. RC5 has always required licensing to use and still does.

5.3.7 Regulatory Considerations

Depending on the industry in which we work, there may be specific guidelines that we must adhere to insofar as it relates to selecting algorithms. Just as we saw that FIPS 140-2 certification played a role in the selection of a library, there are governmental and industry regulations that can assist us in selecting algorithms, and selecting the data that will or will not be encrypted under a particular set of usage constraints. We've selected these constraints based on two factors; some of them tell you *how* to encrypt, and some of them tell you *what* to encrypt. To have them all in one place, we're covering both at this time.

5.3.7.1 FIPS Approved Algorithms

FIPS 140-2 is shorthand notation for the second revision of Federal Information Processing Standard (FIPS) #140, *Security Requirements for Cryptographic Modules.*

NIST (the National Institute of Standards and Technology) maintains a list of cryptographic hardware and software that have undergone validation to meet one of four clearly delineated levels of standards compliance and security specified by the library. Just because we select a library that is FIPS certified does not necessarily mean that any usage with that library will "fly" in a U.S. government context or in an enterprise that stipulates FIPS 140-2 in its security policy. In addition to using a library that is certified for compliance, compliance with the standard also requires that we use only NIST-approved cryptographic algorithms; whether the algorithm implementation has been approved by NIST is listed in the FIPS 140-2 validation certificate located on the NIST Web site.[10] The certificate will have a list of the FIPS-approved algorithms that can be used within the library. For the libraries we are using, here is the breakdown of FIPS approval:

- CAPI (and parts of .NET):
  FIPS-approved algorithms: DES (Cert. #226); Triple-DES (Cert. #192); AES (Cert. #80); SHA-1 (Cert. #176); HMAC-SHA-1 (Cert. #176, vendor affirmed); RSA (PKCS#1, vendor affirmed)—other algorithms: SHA-256; SHA-384; SHA-512; RC2; RC4; MD2; MD4; MD5.
- OpenSSL:
  NIST Pre-Eval (none)
- JCA/JCE: None (third party only) For more information on third-party options, refer to Chapter 9 in the section detailing external service providers. For example, for the IBM add-on:
  —FIPS-approved algorithms: AES (Cert. #78); Triple-DES (Cert. #189); DSA (Cert. #114); SHS (Cert. #259); HMAC-SHA-1 (Cert. #259, vendor affirmed); RSA (Cert. #18); RNG (Cert. #23)
  —Other algorithms: Diffie-Hellman (key agreement); MD5
- BSAFE (Crypto-C)
  —FIPS-approved algorithms: DES (Cert. #131); Triple-DES (Cert. #70); SHA-1 (Cert. #59); DSA (Cert. #49); RSA (ANSI X9.31 and PKCS#1 for Signature; vendor affirmed); ECDSA (vendor affirmed)
  —Other algorithms: RSA Encryption; MD; MD5; HMAC SHA-1; HMAC MD5; AES (Rijndael); DESX; RC2; RC4; RC6; Elliptic Curve (F2&Fp); Elliptic Curve Encryption Scheme; Elliptic Curve Diffie-Hellman (key agreement); Bloom-Shamir; Diffie-Hellman (key agreement)
- BSAFE (Crypto-J)
  —FIPS-approved algorithms: DES (Cert. #168); Triple-DES (Cert. #112); AES (Cert. #45); SHA-1 (Cert. #97); DSA (Cert. #63); RSA (PKCS#1, vendor affirmed)
  —Other algorithms: DESX; RC2; RC4; RC5; MD2; MD5; HMAC-SHA-1 (Cert. #97); Diffie-Hellman (key agreement); Base64

Figure 5.3 summarizes this information.

Library	FIPS-Approved Algorithms	Other Algorithms
JCA/JCE (IBM FIPS provider)	AES Triple-DES DSA HMAC-SHA-1 RSA RNG	Diffie-Hellman MD5
BSAFE (Crypto-C)	DES Triple-DES SHA-1 DSA RSA ECDSA	RSA MD5 HMAC SHA-1 HMAC MD5 AES DESX RC2 RC4 RC6 Diffie-Hellman
BSAFE (Crypto-J)	DES Triple-DES AES SHA-1 DSA RSA	DESX RC2 RC4 RC5 MD2 MD5 HMAC-SHA-1 Diffie-Hellman
OpenSSL	N/A	N/A

FIGURE 5.3 FIPS 140-1/140-2 library certification status.

Note that in some cases, algorithms we would expect to appear on the "approved" list do not (such as AES in some of the libraries). This means that while NIST does approve the algorithm in use, that particular implementation of the algorithm has not gone through the certification process. As such, it is important for implementers who wish to adhere to FIPS 140 to make sure they only use the algorithms that appear on the "approved" section of the certification document. NIST maintains a page at their Web site with the most up-to-date information on the certification status of a number of cryptographic modules, including the ones listed here.

5.3.7.2 CA SB-1386

The California privacy law, SB-1386, requires notification to the affected individual in the event that his or her personal information is or might have been disclosed in an unauthorized way. The text of the law, however, provides special dispensation to encrypted data. Meaning, if the data is encrypted, disclosure is apparently not mandatory.[11] The text of the law does not go on to indicate an encryption algorithm or provide any guidance about what type of encryption is "good enough" to relieve us of the requirement to notify when theft of information occurs. While some individuals will attempt to use this text as impetus to sell their particular encryption product, there isn't any call to use any particular kind of encryption according to the actual provisions of the statute.

5.4 INTEGRATING WITH HARDWARE

Perhaps one of the biggest usage decisions we can make as application designers centers on the task of integrating our application with cryptographic hardware; either hardware used for acceleration or for key storage/key management. We'll discuss a little bit about why we might want to use hardware (especially for key storage), when the use of hardware is appropriate, and (if it is) how we can use the hardware in our application in a transparent way.

5.4.1 Why Use Hardware?

We discussed in the previous chapter that anytime we store data on the filesystem, an attacker can gain access to it if he compromises the underlying OS. In the next section, we'll talk about some strategies we can implement that make this more difficult, but ultimately, if it's on the system, it can be attacked. Obviously, if we have an application that needs to decrypt or encrypt data, we will have to have, at some point, a key that we can read in and understand to kick off the whole decryption process. In most situations, this private key file is stored on the filesystem protected by ACLs or discretionary access control (e.g., SSH without a private key password), or is hidden somewhere on the system in a manner that is difficult to access (e.g., Microsoft DPAPI), or requires a password from which it can derive the key (e.g., SSH with a private key password). However, if we require a password for startup, we will have to have a user present to initially make the key available to our application. If we were to implement a server in this way, we would need to have an attendant on duty to restart the server by typing in the appropriate password anytime the application halted unexpectedly. Since most of the time we want servers to restart themselves automatically, this is obviously undesirable behavior. As such, we need a strategy that both keeps keys off the machine *and* does not require a user to type a password to provide an initial key. The way this is typically done is by using an HSM (hardware security module) to provide that key. Actually, the HSM does not "provide" the key per se—most of the time, it is attached to the server directly (e.g., via the SCSI bus) or it is on a network segment that the server can see, and it performs cryptographic operations on the part of the server using routines that it has built in internally. The advantage of this is that the keys never leave the module. The module will typically implement some kind of antitampering (typically auto-zeroization of the keys) in the even it is under physical attack from an unauthorized party. One of the reasons why we selected the libraries we did is that they transparently can access the majority of the major HSM units on the market today. We'll go into what those HSM units are and how they work, after we discuss acceleration hardware.

In addition to secure key storage, we might want to perform quite a lot of cryptographic operations in rapid sequence. In so doing, we will tremendously impact the system performance due to the extensive overhead required to perform public-key cryptographic operations. In those circumstances, we might wish to use cryptographic accelerator hardware that will offload the cryptographic operations from the CPU for computation on the accelerator. The accelerator has built-in circuitry that can perform cryptographic operations in rapid fashion without using system resources as part of the computation process. In much the same way that the cryptographic libraries support HSM functionality transparently, they also support transparent use of the cryptographic acceleration hardware.

In selecting an HSM or an accelerator for our application, we will want to use one that supports our chosen library transparently. For transparent operation, we want to select one of the hardware providers supported by the OpenSSL ENGINE API (see README.ENGINE in the OpenSSL distribution for a list of hardware products that the OpenSSL currently supports in this way). If we're using CAPI, we'll want to find a hardware provider that supplies a CSP that can be used by CAPI internally. If we're using Crypto-C, we'll want to find a module that supports statically linking against our application (possibly in combination with the addition of the hardware routines to the CHOOSER Crypto-C structures). Lastly, if we are using the JCA/JCE, ideally we will want to find a hardware device that either supports implementing a JCE cryptographic provider or supports PCKS #11 (see sun.security.PKCS11 classes).

5.5 INTEGRATING WITH STANDARDS

In some respects, we are at an impasse when it comes to standards compliance. Many of the standards documents are difficult and confusing to read, we might not often know how to go about implementing the standard, and there may not be tools readily at our disposal (such as in the cryptographic libraries) that make use of the standards in question. To overcome this impasse, we've put together a few tips on standards compliance, particularly the security standards we're likely to come across as we author our applications. The goal of this section is to detail some of the security standards that have prevalence in the development world today, and to provide at least one shortcut to standards compliance that we can readily implement. The goal is to explain what the standard is, what we would want to use it for, how we can use it easily (ideally without having to implement it ourselves), and where we can go to get more information about usage.

5.5.1 Web Services Standards

It is unlikely that any developer living on this planet would have not at least heard of Web services by now. Much like everyone was "Web enabling" their applications in the late 1990s, now everyone is implementing Web services, mostly for application server functionality (e.g., business logic). As we're probably aware, the most common implementation of Web services is for "RPC" and data exchange; although Web services allow all kinds of advanced functionality (such as dynamic location of a service on a large network), most of the time, the implementation provides a framework to request the method of an object over HTTP. Why HTTP? Because it is easy to implement, and the plumbing for supporting it is ubiquitous. As we know, HTTP is both stateless and transparent—not a good start from a security perspective. However, a few standards allow us to implement secure Web-service approaches in our applications. The following are some of those.

5.5.1.1 SAML

SAML stands for Security Association Markup Language, and is an OASIS standard for exchanging authentication state between entities. SAML was developed because it serves a burning need; HTTP is a stateless protocol, so in conducting a session-based transaction, we need the ability to maintain the "state of being authenticated." We typically don't want to have users reauthenticate themselves every time they make a new HTTP request; this would be unbearable. However, since HTTP is stateless, how can we bind an HTTP request to a previous one, such as the one a user made when he or she "logged in" to our application? Typical Web and application servers approach the authentication problem by issuing an HTTP cookie for the session that's being conducted (almost everybody offering a Web or Internet-enabled application does this). Either a Web server will generate a cryptographically authenticated artifact (either signed, MAC'ed, or symmetrically encrypted), or the server will generate an arbitrary nonpredictable "session identifier" that will be used to identify the unique session in progress. However, cookies only work in the context of a single server or set of servers within a single DNS domain. The cookie specification (wisely) prohibits domains from setting cookies for other domains or, for that matter, for issuing a cookie to a DNS root domain (e.g., .com). Since a cookie cannot be used to transmit the "authentication state" (whether a given session has been authenticated), developers using HTTP to implement applications sometimes needed a way to transmit state information outside of a domain. Before SAML, this was usually done by producing a proprietary artifact such as a string or other nonstandard formatted data string and applying cryptography to it in a further nonstandard way. The artifact was then sent as a parameter to an HTTP GET request, as the data to an HTTP POST, as a proprietary HTTP header value, or via some other mechanism. The point is, the implementation was varied and unpredictable. SAML changes that.

SAML allows us to package authentication information in a manner that (ideally) will be verifiable by other parties. As with any standard, SAML supports quite a number of options; however, at its heart, SAML is pretty simple. Simple enough that we can, if we absolutely have to, implement it ourselves in software (although we'll probably want to avoid doing so for the sake of expediency).

SAML: What's in It?

A SAML assertion is XML encoded human-readable text. In a few ways, we can think of a SAML assertion in a similar way that we think about digital certificates. A SAML assertion contains information about an issuer (an entity "vouching" for another individual), a subject (the person who is being authenticated), the time the credential was issued, any number of attributes about the subject, and a cryptographic artifact ensuring the structure is intact and authentic. Perhaps it might also contain information about the cryptographic artifact that allows the receiver to validate it. This is, of course, an oversimplification of the features in SAML, but it is basically the heart and soul of the process.

The current SAML specification is in its second revision (SAML 2.0) and is maintained by the Organization for Advancement of Structured Information Sciences (OASIS) body. Although revision 2.0 of the standard is the most current revision, we'll most often see artifacts from the 1.1 and 1.0 versions of the standard "out in the field."

SAML: Usage

Most of the cryptographic libraries we're covering in this book do not contain intrinsic routines for dealing with SAML. This, again, is an oversimplification. The .NET API does have some limited capability for working with SAML 1.0 (although it is not well documented[12]), and BSAFE ships with a Web services component that provides some functionality in this arena. However, for the most part, using SAML is outside the usage scope of a cryptographic library per se. Therefore, if we want to use it, we'll either need to implement it ourselves, which although not impossible is certainly "the hard way," or use a tool that implements it for us. The tool that is probably the easiest to use, with the most built-in functionality, is the open source "opensaml" tool (*www.opensaml.org*). The tool *is* easy to use, but developers should be forewarned that there is no user documentation for the tool. The scope of this chapter isn't detailed usage information, but the companion CD-ROM contains an OpenSAML usage example (generating an assertion and validating an assertion) developers can use to get started in supporting SAML in their applications (in the

ON THE CD

/Examples/Chapter 5/saml_usage folder). We've used the Java API to OpenSAML in this example (the Java API is easier to use), but a C++ API is also available in OpenSAML.

5.5.1.2 XACML

XACML (eXtensible Access Control Markup Language) is the "other side of the coin" to SAML; it is also an OASIS standard, but XACML provides the capability for entities to exchange access control information. Referring back to what SAML does and how it works, we can use SAML to pass authentication state information from point A to point B, but this does not account for "Access Control" functionality. In other words, while SAML does a good job of saying "who" someone is, it really doesn't do much in the way of saying "what" that person can do once we know who he or she is. XACML is the answer to that; literally, any policy decision involving access control can be represented as XACML (although it might not be useful to anybody else). For example, if we are on a Windows box and create an ACL for Administrator that says they have "full control" to the contents of the "C" drive, that is an access control policy decision that we can represent in XACML if we so desire. Basically, any decision that takes the form "*person or group* has access to perform some *action* on some *resource*" is a candidate for use of XACML. We might also wish to apply particular "caveats" to the rule, such as "Administrator has full control to the C drive only on weekdays." This also, can be done.

XACML: Usage

XACML is a newer standard than SAML is; it is also significantly more complicated to generate and more complicated to parse. As such, our options on implementations of the standard are a bit slim. Support for XACML is limited in the libraries we're working with, but there are a few good free implementations available that make supporting it easier. The easiest one to use is the SUN *SUNXACML* implementation; it is open source and it is Java. Usage is complex, but not unapproachable. Again, the goal of this section is not usage, but rather informative. Therefore, we've left the specifics of the API out of this chapter. There is a simple usage example on the companion CD-ROM in the material for this chapter using the freely available Sun implementation (located in the /Examples/Chapter 5/xacml_usage folder).

ON THE CD

5.5.2 Secure File Transmission

We've discussed how SSL/TLS can be used for the secure transmission of data, and we've further elaborated on that by pointing out that SSL/TLS is one of the most versatile tools to use from a development perspective, primarily because it provides the most easily accessible and common set of APIs. However, as we design our applications, we will find that very commonly our applications will have to send files from point A to point B in a secure way, and we do not want to have to programmatically implement that every time. For example, our application requirements might dictate that a batch transfers a file across a network, and our security requirements might dictate that we do that file transfer in a secure way; however, neither requirement specifies that we have to write the functionality ourselves from scratch. In fact, given that there are numerous tools available to assist in the secure transfer of files, we can very likely save ourselves quite a bit of work by using such a tool or protocol rather than implementing it ourselves.

In saying "secure file transmission," we mean it to apply to both "store and forward" protocols (such as email) and real-time transmission of data over a network. Either way, we'll want to use standard methodologies for encrypting these files when called upon to do so if we require our applications to interact with other applications that might need access to the files. There are a few approaches we can use; some we can use directly within our application through external APIs, and some we'll need to implement ourselves. The easiest scenario, of course, is when our application does not need to communicate at all with applications outside its sphere of function. We'll cover some of the more common implementations of secure file transmission and how we can use them in the following subsection.

5.5.2.1 SCP/SFTP

SCP (Secure Copy) and SFTP (Secure File Transfer Protocol) both use SSH (Secure Shell) for enciphered transmission of data. Within the Unix world, SSH is ubiquitous; SSH uses a combination of symmetric and asymmetric cryptography to provide confidentiality between two parties for the purposes of exchanging arbitrary data such as files. From an application design perspective, all we really need to know about SCP and SFTP are that files are *transmitted* in encrypted form, but are *stored* on the remote host in whatever format we originally sent them in. Therefore, these protocols would not be appropriate for a "store and forward" context. From an application development point of view, SCP and SFTP provide excellent capability for secure transmission of files in a script (such as a bash, sh, ksh, etc.). While the typical usage requires specification of a user password (the user password at the remote host), other usage scenarios are possible that facilitate alternative logon (such as the use of asymmetric keys for remote logon). It is difficult to use SCP and SFTP from a nonscript application.

5.5.2.2 Microsoft EFS

Microsoft includes the EFS (Encrypted FileSystem) feature on newer versions of Microsoft Windows (Windows 2000, Windows XP). EFS uses a combination of symmetric and asymmetric cryptography to encrypt file contents. While a detailed discussion on the internal mechanics of EFS is outside the scope of this discussion, from an application design perspective it is useful to note that EFS *stores* the data in encrypted form, but does not provide a mechanism to *transmit* the data as such. Therefore, this mechanism is most useful for the "store" part of "store and forward" applications or for encryption of application data "at rest," and not necessarily appropriate for protection of information in transit.

5.5.2.3 PGP and GPG

PGP (Pretty Good Privacy) and GPG (GNU Privacy Guard) are both utilities for encryption of data such as email and files. The two applications interoperate to a high degree, and we felt it was important to mention their existence given the ubiquity of the tools coupled with the long history of PGP, but there is not much in the way of a programmatic interface to either (at least not directly). These utilities use a combination of symmetric and asymmetric cryptography to encrypt data during an exchange between two parties. Since we do not have an easily accessible programmatic interface, we will likely not need (or desire) to support these utilities. However, there might be situations in which we could require application data to be encrypted using one of these tools as part of ancillary application functionality. For example, we might require that initialization files be decrypted or verified using one of these tools as part of the application initialization procedure.

5.6 ENDNOTES

1. *https://eval.rsasecurity.com.au/cgi-bin/external/eval_prod.cgi#4*
2. Note that "out of the box support" might be stretching it a bit with respect to enabling JCE support. Newer releases of the board may differ, but the version we used utilized a custom PKCS #11 "pass through" wrapper via JNI. This interface was problematic.
3. *www.gotdotnet.com/team/clr/cryptofaq.htm*
4. *http://theory.csail.mit.edu/~yiqun/shanote.pdf* and *www.schneier.com/blog/archives/2005/02/cryptanalysis_o.html*
5. *http://cryptography.hyperlink.cz/md5/Vlastimil_Klima_MD5_collisions.pdf*
6. *www.openssl.org/docs/apps/genrsa.html*
7. *http://msdn.microsoft.com/library/default.asp?url=/library/en-us/seccrypto/security/key_length_comparison.asp*
8. *http://jce.iaik.tugraz.at/sales/algorithms/index.php*
9. *www.rsasecurity.com/rsalabs/node.asp?id=2251*
10. *http://csrc.nist.gov/cryptval/140-1/140val-all.htm*
11. I am not a lawyer. This is not legal advice.
12. *http://msdn.microsoft.com/library/default.asp?url=/library/en-us/wseref/html/T_Microsoft_Web_Services2_Security_SAML.asp*

6 Application Development Strategies

In This Chapter

Every developer knows that the "right way" to develop software is to follow a reproducible and repeatable process; we're all familiar with the software development lifecycle (we're probably familiar with a few different models and a number of development frameworks). The typical process requires us to record the application's requirements, interview the user population, document/record what the user expectations are, get a representative of the user community to sign off on their expectations, and so forth. We also know that we should thoroughly document a detailed design before we even start development so we can ensure that our application meets the user requirements, is fully tested, is maintainable, and is scaleable. That's the theory, anyway. As any developer knows, in the current workplace, it very rarely works this way.

Most of the time, developers do not have the luxury of sufficient time to follow all the "best practice" development steps with the rigor and thoroughness we would like. It is possible that some developers reading this book might work within a development shop that meets a high level of maturity and discipline (we've heard such shops exist), but in practice, developers and all personnel involved in the software development lifecycle (testers, project managers, etc.) are usually hard-pressed for time, personnel, and resources. In short, we do our best to maintain the highest level of development process maturity—but within the parameters of a set of constraints imposed on us by factors outside our control, such as the need to be "first to market," time commitments by marketing personnel or salespeople, or the need to achieve profitability in a rapid time. In other words, the need to meet aggressive deadlines often forces developers to implement whatever time-saving strategies they can find along the way, when and where they can find them. This section attempts to provide developers with some of these strategies as they approach their security functionality, strategies they can (best case) cut and paste into applications or hopefully otherwise reuse to save time and energy in building secure applications.

We've tried to approach this section from the point of view of "return on investment"; in other words, these strategies oftentimes require an up-front investment in time, but will return time savings over time. We've also tried to provide strategies we can make an investment in designing/developing/implementing once and then reuse that functionality over and over again throughout the application (a time hit today, but payback every other time we need to do the same task). We also want to provide strategies that are "fire and forget" where possible; by "fire and forget," we mean that we won't have to remember to do difficult to remember tasks during our application development.

For example, we know that not deallocating memory when we're done with it (if we're using C) can lead to a memory leak; yet, most applications have at least one memory leak that we have to fix during QA. Why does this happen when we all know to do it? Because sometimes we forget to put in the call to "free" or "delete." The unfortunate reality of software development is that anytime we have to "remember" to do something, sometimes we'll forget—especially if we're pressed for time. Part of the timesaving strategy is to manipulate our "code environment" (e.g., the structures and routines we work with in building our applications) in such a way that we have to remember as little as possible. If a structure needs to be "cleaned up" after use, for example, we'll write a little extra code so the structure cleans up itself without our having to worry about it. The process of developing security software is filled with hundreds of difficult-to-remember ancillary tasks that we have to remember to do. For example, we have to remember to zeroize buffers containing keys, we sometimes have to remember to seed the random number generator, and we have to remember to free quite a few structures and values internal to the libraries with which we're working. The list is extensive. Therefore, first, we want to demuddy those waters a little bit—ideally in an easy to implement way.

Sometimes, individuals will make the claim that they have stumbled upon a unique and grandiose achievement; they have developed a new "secret sauce" that will revolutionize a given industry. These techniques are not in that category. None of what we are going to discuss is a "secret sauce" recipe; they're not particularly new or innovative, and they probably don't spell out anything a developer reading this book doesn't already know.

They do, however, lay out techniques that are a rarity in commercially developed applications, both in the enterprise and on the market. Day after day, we see usage errors in commercial code that could have been avoided by using a simple technique, a simple class or structure that would have prevented a security vulnerability or memory leak from being introduced into a piece of software. The most often reason we hear for why automated techniques were not used in the application is "time"; we hear time and again that there just wasn't sufficient time to implement automation into an application. Therefore, to save you some time, we've implemented them here. Feel free to cut and paste, statically link against the .lib on the companion CD-ROM (found in the Platform folder, copied during the platform-specific installer operation; can be built for other architectures using the included source) build the classes as a .dll, and dynamically link against it, or even write your own classes that do the same thing using some of the concepts we've outlined. The goal is to save you time, so whatever saves the most, use it.

As a final word of caution, since our intent is to save time, if any of the examples proves unfamiliar or is not appropriate for your application, feel free to skip over it. As the old saw goes, "the shortest distance between two points is the route you know." This is no less true with these strategies; if a strategy is completely unfamiliar and would increase rather than alleviate difficulty, we encourage you to skip it and use what's familiar. However, these strategies have proven themselves, in our experience, to greatly streamline development over the *long term* (some strategies might require a short-term investment, but will save time later on in the process). We recommend that developers read this chapter, assess the strategies on their own merit in the context of their particular development environment and needs, and choose ones that make sense for them. Obviously, not every technique will work in every context.

ON THE CD

We've split the examples in this chapter into category rather than by technique. For example, we'll be talking about ways to automate key management, ways to automate the protection and zeroization of memory, ways to do automated policy enforcement, and so forth, in each its own section. For the most part, the text in the chapter is focused on the conceptual, and the library on the companion CD-ROM (/Examples/Chapter 6/Framework) contains the actual implementation. We will point out implementation considerations inline in the text as appropriate, but our primary goal is to lay out the concepts with the assumption that developers will likely want to "tweak" what we've provided in the implementation to suit their own usage and applications.

6.1 KEY MANAGEMENT DESIGN STRATEGIES

In previous sections, we've said that key management is by far the most difficult task we will have to undertake in writing secure applications. "Key management" in this context does not mean distribution of keys, generating keys for individuals or entities in our applications, and so forth. Instead, the "key management" referred to here is the low-level "bits and bytes" of doing very simple tasks with keys, such as storing them on the filesystem, reading them into memory, supplying them to the cryptographic libraries, and so on. This section will review some of the things we need to consider when working with keys from a design perspective, and subsequent sections will outline some strategies on how to implement automated techniques where we can make sure they get done without having to consciously implement them every time.

These seemingly insignificant details of normal program operation become infinitely more complex once we realize that we have to "micromanage" everything about the key, such as its lifetime in memory, whether it gets written to the paging file, and so forth. For example, a very valid design consideration in our applications would be to prevent the object from being written to virtual memory, but the mechanisms required to prevent it are severely platform dependent. On a Windows system, for example, we might choose to use the API functions `VirtualLock` and `VirtualUnlock` to make sure the keys are not written to the swap file, but in a POSIX world (in C), we would need to use `mlock` and `munlock` instead. With the goal in mind of preventing unauthorized access to keys, passwords, and other sensitive buffers, let's look at some of the main areas of concern where such a buffer could be accidentally disclosed; these issues are of concern no matter what language we are writing in:

- Accidental disclosure of the sensitive material in the paging/swap file
- Remnants of the sensitive material on the heap following `delete` or `free()`
- Remnants of the sensitive material on the stack after having been stored in a local variable or returned from a function/subroutine
- Stored sensitive material on the filesystem

We will need to design and implement mechanisms to control all these possibilities—obviously, not a simple task. To make the matter even more complex, we might want to incorporate functionality within our application logic that enforces limited "authentication" in a limited way; for example, we might want to ensure:

- A particular key is only accessible on a particular host.
- A particular key is only available to a particular application.

Introduce support for more than one platform (with the recognition that we might need to support more than one cryptographic library), and you can start to get a feel for the scope of the problem. Fortunately, there are a few things we can do. We've somewhat arbitrarily grouped the concerns relating to key disclosure into the following sections: environmental issues, access issues, and storage issues.

Environmental issues: Refers to areas of concern we must specifically address related to how our software will operate in the context of a general-purpose operating system platform. Leakage of key material to a paging file, leakage of information due to the nuances of stack and heap management would be classified in this category.

Access issues: Areas relating to limiting the accessibility of sensitive material are listed in this category. For example, limiting access to keys on a host-by-host, user-by-user, or application-by-application basis is grouped in this category.

Secure storage: Areas relating to protecting secrets outside our application boundary. For example, long-term or transient storage of keys to the filesystem resides in this category.

Let's address each issue one at a time.

6.1.1 Environmental Issues

The fact of the matter is, most of the time, we will be working on a general-purpose operating system. A few of us have the luxury of writing applications on specialized hardware where day-to-day trivialities such as how to make sure a buffer is "really deleted" don't matter, but this is the rare exception rather than the general rule. Since our applications do have to run in the context of a general-purpose operating system, we need to recognize that these operating systems were not primarily designed to facilitate security; instead, they are optimized for alacritous program execution, ease of use, "flashy" graphics, and a whole host of other things. As a result, as developers of security software, we'll need to work around some of the security issues inherent in the way modern operating systems work.

First, in writing secure applications, we need to start with the assumption that the operating systems on which our applications run are optimized for *public* or "nonsecret" data. This is a valid engineering decision on the part of the OS designers. If the operating system had to assume that all data was secret, modern computer systems would function much more slowly than they do. All heap memory would be purged on deallocation, the stack would have to enforce a protection and cleanup mechanism, the swap file would either not exist or would need to be protected somehow (thus slowing down virtual memory operations tremendously), and so on. Second, we need to also recognize that even if an OS was designed with prevention of information disclosure as a priority, there is no way for an OS designer to account for everything we could possibly do in our application. In other words, if we allocate a buffer, fill it with sensitive information, and then "leak" it (meaning we don't deallocate it), how could an operating system know that we're "really" done with the buffer in question until the process terminates? In short, it could not. Knowing that the platform is optimized for public data, we must therefore account for the environmental issues and ensure that our applications enforce a level of protection and confidentiality not guaranteed or even necessarily facilitated by the operating system itself.

6.1.1.1 Memory Purging

In using memory on a general-purpose operating system, we must keep in mind a few realities associated with the way buffers are treated on the stack and on the heap. For those of us working in a lower level language like C or C++, we are already familiar with the allocation and deallocation of memory. For example, we understand that when we wish to store something in memory, we can create a variable on the stack by specifying how big it will be and defining it as a local variable. For example, we know we can create a 10-byte block on the stack by specifying something similar to:

```
unsigned char arbitrary[10];
```

In a stack context, we know we need to initialize the array before we use it, since we are not guaranteed what the value will be. When the variable "scopes out" (leaves the scope of the execution context), we don't have any guarantees as to what the underlying operating system will do with the memory location we just used. In practice, values on the stack tend to get rapidly overwritten by other values that our application uses, but still, we don't know for sure exactly where it will go or how quickly it will get erased.

In a heap context, if we don't know how big the buffer will need to be at runtime, we can allocate a buffer dynamically using an operator like `new` or a function like `malloc()`. We also know that we'll need to specifically initialize the content of these buffers before we use them, because there is no guarantee what the contents of the buffer will be when we create them since the memory may contain whatever was in that particular area of memory before we allocated it. When we're done with the memory in question, we call either `delete` or `free()`, which informs the operating system that we are done with the memory and it returns to the pool available for some other application. The memory is marked as "no longer in use" and goes back to the heap for later use; with the heap, there is no guarantee when (or if) the data will get overwritten, and in practice, heap-based buffers can persist (their contents intact) for relatively long periods of time. Obviously, if we are dealing with secret information we wish to protect from other applications on the same machine, or from an attacker with a debugger, or from a rogue administrator, we want to make sure that any memory we use for critical information is marked as "inactive" and scrubbed before we allow it to go back to the pool.

In C and C++, we would only need to do something like:

```
memcpy(arbitrary, 0x0, sizeof(arbitrary));
```

for a stack-based variable. For heap-based buffers (since `sizeof()` would only tell us the size of the pointer and not the size of the buffer), we would use something like:

```
memcpy(arbitrary, 0x0, arbitraryLen);
```

where `arbitraryLen` is the stored size of the buffer in bytes from when we created it. In languages in which direct memory manipulation is not presumed (such as scripting languages, Visual Basic, Java, etc.), we'll need to implement other approaches. Most of the time, individually setting each byte in the buffer to zero in a loop will do the trick unless a specific function is explicitly made available to us for this purpose (e.g., the `SecureZeroMemory` routine in the Microsoft Platform SDK that performs the procedure illustrated earlier).

6.1.1.2 Swap Files and Virtual Memory

Once we make sure we're scrubbing all our secrets after use, we'll also need to make sure we keep the secrets out of the paging file. We're probably familiar with the concept of paging or the moving of particular regions of memory out of physical memory and onto a fixed storage device so the operating system is not constrained by the actual amount of physical RAM present on the system. The operating system will periodically move pages of memory on to and off of the hard disk in a "managed" fashion without our involvement and (in general) without notification to our application. This is an issue, because if we happen to have a plaintext key in memory at the time paging takes place, our key could be written to the filesystem. Further, our application has no control over where it gets written or when/if the operating system will write over it once it's there. To mitigate this, we'll take two approaches in parallel: first, we will take measures to make sure we keep any sensitive values in memory only for the shortest possible time required by our application. Second (where we can), we'll use the inherent features of the operating system to prevent the data from being written to the physical disk as part of virtual memory management. In the Microsoft Windows world, the SDK function `VirtualLock()` will prevent a given area of memory from being written to the filesystem, and `mlock()` will do the same on most Unix systems (it's defined in POSIX). Note that in both cases, we'll have to explicitly unlock the buffer when we're done with it—in Windows using `VirtualUnlock()`, and on a Unix machine using `munlock()`.

6.1.2 Access Issues

In many cases, it is desirable to attempt to restrict access to *who* can get keys through our application. Sometimes, we might want to only allow certain keys to be used on a particular host (e.g., to ensure that keys used in the QA environment don't wind up in a production environment or vice versa). Additionally, we might want to make sure that if our application supports more than one user, that the users don't have access to each other's keys. Most of the time, we will have to enforce these protection measures both during our program's execution and anytime we store the material outside our application (e.g., on the filesystem). Implementing these types of key access scenarios isn't easy, but is not insurmountable. To select an approach governing how we'll make this happen, we first need to set the requirements; specifically:

- In what circumstances will our application need to use keys?
- On whose behalf are we accessing the keys (e.g., on behalf of a user, on behalf of our application, or something else)?
- What is the "scope" of our key? Who needs to access it, and from where?
- What is our level of enforcement? In other words, what are we trying to protect the key *from*?

Once we decide what the access control requirements are (e.g., the answers to these questions), we can begin to consider *how* we plan to protect the keys. In general, we can use three approaches, either alone or in combination for protection:

- Operating system inherent access control measures
- Application access control measures
- Cryptographic access control measures

Following is an explanation of each of these measures and some information about what they protect against.

6.1.2.1 Application Access Controls

One approach we can use is to enforce access to keys and other confidential information within our application. This approach means that our application will have to authenticate a user, ensure that he or she possesses the appropriate authority to gain access to the data, and enforce that only authenticated, entitled individuals (or components) have access to it. In this scenario, we will build in application controls that enforce when and to whom the keys will be relinquished; in other words, we are building in the controls ourselves "from the ground up." This approach can be useful, since this is the most flexible approach; in other words, no matter what criteria we want to put in to govern access control, we can do so. If we want the keys to only be used on the weekend, for example, we can author software that checks to see if it is after 5:00 P.M. on Friday and before 8:00 A.M. on Monday before performing cryptography. On the downside, this approach comes with tremendous complexity and is less robust than the others from a security perspective. Specifically, the new functionality can slow our development process (since it is more functionality we have to write, debug, and test), and it does not prevent an attacker who is able to compromise our application. In other words, if an attacker is able to "break" our application or anything upon which our application relies (such as the operating system), any facility we build in to control access (and any data that has been protected using that methodology) is compromised. Therefore, *if we want to prevent our data from being compromised when the application is compromised, we need another protection mechanism.*

6.1.2.2 Operating System Access Controls

In this approach, we leverage the facilities of the operating system to govern access to the data. While not as flexible as building in controls to the application ourselves, we do have at our disposal a number of built-in protection mechanisms and criteria for access. Quite a few criteria are provided by the operating system to govern access to data (particularly files), such as group, owner, ACLs, and so forth. While this approach will provide some degree of assurance, it can only ensure that unauthorized access has not taken place to the extent that the operating system has not been compromised. In other words, the inherent access control capacities of the operating system will not secure our application's keys against access by users such as administration personnel who have superuser or equivalent access on the machine, or attackers who gain administrator-level access to the machine through alternative means (such as exploiting a buffer overflow in an application that runs with administrative privilege). As an example of this kind of approach, if we were to write our key data to a file and set ACLs or discretionary access control permissions on that file, we would be leveraging the inherent capabilities of the filesystem to provide some level of assurance to us. However, anyone who has access to that file can gain access to our keys. Keeping this in mind, *if we want to prevent our data from being compromised when the underlying operating system is compromised, we need another protection mechanism* either different from or in addition to the native access control capability of the operating system on which our application runs.

6.1.2.3 Cryptographic Access Controls

Lastly, we can to some extent, employ cryptography as an access control mechanism. This sounds like an exercise in "circular logic" (using cryptography to control access to the cryptography), but it really isn't when we look at it. Specifically, this approach would entail tying the keys our application uses to possession of a single secret; if we were to employ this approach, we could then use that initial secret to "unlock" all of the other secrets our application will have access to within that particular context. This can be done on a user-by-user basis (meaning that each user has his or her own key that he or she unlocks), or at an application-global level (such as a server application that requires an administrator or HSM device to supply a key at startup). Microsoft EFS on Windows XP employs this type of protection mechanism: an EFS key on Windows XP is tied to the password used by the user to log in to the system; the key to unlock the EFS key is derived from the user's logon password, and that key is subsequently used to encrypt and decrypt files. Anyone who does not have access to the user's key, can't get the EFS key (at least not while it's stored on the disk). This is a fruitful methodology to employ when we are trying to make sure only an authorized party can "unlock" all the other keys we plan to use, but it still doesn't protect against an attacker from exploiting the application or the underlying operating system to gain access. For example, someone could compromise the operating system and install a keystroke recorder, or someone could install a Trojan to steal files after the user has logged on.

In practice, we'll usually want to employ more than one access control strategy when it comes to controlling access to cryptographic keys. Specifically, we'll probably want to enforce enough control to meet the requirements by using these strategies in combination. If, for example, we need to protect keys in a server application, and we need those keys to be accessible and constant from one instance of the application to another (i.e., if the server restarts, we need to have it use the same keys every time), we could use a strategy of combining operating system controls to restrict access to the key file (or other storage repository) with relatively weak cryptographic controls to prevent casual viewing of the contents by an administrator, and application controls to enforce that development keys don't wind up in production.

6.2 USEFUL TECHNIQUES FOR PROTECTING KEYS

Probably the best way to illustrate some of the design considerations we've been reviewing is to go through some implementations of these designs in practice. The best way to save time during the implementation phase is to consolidate and reuse code, specifically in areas of our software that are highly error prone, are particularly verbose, or will be done frequently. It is surprising when we look at how many developers don't do this in practice. In writing software, reuse and consolidation of code reduces the number of changes we have to make in the event of a bug, reduces the first-time debugging effort associated with implementing functionality, and streamlines the testing of software that uses the routine. In short, it is a long-term timesaving measure. So, recognizing this, let's attempt to shave time off the development process by centralizing some of the more laborious (and error-prone) tasks we will have to do over and over again no matter which canned cryptographic functionality we ultimately choose. Hopefully, this in itself will prove useful. Additionally, though, we've tried to provide strategies that mitigate some of the common "bug zones," places in our code that are "hotbeds of delay" in our software that can often bring about unanticipated delay as we track down and debug problems in the implementation.

The difficult part about delineating these techniques involves the language and platform differences within which our applications will run; for example, a given technique might only be applicable in one language and not in another, or it might only apply in a particular context. Therefore, we've attempted to provide techniques in the different contexts we will be working in, but it should be noted that not all techniques will apply in every environment, on every platform, or in every development shop. For example, the first thing we are going to discuss is creation of "self-scrubbing" memory buffers in C++. This specific implementation presumes object orientation, and, moreover, it won't work in Java (we'll talk about why when we get into the specifics). These buffers will initially save us some development time, but will become part of a larger C++ security framework as we move along.

6.2.1 Self-Protecting Structures (C++ Strategies)

The first of the application design strategies we considered was how to make sure that buffers we use to store sensitive data do not "leak" information outside of our application. Unless we are working in the most controlled (and arguably "contrived") conditions, we will need to handle sensitive data in our applications, and given the nature of the languages in which we work, oftentimes we don't have a secure and convenient structure within which to store this data. In other words, we will often be called upon to hold key data, password data, plaintext data, or other sensitive information within a structure of which we will have little control—this structure might be a stack-based or heap-based buffer (in C++), or in a more opaque structure (such as a string or a byte array) in Java. A productive place to streamline development is in how we approach the most basic of tasks required for any application: manipulation of memory.

6.2.1.1 Self-Purging Memory Structures–Null Bytes

The documentation for each of our cryptographic libraries recommends that we take a few precautions with respect to data in our application's memory space; the instructions, while each is phrased differently, basically call for the following:

- When library operations are complete, overwrite the contents of the memory with null-bytes or random data.
- Ensure that any transient copies of the data are overwritten as discussed previously.

This procedure makes sense from a security standpoint, because we know that it might be a long time before a given buffer is overwritten with other data by the operating system. As with any routine we write, we have a choice of how to implement the "scrubbing" functionality: we could try to remember to implement the data scrubbing each time we use a buffer that contains sensitive data (including transient copies of data). However, in doing this, we have to account for the possibility of human error. In other words, there is the very real possibility that if we are required to `memset` every sensitive buffer back after using it, we might forget to apply it (or perhaps a maintenance programmer might not know to apply the data scrubbing functionality if he is modifying our code at a later time). As an alternative choice to writing this functionality every time, we might create a single place where we implement functionality for creating, managing, and purging these buffers in a safe way, and we can then call the reusable routine anytime we are called on to purge a buffer.

This type of functionality could (of course) be implemented in an infinite number of different ways; however, one way that has a number of advantages is in the creation of a semitransparent class that abstracts the developer away from the details of having to purge the buffer, string, or array. The fact that we are choosing to implement this as a class clearly limits our language selection in employing this technique; equivalent mechanisms can be explored in procedural-based environments as alternatives to this approach as well.

In the context of C++, let's go about creating a class that "automagically" scrubs the buffer for us when the object scopes out; that way, we don't have to worry about scrubbing the buffer once we have written the code the first time. Primarily, we are interested in creating a class that encapsulates the buffer type required by our cryptographic library and ensures that appropriate discipline is enforced with respect to the purging of the data. For example, if our library requires us to specify key data as an unsigned char array, we would want to make sure that we can easily convert between unsigned char and our new type.

Let's create a specify map of the function points we want to make sure we include:

- Easily translate between the library-required types and the encapsulated type—in C++, most of the time, unsigned char will be the type for which we will wish to provide a convenient extractor.
- Ensure that we completely purge the memory buffer as part of the destruction process.
- Ensure that transient (or other) copies of the data are purged on destruction of the instance.

Therefore, the bare minimum of behavior we would want to provide in a C++ class would have behavior similar to that described in the following template:

```
class SCBASE_CALL Data {
public:
```

```
    Data(unsigned char * buffer, unsigned int len);
    Data(const Data & data);
    Data();
    ~Data();
    const unsigned char * GetBuffer() const;
    unsigned int Length() const;
private:
    void Init();
    void Purge();
    void SetData(const unsigned char * buffer, unsigned int len);
    unsigned char * theBuffer;
    unsigned int theLength;
};
```

In this example, `SCBASE_CALL` can be conditionally defined within our utility software to allow us to import or export the class from a dll (using, for example, an export declaration such as `__declspec(dllexport)` or `__declspec(dllimport)`). Implementing that functionality in a "quick and dirty" way is easy; in fact, the easiest part of developing this class is the destructor (the actual purging of the memory). The private members of the class would be set up to hold the internal buffer, and the `SetData()` method would concern itself with the allocation of memory and the copying of the incoming values to the data on the heap. Leaving the incidental portions of the class out, the useful methods would be implemented along these lines:

```
Data::Data(unsigned char * buffer, unsigned int length) {
Init();
SetData(buffer, length);
}

Data::Data(const Data& newData){
    Init();
    SetData(newData.GetBuffer(), newData.Length());
}

Data::~Data() {
    Purge();
}

void Data::Purge() {
    if(theBuffer&&theLength) {
            memset(theBuffer, 0x0, theLength);
            delete theBuffer;
    }
```

```
        theLength = 0;
        theBuffer = 0;
    }

    void Data::Init() {
        theLength = 0;
        theBuffer = 0;
        useRandomData = false;
    }


    void Data::SetData(const unsigned char * buffer, unsigned int
length) {
        if(!buffer||!length) {
            return;
        }
        theBuffer = new unsigned char[length];
        memcpy(theBuffer, buffer, length);
        theLength = length;
    }
```

While that thin wrapper is obviously the easy part, the hard part involves what to do during the creation of transient copies of the object (such as transient copies made when returning an object from a function). Here, the strategy we've used is to make a copy of the internal buffer in implementing the copy constructor. The new copy will itself be scrubbed when the object is destroyed (e.g., when the object leaves scope). The fact that we are copying a buffer during the copying of a buffer means that we have to exercise caution in when/how we use these objects, since normal operation of our software can have some unfortunate performance consequences unless we implement a more intelligent mechanism. Note that later we will improve upon this class to implement strategies for removing this performance impact. However, simply for solving the problem of self-purging memory structures, this approach has appeal. We will build on this class throughout this section to add more functionality and to solve other development challenges.

6.2.1.2 Self-Purging Memory Structures–Random Bytes

In some of the security literature, it is recommended that we scrub memory used to store sensitive material with random data rather than zeroes; this makes a good deal of sense when dealing with permanent storage such as the filesystem (where information can be recovered once written over), but can prove very burdensome to implement. In practice, our organization's security policy might require the "random data" approach for both volatile and permanent memory instead of simply writing over the memory with zeroes. While purging memory with random data comes with an associated performance impact, we can alleviate some of that impact by making a few smart design decisions and implementing the procedure centrally. In this example, we can build upon the class we outlined in the previous section and couple it with a central application pseudorandom number generator. Let's go ahead and start building a class that implements random number generation for that purpose. There are a few design considerations we need to make ahead of time for the purposes of minimizing performance impact and for providing additional functionality we might want the class to have for other uses later:

- Having a unique application-global instance of the PRNG that can be seeded during application startup and freed during application cessation
- Use of the random number generator to scrub the data

Since we don't want to implement a PRNG from scratch, we'll need to commit to a library in implementing this. Since doing so can have an associated platform constraint, we'll introduce a layer of abstraction in our global random number generator and use conditional compilation to include and link to the appropriate library we need and call the appropriate routine from it. In making these modifications, we'll introduce a new class called `RandomSource`, and all we need do is make reference to it in the destructor of our original `Data` class. Making these changes, the updated class signature would remain the same as the previous example, but we would want to update the `Purge()` method to make use of our new functionality:

```
void Data::Purge() {
    if(theBuffer&&theLength) {
#ifdef USESZEROES
        memset(theBuffer, 0x0, theLength);
#else
        const RandomSource* rand = RandomSource::
            GetGlobalRandomSource();
        for(unsigned int i = 0; i < theLength; i++) {
            theBuffer[i] = rand->GetByte();
#endif
        }
        delete theBuffer;
    }
    theLength = 0;
    theBuffer = 0;
}
```

The `RandomSource` class would have, at a minimum the following method signature:

```
class SCBASE_CALL RandomSource {
public:
    RandomSource();
    ~RandomSource();
    unsigned char GetByte() const;
    Data GetBytes(unsigned int numBytes) const;
    static const RandomSource* GetGlobalRandomSource();
private:
    static RandomSource globalRandom;
    mutable unsigned char * lib_reqs; //used for library structures
};
```

Obviously, the implementation of `GetByte()` and `GetBytes()` will vary according to the underlying cryptographic library we're using; we can use conditional compilation to switch between various random number generator implementations within our software. Specifics of implementation of this approach are demonstrated in full on the companion CD-ROM within the framework (/Examples/Chapter 6/Framework); for the purposes of demonstration, the following "highlights" from the implementation are listed here:

ON THE CD

```
RandomSource::RandomSource() {
#ifdef WIN32 //windows CAPI for demo
    HCRYPTPROV providerHandle;
    int status =
        CryptAcquireContext(&providerHandle,
        "myContainer",
        MS_ENHANCED_PROV, //use the enhanced provider
        PROV_RSA_FULL, //provider type (RSA full)
        0); //no flags
    if(!status) { //no existing provider, need to create one
        status = CryptAcquireContext(&providerHandle,
            "myContainer",
            MS_ENHANCED_PROV,
            PROV_RSA_FULL,
            CRYPT_NEWKEYSET);
    }
    lib_reqs = (unsigned char*)providerHandle; //typesafety issue
#endif
}

RandomSource::~RandomSource() {
    if(lib_reqs) {
        HCRYPTPROV ctx = 0;
        ctx = (HCRYPTPROV)ctx;
```

```
            CryptReleaseContext(ctx, 0);
        }
    }

    unsigned char RandomSource::GetByte() const {
        unsigned char c = 0x0;
    #ifdef WIN32
        HCRYPTPROV ctx = (HCRYPTPROV)lib_reqs;
        CryptGenRandom(ctx, sizeof(c), &c);
    #endif
        return c;
    }

    const RandomSource* RandomSource::GetGlobalRandomSource() {
        return &globalRandom;
    }

    RandomSource RandomSource::globalRandom;
```

Note that in this example, the use of a global random number generator prevents us from having to reinitialize the library any time we want random data; since the goal is to use the random data any time a buffer is destroyed (which could be frequently), we would obviously want to further optimize this approach. Another way to optimize would be to implement a routine that gathers more than one byte at a time from the `RandomSource` class. However, in implementing a routine that does this, it would obviously be desirable to use the `Data` class to do so, which means we have to solve some of the performance issues associated with the current implementation before we can readily do so.

6.2.1.3 Self-Locking Memory Structures

Just as we created self-zeroizing memory structures, so too can we use object orientation to help reduce the complexities associated with managing how our platform's virtual memory subsystem handles sensitive information such as keys or passwords. More specifically, we discussed earlier in this chapter that anytime we work with a key or a sensitive buffer, we should consider locking that buffer to prevent any potentiality of the operating system's virtual memory manager from writing the contents of those buffers to the paging file. Using the same methodology we employed previously, we can seamlessly incorporate the requisite locking and unlocking functionality into the allocation and deallocation portions of the class. Further, with a little conditional compilation, we can implement this both within a Windows context and within a POSIX context without much additional effort. To support this, all we need do is adjust the constructor of our `Data` class to accept a `boolean` to lock if the value is true, and to not lock if the value is false. Additionally, we'll need to modify our data initialization methods to use the new functionality, and we'll need to modify the places where we delete the buffers to make sure these are accounted for as well. Since the goal is to protect the data, we'll want to make sure the memory regions are locked *before* we set the sensitive data in them, and unlocked *after* we've purged them.

In practice, we would do something similar to the following; updating the constructor that sets data to be something like:

```
Data(unsigned char * buffer, unsigned int len, bool lock = false);
```

We would also adjust the private method that sets data as follows:

```
void SetData(const unsigned char * buffer, unsigned int len,
    bool lock = false);
```

Finally, we would add the following private methods to actually do the work, and the following private data member:

```
void UnlockBuffer(void * buffer, unsigned int length);
void LockBuffer(void * buffer, unsigned int length);
bool isLocked;
```

Aside from some minor adjustments to reflect the new method signatures and to initialize the flag we're using to track the locked/unlocked state, the only points we would have to modify the code are shown here:

```
void Data::SetData(const unsigned char * buffer, unsigned int length,
                   bool lock) {
    if(!buffer||!length) {
        return;
    }
    if(theBuffer) {
        //resetting
        if(isLocked) {
            UnlockBuffer(theBuffer, length);
        }
        delete theBuffer;
        theLength = 0;
    }
    theBuffer = new unsigned char[length];
    if(lock) {
        LockBuffer(theBuffer, length);
    }
```

```
    memcpy(theBuffer, buffer, length);
    theLength = length;
}

void Data::Purge() {
    if(theBuffer&&theLength) {
#ifdef USESZEROES
        memset(theBuffer, 0x0, theLength);
#else
        const RandomSource* rand = RandomSource::
            GetGlobalRandomSource();
        for(unsigned int i = 0; i < theLength; i++) {
            theBuffer[i] = rand->GetByte();
#endif
        }
        if(isLocked) {
            UnlockBuffer(theBuffer, theLength);
        }
        delete theBuffer;
    }
    theLength = 0;
    theBuffer = 0;
}

void Data::LockBuffer(void * buffer, unsigned int length) {

#ifdef POSIX
    mlock(buffer, length);
#endif
#ifdef WIN32
    VirtualLock(buffer, length);
#endif
    isLocked = true;
}

void Data::UnlockBuffer(void * buffer, unsigned int length) {

#ifdef POSIX
    munlock(buffer, length);
#endif
#ifdef WIN32
    VirtualUnlock(buffer, length);
#endif
    isLocked = false;
}
```

And that's it. Now, we have a structure we can use anywhere we need to store sensitive information that will automatically "do the right thing" even without our explicit intervention (aside from instructing it appropriately). Depending on the application we're writing and the extent to which we anticipate using this class, we could actually set the default state to locked rather than unlocked—then it requires no intervention on our part. However, since we're still working on the framework, we're going to leave the default state alone for now, the goal being to use this class for more than just keys and passwords.

6.2.1.4 Safety and Performance Considerations

In developing our framework, if we want to extend our implementation to solve some additional security challenges, we'll need to address both the performance and the lack of functionality within the current `Data` implementation. Specifically, the "quick and dirty" implementation we used earlier does not make it convenient to return an object of type `Data` from a method or function. Returning such an object will make a copy of the internal buffer, and there are other things we might like to do with buffers besides storing them (such as searches within a buffer, concatenation, tokenization, etc.). Being able to increase the performance is desirable because ubiquitous use of the new buffer class we've implemented can centralize memory management and thereby decrease the likelihood of certain application vulnerabilities within our applications. In other words, we can "kill two birds with one stone" and potentially realize a security benefit by encapsulating all memory manipulation within one class. To be more specific, a recurring issue in the security industry today is the ubiquity of application software vulnerable to "buffer overflow" conditions either on the stack or on the heap. To increase the resilience of our software to this type of application vulnerability, we can centralize memory management and make it easier to make sure all boundaries are checked "automagically" within our application.

For developers who are unfamiliar with buffer overflow conditions, we'll do a quick walkthrough just to illustrate the point. Of course, this is not an exhaustive description of the problem; fully understanding the cause and ramifications of this problem is a discipline unto itself that would extend beyond our scope. However, very cursorily, buffer overflow conditions are caused by application software that writes beyond the boundaries of a stack- or heap-based buffer. Overflow of the buffer can have undesired consequences, such as allowing an attacker to execute arbitrary code, manipulating our application's memory space, or other undesired consequences.

As an example, consider the following code:

```
char aBuffer[15];
strcpy(aBuffer, "some long string that is bigger than that.");
```

The preceding code is simplistic, but should serve to illustrate the point. In this example, we've allocated only 15 bytes for the variable `aBuffer`, and we've attempted to copy the long string into the small space we've allocated. Unless we're doing something unusual (e.g., using a product that helps us locate this type of issue), the compiler and underlying string library routine will "take us at our word" that the buffer is big enough to handle the data we've submitted and will attempt to copy the second string onto the too-short buffer. In so doing, the memory space after the end of the `aBuffer` variable will be overwritten with the end of the string we've supplied. In and of itself, this would only be a "logic error" (perhaps causing our software to crash), but when we put this in the context of the specific data we're overwriting (particularly on the stack), the problem gets much nastier.

On most computing platforms, the stack is laid out for maximum efficiency; when passing functions, for example, only a few words away from the end of our buffer is the return address of the function that's being entered. This means that if someone knew the "right" return address to supply, he could deliberately manipulate where in our software the CPU resumes execution at the end of the function. That's one way a security problem could be introduced: someone with knowledge of the platform we're running on and access to a debugger to help locate the "right" address could write a string that overwrites the return address with a new return address pointing to instructions that person specifies (maybe within the buffer itself). This would cause the machine to execute the "bogus" instructions rather than the instructions we intend. Obviously, that would be a problem. In practice, every buffer overflow situation is different; the overwritten buffer might be farther away from a "target" that a hostile party could use to run arbitrary code, or there might be other qualities of the software the overflow is in that might limit the damage that can be done via exploitation (maybe an attacker can only crash our process and not run arbitrary software on the machine). The problem affects heap-based buffers as well; granted, the damage that can be done from a heap-based overflow is potentially less than a stack-based one (or at least it's harder to exploit it to "maximum advantage"), but it can still be a problem.

The most popular approach today is "developer education" to help bring about a reduction in buffer overflow conditions. In essence, "developer education" seeks to instruct developers about which functions to call and which not to (the "thou shalt not" approach). Basically, developers are instructed on a periodic basis about the "dangers of strcat" (or "strcpy," or any other buffer manipulation routine that doesn't check boundaries). However, time and experience have demonstrated that telling C/C++ programmers not to use "unsafe" functions doesn't work for a variety of reasons; specifically:

- Not every developer in an organization will be present at the training.
- "Indoctrinating" new personnel on a project team is expensive.

- The "dangerous" functions are ubiquitously provided and don't come with warning labels.
- Other routines that *do* perform boundary-checking can still cause the same problem (just not as easily).

To understand specifically why this training approach doesn't work, let's look at what exactly is being proposed. First, we would have to get all of our developers into training classes (or barrage them with memos) telling them about the functions they should and should not use. Not only do we have to make sure existing developers are trained, we would have to make sure that new developers coming onto the team are also briefed. Let's assume that the developers we're educating get over their distaste for the education process and agree not to use the functions in question (not many developers we know like being told how to do their job). Let's further assume that we indoctrinate and train all incoming personnel, all maintenance personnel, anybody doing professional services with clients, and so on. How much money have we spent by this point? Millions? And as soon as we stop spending money, people start to forget, new personnel join the team, and all sorts of other things happen to cause the "bad functions" to start creeping back in.

So, understanding that centralization of memory management is desirable, how can we make the `Data` class robust enough in functionality and performance that one can consolidate the majority of buffer handling within a large application? To start with, we can improve the performance associated with returning a `Data` instance from inside a function or method by having `Data` support a `Return()` method. In this manner, we can inform the data class that we will be returning the value and therefore "hand ownership" of the internal buffer over to the receiver rather than making a copy. The internal logistics of this aren't complicated—we're using a `boolean` as a flag to control a private member named "`isReturning`," and we just make a copy of the pointer if the internal value is true, and a copy of the full buffer if the value is false. The internal mechanics are relatively simple to implement, so they are not included verbatim in this section (although they are included in the sample framework.

6.2.1.5 Centralizing the Functionality

The goal of this approach is partially to make it harder for developers to do a task the "unsafe way" (using unsafe buffer manipulation functions) than it is to do it a "safer way." Obviously, we can't discourage the use of strcpy by making it any harder to use than it already is, but we can work in reverse; in other words, we can create alternative constructs that are easier to use than these routines and encourage their use throughout the application. This is not a new concept; for example, most C++ textbooks start by teaching the developer how to create a string class (a class that encapsulates string functionality), but how often do we see this done in practice? In shops that do supply and encourage the use of an underlying framework, how often do we see them circumvented in practice? Alternatively, we could use something that already exists (such as MFC's CString), but let's face it: CString is cumbersome to use and has a heavy footprint (the same could be said about all of MFC in general). So, let's consolidate all of our buffer manipulation in one place and use that instead of the unsafe string routines. To make it (arguably) even safer, let's add some more functionality to our standardized heap-based buffers to attempt to obviate the majority of the need to use a traditional memory allocation and deallocation approach.

To maximize the potential usefulness of our structure, methods to concatenate buffers, set buffers equal to each other, compare buffers for equality or "less than" or "greater than" relationships, find positions of characters within buffers, and so forth are all useful. Adding this functionality, our updated class signature would be adjusted to contain the following methods as well:

```
Data& operator=(const Data& toCopy);
bool operator>=(const Data& toCompare) const;
bool operator<=(const Data& toCompare) const;
bool operator<(const Data& toCompare) const;
bool operator>(const Data& toCompare) const;
bool operator==(const Data& toCompare) const;
unsigned char operator[](unsigned int pos) const;
Data GetSubBuffer(unsigned int start,
    unsigned int end) const;
```

And we don't need to stop there; as we continue to update our application software, we can add more and more functionality to this class. If the class doesn't do what we want right now, we can just add it in. That way, as our application progresses, so will the underlying functionality (which becomes available for other uses besides just this application). Rather than having to rewrite the same tired buffer manipulation code over and over again, we can very quickly build a structure that becomes ever more useful as we keep writing other software around it. As we can see, at the end of the day, this is a useful technique for consolidation of memory management all in one central locality; there are good security reasons for doing so, and it leads to less development headache in the long term.

6.2.2 Self-Purging Memory (Java Strategies)

Implementing a self-purging memory strategy as we did in C++ is much more difficult in Java; the specifics of the way Java is implemented make it difficult for us to manipulate sensitive material in this language. Specifically, when manipulating a password or cryptographic key *bytes* (but not key-related objects), we might be tempted to store these sensitive values in a `String`, but here's where the complexity comes in. First, we can never guarantee when (if ever) objects in Java will get garbage collected; and second, once we put data in a `String`, we lose our capacity to overwrite it. In other words, strings are "immutable," meaning that we don't get to control the internal buffer within the class to overwrite it with zeroes or random data. Because of these facts, we must *never* use `java.lang.String` for anything we want to make sure is zeroed out after use. This sounds like less of a problem than it actually is; for example, we might decide that because of this, we'll just use a command-line application to read data in to our application, and we'll make sure that everywhere we use the password we zeroize the buffer. However, when we look at the code recommended by Sun to do this, we realize that this might be harder to do than we originally anticipated. The Sun documentation (specifically the "Java Cryptography Extension (JCE) Reference Guide")[1] instructs us to call the `System.read()` method in a loop to obtain the contents of the password from the user via the console and to use the `Array.arraycopy()` method to zeroize any transient buffers that we might use during the password reading process. The resultant character array can then be directly passed into the key generation process.

Obviously, this makes for some pretty complex code to write and not something we would want to implement more than once in our application; therefore, if possible, we'll want to go ahead and centralize the routine. One of the things this code snippet does not provide is portability of the resultant byte array (by design). In other words, in using this code, we have to keep track of the returned byte array, where it goes, and any transient copies of the buffer that might be created along the way during our usage. We would not, for example, want to store the byte array in a local variable within the method that calls this routine unless we then zeroize that buffer as well. All in all, the usage issues get fairly problematic once we want to do anything more than just read a password in from the command line and use it immediately. What makes this problem most difficult to solve is the lack of a destructor in Java; while we could implement our own buffer class that zeroes memory after use (using, for example, a `finalize()` method to overwrite the data), we can't reliably control when and if garbage collection will take place to actually zero out the data.

Even though we can't use the same approach in Java that we did in C++ earlier, we can at least write a central class that consolidates the password reading functionality, allows us to not have to write the same zeroizing code over and over again, and "does its best" to clean up after accidental usage. Such a class would be relatively simple to implement; incorporating the Sun sample material as a static method, the following class implements this simple bare-bones functionality:

```
import java.io.PushbackInputStream;
import java.io.IOException;
import java.io.InputStream;
import java.util.Arrays;
```

```
public class Password {

    public Password() {
    }

    public Password(char[] password) {
        myPassword = password;
    }

    private char[] myPassword;

    protected void finalize() throws Throwable {
        try {
            Arrays.fill(myPassword, ' ');
        } finally {
            super.finalize();
        }
    }

    public void Zeroize() {
        Arrays.fill(myPassword, ' ');

    }

    public static char[] readPasswd(InputStream in) throws
IOException {
        char[] lineBuffer;
        char[] buf;
        int i;

        buf = lineBuffer = new char[128];

        int room = buf.length;
        int offset = 0;
        int c;

loop:   while (true) {
            switch (c = in.read()) {
              case -1:
              case '\n':
                break loop;

              case '\r':
                int c2 = in.read();
                if ((c2 != '\n') && (c2 != -1)) {
```

```
                        if (!(in instanceof PushbackInputStream)) {
                            in = new PushbackInputStream(in);
                        }
                        ((PushbackInputStream)in).unread(c2);
                    } else
                        break loop;

                default:
                    if (--room < 0) {
                        buf = new char[offset + 128];
                        room = buf.length - offset - 1;
                        System.arraycopy(lineBuffer, 0, buf, 0, offset);
                        Arrays.fill(lineBuffer, ' ');
                        lineBuffer = buf;
                    }
                    buf[offset++] = (char) c;
                    break;
                }
            }

            if (offset == 0) {
                return null;
            }

            char[] ret = new char[offset];
            System.arraycopy(buf, 0, ret, 0, offset);
            Arrays.fill(buf, ' ');

            return ret;
        }

    }
```

Obviously, we still have to be careful when and how we use this. On the plus side, however, at least this class will attempt to zeroize the memory on garbage collection in case we forget to do it or if another developer on our team modifies our code and does not anticipate the zeroization requirement.

6.2.3 Policy Enforcement

In our software, it is useful to enforce policy that governs how cryptographic keys can be used; as the developers of the application, it is imperative for us to understand how our software is intended to function and do our best to ensure that it functions according to “spec” programmatically. For example, we might note during development that the keys we’re using should be changed every year; a fruitful approach to maintaining the security of our application is to enforce that they be changed at a regular interval. For example, when the keys are getting "stale," we could prompt the user to change them; depending on the nature of the application, we could even programmatically stop using them if they continue to be used after an appropriate period of warning the user. There might be other policies we wish to enforce as well; we might, for example, specify that a particular set of keys can only be used on a certain host (e.g., in the development environment but not in the production environment). In short, defining a policy that should be followed ahead of time and enforcing it within the application helps to protect the investment in time and manpower we've made in building the secure application in the first place.

There are a few frequently used controls that we might want to consider for inclusion in a policy-enforcement engine:

- Implement software restrictions limiting where keys can be used.
- Put restrictions in place limiting the lifetime of development keys.
- Authenticate the application prior to allowing access to keys.
- Authenticate the user prior to allowing access to keys.
- Enforce restrictions about when a user can use keys.
- Implement a strategy involving a combination of the above.

Although it might not seem that way, using application controls to prevent unauthorized access (to keys, to data, to anything) can be a bit of a controversial subject. In determining why this is, we must understand both where the criticism is coming from, and what we are trying to do in our application. In other words, a clear delineation of the goal in light of the potential objections will enable us to see why the criticism exists, why some individuals (particularly those trained in security) might object to it, and why we should consider doing it anyway (at least in certain situations). The controversy comes about in light of our previous discussions about "security by obscurity." In other words, we cannot rely on an attacker not knowing about some Boolean we're using to allow or deny access, a hard-coded key in our source we're using to encrypt an initialization file, data "hidden" in some file on the filesystem, or any other approach where we assume "an attacker doesn't know xyz, so we're safe." These naysayers are absolutely right in what they say. Specifically, the use of application logic as a *protection* for keys, data, or anything else will receive well-deserved criticism. After all, couldn't a determined adversary use a debugger or other mechanism to manipulate the Boolean while the application's running and thereby completely bypass our protection? Couldn't an attacker reverse engineer our software and modify the instructions that do the checking in the first place? The answer is "yes" to both these questions; in fact, if the goal of enforcing an application control were to prevent deliberate attack from a knowledgeable party, there would be no point in implementing the controls using the methodologies available to us in a software application. However, that's not our goal. Instead, the goal in these scenarios is to prevent *accidental misuse*, not to prevent *deliberate attacks*; preventing accidental misuse is much easier than preventing an intentional attack, but it does solve a very real problem using a minimum of additional software. So, understanding that the goal is not to prevent attack but to prevent misuse, let's look at two of the more frequent key policy items we would want to enforce programmatically, and then discuss some implementation options.

6.2.3.1 Location-Specific Policy

Probably the easiest way to ensure that development keys stay in development and production keys stay in production is to limit the locality (hostname, domain, etc.) in which the keys are valid. There are, of course, numerous other ways to do this, but limiting a given key to a particular hostname (such as the FQDN of the production server, for example) does not require any additional engineering beyond knowing the name of the machine in question. One way this can be done (as we will demonstrate) is by creating a wrapper class that "envelops" the actual key data, and enforces the predefined policy.

6.2.3.2 Key Expiration Policy

All keys have a limited useful lifetime; over time, the likelihood that our keys will be compromised goes up. To preserve the security of the applications we build, we'll often need to enforce "key rollover," where keys that have been in use for a long period of time are replaced with new keys. This may not sound like much of a challenge until we consider what happens when an application "goes legacy" and support for it drops off—in that situation, long periods of time might elapse before the keys are changed (decades, potentially). One of the most useful things we can do is to build into our policy enforcement engine the capacity for the application to warn users or administrators ahead of time that the keys are about to expire, and actually expiring them after a certain period of time. We'll implement a `KeyPolicy` class that keeps track of those values. How we implement them is a matter of personal preference (the framework on the companion CD-ROM uses strings, but they could be implemented as constant integers for better performance if a developer so desires). We've chosen strings for expediency, to allow rapid printing of the strings and for ease of serialization primarily.

ON THE CD

6.2.3.3 Policy Enforcement Implementation

In building policy enforcement into our application, we need to first investigate if our application can leverage standard structures for policy enforcement. For example, X.509 digital certificates contain expiration information (thus enforcing that appropriate rollover take place at a specified interval), and in some cases are bound to the hostname of the device on which they are to operate (server certificates, for example, contain the DNS name of the server in the Common Name field). If our application uses public keys, and we have the facility to use certificates bound to those keys, so much the better (since it lessens our workload quite a bit). If, as is more often the case, we will be using symmetric cryptography and we need to retain and use symmetric keys over a long period of time, we will need to build the implementation ourselves outside the purview of standardized structures. If this is the case, it behooves us to use an approach similar to the way we approached the protection of buffers: namely, we'll want to automate the approach so we do not have to worry about implementing this code over and over again every time we use a key. In object-oriented languages, we'll probably want to develop a centralized key class that does the enforcement internally, and in procedural-based languages, we'll probably want to implement routines that will supply the key and do policy enforcement at the time the key is requested.

6.2.3.4 Sample Implementation—C++

A hypothetical class that implements this type of policy enforcement and incorporates the previous self-purging memory structures we outlined earlier could be implemented in a manner similar to the following. To preserve state, we'll create a hypothetical "Serializable" parent class that will behave in much the same way as the Java Serializable interface (namely that the contents of the object can be written to a string and read back in from that string at a later time):

```
#ifndef SCKEY_H
#define SCKEY_H

#include "SCGlobal.h"
#include "SCData.h"
#include "SCSerializable.h"
#include "SCKeyPolicy.h"

class SCBASE_CALL Key : public Serializable {
public:
    Key();
    Key(Data & keyBytes, KeyPolicy & policy);
    ~Key();
    const unsigned char * GetKeyBytes() const;
    //serializable functions
    Data Serialize() const = 0;
    void Deserialize(const Data & value) = 0;
    bool CheckPolicy();
private:
    Data keyValue;
    KeyPolicy keyPolicy;
};

#endif
```

The only thing we've done here is used the safe `Data` structure we created before for storing of the actual bytes of the key value; this allows us to make sure the memory buffer used is locked, zeroized (or filled with random data), and so forth.

6.2.4 Cryptographic Protections of Keys

In addition to strategies allowing the segregation of the key information, in scenarios in which we cannot prompt a user for key information (e.g., for password-based key derivation), we may wish to implement cryptographic protection for the keys. This can be done via a hardware device (Hardware Security Module) if we desire extremely robust protection of the key information, or we can attempt to implement an HSM-like protection strategy in software. Both strategies, using an HSM or a software-like protection methodology, have appeal in that they limit the extent to which the key information is divulged to casual observance by administrator personnel, and the first (HSM) strategy has appeal in that it further limits the degree to which the keys are exposed even in the face of a determined adversary with physical access to the equipment. However, both strategies have an impact in terms of cost, both from a dollar perspective and from a development time perspective. A software implementation will most likely be the preferred scenario since it is unusual to encounter a context where the default implementation of an application will require an HSM to function. In outlining a strategy of this type, it is useful to differentiate between libraries that provide useful mechanisms to assist in this endeavor and those that do not. For example, if we are using Microsoft CAPI or the .NET framework, we can use the DPAPI (Data Protection API) to assist us in developing a secure storage framework for cryptographic keys. If we are using the JCE, some providers will allow us to leverage the inherent private key storage facility of the KeyStore functionality to store session keys. In other contexts where a specific API for protection of keys is not directly laid out, we can build such a mechanism programmatically. Again, it is not the purpose of this section to go into the details of implementing such a protection mechanism, rather to lay out the concepts (going into a specific implementation would probably be confusing, since we haven't yet covered usage of the specific libraries or what functionality is available in them).

Let's discuss what properties will be most useful in implementing a cryptographic software protection mechanism for our key data. First, we'll want to build the mechanism to allow either password-based key derivation for access to the other keys, or we will want to implement some type of application password that allows only a certain application to gain access to its own keys. Binding the protection key to a password is useful, because in the situation in which a user will be prompted for the password, it provides protection against attack, and in other cases (using an application password, for example), it protects against casual observation of the key data. This is a useful feature to highlight: we are implementing a security feature that can provide different levels of "assurance" depending on the application context. In other words, we can author it once and make application design decisions that either heighten the security of the usage or heighten the flexibility of the usage. Additionally, in designing a general-purpose tool, we will want the structure we build to be transferable from one application instance to another. For example, it is useful to design the protection structure in such a way that we can use it to share keys among applications if we so desire.

So, from an implementation perspective, how can we effect these goals? The simplest way is to couple the cryptographic primitives we've used already to incorporate both password-based key derivation and symmetric cryptography. To do this, we'll have to satisfy the Serialization prerequisite that will allow our objects to be saved as a string. In other words, first we'll need to implement a mechanism that allows us to transform keys into a contiguous byte string (including any associate policy information), and we'll need something that groups keys together in a structured way so keys can be readily located and serialized together. From a functional perspective, when an application instantiates, it will look for the grouped key structure, obtain a password from the user or application, decrypt the serialized group key structure using the derived key, and load the high-level decrypted structure and the individual keys within it. Of course, we will want to ensure that each of the keys within the structure is created in such a way that memory is purged upon completion, that it is not written to the pagefile, and so forth. All this sounds like complicated functionality to implement, but in reality, it isn't. Using the classes we've come up with so far in addition to some of the basic functionality offered by the library, the implementation is really not that difficult. In fact, the implementation is a snap:

```
#ifndef SCKEYSTORAGE_H
#define SCKEYSTORAGE_H

#include "SCGlobal.h"
#include "SCList.h"
#include "SCSecureSerializable.h"


class SCBASE_CALL KeyStorage : public SecureSerializable {
public:
    KeyStorage();
    ~KeyStorage();
    void AddKey(Key & toAdd);
    void RemoveKey(const Data & name);
    const Key * GetKey(const Data & name);
    Data Serialize(const Data & password) const;
    void Deserialize(const Data & sObject,
        const Data & password);
private:
```

```
        List keys;
    };

    #endif
```

Of course, we need a few helper classes to drive this. First, we'll need a secure serialization interface; we'll extend the Serialization interface we borrowed from the Java API, and we'll add a SecureSerialize interface that takes a password. Internal to this interface, we can implement the functionality to do password-based key derivation and encryption. We'll need to give our keys names, which they didn't have before, so we can look them up in the structure. Those with some familiarity with the Java API might intuit that this is starting to look quite a bit like a KeyStore; as a matter of fact, it is. The KeyStore is an extremely useful piece of software engineering; while the Java API doesn't include the same type of policy we're putting in (e.g., for symmetric key policy checking) the API is a solid one to emulate, and can be used to solve a number of security challenges, particularly with respect to administrative access to key material.

6.3 LIBRARY INTEGRATION STRATEGIES

While building in automation protection for keys and data significantly reduces our workload during the application development phase, it does not go as far in lessening our workload once the application is deployed. It is inevitable that our code will need to be maintained after deployment, and every developer knows that maintenance can be a hassle. However, when we are called upon to interface with external libraries, that hassle can be huge unless we anticipate and plan accordingly in our application design. This subsection walks through some small steps we can introduce early in the process, and pay for themselves to a great degree in the long term.

6.3.1 Encapsulate Integration Points

We discussed in Chapter 5 the benefits of encapsulation/consolidation of library code; specifically, we laid out why it is beneficial for our software to make use of centralization for the purposes of creating a layer of abstraction between our software and the libraries. It is neither our intention to "beat a dead" horse nor to "preach to the choir" about the benefits of these design practices; therefore, we will take it as a given that you are using some sort of centralized encapsulated framework to shield your application from the cryptographic libraries' interface points. However, one thing that does bear mentioning specifically is the degree to which this design strategy minimizes the impact of having to change libraries after initial application deployment. Although it sounds unlikely before the application is written, it is almost inevitable that we will have to (depending on the lifetime of the application) change libraries at some point, update the way our application calls those libraries, or significantly enhance the cryptographic processing capability of our application. There are a number of reasons for this, including:

Evolution of the library: The libraries are not stagnant; they evolve over time and new releases of the libraries contain bug fixes, feature enhancements, deprecated functionality, and so on. We may need to update our integration points to remove deprecated functionality or to take advantage of new features.

Evolution of our application: Requirements can and do change. Our application may evolve over time, and the library that was "good enough" for today's requirements may not fit the new requirements that will be added as the application matures. For example, if we are working on a logistics application that will be sold to retail stores, we may not consider FIPS 140 compliance in our original application design; if the sales department discovers that our software will sell like hotcakes to the military, however, we may find that it will become a requirement.

Evolution of the underlying platform: Some of the libraries make use of operating system features and functionality. In the case of Microsoft CAPI, for example, particular versions of Windows support particular cryptographic functionality. What was available on Windows 2003 Server may or may not continue to be available on Longhorn. As such, we may find that platform considerations force us to update our software.

Newly discovered attacks: Vulnerabilities discovered in the library we are using, or weaknesses in the underlying algorithms themselves may force us to change our usage.

New standards: New standards are constantly evolving. If we are a product company, our clients will most likely demand that we use the standards they are comfortable with, and if we are a nontechnology enterprise, our security organization will like enforce that our software stay up to date with current standards. Staying up to date may very well necessitate changes in the underlying security support software.

Understanding that we may need to change the way we call the underlying libraries, a layer of abstraction between our software and those libraries is a very useful practice.

6.3.2 Updates and Patches

Any application that uses external software needs to keep abreast of patches and updates for that software; this is particularly true when the external software in question drives the security of our entire application. Depending on the library we use, and depending on how we make use of that library (e.g., static or dynamic linkage), changes in the underlying cryptographic libraries may require that we recompile our application, retest the security functionality, and write additional code. This maintenance effort is compounded if we decide to "double up" on library usage (i.e., we use more than one library); using more than one library is a useful technique for ensuring portability and for satisfying certain sets of requirements that are not directly addressed by one library alone. Therefore, given the fact that we will have to keep abreast of these updates, it pays to prepare a plan ahead of time for how we keep up, how we will roll out changes, and how we will coordinate those changes with different components within our infrastructure.

For example, having two components in different infrastructures does not sound like a threatening maintenance situation at first glance; for example, our application might encrypt messages at the sales department's datacenter and send those messages for decryption to the marketing department's datacenter by means of a shared key. However, without foresight and planning, this situation can be a nightmare! Specifically, what happens if a newly published algorithm weakness makes us want to change the algorithm? Do we have to update both components at the same time? That may prove extremely difficult to do if they are in different infrastructures as specified. Therefore, we'll want to have a plan in place for how we will coordinate the update. There are a number of strategies we can use to do this; the important part is not so much how we do it, but that we spend some time thinking about how it will be done ahead of time. We don't want to be caught by surprise after the application is already deployed.

6.4 SUMMARY

Within this chapter, we've looked at a few techniques that (hopefully) you can use during the design and development phases of your application to lighten the workload over the long term. Of course, not every technique will work in every context. We've also included a framework on the companion CD-ROM implementations of each of the techniques discussed here (/Examples/Chapter 6/Framework.) The biggest timesaver is "cut and paste," so hopefully you'll be able to do that with some of what we've put together.

ON THE CD

6.5 ENDNOTES

1. *http://java.sun.com/j2se/1.4.2/docs/guide/security/jce/JCERefGuide.html*

7 Developing with OpenSSL

In This Chapter

- Chapter Goal
- Preparing the Environment
- Using the Library
- Symmetric Cryptography Using OpenSSL
- Message Digests (Hashing) Using OpenSSL
- MACs (Keyed Hashes) Using OpenSSL
- Digital Signature Using OpenSSL
- Asymmetric Encryption
- Secure Communications
- Endnotes

OpenSSL is an extensive and easy-to-use interface to security functionality. Unlike some of the other libraries, OpenSSL provides both a command-line interface that exposes cryptographic and communication-security functionality via a highly flexible command-line application, and the standard library capability. This, in and of itself, is an extremely powerful capability; however, OpenSSL does not skimp in other areas of functionality: the library features available in OpenSSL are every bit as robust and easy to use (if not more so) than any of the other libraries covered in this book. Since the library is so easy to use, it is free from software licensing costs, and the terms of the license are extremely forgiving, this library is a wise choice for application developers to consider in building new applications.

As we've stated in other sections of this book, there are a few situations in which we *cannot* use the library in its current form. In particular, enterprises that require commercial support are likely to want to look to another library, and organizations that require FIPS 140-2 certification will need to look elsewhere. Currently, the OpenSSL library is undergoing FIPS certification, but as of the time of this writing, such certification is "in process" (preevaluation) and has yet to complete the certification process. While this will mostly apply to developers working in a U.S. government context, some firms use FIPS 140-2 as a baseline for cryptographic components they bring in house; if your organization is such an entity, another library should be considered.

7.1 CHAPTER GOAL

As with all the libraries, it is not our goal to replace the excellent documentation available in OpenSSL; numerous individuals have contributed many hours in preparing detailed descriptions of the functions in the library, excellent usage examples, annotated source, and other usage-centered learning materials. In addition to the excellent documentation, there are numerous mailing lists (and archives of those mailing lists) such as the openssl-users list that are an excellent resource for asking questions of experienced OpenSSL users and for finding answers to previously asked questions. This chapter is not a replacement for any of that material. Instead, it is our only goal to provide one learning path to the developer who is currently working on a project. We're assuming an "80/20" stance, meaning that 80 percent of the time, we'll be using 20 percent of the functionality of the toolkit. Twenty percent isn't that hard to cover, and is likely to be adequate for the basic tasks we'll encounter in writing "everyday" enterprise and consumer applications.

In other words, the manual pages supplied by OpenSSL are excellent, and the APIs described therein contain explanations of the various features and a function-by-function breakdown of what each function does and how it is used. Our goal here is only to describe the "bare minimum" approach required for developers to make use of the functionality they will encounter in the majority of usage scenarios. We do not make the claim that the descriptions contained in this chapter are more thorough than the OpenSSL documentation (they aren't) or that they are more easily understood by a developer (that's open to interpretation). Instead, if the OpenSSL is the "road atlas" of the library API, we hope to provide a set of abbreviated driving directions through the API that a developer can pick up and use *in a hurry*.

Getting that out of the way, let's get to the point of learning the library's basic features. To help the developer understand the powerful features of the tool, we will start with a description of the command-line capabilities of the tool and some basic usage from shell scripts or batch files. We will then progress to basic cryptographic functionality such as the primitives we covered in previous sections as available through C (or exported in to other languages via dynamic link). Finally, we will move to establishing secure connections using SSL/TLS, which (arguably) is where the real strength of the library lies. However, before we can do any of that, we'll need to make sure we can obtain, compile, and run the current versions of OpenSSL. Moreover, we'll need to prepare our environment in such a way that we can compile in the right headers and link against the right libraries.

7.2 PREPARING THE ENVIRONMENT

The first thing we need to do is prepare our environment so the applications we write can compile and link cleanly. However, a prerequisite to preparing the environment is ensuring that we have a version of OpenSSL to use in our applications and to prepare our environment for. As of the time of this writing, the most recent version of OpenSSL is 0.9.7g; we'll use that for our testing, but a developer reading along might wish to obtain the most recent version, as subsequent releases might contain important bug fixes (including security fixes). To obtain the files, we'll want to navigate to the homepage of the OpenSSL project, and download the right files. We'll download the file openssl-0.9.7g.tar.gz since it corresponds to the most recent release at the time of this writing. Having obtained this file, we'll go ahead and unpack it to a working directory where we can build the resulting files.

7.2.1 Building for Unix

Having obtained the file, we'll need to go ahead and compile it. Doing so is easiest on a Unix platform such as Solaris, Linux, BSD, or Mac OS X. Note that we can also build it for cygwin using this methodology, but we get a bit more flexibility on the Windows platform by building it using the method described in the next subsection, since by doing so we won't be dependant on the cygwin dlls. To build for Unix, we'll just go ahead and extract it in a working directory:

```
[emoyle@elysium:~]$ gzip -dc openssl-0.9.7g.tar.gz | tar xvf -
```

This will extract the contents of the gzipped tarball into a directory for us. Once we've done this, we'll want to change to the created directory:

```
[emoyle@elysium:~]$ cd openssl-0.9.7g
```

Next, we'll use the `config` command to configure the tool to build on our platform. Note that we'll have to have a compiler, linker, and a usable version of `make` on our machine and locatable by the config script (i.e., in our path) for this to work:

```
[emoyle@elysium:~/openssl-0.9.7g]$ ./config
 Operating system: sun4u-whatever-solaris2
 NOTICE! If you *know* that your GNU C supports 64-bit/V9 ABI
         and wish to build 64-bit library, then you have to
         invoke './Configure solaris64-sparcv9-gcc' *manually*.
 Configuring for solaris-sparcv9-gcc
 Configuring for solaris-sparcv9-gcc
 IsWindows=0
 CC             =gcc
 […]
```

If we have any unsatisfied dependencies such as missing libraries or anything that might be required by the library (e.g., a functional /dev/random or an up-to-date instance of flex), the configuration script should indicate them at this time. However, encountering a difficulty at this point is unlikely (the config script runs without complaint on the majority of "vanilla" Unix systems tested in preparation for this chapter). Having obtained the files and run the config script, we will now build the library using the `make` command:

```
    [emoyle@elysium:~/openssl-0.9.7g]$   make
    making all in crypto...
    ( echo "#ifndef MK1MF_BUILD"; \
    echo '  /* auto-generated by crypto/Makefile for crypto/cversion.
c */'; \
    echo '  #define CFLAGS "gcc -DOPENSSL_SYSNAME_ULTRASPARC
-DOPENSSL_THREADS -D_RE
    ENTRANT -DDSO_DLFCN -DHAVE_DLFCN_H -DOPENSSL_NO_KRB5 -m32
-mcpu=ultrasparc -O3 -
    fomit-frame-pointer -Wall -DB_ENDIAN -DBN_DIV2W -DMD5_ASM"'; \
    echo '  #define PLATFORM "solaris-sparcv9-gcc"'; \
    […]
```

As a result of this operation, we should have successfully built the required shared objects and the OpenSSL applications. We're now ready to configure our projects to use these shared objects, and use the compiled application to perform tasks.

7.2.2 Building for Windows

Building the OpenSSL library for Windows is a little bit more difficult. First, to do so, we'll need access to a few tools such as Perl, a C compiler, and an assembler. For most Windows developers, the last two choices will be obvious (although other choices work as well): Visual C++ and the Microsoft Macro Assembler (MASM). Actually, you need to be able to run the ml.exe executable file, which is available in a number of places. For our testing purposes, we'll be using the MASM 6.11 that is available via the Windows DDK via MSDN subscription; however, just about any version of the assembler will do. We'll want to make sure that ml.exe can be located in our PATH environment variable (settable from the "Environment Variables" button in the "Advanced" pane of the System property pane). Using the 6.11 version installed in c:\, the addition of ";c:\masm611\bin" to the system path would do the trick. Once we've configured it, we should be able to run ML from the command line, like so:

```
Microsoft Windows XP [Version 5.1.2600]
(C) Copyright 1985-2001 Microsoft Corp.
C:\Documents and Settings\emoyle>ml
Microsoft (R) Macro Assembler Version 6.11
Copyright (C) Microsoft Corp 1981-1993.  All rights reserved.
usage: ML [ options ] filelist [ /link linkoptions]
Run "ML /help" or "ML /?" for more info
C:\Documents and Settings\emoyle>
```

Having verified that we can find and run the assembler, we'll also need to make sure the C/C++ compiler is accessible from the command line; this tool is cl.exe and is provided by way of Visual C++ or Visual Studio. For these examples, we'll be using Visual C++ 6.0, although any version will do. In this case, we would add the location of cl.exe and the supporting .dlls to the path. For this version of the Visual Studio, we would add the value ";C:\Program Files\Microsoft Visual Studio\VC98\Bin;C:\Program Files\Microsoft Visual Studio\Common\MSDev98\Bin", which happens to be the location of cl.exe and the supporting libraries. However, for a newer release, we might use a different locality such as "C:\Program Files\Microsoft Visual Studio 8\VC\bin" or whatever is appropriate for the version we're using. Having done this, we should be able to find the cl.exe from the command line, like so:

```
    Microsoft Windows XP [Version 5.1.2600]
    (C) Copyright 1985-2001 Microsoft Corp.
    C:\Documents and Settings\emoyle>cl
    Microsoft (R) 32-bit C/C++ Optimizing Compiler Version 12.00.8804
for 80x86
    Copyright (C) Microsoft Corp 1984-1998. All rights reserved.
    usage: cl [ option... ] filename... [ /link linkoption... ]
    C:\Documents and Settings\emoyle>
```

The last remaining component is a functional version of Perl; this is not included in any of the Microsoft distributions, so we'll need to download a version of Perl for the Windows platform. One good choice is ActivePerl from ActiveState corporation; the interpreter is free for use, and it's easy to install. Provided we have obtained and installed it, we should be able to run `perl` from the command line; of course, just running `perl` without arguments will cause it to hang, so to detect if it is installed, we'll run it with the "—version" argument like this:

```
    C:\Documents and Settings\emoyle>perl --version
    This is perl, v5.8.0 built for MSWin32-x86-multi-thread
    (with 1 registered patch, see perl -V for more detail)
    Copyright 1987-2002, Larry Wall
    Binary build 806 provided by ActiveState Corp.
http://www.ActiveState.com
    Built 00:45:44 Mar 31 2003

    Perl may be copied only under the terms of either the Artistic
License or the
    GNU General Public License, which may be found in the Perl 5 source
kit.
    Complete documentation for Perl, including FAQ lists, should be
found on
    this system using `man perl' or `perldoc perl'.  If you have access
to the
    Internet, point your browser at http://www.perl.com/, the Perl Home
Page.

    C:\Documents and Settings\emoyle>
```

So now we have everything we need to compile OpenSSL; all of the instructions to configure and build for Windows are in the INSTALL.W32 file included with OpenSSL, but we'll just walk through it quickly anyhow for completeness. To build the library, there are just a few configuration scripts we have to run before we compile it; first, we need to configure the build process to use Visual Studio by running `perl Configure VS-WIN32` as follows:

```
    C:\Documents and Settings\emoyle\Desktop\openssl-0.9.7g>perl
Configure VC-WIN32
```

Then, we need to configure the library to use the appropriate assembler by running the appropriate script in the OpenSSL "ms" directory; for MASM, we would run the `do_masm` script like so:

```
    C:\Documents and Settings\emoyle\Desktop\openssl-0.9.7g>ms\do_masm
    Generating x86 for MASM assembler
    Bignum
    DES
```

```
"crypt(3)"
Blowfish
CAST5
RC4
MD5
SHA1
RIPEMD160
RC5\32
[…]
```

Now that we've done all this, we'll use `nmake -f` to build the appropriate version of the library. We have the option of either building statically linkable libraries (.lib) or dynamically linked libraries (.dll) from here. For the most part, we'll want to use the .dll build, but there might be circumstances where we'll prefer a static .lib instead. Either way, use `nmake -f <file>`, where `<file>` is either `nt.mak` for static libs or `ntdll.mak` for dynamic libs. Of course, don't forget that we need to set up our variables for command-line compilation using our tool of choice if we didn't elect the setup file to do this for us at install time; this .bat file just ensures that the libraries, headers, and executables can be found from the command line:

```
C:\Documents and Settings\emoyle\Desktop\openssl-0.9.7g>vcvars32.bat
Setting environment for using Microsoft Visual C++ tools.
```

and then we can build:

```
    C:\Documents and Settings\emoyle\Desktop\openssl-0.9.7g>nmake
-f ms\ntdll.mak
    Microsoft (R) Program Maintenance Utility   Version 6.00.8168.0
    Copyright (C) Microsoft Corp 1988-1998. All rights reserved.
    Building OpenSSL
            copy nul+ .\crypto\opensslconf.h inc32\openssl\opensslconf.h
    nul
    .\crypto\opensslconf.h
            1 file(s) copied.
            copy nul+ .\crypto\ebcdic.h inc32\openssl\ebcdic.h
    nul
    .\crypto\ebcdic.h
            1 file(s) copied.
            copy nul+ .\crypto\symhacks.h inc32\openssl\symhacks.h
    nul
    […]
```

As a result of this process, we'll have the library and tools built and ready to run.

7.2.3 Finding Include Files, Libraries, and Shared Objects

Of course, building the library is only half the story. Now that we have the tool built, we'll need to configure our development environment to find the appropriate artifacts if we're going to be working in C or C++. The paths to doing this are different depending on our compiler, linker, and IDE (if any). Obviously, we can't go through detailed instructions on how to configure every possible development environment, but we can pick the most common set of tools and give instructions for them. Specifically, we'll provide instructions for Microsoft Visual C++ on the Windows platform and gcc/g++ in the Unix world.

7.2.3.1 Windows: Visual C++ 6.0

In Visual C++, there are two ways to include additional include (header) files. We can adjust the environment on a global basis so all projects will be able to by default find the include files, or we can selectively update each project on a project-by-project basis. Oftentimes, it is desirable to update each project individually to lead to more portable projects and to reduce confusion with other developers (so their global environment is the same or similar to our global environment), so this is the approach we'll use. To do this:

1. Update the project's "Additional Include Files" to reference the OpenSSL include directory ("inc32"). This configuration is set under the "C++" pane of the "Project->Settings" dialog box under the category "Preprocessor." The value to update with the full path of the include directory is the edit box labeled, "Additional include directories" (see Figure 7.1).

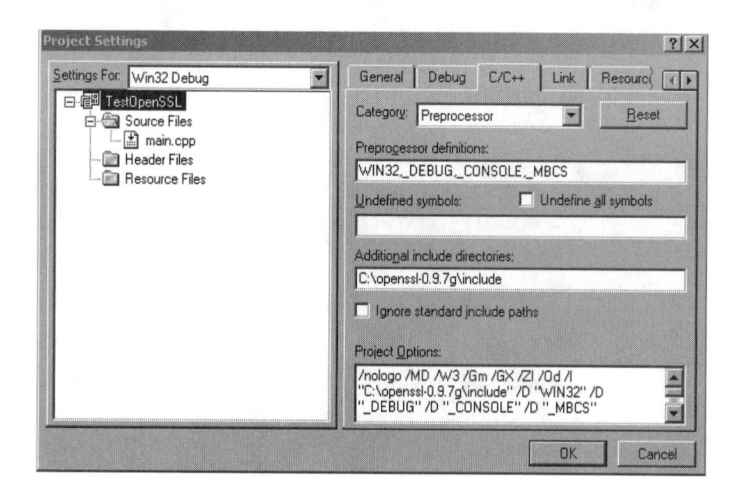

FIGURE 7.1 Update Include directories.

2. Update the project's library includes to reference the OpenSSL static libraries (either stubs or static libs depending on our build configuration) located in the output directory from the build process. This setting is configurable under the "Link" pane of the "Project->Settings" dialog under the category "Input." The value to update with names of the libraries (ssleay32.lib and libeay32.lib) is the edit box labeled, "Object/Library Modules" (see Figure 7.2).

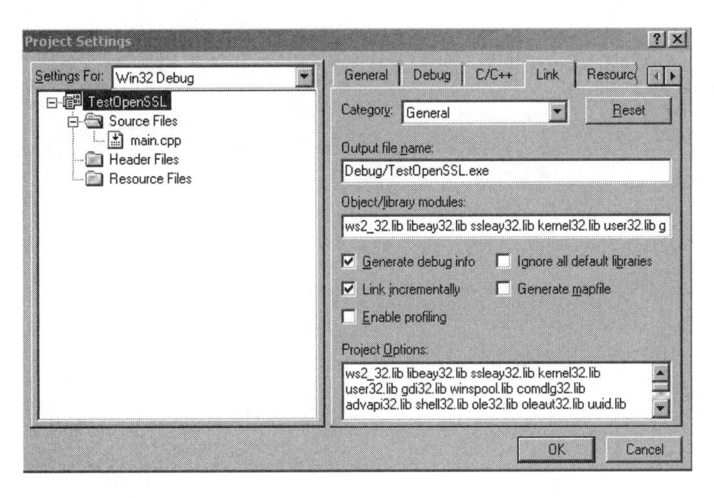

FIGURE 7.2 Add library to linkage.

3. Update the project's "Additional Library Path" to reference the location of the OpenSSL static libraries (either stubs or static libs depending on our build configuration) located in the output directory from the build process. This setting is configurable under the "Link" pane of the "Project->Settings" dialog under the category "Input." The value to update with the full path of the library directory is the edit box labeled, "Additional Library Path" (see Figure 7.3).
4. Update the project's global settings to include the additional OpenSSL .dlls if we've elected to build the dynamically loaded library version of the OpenSSL project. This setting is most easily configured on a global basis through the "Directories" pane of the "Tools->Options" dialog box.
5. Lastly, ensure that our project uses the multithreaded DLL version of the runtime library; this setting can be found under the heading "Code Generation" in the "C/C++" pane of the "Project->Settings" dialog box. This is a very important step, as software we write may crash (access violation) if we do not do so (see Figure 7.4).

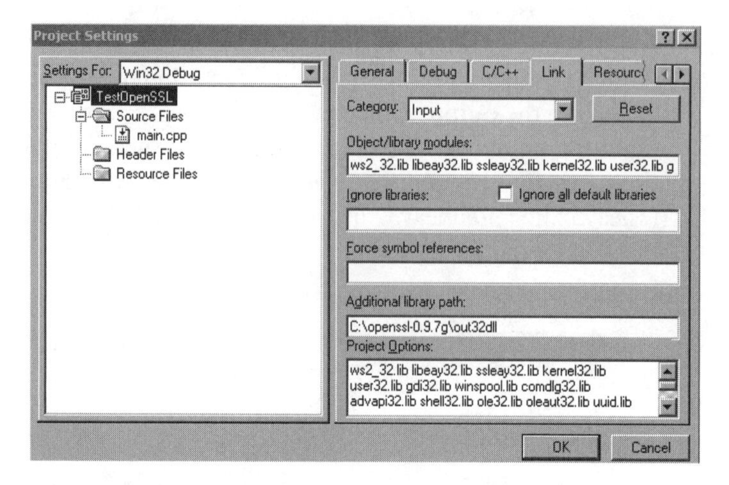

FIGURE 7.3 Update linker path.

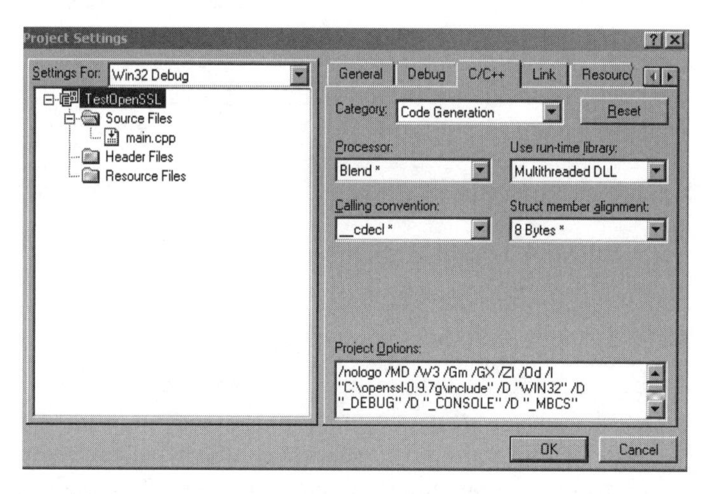

FIGURE 7.4 Set runtime threading.

Once we have done these things, we should be ready to build applications that make use of OpenSSL.

7.2.3.2 Windows: Visual C++ 2005

Since more recent versions of C++ have a fully redesigned UI, we've opted to include a more recent version of the tool for a more complete set of instructions. The steps are the same, but the mechanics of changing the settings are different. Again, we can change the settings for all projects, or just for the project we're currently working on. We'll go ahead and just change the project we're working on:

1. In the Project Properties dialog box, under the "Configuration Properties" leaf item in the left-hand tree control, add the OpenSSL include directory ("inc32") to the "Additional Include Directories" item under the "General" section of the "C++" item (see Figure 7.5).

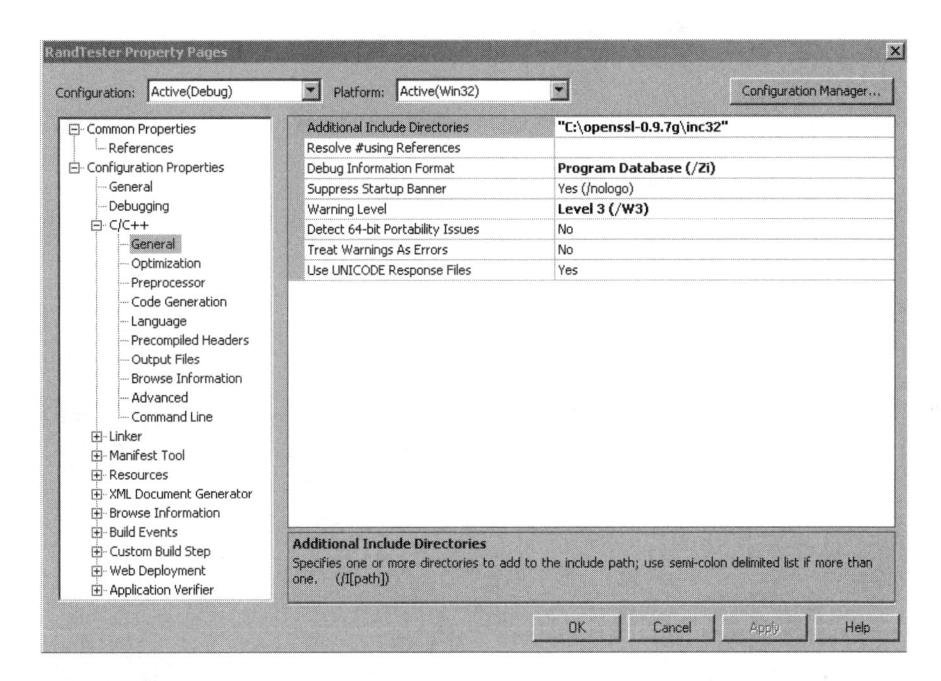

FIGURE 7.5 Update Include directories.

2. In the Project Properties dialog box, under the "Configuration Properties" leaf item in the left-hand tree control, add the OpenSSL libraries (either the stubs or the static libraries) to the "Additional Dependencies" item under the "Input" section of the "Linker" item (see Figure 7.6).
3. In the Project Properties dialog box, under the "Configuration Properties" leaf item in the left-hand tree control, add the OpenSSL "output" directory (containing the static libs) to the "Additional Library Directories" item under the "General" section of the "Linker" item (see Figure 7.7).
4. Update the project's global settings to include the additional OpenSSL .dlls if we've elected to build the dynamically loaded library version of the OpenSSL project. This setting is most easily configured on a global basis through the "VC++ Directories" pane of the "Tools->Options" dialog box under the heading "Projects and Solutions" (see Figure 7.8).

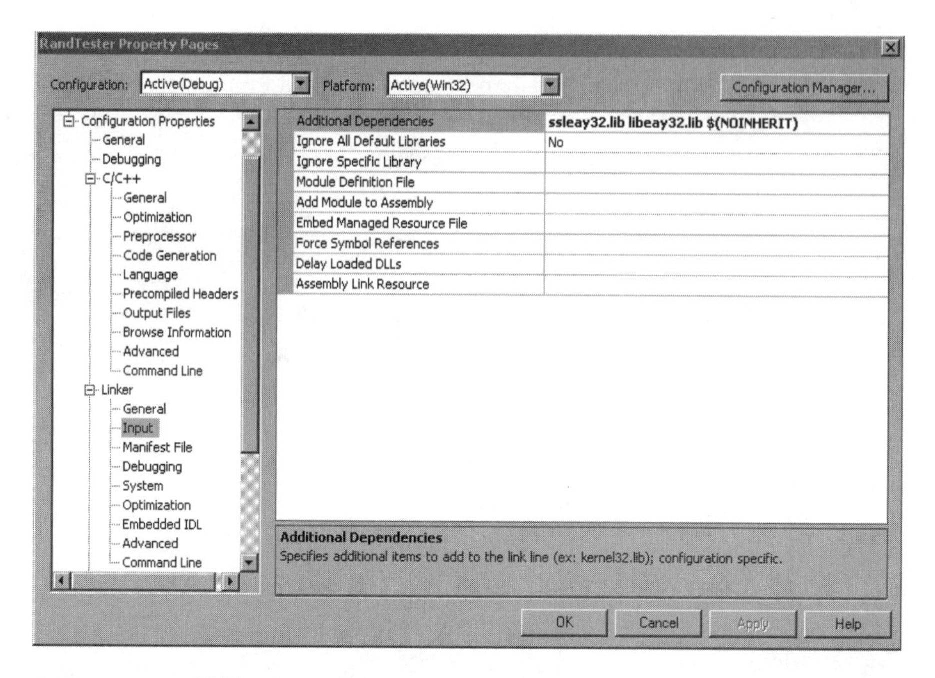

FIGURE 7.6 Add libraries to linkage.

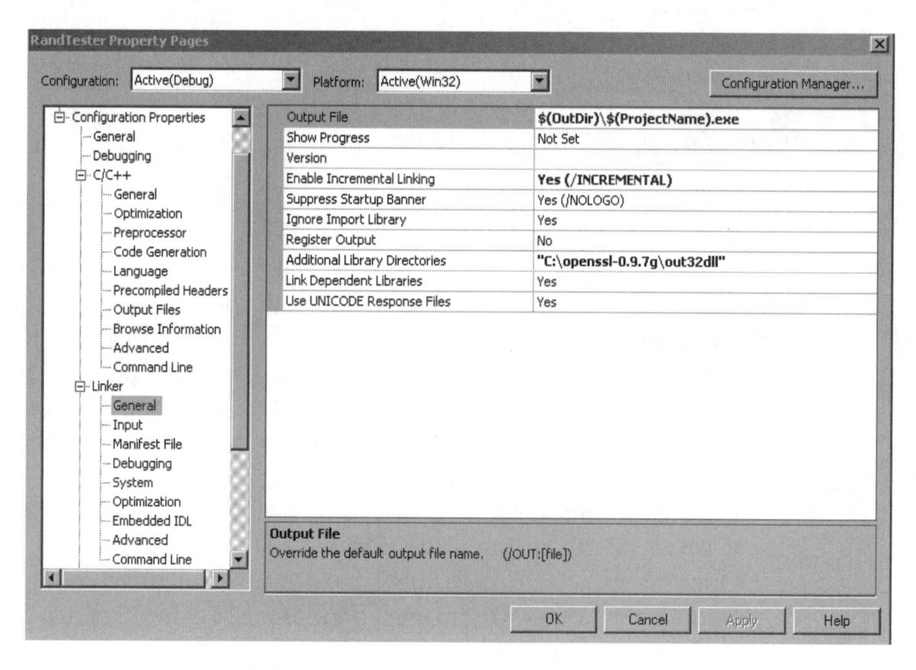

FIGURE 7.7 Update linker path.

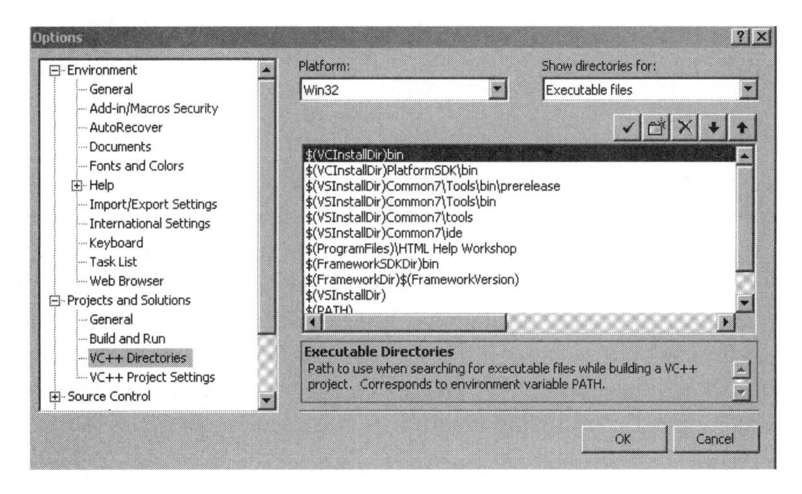

FIGURE 7.8 Add binary image to path.

5. Lastly, ensure that our project uses the multithreaded DLL version of the runtime library; this setting can be found under the heading “Code Generation” leaf of the “C/C++” node in the “Project->Properties” dialog box. This is a very important step, as software we write may crash (access violation) if we do not do so (see Figure 7.9).

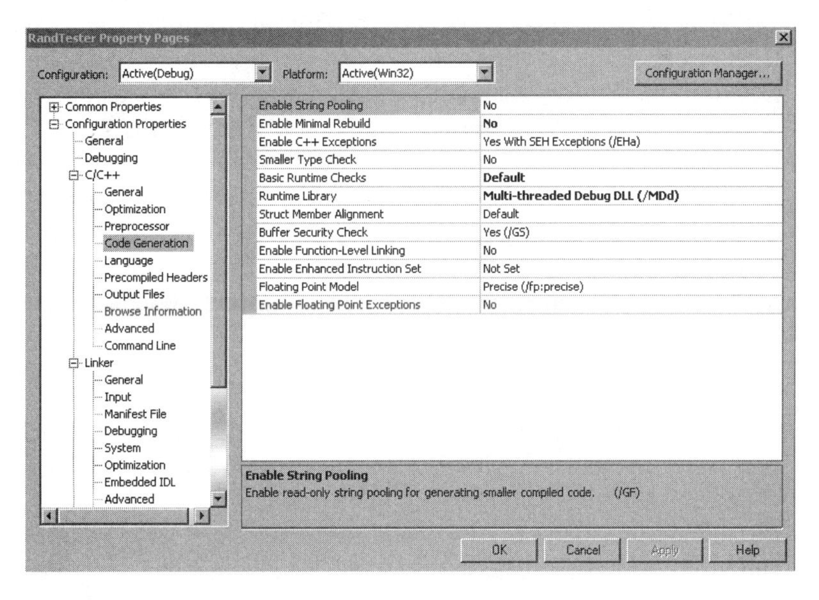

FIGURE 7.9 Update runtime threading.

Once we have done these things, we should be ready to build applications that make use of OpenSSL.

7.2.3.3 Unix/Linux: gcc/g++

If we're using the ubiquitous gcc utility for compilation on a Unix platform, we'll need to update the compiler arguments to include the OpenSSL include directory, update the linker to find the shared objects, and configure our user environment so we can find the shared objects at application runtime. However, before we do any of this, we'll need to decide if we want to install the OpenSSL library to the system, or if we'd rather just have the shared objects, libs, and includes available to certain users. If we desire to "deploy" OpenSSL to our Unix machine, we'll just run the `make install` command as root in a manner similar to the following:

```
[emoyle@elysium:~/openssl-0.9.7g]$ su
Password:
# /usr/ccs/bin/make install
```

Of course, this requires that we have root access to the box; if we don't, we don't need to deploy the binaries to make use of the library on the system or to run the command-line applications. By default, `make install` will install the library to /usr/local/ssl/, and it will create a number of subdirectories within it. The binaries including applications will be placed in /usr/local/ssl/bin, the includes will be placed in /usr/local/ssl/include, and the shared objects will be placed in /usr/local/ssl/lib. We'll want to remember those locations for our compiler and linker settings later. If we do not wish to install the library, we'll just need to put the files we need (application, include, shared objects) somewhere our application has access to and remember that location for our compiler and linker settings.

Specifying the location for the files to the compiler is easy; if we intend to use the C/C++ API, first we'll want to make sure the compiler can find the include files that contain the OpenSSL includes. This will be done using the `-I` directive to `gcc/g++` in combination with the `-c` (compile) directive. We'll want to provide the full path to the include directories when compiling, as demonstrated:

```
[emoyle@elysium:~]$ g++ -I~/openssl-0.9.7g/include/ -c main.cpp
```

The preceding assumes we didn't deploy OpenSSL to the machine using `make install`. If we did, we'll just substitute the /usr/local/ssl/include directory instead of the reference to the include files in our home directory. During the linking process, we'll also want to update our linker arguments to specify the location of the "crypto" and "ssl" library files (usually libcrypto.a and libssl.a) by using the `-l` (library) and `-L` (library path) linker directives similar to the following:

```
[emoyle@elysium:~]$ g++ -omain main.o -lcrypto -lssl \
--> -L/export/home/emoyle/openssl-0.9.7g/
```

Again, if we deployed the files to the machine, we'll just specify /usr/local/ssl/lib instead of the entry in our home directory.

Having done this, we are now ready to build applications that use OpenSSL on the Unix platform. To run them, however, we'll need to perform one last step: update our environment so the shared objects can be found at runtime. If we've installed the files using `make install`, we'll just add /usr/local/ssl/bin and /usr/local/ssl/lib to the path and that should be all we need to do. If we have not done this, we'll need to add the contents of the lib and bin directories to a locality that can be located from the path or adjust the path so it can find those directories.

7.3 USING THE LIBRARY

There are two different ways to access the OpenSSL functionality: we can write software that uses the shared objects, .dlls, or static libraries (depending on our platform and how we've built the library), or we can access the command-line interface. Using the non-command-line libraries requires that we use a language that can load and execute a shared object (e.g., Perl, Python, etc.), load and run routines within dynamic link libraries (e.g., Visual Basic, C#, and so on), directly use any of the preceding (e.g., C or C++), or a language like Java that can use a "bridging" mechanism (e.g., JNI) to make use of the routines. However, to make use of the command-line interface, we'll only need to be able to execute the "openssl" process using (for example) the Windows "cmd.exe", `CreateProcess()` Platform SDK function, a shell environment (bash, ksh, sh, zsh, csh, etc.), or a routine such as `execl()` in C.

7.3.1 About the Command-Line Interface

One of the great things about OpenSSL is that we don't always have to use the shared objects to perform a great deal of cryptographic functionality; as stated, a very robust command-line interface comes with it. Like all of the other specific-usage library chapters, this chapter is broken down by task. We'll go through the more common usage of the library (in particular, the cryptographic primitives), and in keeping with laying out the "easiest to use first" methodology, we'll be covering the command-line mechanisms for doing the task first. To access the command-line interface, all we need to do is ensure that we can find and load the "openssl" binary. If we've deployed OpenSSL on Unix using `make install`, the library will be by default, located in /usr/local/ssl/bin and will be called "openssl." We can run it with the `version` argument to ensure it is installed and operational:

```
[emoyle@elysium:~]$ /usr/local/ssl/bin/openssl version
OpenSSL 0.9.7g 11 Apr 2005
[emoyle@elysium:~]$
```

Just typing the command `openssl` brings us to an `OpenSSL>` prompt, from which we can obtain valid commands by typing "?" (or any other invalid command). From this prompt, we can perform any of the listed commands; alternatively, we can pass commands directly on the command line to have them executed by the `openssl` application. According to the help/usage information, the usage for the command-line interface is divided into three parts: "Standards Commands," "Message Digest Commands," and "Cipher Commands." Obviously, we won't be covering how to use all this functionality here, but the help information provided by the developers is very friendly and easy to follow, so usage information is never far away. Usage surrounding other commands that we're not going to cover in this chapter is simply a matter of referring to the corresponding man pages or to the online documentation at the project homepage at *www.openssl.org*.

7.3.2 About the API

The API consists of a crypto library, including all representations of most of the primitives we've covered so far, "support" routines that (for example) allow us to convert between commonly used formatting types, and functionality that allows us to deal with higher level protocols such as SSL/TLS. The functionality is easily accessible to most developers with a working knowledge of C, and the structures/functions are seldom complicated or difficult to intuit how to use.

7.3.2.1 Using the Crypto API

Using the cryptographic primitives supplied with the OpenSSL library is straightforward, but a little different from some of the other libraries we'll cover—in particular, because of the open nature of the library. OpenSSL provides high-level abstractions that we can use to perform most tasks, and provides lower level interfaces to those same routines. In other words, most of the other libraries force us to use a "universal interface" that abstracts the developer away from the underlying cryptography—this "universal interface" is immutable no matter what underlying algorithm is being used in the other libraries. However, OpenSSL does not force us to use this. We can, if we like, use the higher level API provided by the library, or we can interface with the cryptographic primitives concisely depending on the algorithm we are interested in using. For example, if we want to encrypt with AES, we can tailor our application to use it specifically. Of course, we'll need to include the right AES header files to resolve the right AES-specific functions, understand how the AES API works, and call the right AES functions in the right order for our usage. However, in practice, most of the time we'll know ahead of time what algorithm we want, so this isn't an obstacle to usage. Worst case, a little trial and error with the API will help us iron out any kinks and get our application up and running.

7.2.3.2 Using the SSL API

Use of the SSL API is very "abstract"— the SSL API does not use a different interface depending on ciphersuites we select, protocol versions we wish to use, or for any other reason. We do have some options about at what level of abstraction we use to call the SSL API, though. We can either use the SSL "socket" API (mirroring the Berkeley socket API), or the underlying "BIO" IO abstraction directly that has been extant in the library since before it was OpenSSL. Which we choose is mostly a matter of preference; functionality is pretty much the same since they both do the same thing under the hood. Both methods will be covered in this chapter, but in general, we find using the pseudo-Berkeley interface preferable, because it uses calls we're already familiar with if we're accustomed to working with sockets (e.g., `SSL_connect() mirroring connect()`, `SSL_accept() mirroring accept()`, etc.). We won't be going into detail into this portion of the API until after we've discussed the cryptographic primitives available in OpenSSL.

7.2.3.3 OpenSSL Error Reporting

In making calls to the OpenSSL library, error conditions can occur in numerous situations. OpenSSL makes a few functions available to us to obtain extended error information, which we will delve into first before we cover any of the functionality of the library. Developers who are familiar with the Windows Platform SDK will have an immediate familiarity with the OpenSSL error-reporting methodology, since it is strongly akin to the routines and functionality available in that API for handling error conditions. Briefly, OpenSSL maintains an internal stack of error codes that occur within our usage. At any time, we can call routines within the library to determine what went wrong in the form of an error code and/or additional error information (reason code and location in the source that the error transpired). Additionally, OpenSSL allows us to make use of an internal lookup table that maps error codes to human-readable strings; we can use this mapping functionality for debugging purposes to determine what occurred, where, and why. Although the error API is quite extensive, more often than not, we need only call a few functions within it for the majority of our usage. These functions are summarized as follows:

`ERR_get_error()`: This function returns an error code indicating the most recent error entry (the error on the top of the stack).

`SSL_load_error_strings()`: Load all the error strings, including those used in the cryptographic API and those used in the SSL API. Note that we can selectively load only the crypto error strings if we so desire using `ERR_load_crypto_strings()` instead.

ERR_free_strings(): Release the error strings previously loaded.

ERR_print_errors_fp(FILE*): Print all errors contained in the error stack to the file specified in the argument. Note that a useful application of this function is to use stderr as the file pointer and thus cause the library to write the errors in the typical manner. Note, however, that this can be a log file, stdout, or any other file pointer we desire.

We'll see these routines used repeatedly throughout this section and throughout the examples on the companion CD-ROM.

7.4 SYMMETRIC CRYPTOGRAPHY USING OPENSSL

Symmetric cryptography is readily accomplished no matter if we are using the command-line interface or we are calling into the crypto library directly.

7.4.1 Symmetric Cryptography Using the Command Line

The "openssl" provides a full-featured interface to the symmetric cryptographic routines. The primary mechanism for using symmetric ciphers in this way is to use the `openssl enc` command, which does both encryption and decryption. According to the openssl documentation[1], the following is the syntax for using the `openssl` command-line utility encryption capability:

```
openssl enc <options> <arguments>
```

where `<options>` is one of:

```
-in <file>       input file
-out <file>      output file
-pass <arg>      pass phrase source
-e               encrypt
-d               decrypt
-a/-base64       base64 encode/decode, depending on encryption flag
-k               key is the next argument
-kfile           key is the first line of the file argument
-K/-iv           key/iv in hex is the next argument
-[pP]            print the iv/key (then exit if -P)
-bufsize <n>     buffer size
-engine e        use engine e, possibly a hardware device.
```

In supplying arguments to the utility, we will need to specify a few things governing the operation of the program; the following are the most commonly used usage arguments:

- We will need to specify either "encrypt" or "decrypt" mode; -e is the argument specifying encryption, -d is the argument specifying decryption. Encryption is the default if no argument is specified.
- We have the option of either specifying a key and IV (if needed) using –K (key in hex), -k (raw key), -iv (IV in hex), or –kfile (read the key from a file). Alternatively, we can allow the routine to generate a key and IV for us from a supplied passphrase using the `–pass` argument. We can supply the passphrase to the openssl utility from a number of sources: from the command line using "–pass:<password>", from a file using "-pass file:<file>", from stdin (the default), or from an environment variable using "-pass env:<var>". The default is to read a passphrase in from the user.
- We have the option of specifying input and output files. By default, "openssl enc" will read data from stdin and write data to stdout (like just about any other Unix application). Either or both defaults can be overridden using "–in <file>"and "–out <file>" to specify input and output files, respectively.
- We will need to specify a symmetric algorithm to use; this value is specified directly on the command line (e.g., "-rc4"). The choices are too numerous to list, but providing an invalid argument to "openssl enc" (such as "?") will cause them to be listed under the heading "Cipher Types:" The ones we'll probably want to use for most instances are:

  –aes-128-cbc: 128-bit AES in CBC mode

  –des-ede3-cbc: Triple-DES in ede (encrypt, decrypt, encrypt) CBC mode

We can use this extremely useful, flexible, and easy functionality for a variety of purposes. We can encrypt or decrypt files, use the encryption functionality to protect backups, use it to protect data we send over the network, or for just about any purpose we can think up. Since we can "chain" commands together through pipes and/or redirection, we can come up with a nearly infinite number of ways to use this functionality. In fact, since we can chain multiple `openssl` commands together, we can use this functionality in combination with other features offered by the tool to extend the flexibility. As an example of the power of the tool, the following quick examples demonstrate some of the flexibility.

7.4.1.1 Encrypting Files Example

Obviously, the most common scenario for this command is the encryption of files. The following example demonstrates encrypting a file stored in a user's home directory that he wishes to prevent others from reading; we've picked a large file that was handy in the user home directory, which just happens to be the OpenSSL distribution.

```
[emoyle@elysium:~]$ openssl enc -e -aes-128-cbc \
--> -in openssl-0.9.7g.tar.gz > openssl-0.9.7g.tar.gz.enc
enter aes-128-cbc encryption password:
Verifying - enter aes-128-cbc encryption password:
[emoyle@elysium:~]$
```

Note that the password does not echo, but it must be the same password provided in both prompts and during the decryption process. To decrypt the file, we would perform the operation in reverse:

```
[emoyle@elysium:~]$ openssl enc -d -aes-128-cbc \
--> -in openssl-0.9.7g.tar.gz.enc > openssl-0.9.7g.tar.gz.2
enter aes-128-cbc decryption password:
[emoyle@elysium:~]$
```

We can ensure that the files are identical by using the ubiquitous "diff" utility:

```
    [emoyle@elysium:~]$ diff openssl-0.9.7g.tar.gz openssl-
0.9.7g.tar.gz.2
    [emoyle@elysium:~]$
```

7.4.1.2 Backup Example

Of course, since we can use OpenSSL's command-line utility in combination with other commands such as those used for backup, compression, or other tasks, we have a convenient mechanism for ensuring that backup tapes are encrypted prior to storage and decrypted when they are read back in. Using this functionality is as easy as the previous file encryption example. For example, assuming we have a backup tape ready and waiting to receive our data (assuming the tape is at /dev/rmt/0n), we could insert the encryption command into our backup process like so:

```
    [emoyle@elysium:~]$ tar cvf - openssl-0.9.7g | gzip | openssl enc
-e \
    --> -aes-128-cbc -pass file:.backup_password | tar cf /dev/rmt/0n -
    a openssl-0.9.7g/ OK
    a openssl-0.9.7g/apps/ OK
    a openssl-0.9.7g/apps/app_rand.c 8K
    a openssl-0.9.7g/apps/apps.c 47K
    [...]
```

and of course, restoring it from backup would be the reverse of that operation:

```
[emoyle@elysium:~]$ tar xf -O /dev/rmt/0n | openssl enc -d \
--> -aes-128-cbc -pass file:.backup_password | gzip –dc | \
tar xf –
```

Note that this assumes that our version of tar accepts the –O (output to stdout) option, which might not be the case on all versions of the command (such as those provided by default on all versions of Solaris). If we are using a version of tar that does not do this, we'll need an intermediate step to extract the restore file first, decrypt it, and then extract it.

Obviously, the command-line approach is extremely flexible. In fact, given the number of challenges this tool helps alleviate, it is surprising that only this library provides a utility such as this one.

7.4.2 Symmetric Cryptography Using the Crypto API

Despite the flexibility of the command-line utility, however, encryption via this mechanism will not always fit our application's needs. The performance and overhead of executing a child process, the lack of control over child processes, or any number of other reasons might preclude our application from availing itself of this functionality directly. If this is the case, we'll need to use the C API (or call the C API via the dll/shared object). There are a few ways we can use the OpenSSL API to encrypt data; OpenSSL provides a high-level cryptographic interface documented in the "evp" (stands for "envelope") section of the OpenSSL user documentation. We'll cover the EVP interface, since it is a useful way to interface with the message digest functions, the signature functions, and the symmetric encryption functions. However, one of the nice things about OpenSSL is that we can interact with the library at a number of abstraction levels. We can use the EVP API if we like, or we can interact directly with the cryptographic functions themselves. Since in some cases, the lower level APIs are easier to use than the EVP API, we'll cover both ways of doing the same thing within this section.

7.4.2.1 Using the EVP API

The EVP API is the primary OpenSSL programmatic mechanism for abstract symmetric encryption functionality. The API allows us to encrypt via a single interface no matter what the algorithm in use might be, and attempts to abstract the developer away from algorithm-specific nuances such as key lengths, block sizes, implementations, and so on. Using the EVP interface for encryption consists of a few overall steps, which "parallel" numerous other encryption APIs we'll cover in this book. From the highest of levels, the steps to use the API are:

1. **High-level initialization**: Initialization of the library's internal state will take place at this time.
2. **Cipher initialization**: Initialization of the particular cipher "instance" we will be using will take place at this time. Also in addition, the key and IV will be bound to the cipher "instance" our application will be working with.

3. **Iterative cipher update:** We will pass our data through the cipher a buffer at a time. We will likely want to break larger data blocks or IO-bound artifacts (such as files, network activity, etc.) into smaller "chunks," which we will encrypt a piece at a time.
4. **Cipher finalization:** We will need to instruct the cipher that we are done using it and that the last "chunk" of data has been reached. This allows the underlying implementation to provide padding to us if necessary and to do any cipher-specific cleanup that may be required.
5. **High-level cleanup:** At this time, any constructs not bound to a particular cipher will be freed/released.

These high-level steps are analogous to what we will see in almost every library, so it bears getting familiar with them now. Note that the same API applies if we are using a stream cipher or a block cipher. Mapping the high-level steps to actual functions present in the EVP API, we come up with the following specific steps (and function calls) we will need to use in our applications. Note that these steps are provided here as an overview; a more complete "drill-down" on usage and arguments will immediately follow.

1. **High-level initialization steps:** Declare a variable of type `EVP_CIPHER_CTX` to use for storing the "cipher context" or the internal resources and variables associated with a particular cipher operation. Call `EVP_CIPHER_CTX_init()`to initialize the "EVP context."
2. **Cipher initialization steps:** Call `EVP_CipherInit_ex()` to bind the created context to the key we supply, the IV we supply, and the algorithm we specify; additionally, this call takes a flag specifying an encryption operation or a decryption operation. We can also optionally use `EVP_EncryptInit_ex()` and `EVP_DecryptInit_ex()` to segregate encryption operations from decryption operations. These calls are used in an identical manner to `EVP_CipherInit_ex()` with the exception that they do not require an encryption/decryption flag to indicate in which manner the algorithm should operate.
3. **Iterative cipher update steps:** Iteratively call `EVP_CipherUpdate()` one or more times, passing in the plaintext/ciphertext buffer that is to be encrypted/decrypted in piecemeal fashion. Optionally, we can use `EVP_EncryptUpdate()` and `EVP_DecryptUpdate()` to segregate encryption and decryption operations.
4. **Cipher finalization steps:** Call `EVP_CipherFinal_ex()` to "finalize" the encryption operation, performing any padding that may need to transpire at this time. Again, we can be more specific in usage by using as an alternative `EVP_EncryptFinal_ex()` and `EVP_DecryptFinal_ex()` for encryption and decryption operations, respectively.

5. **High-level cleanup steps:** Clean up the resources and state used by the library internally by calling `EVP_CIPHER_CTX_cleanup()`.

Obviously, there are quite a few new data types here and a few functions we'll need to become familiar with before we can use the routines; following is a list of the functions we'll call and their required arguments:

`EVP_CIPHER_CTX_init()`: This function will prepare a cipher "context" for use by the library. The cipher context is used internal to the library to keep track of all the state information associated with a current algorithm's operation. This context is the primary "handle" we will pass to encryption (or decryption) operations to differentiate different potentially simultaneous cipher operations. According to evp.h, this function has the following signature:

```
void EVP_CIPHER_CTX_init(EVP_CIPHER_CTX *a);
```

There is only one parameter, which is the context that will be initialized. The function does not differentiate success versus failure, as the return from this function is void.

`EVP_CipherInit_ex()`: This function will "bind" the right key, IV, algorithm, algorithm implementation, and manner of algorithm operation (encryption or decryption). According to evp.h, this routine has the following signature:

```
int    EVP_CipherInit_ex(EVP_CIPHER_CTX *ctx,
 const EVP_CIPHER *cipher,
             ENGINE *impl,
          const unsigned char *key,
 const unsigned char *iv,
          int enc);
```

The integer return value is used to indicate failure (zero) or success (nonzero). The parameters to the function are described as follows:

ctx: The context created using the `EVP_CIPHER_CTX_init()` function.

cipher: An EVP_CIPHER object corresponding to the cipher we wish to use. In other words, this parameter governs which cipher will be used. We will need to locate and call the correct cipher creation function to supply an appropriate value to this parameter. There's a full list of these functions in evp.h and a (slightly outdated) list in the EVP user documentation on the OpenSSL Web site (and included in the OpenSSL manual pages); a full listing of all the supported algorithms would be much too voluminous to list in this chapter. For our purposes, we will typically use either AES in CBC mode (`EVP_aes_128_cbc()`) or Triple-DES in CBC mode (`EVP_des_ede_cbc()`).

ipml: The implementation of the algorithm to use; unless we are using cryptographic accelerator hardware, we'll usually just leave this parameter as NULL.

key: The key we will use for the encryption or decryption. Note that this value should be of appropriate size for the algorithm we've selected.

iv: The initialization vector that will be used. Note that this value should be of the appropriate size for the algorithm being used.

enc: The encryption/decryption flag. This value should be set to 1 for encryption or 0 for decryption.

`EVP_CipherUpdate()`: This function passes data into the cipher for encryption. We will want to call this in an iterative manner, calling it at least one time with the data we wish to encrypt. The padding will not be applied by calling this function, and the function does not guarantee that all the input data will be encrypted. According to evp.h, this routine has the following signature:

```
int     EVP_CipherUpdate(EVP_CIPHER_CTX *ctx, unsigned char *out,
        int *outl, const unsigned char *in, int inl);
```

The integer return value is used to indicate failure (zero) or success (nonzero). The parameters to the function are described as follows:

ctx: The context created using the `EVP_CIPHER_CTX_init()` function.

out: The output buffer that will be used to store the ciphertext (in the case of encryption) or the plaintext (in the case of decryption).

outl: A pointer to an integer value that will be updated by the function to contain the length of the resultant output data.

in: The input buffer that will be operated on by the cipher operation. This will be the plaintext (in the case of encryption) or the ciphertext (in the case of decryption).

inl: The length of the input data in bytes.

`EVP_CipherFinal_ex()`: This function passes terminating data into the cipher for encryption. Padding will be applied at this time. According to evp.h, this routine has the following signature:

```
int     EVP_CipherFinal_ex(EVP_CIPHER_CTX *ctx, unsigned char *outm,
int *outl);
```

The integer return value is used to indicate failure (zero) or success (nonzero). The parameters to the function are described as follows:

ctx: The context created using the `EVP_CIPHER_CTX_init()` function

outm: An output buffer that will hold the finalized end of the ciphertext buffer (including any required padding).

outl: A pointer to an integer that will be updated by the function to contain the length of the valid ciphertext data contained in outm.

`EVP_CIPHER_CTX_cleanup()`: Release the cipher context structure allocated by the `EVP_CIPHER_CTX_init()` function. According to evp.h, this routine has the following signature:

```
int EVP_CIPHER_CTX_cleanup(EVP_CIPHER_CTX *a);
```

There is only one parameter, which is the context that will be released. The integer return value is used to indicate failure (zero) or success (nonzero).

Sample: Simple EVP Symmetric Cryptography

Having laid out the nuances of the EVP symmetric crypto API, let's go ahead and use it to encrypt some data. We'll just encrypt and decrypt some test data here to show how the functions would be used in practice. We'll use this approach throughout this book. First, we'll show some samples of the libraries in use in a limited-use sample case, and then we'll apply them in a larger context to see how they would fit into a typical application. Additionally, a number of samples included on the companion CD-ROM located in the /Examples/Chapter 7/EVP/ folder provide more usage examples.

ON THE CD

For now, let's just encrypt some sample data using the simplest and most forthright library functionality:

```
EVP_CIPHER_CTX ctx;
EVP_CIPHER_CTX_init(&ctx);

unsigned char theKeyBytes[16]; //16 bytes = 128 bit key
GetRandomKeyBytes(theKeyBytes, sizeof(theKeyBytes));

unsigned char IV[128/8]; //128 bit block
GetIV(IV);
int result = EVP_CipherInit_ex(&ctx, //context
    EVP_aes_128_cbc(),  //use AES
    NULL, //use default implementation
    theKeyBytes, //key
```

```
        IV, //IV
        1); //encrypt mode
    if(!result) {
        bomb_out();
    }

    char * plaintext = "This is the plaintext.";
    int outputLength = 0;
    int totalLength = 0;
    //buffer of sufficient size to hold the output
    unsigned char cipherText[128];
    result = EVP_CipherUpdate(&ctx, //context
                              cipherText,
                              &outputLength,
                              (unsigned char*)plaintext,
                              strlen(plaintext)+1);
    if(!result) {
        bomb_out();
    }
    totalLength += outputLength;
    result = EVP_CipherFinal_ex(&ctx,
                              cipherText+totalLength,
                              &outputLength);
    totalLength += outputLength;
    if(!result) {
        bomb_out();
    }
    EVP_CIPHER_CTX_cleanup(&ctx);
```

The decryption process for this is the same, except we would switch the "1" as the last parameter to the initialization function (signaling encrypt mode) to a zero (0) signaling decrypt mode.

7.4.2.2 AES without the EVP API

Sometimes, we'll want to use and access the algorithm-specific API for the algorithms we are using. The documentation mentions that we should preferably use the EVP API since the underlying cryptography is opaque by doing so—this is true and useful guidance. However, we might decide that we want to directly wrap the underlying cryptography to minimize the interface points with OpenSSL, to develop specialized usage, or to author a single highly efficient class for a given algorithm. For example, we might decide that we only want to support AES for our application, and we might find that the usage of the AES low-level interface requires a great deal less software on our part than using the high-level API. By tailoring our usage directly to the AES API, we can accomplish with two calls to the AES API what would take us five or more calls using the EVP API. The ability to interface with the library at this lower level is one of the advantages of using OpenSSL, so it is useful to discuss how to avail ourselves of the capability. For our purposes, we'll concentrate on encryption using AES in this way. Other algorithms might be appropriate for our application, but since dozens are provided in OpenSSL, we're choosing the one that developers will most likely want to use for new applications.

To use AES, first we'll need to include the AES header file so our application can resolve the appropriate AES function declarations. The AES functions are defined in aes.h. OpenSSL has a convention of using an openssl subdirectory under the include directory, so we'll want to put in a line like `#include <openssl/aes.h>` in our application. A quick breeze through the header file reveals a straightforward API. The function `AES_set_encrypt_key()` is used (intuitively) to create a key structure that can be used by the library from a buffer we supply, and a corresponding `AES_set_decrypt_key()` is used to set a decryption key. The actual work is done via functions named in the form `AES_<mode>_encrypt()` and `AES_<mode>_decrypt()`, where `<mode>` corresponds to the algorithm mode we wish to employ (e.g., CBC mode).

Preparing the Data for Encryption

There are a few reasons why it is helpful for us to implement our own padding in calling the OpenSSL AES encryption API. The other libraries covered in this book don't require that we do so (and, in fact, we don't strictly have to do this with the OpenSSL library either), but there are a few reasons why we might wish to do so. The primary reason for this is that the API does not provide a convenient mechanism to retrieve the size of output once decryption is completed. For example, if we encrypt a block of data, unless we implement something ourselves, we won't have a way to determine which of the output text is real data and which isn't. It sounds hard to pad ourselves, but it's only a minor inconvenience. In fact, we can usually just add a padding routine once and never worry about it again. Unless we have a particular legacy padding mechanism that we need to be compatible with, it's a good idea to use PKCS #5 padding, which (as a memory refresher) uses the size of the padding as the padding byte (as an 8-bit quantity) and ensures that there is always padding. We'll just add it once and use it over and over again. Since we might want to use the same padding mechanism with other block ciphers, the padding mechanism should be flexible enough to handle multiple block sizes in our initial implementation. A quick and dirty implementation could be something like the following:

```
unsigned long SizeWithPadding(unsigned long dataLen,
                              unsigned int blockSize) {
    unsigned long requiredExtra = blockSize - (dataLen % blockSize);
    if(!requiredExtra) {
        requiredExtra = blockSize;
    }
    return dataLen + requiredExtra;
}
void CopyWithPadding(unsigned char * newBuffer,
                     const unsigned char * oldBuffer,
                     unsigned long dataLen,
                     unsigned int blockSize) {
    unsigned long requiredExtra = blockSize - (dataLen % blockSize);
    if(!requiredExtra) {
        requiredExtra = blockSize;
    }
    memcpy(newBuffer, oldBuffer, dataLen);
    memset(newBuffer+dataLen, requiredExtra, requiredExtra);
}
int DataNoPadding(unsigned char * buffer, unsigned int len) {
    char c = buffer[len-1];
    int paddingSize = (int)c;
    return len - paddingSize;
}
```

Perfection is not an issue here; we're mostly just interested in passing even block-size buffers to the library and being able to tell which pieces of the last block are data and which aren't after the call to the decryption routine.

Overview of the AES API

Using a padding mechanism we implement ourselves in combination with the routines supplied by the library is all that's required to actually encrypt and decrypt the data. Following is a detailed description of the functions we'll need to call, in order, for encryption to take place:

`AES_set_encrypt_key()`: For the library to complete the encryption process, it will need to render the keys we supply it as byte buffers (e.g., contiguous blocks of unsigned chars) into structures that it uses internally (`aes_key_st`). The following is the function signature as specified in aes.h:

```
int AES_set_encrypt_key(const unsigned char *userKey, const int bits,
    AES_KEY *key);
```

The function returns 0 (success) or nonzero (failure). The following is a description of the parameters:

userKey: Our key as a contiguous block (buffer) of unsigned chars.

bits: The desired size (in bits) of the key. This should match the size of the buffer we supply in most circumstances.

key: An output from this function, key is the structure used internally by the library to handle the key.

`AES_cbc_encrypt()`: Assuming for the moment that we intend to encrypt data in CBC (cipher block chaining) mode, we'll want to call this function. This function will perform the actual encryption transformation on the data. The following is the function signature as specified in aes.h:

```
void AES_cbc_encrypt(const unsigned char *in, unsigned char *out,
     const unsigned long length, const AES_KEY *key,
     unsigned char *ivec, const int enc);
```

The function does not have a return value. The following is a description of the parameters:

in: The input buffer to the encryption function.

out: The ciphertext output.

length: The amount of data for encryption (or decryption).

key: The key structure obtained via the `AES_set_encrypt_key` call.

ivec: The initialization vector; note that this will be updated by the call so we should not assume that the parameter we supply is the same before the call as after it.

enc: The "operation" to perform; either AES_ENCRYPT or AES_DECRYPT.

And that's all that there is to it. Decryption is just as easy using the following functions:

`AES_set_decrypt_key()`: Just as we needed to render the encryption key into a format usable by the library, we will need to do the same with the decryption key; this function will render the keys we supply it as byte buffers into structures that the library uses internally. The following is the function signature as specified in aes.h:

```
int AES_set_decrypt_key(const unsigned char *userKey, const int bits,
    AES_KEY *key);
```

The parameters are the same:

userKey: Our key as a contiguous block (buffer) of unsigned chars.

bits: The desired size (in bits) of the key. This should match the size of the buffer we supply in most circumstances.

key: An output from this function, key is the structure used internally by the library to handle the key.

`AES_cbc_encrypt()`: We'll use this same function for decryption as well as decryption. This time, however, the input buffer is the ciphertext and the output buffer is the plaintext. We'll also need to specify AES_DECRYPT as the encryption mode rather than AES_ENCRYPT, which we specified for encryption.

Using the AES API

Now that we know what functions to call and in what order, incorporating them into an application is a snap. Leaving out key and IV generation for now and using the padding functions we authored earlier, the following encrypts and decrypts data using AES via OpenSSL:

```
//populate with the key
unsigned char theKeyBytes[16]; //16 bytes = 128 bit key
GetRandomKeyBytes(theKeyBytes, sizeof(theKeyBytes));
//transform the key into appropriate struct
AES_KEY myKey;
int result = AES_set_encrypt_key(theKeyBytes, //key buffer
    sizeof(theKeyBytes)*8, //key size in bits
    &myKey);
//set up input buffer and pad
char * plaintextNoPadding = "The data.";
char plaintext[64];
int dataLen = SizeWithPadding(strlen(plaintextNoPadding)+1,
    128/8);

//copy to new buffer and pad
CopyWithPadding((unsigned char*)plaintext,
    (unsigned char*)plaintextNoPadding,
    strlen(plaintextNoPadding)+1, 128/8);

//set up output buffer
unsigned char ciphertext[128];
//set up IV
unsigned char IV[128/8]; //128 bit block
GetIV(IV);
```

```
//do the work
AES_cbc_encrypt(
    (unsigned char*)plaintext,
    ciphertext,
    dataLen,
    &myKey,
    IV,
    AES_ENCRYPT);
```

Not a very difficult API to use; obtaining the decrypted data is just as easy:

```
unsigned char reverted[256];
AES_set_decrypt_key(theKeyBytes,
    sizeof(theKeyBytes)*8,
    &myKey);
GetIV(IV);
AES_cbc_encrypt(
    ciphertext,
    reverted,
    dataLen,
    &myKey,
    IV,
    AES_DECRYPT);
int validLen = DataNoPadding(reverted, dataLen);
```

Of course, we'll need to generate a key to use the function in a secure way, but we'll save that discussion until we've had a chance to discuss the random number generation capability.

7.4.2.3 Opaque Ciphers with EVP

One of the useful things about the EVP API is that our usage does not have to change depending on the algorithm we select. Obviously, writing directly to the algorithm-specific APIs as we did with AES requires fewer calls, but we're locked into AES. If we need to incorporate Triple-DES into the application on a moment's notice, we'll have to change all the calls we implemented in this way to use the new algorithm. This is definitely not a desirable situation. However, in using the EVP API, we still had to know what algorithm we're using—both to instantiate the right type of algorithm struct and determine what the required key size should be, what the block size was, and so on. To achieve true opacity with respect to the ciphers we select, we'll need to add support for our applications for a few different functions that allow us to work around this. Specifically, we'll need to use the EVP functions that allow us to retrieve a cipher by name, and functions that allow us to determine the block size and key size for algorithms we select. The following functions are provided to do just that:

OpenSSL_add_all_algorithms(): This function will build the internal state table allowing symmetric ciphers to be queried at runtime. One characteristic we can use to query individual algorithms is the algorithm's name.

EVP_get_cipherbyname(): Return a cipher instance (`struct EVP_CIPHER*`) given a unique cipher name.

EVP_cleanup(): Deallocate the internal resources created in the call to `OpenSSL_add_all_algorithms()`.

We can use these internal functions to query a cipher at runtime to determine how we should use it. We will use these functions in combination with a few macros to get at the data relevant to us. It's useful to point out that they are macros rather than functions, since the compiler messages we will receive from incorrect usage are much different from what we would receive given a function with the same signature (for example, if we don't close a parenthesis, CL.exe will tell us "unexpected end of file during macro expansion" rather than "missing"). The following macros will provide the information we need to determine key and IV lengths at runtime:

EVP_CIPHER_iv_length(): Given a pointer to an `EVP_CIPHER` struct, return the length in bytes of the initialization vector.

EVP_CIPHER_key_length(): Given a pointer to an `EVP_CIPHER` struct, return the length in bytes of the key.

Using these functions in combination with our previous sample yields:

```
OpenSSL_add_all_algorithms();
EVP_CIPHER_CTX ctx;
EVP_CIPHER_CTX_init(&ctx);
const EVP_CIPHER * cipher = EVP_get_cipherbyname("DES-EDE"//);
int ivLen = EVP_CIPHER_iv_length(cipher//);
int keyLen = EVP_CIPHER_key_length(cipher);

//allocate key and IV
unsigned char * theKeyBytes = new unsigned char[keyLen];
GetRandomKeyBytes(theKeyBytes, keyLen);
unsigned char * IV = new unsigned char[ivLen];
GetIV(IV);
int result = EVP_CipherInit_ex(&ctx, //context
```

```
        cipher,  //use whatever was obtained by name
        NULL, //use default implementation
        theKeyBytes, //key
        IV, //IV
        1); //encrypt mode
    if(!result) {
        bomb_out();
    }
    delete theKeyBytes;
    delete IV;
    char * plaintext = "This is the plaintext.";
    int outputLength = 0;
    int totalLength = 0;
    unsigned char cipherText[128];
    result = EVP_CipherUpdate(&ctx, //context
                              cipherText,
                              &outputLength,
                              (unsigned char*)plaintext,
                              strlen(plaintext)+1);
    if(!result) {
        bomb_out();
    }
    totalLength += outputLength;
    result = EVP_CipherFinal_ex(&ctx,
                             cipherText+totalLength,
                             &outputLength);
    totalLength += outputLength;
    if(!result) {
        bomb_out();
    }

    EVP_CIPHER_CTX_cleanup(&ctx);
    EVP_cleanup();
```

7.4.2.4 Generating Random Keys Using the PRNG

The PRNG (Pseudo-Random Number Generator) provided by OpenSSL is important for us to address early on. We'll use it to generate random keys, random initialization vectors, and any other cryptographically secure random data our application needs. We discussed early in this book the need to ensure a good source of randomness for everything from key generation, to certain signing operations. We also stated that sometimes we will be called upon to seed a random number generator ourselves from a good source of relatively unpredictable data on the machine on which our application is running. All these points are true. However, sometimes a library will attempt to seed itself transparently without our intervention; OpenSSL is one of these. Under many circumstances, we will not have to directly seed the internal random number generator in OpenSSL before we use it; like the JCE and the Microsoft cryptographic implementations, OpenSSL attempts to make use of internal routines to gather and maintain a pool of randomness information that we can draw on within our applications. However, unlike the JCE and CAPI/.NET, OpenSSL does *not always* do this—seeding behavior will vary depending on the version of the library we are using, the platform we are using, and so on. Knowing ahead of time exactly when and if the random number generator will seed itself is a difficult exercise without referring to the underlying source code, but luckily for us, recent versions of the library provide a mechanism whereby we can query the state of the PRNG and determine if sufficient randomness exists for us to use it.

The default random number generator implementation supplied with OpenSSL will attempt to seed itself if a functional /dev/random or /dev/urandom exists on the current machine or the native routines on that platform attempt to gather randomness information. If the generator cannot acquire its own seed "automagically," the library provides us with three shortcuts depending on the host operating system on which we run:

Hardware: If we are using any platform that has a hardware security module (i.e., cryptographic hardware), we can use that for randomness information (through the OpenSSL ENGINE API, OpenSSL will even call it for us).

EGD/PRNGD: On Unix platforms that do not have a kernel-level structure for gathering random numbers, the OpenSSL can query[2] one of a few daemons to obtain randomness information (either EGD, the "Entropy Gathering Daemon,"[3] or PRNGD, the "Pseudo-Random Number Generator Daemon"[4]).

On Windows, if we are running in the context of a windowed application, functionality is supplied to allow us to pass window messages to OpenSSL from which OpenSSL will derive entropy. Additionally, if we are running in the context of a heavily used system, another routine is supplied to allow us to pass the contents of the screen to the random number generator. Note that on a server system, both of these functions are problematic, since we will not receive numerous messages and there will be infrequent screen updates.

OpenSSL provides an API that will allow us to query the PRNG so we can determine if additional seeding is required. This is useful to know, since newer versions of OpenSSL will actually *prevent* us from using certain portions of the API if the random number generator is not seeded sufficiently; this is useful functionality not present in earlier versions of the library. It's useful because the library tries to prevent us from shooting ourselves in the foot through improper usage.

The following are some useful functions to determine if the randomness source is seeded and to add to it if necessary. Note that to make use of these, we will have to incorporate a reference to "rand.h" in our source in order to resolve them (e.g., `#include <openssl/rand.h>`):

`RAND_status()`: No arguments. Returns 0 if the random number generator is not sufficiently seeded, and returns 1 otherwise.

`RAND_event()`: Accepts a "window message" (control message) sent to an application that uses windows in its interface. Both window messaging parameters (WParam and LParam) are provided as input. Returns 0 if the random number generator is not sufficiently seeded, and returns 1 otherwise.

`RAND_screen()`: Adds the contents of the screen to the randomness state. The function does not return a value (return is void).

`RAND_add()`: Adds a block of data to the internal randomness state. The function accepts a buffer, the length of that buffer, and a byte estimate of how much data the buffer contains. The function does not return a value (return is void).

Making use of these functions obviously varies on the platform we are using. If we are using a platform that the library can gain enough randomness information from, calling these functions at all is unnecessary.

Using the PRNG

Once we've seeded the random number generator (or it has seeded itself, as the case may be), we can then go ahead and use it to generate random values such as keys and IVs. The primary method for gaining access to the random bytes is through a call to the API function `RAND_bytes()`. According to rand.h, this function has the following signature:

```
int  RAND_bytes(unsigned char *buf,int num);
```

The function returns 1 (success) or 0 (failure) and fills the buffer indicated in the `buf` parameter with the number of bytes specified in the `num` parameter. As such, it is extremely simple to use. Putting this information together with the previous information for updating the random state, we can concoct some simple usage to retrieve a random session key to use with a symmetric cipher, and can retrieve an IV as well in doing so:

```
int canContinue = RAND_status();
while(!canContinue) {
    platform_add_random();
    canContinue = RAND_status();
```

```
}
unsigned char TestAESKey[16];
unsigned char IV[16];
RAND_bytes(TestAESKey, sizeof(TestAESKey));
RAND_bytes(IV, sizeof(IV));
```

7.4.2.5 Password-Based Key Derivation

For the most part, password-based encryption or PBE is performed in an identical manner through the EVP API as symmetric encryption. While there is a call to bind a derived key to a cipher context directly (`EVP_PBE_CipherInit()`), actually using the call in practice is difficult. Therefore, to generate a key from a password, we can use an easily called lower level API key derivation function that implements PKCS #5 PBKDF2 and bind the key buffer obtained as a result of that to the cipher context. The signature for the function is as follows:

```
int PKCS5_PBKDF2_HMAC_SHA1(const char *pass, int passlen,
             unsigned char *salt, int saltlen, int iter,
             int keylen, unsigned char *out);
```

The function returns 0 (failure) or nonzero (success). The following parameters are accepted:

pass: The password bytes as a character array.

passlen: The size, in bytes, of the password specified in pass.

salt: A pointer to a byte array containing a salt value (salt is used to prevent dictionary attacks against passwords; it is useful to have a random salt value for each key we generate in this way).

saltlen: The length in bytes of the salt buffer.

iter: The number of "iterations"; we'll want this number to be large, although note that there is a performance impact for making the number too large. Anywhere between 4000 and 10000 is probably sufficient for most purposes.

keylen: The length of the key we wish to generate.

out: The key output value.

Calling this function first before the call to `EVP_CipherInit_ex()` will allow us to obtain our password-derived key readily; note that the IV is not generated for us, so we will likely want to store a random IV in a structure somehow serialized with (e.g., prepended or appended to) the encrypted data.

7.5 MESSAGE DIGESTS (HASHING) USING OPENSSL

Just like symmetric cryptography, there is both a command-line interface to message digest functionality and a C API; also like symmetric cryptography, the command-line interface is much easier to use than the programmatic API, but does not provide the same flexibility to the developer. We'll cover the command-line usage first, seeing as how it is easier to use, we'll go through a few examples, and then we'll get into the programmatic API.

7.5.1 Message Digests Using the Command Line

Again, we will be using the `openssl` command-line application; this time, however, instead of using the `enc` command to encrypt, we will use the `dgst` command to create message digests. In an intuitive fashion, the `dgst` command reads data off stdin and outputs the digest to stdout in one of a few formats. The `dgst` usage information (available by running `openssl dgst` with an invalid command such as `openssl dgst –help`) is as follows:

```
options are
-c                to output the digest with separating colons
-d                to output debug info
-hex              output as hex dump
-binary           output in binary form
-sign   file      sign digest using private key in file
-verify file      verify a signature using public key in file
-prverify file    verify a signature using private key in file
-keyform arg      key file format (PEM or ENGINE)
-signature file   signature to verify
-binary           output in binary form
-engine e         use engine e, possibly a hardware device.
-md5 to use the md5 message digest algorithm (default)
-md4 to use the md4 message digest algorithm
-md2 to use the md2 message digest algorithm
-sha1 to use the sha1 message digest algorithm
-sha to use the sha message digest algorithm
-mdc2 to use the mdc2 message digest algorithm
-ripemd160 to use the ripemd160 message digest algorithm
```

The most useful switches pertinent to this discussion are the switches indicating which hashing algorithm to use (e.g., –md5, -sha1, etc.) and the format to put the digest into (e.g., binary, -hex, or –c to separate the output with colons). You'll notice that there are switches dealing with signing and verification, but we'll skip over them for the moment since we are interested only in digests at this time (we will discuss the signing options in more detail later). To compute a digest from a stream of data on stdin, we will structure the command such that we indicate an algorithm and an output format; we'll also give it an input stream to compute the digest of. To produce a digest of an arbitrary file, we would structure the command like so:

```
[emoyle@elysium:~]$ openssl dgst -sha1 < openssl-0.9.7g.tar.gz
2134880b8f279453009ac5c506e289aa69f65b56
```

Using the library in this way is a useful mechanism for validating the authenticity of downloaded files, verifying that files read from a storage device (such as a tape backup) are error free, or for any other purposes we might wish to put it to.

7.5.2 Message Digests Using the EVP API

Just as we used the EVP API to make opaque calls to the symmetric cryptographic routines, we can use the EVP message digest interface to opaquely compute digests of input data. Much of the API will appear familiar when compared with the encryption interface. Just as we used a context "handle" to maintain the internal state of our encryption state, we will use a similar context handle to maintain the state of the message digest operation. We will also use the sequence of "initialize, update, finalize" just as we did with symmetric cryptography. Similar to symmetric cryptography, the following are the high-level steps required for message digest use:

1. **High-level initialization**: Initialization of the library's internal state will take place at this time.
2. **Digest initialization:** Initialization of the particular digest "instance" we will be using will take place at this time.
3. **Iterative digest update**: We will pass our data through the digest a buffer at a time. We will likely want to break larger data blocks into smaller "chunks," which we will operate on a piece at a time.
4. **Digest finalization**: We will need to instruct the digest that we are done using it and the last "chunk" of data has been reached.
5. **High-level cleanup**: At this time, any constructs that were created will be freed/released.

Bringing this usage down one level of abstraction, the following list maps these high-level steps to the specific usage required by and provided by the library:

High-level initialization steps: Declare a variable of type `EVP_MD_CTX` to use for storing the "digest context"—this context consists of the internal resources and variables associated with a particular operation. Call `EVP_MD_CTX_init()` to initialize the "EVP context."

Digest initialization steps: Call `EVP_DigestInit_ex()` to bind the appropriate implementation and algorithm to the context we supply.

Iterative digest update steps: Iteratively call `EVP_DigestUpdate()` one or more times, passing in the buffer that is being hashed in piecemeal fashion.

Digest finalization steps: Call `EVP_DigestFinal_ex()` to "finalize" the digest operation.

High-level cleanup steps: Clean up the resources and state used by the library internally by calling `EVP_MD_CTX_cleanup()`.

The following functions are used during the creation of message digests:

`EVP_MD_CTX_init()`: This function is used to create the message digest context. The context is required to store "state" associated with the digest operation we are performing. The return is void, so there is no differentiation between success and failure.

`EVP_DigestInit_ex()`: Used to bind an implementation and an algorithm to the digest context. The function returns 0 (failure) or nonzero (success). The function accepts a context pointer (`struct EVP_MD_CTX*`) as input, as well as a message digest algorithm pointer (`struct EVP_MD*`) and an implementation, which (unless we are using specialized hardware) will usually be NULL.

`EVP_DigestUpdate()`: Used to send data "through" the hashing algorithm. We will want to send the data through in a "buffer by buffer" fashion. Being able to call this routine more than once for a particular message digest operation allows us to separate large buffers and to perform incremental operations on incomplete data streams (such as files). The function returns 0 (failure) or nonzero (success). According to evp.h, this function has the following signature:

```
int EVP_DigestUpdate(EVP_MD_CTX *ctx, const void *d, size_t cnt);
```

The function accepts the following parameters:

ctx: The context that should be used for the current operation.

d: The data over which to compute the digest.

cnt: The size of d in bytes.

`EVP_DigestFinal_ex()`: Used to retrieve the completed hash resultant from the hashing process. The function returns 0 (failure) or nonzero (success). According to evp.h, this function has the following signature:

```
int EVP_DigestFinal_ex(EVP_MD_CTX *ctx, unsigned char *md,
        unsigned int *s);
```

The function accepts the following arguments:

ctx: The context that should be used for the current operation.

md: A buffer into which to place the output message digest.

s: A pointer to an unsigned int that will be used to store the size of the resultant message digest in bytes.

`EVP_MD_CTX_cleanup()`: Used to release any internal structures in use by the message digest context. The function returns 0 (failure) or nonzero (success), and takes only one argument: the context that is to be released.

Using these functions to create a sample usage, we would get software similar to the following:

```
char * message = "This is the message.";
EVP_MD_CTX dgCtx;
EVP_MD_CTX_init(&dgCtx);
EVP_DigestInit_ex(&dgCtx, EVP_sha1(), NULL);
EVP_DigestUpdate(&dgCtx, message, strlen(message));
//using 20 bytes for SHA-1.  Other digest sizes will vary
unsigned char theHash[20];
unsigned int hashLen;
EVP_DigestFinal(&dgCtx, theHash, &hashLen);
EVP_MD_CTX_cleanup(&dgCtx);
```

This is just a very simple example; within it, we request SHA-1 specifically (`EVP_sha1()`), and we created a buffer exactly big enough to hold an SHA-1 hash. In practice, we do not have to know these things ahead of time to use the EVP API to generate message digests.

7.5.3 Opaque Message Digests Using the EVP API

Just as we could use the EVP API to "late bind" a symmetric encryption algorithm to a particular context, we can do the same thing with message digests. OpenSSL allows us the same opacity with respect to algorithm use that symmetric cryptography did. Once we incorporate the support functions into our usage, we can dynamically bind to a message digest algorithm by name at runtime, query it to find out how big the resultant digest will be, allocate our digest buffer in concordance with that size, and compute the hash. To do this, all we need do is make use of two of the same functions we used in symmetric encryption EVP usage, and one new one; the functions we've already discussed are the `OpenSSL_add_all_algorithms()` and the `EVP_cleanup()` routines to load and free the internal algorithm lookup table. Whereas we used `EVP_get_cipherbyname()` in the context of symmetric encryption, we will substitute instead the EVP_get_digestbyname() as the analogous function for returning the message digest artifact. Including the two functions we've already covered (included here for clarity), the following summarizes the additional functions we'll use in doing run-time lookup:

OpenSSL_add_all_algorithms(): This function will build the internal state table, allowing symmetric ciphers to be queried at runtime. One characteristic we can use to query individual algorithms is by the algorithm's name.

EVP_get_digestbyname(): Return a digest instance (struct EVP_MD*) given a unique digest name.

EVP_cleanup(): Deallocate the internal resources created in the call to OpenSSL_add_all_algorithms().

In conjunction with these functions, the following macro may also be used to determine the size of the message digest:

EVP_MD_size(e): Given a digest instance (struct EVP_MD *), provide the size of the message digest that will be computed.

Incorporating this methodology into our previous example, we get:

```
char * message = "This is the message.";
EVP_MD_CTX dgCtx;
EVP_MD_CTX_init(&dgCtx);
//load the lookup table
OpenSSL_add_all_algorithms();
//get the digest by name
const EVP_MD * digestAlg = EVP_get_digestbyname("SHA1");
if(!digestAlg) {
    //unknown digest, use default? throw exception?
}
//init and update as usual
EVP_DigestInit_ex(&dgCtx, digestAlg, NULL);
EVP_DigestUpdate(&dgCtx, message, strlen(message));
//allocate hash buffer based on size
unsigned char * theHash = new
    unsigned char[EVP_MD_size(digestAlg)];
unsigned int hashLen;
//complete
EVP_DigestFinal(&dgCtx, theHash, &hashLen);
//free and cleanup
delete theHash;
```

```
EVP_MD_CTX_cleanup(&dgCtx);
EVP_cleanup();
```

Note that it is *extremely important* for us to check that the pointer returned from `EVP_get_digestbyname()` is not null; the subsequent calls (digest init, digest update, etc.) *will* try to access the pointer (even if it's null) and cause an access violation in doing so in the case of a bogus pointer. Situations can arise, for example, in which we might author our application to read a value from the environment or from an initialization file; leading to a situation in which our application runs fine until something in the environment occurs that we did not expect. This kind of situation can be difficult to diagnose in the field, so it helps to plan for it ahead of time during the code-authoring portion of our development process.

7.5.4 Digests without the EVP API

Again, we have the option of avoiding the EVP API in situations in which we know what the message digest algorithm will be ahead of time. The documentation for OpenSSL encourages us not to do this, because in so doing, we limit ourselves to only the algorithm we've selected. However, it is a useful feature of the library that we can choose how we want to interact with it. For example, given some of the weaknesses recently pointed out in SHA-1 and MD5, our application might require that we use the updated SHA algorithms such as SHA-256 or SHA-512. As of the writing of this book, these updates are not in the latest "stable" distribution of the OpenSSL library; they are, however, present in the "development" versions of the library. We might want to experiment with adding support for these algorithms in our application, but we might not want to "install" a nonrelease version of the library to do so in a way that globally impacts all of our cryptographic functionality. As such, having the option to interface with the library according to both high- and low-level APIs would allow us to "pull down" just the updated files we need (e.g., SHA256*.c, SHA512*.c, and the modified sha.h header) to perform our experimentation. In other words, if our proverbial "back is to the wall" and we absolutely have to use an algorithm like this one, it is nice to know that the library developers have left us with an escape route that we can try (even if it is just a short-term solution) to get our application up and running. If they did not allow this, and only provided a high-level API, we would have to wait for a subsequent release or use a different library entirely if our application required support for one of these algorithms.

7.6 MACS (KEYED HASHES) USING OPENSSL

Although quite a bit of functionality is provided from the command line, implementation of MAC functionality is not provided directly. "Provided directly" doesn't mean that we couldn't implement MAC using the digest commands that already exist (indeed we could), it just means that there's no "MAC" command or something like it that we can use for generation of standard MACs. Since implementing MACing functionality using the digest functionality available from the command line is probably more difficult than writing our own command-line application that wraps the MAC functionality already provided by the library, we'll skip a command-line interface description for this functionality and proceed directly to how to use the C API MAC functionality.

7.6.1 HMAC Using the OpenSSL Crypto API

Creating and using MAC functionality is similar to the EVP API we've covered in the symmetric and message digest examples throughout this chapter. To make use of the functionality, we will need to initialize a structure of type `HMAC_CTX` (analogous to the `CIPHER_CTX` and `MD_CTX` used in symmetric cryptography and message digests, respectively). Once we have a context, we will repeat the pattern of initialize, update, and finalize according to the following steps:

High-level initialization steps: Declare a variable of type `HMAC_CTX` to use for storing the "hmac context"—this context consists of the internal resources and variables associated with the hmac operation. Call `HMAC_CTX_init()`to initialize this context.

HMAC initialization step: Call `HMAC_Init_ex()` to bind the appropriate implementation, key, and hash algorithm to the context we supply.

Iterative HMAC update steps: Iteratively call `HMAC_Update()` one or more times, passing in the buffer that is being hashed in piecemeal fashion.

HMAC finalization step: Call `HMAC_Final_ex()` to "finalize" the HMAC operation.

High-level cleanup step: Clean up the resources and state used by the library internally by calling `HMAC_CTX_cleanup()`.

The functions used throughout this process are described as follows:

`HMAC_CTX_init()`: Used to prepare an HMAC context for use in maintaining the internal state of the HMAC operation. The return type is void, and the only parameter is a pointer to the HMAC_CTX struct we wish to initialize.

`HMAC_Init_ex()`: Used to bind the key and the message digest (hashing) algorithm to the context. According to hmac.h, the function has the following signature:

```
void HMAC_Init_ex(HMAC_CTX *ctx, const void *key, int key_len,
                  const EVP_MD *md, ENGINE * impl);
```

The parameters to this function are as follows:

ctx: The context we wish to bind the parameters to. This is the value previously initialized through the call to `HMAC_CTX_init()`.

key: The key that will be used for the HMAC.

len: The length in bytes of the key.

md: The message digest algorithm used for the HMAC operation; this should be supplied as a pointer to a valid EVP_MD structure.

impl: The implementation that will be used. Unless we require specialized hardware support, the default implementation can be used by passing NULL in this parameter[5].

`HMAC_Update()`: Used to iteratively supply the data that will be hashed in preparation for the computation of the MAC. This function will be called at least once, specifying the data that will be submitted as input to the hashing function. According to hmac.h, this function has the following signature:

```
void HMAC_Update(HMAC_CTX *ctx, const unsigned char *data, int len);
```

The parameters to this function are:

ctx: The context we wish to use to compute the MAC. This is the value previously initialized through the call to `HMAC_CTX_init()`.

data: The data to process through the MAC function.

len: The length of the data indicated in the "data" parameter.

`HMAC_Final()`: Used to complete the HMAC operation and compute the final MAC value. According to hmac.h, this function has the following signature:

```
void HMAC_Final(HMAC_CTX *ctx, unsigned char *md, unsigned int *len);
```

The parameters to this function are:

ctx: The context we wish to use to compute the MAC. This is the value previously initialized through the call to `HMAC_CTX_init()`.

md: The message digest output. This parameter should consist of a pointer to a buffer that will be populated by the library with the results of the MAC.

len: A pointer to an unsigned integer that will receive the length of the output placed in md specified in bytes.

`HMAC_CTX_cleanup()`: Used to release the HMAC context previously allocated. This function takes only one parameter, which is the pointer to the previously generated context struct.

Using the preceding functions to compute an HMAC in a very simple situation would yield code similar to the following:

```
char * message = "This is the message.";
//set up structures and initialize
HMAC_CTX hmacCtx;
HMAC_CTX_init(&hmacCtx);
unsigned char key[20];
GetRandomKeyBytes(key, sizeof(key));
HMAC_Init_ex(&hmacCtx, key, sizeof(key), EVP_sha1(), NULL);
//pass the data in
HMAC_Update(&hmacCtx, (unsigned char*)message, strlen(message));
unsigned char hmac[20];
unsigned int macLen;
//finalize (generate HMAC)
HMAC_Final(&hmacCtx, hmac, &macLen);
//cleanup
HMAC_CTX_cleanup(&hmacCtx);
```

Of course, we could use another message digest algorithm other than SHA-1 if we have a particular requirement to which our application must comply. The relevant standards documentation (e.g., RFC 2104 and by association 2404) recommend using a key length equal to the digest size of the underlying message digest function; therefore, for SHA-1, the preceding example used a 20-byte (160-bit) key. If we were using MD5, we could substitute a 16-byte (128-bit) key instead and so remain compliant with the guidance available to us.

7.7 DIGITAL SIGNATURE USING OPENSSL

Signing is perhaps the most complex operation in all the libraries we'll cover. Key generation is always difficult and time consuming to effect, ensuring that we maintain compliance with the appropriate standards (e.g., in matters such as padding) is burdensome, and there are usually numerous constraints we must keep in mind during usage. As with all the libraries in this book, the OpenSSL API to the signature functionality is no exception; both the command-line API and the C API are more complicated than any of the material we have covered in this chapter. The intention is not to scare anyone away in stating this; we merely state it because we place a great deal of emphasis on signing and validation in this chapter (as well as in subsequent chapters) due primarily to the comparatively increased complexity of this functionality compared to the other tasks we'll cover. In fact, from a usage developer's perspective, most of the time, even connecting to an SSL socket is much simpler no matter what library we use (with the possible exception of the Microsoft SSPI API) than generating a basic digital signature.

7.7.1 Command-Line Digital Signatures

OpenSSL uses the `openssl` command-line utility for creation of digital signatures in addition to all the functionality we've highlighted already throughout this chapter. In fact, we've already seen some glimpses as to how that functionality might be used in our discussion of creating message digests from the command line. However, before we can sign anything, we need to have a key to sign it with. In other words, from the command line, we will need to first generate a key pair specific to the algorithm we intend to use for signing, and we will need to extract the public key into a useful format that we can share with individuals who wish to verify the signatures that we produce.

7.7.1.1 Command-Line Key Creation

For creating digital signatures using the command-line interface, we have the choice of creating and using RSA or DSA. Each of these algorithms has a different command-line option to the `openssl` command-line application for key creation, although the parameters to each and usage for each is thankfully similar. To create an RSA key, we will use the `genrsa` command, and to generate a DSA key, we will use either the `gendsa` command or the `dsaparam` command. We'll cover the usage information for both RSA and DSA in this section.

The `genrsa` command is used to generate an RSA key that we can use for both encryption and digital signature from the command line. Most of the time, we will want to place the private key in a file that only we have access to, and unless we have a good reason for not doing so, we will want to protect the private key contents with a symmetric cipher derived from a password. Don't worry, though, the utility will do all this work for us. According to the usage information, the following arguments are supported by the `genrsa` command:

```
    usage: genrsa [args] [numbits]
     -des            encrypt the generated key with DES in cbc mode
     -des3           encrypt the generated key with DES in ede cbc mode
(168 bit key
    )
     -aes128, -aes192, -aes256
                     encrypt PEM output with cbc aes
     -out file       output the key to 'file
```

```
-passout arg    output file pass phrase source
-f4             use F4 (0x10001) for the E value6
-3              use 3 for the E value
-engine e       use engine e, possibly a hardware device.
-rand file:file:...
                load the file (or the files in the directory) into
                the random number generator
```

However, most of the time, our usage will be both limited and straightforward. Of the parameters supported, the ones we are most interested in are the –out parameter (allowing us to create a file containing the newly generated key) and the symmetric cipher to encrypt it with (such as –aes128, for example). Additionally, we will want to avail ourselves of the opportunity to specify the modulus bit length as the final parameter to the key generation process; the default size, 512 bits, should be avoided under most circumstances. The following usage will create a key in the specified file and protect it with an AES-128 key derived from a password we supply; we will be prompted to specify a password, which we will do when indicated:

```
[emoyle@elysium:~]$ openssl genrsa -aes128 -out .rsakey 1024
Generating RSA private key, 1024 bit long modulus
.......++++++
.....................................++++++
e is 65537 (0x10001)
Enter pass phrase for .rsakey:
Verifying - Enter pass phrase for .rsakey:
[emoyle@elysium:~]$
```

Provided this command runs successfully, something similar to the following will be created and placed in the .rsakey file:

```
[emoyle@elysium:~]$ cat .rsakey
-----BEGIN RSA PRIVATE KEY-----
Proc-Type: 4,ENCRYPTED
DEK-Info: AES-128-CBC,EBEADBBB629CA1AEE166A56292A050DD
Hh2s/8YJQUn5rDZxTZGVmrfgVgABvaB99Upbq+OsacuFg153NJCOZQAvBAq1gpgu
b88nMcnJF1eT74Nv5lgjMOJQgFQxxx/DxXsoLXXL7p1KCcGtaZkDekM5EOgJ8lXD
TXDq27rFOsSuPkfQ9T7T9HgWTnhFSCOn+foPhzLBmkq7LpH8wj8bWRLz//A7Letd
Ixw4MdMsx/dW2oXNHiPmhK4TMwWN42Cxu9kJ+OQteJ/SgThkbB8mOAWik5hKlqSP
9pjOPPpFdDo45IJK7WjaOieTsvODLXlYcRanYOIe4sGrAt/AvJlbnOeEZQs3vzSQ
9ePXIFOSvd1pci1JL2TnUQx19Ht37squN4eKz9FEkSkk/J3TV9h+VJmiok5DUABP
dmUVEbqtv+KWcMbm1oOp35EqKnR7UtSSRFMPbSN1SWkJoNQPCqj9+6r53BjCK4q5
d89OAJnvBG7pCSOkAUDLYKp98ORKVz2hT/bQJ5BxJWjtVIszpaaEmGAbPIgWBUta
h5Vrbthu3NnzCzFURVeOX1lotOIMeqCDNb5ctvoJFUGt2MSq7Pb3QWUI2jddQhSX
2vNpWKYa/YKl4IAE1CsVu5wqZkESiOOEGpqPelQq2/IBetOU7fs8RPKmFXKa+MLF
```

```
eqtFRxh7+Yme6OssKRKWW449Aj/M9VU6QL7XtxJh2DujbMV2eZ7OvfZaH3oHdgfT
2oooKBJnaAppXoDIdH5rLsax76kOTxdLdDXK5LSxhDFzZtIGdVENM31FxNfPyhW1
gSO7C935VzjBL+yfsFICkifnqhK5NfRzTJ+7Vgo6WXfYYYY6sJhyMSa2gAUm1UuP
-----END RSA PRIVATE KEY-----
[emoyle@elysium:~]$
```

Using `gendsa` is similar to `genrsa`, although it does require a “dsa parameter file” that we will need to submit to the key generation process. DSA parameter generation is time consuming, so if we are going to create more than one key in the near future, we’ll probably want to build the parameters file once and use it over and over again. A convenient shortcut if we are generating only one key is to bypass the parameters file entirely and use `dsaparam` to generate the key. Obtained by running `openssl dsaparam` with an invalid argument, the usage for `dsaparam` is:

```
dsaparam [options] [bits] <infile >outfile
where options are
 -inform arg    input format - DER or PEM
 -outform arg   output format - DER or PEM
 -in arg        input file
 -out arg       output file
 -text          print as text
 -C             Output C code
 -noout         no output
 -genkey        generate a DSA key
 -rand          files to use for random number input
 -engine e      use engine e, possibly a hardware device.
 number         number of bits to use for generating private key
```

To bypass the parameters file entirely, we can use the `–noout` flag in combination with the `–genkey` flag to do so, but note that we won’t be able to specify a symmetric cipher to encrypt the private key with in doing so. No matter how we use this operation, we’ll want to specify the size in bits of the prime number that will be used. To generate a DSA parameters file using this function, we can just go ahead and call the `dsaparam` command using syntax like the following to generate the parameters file:

```
    [emoyle@elysium:~]$ openssl dsaparam -out .dsaparams 1024
    Generating DSA parameters, 1024 bit long prime
    This could take some time
    .+....+................+.........+++++++++++++++++++++++++++++++++++
+++++++++++++
    ++++*
    +....+........................+..........+............+
....................
```

```
    ....+...............+....+......+...........+...................
+.+.+..........
    ..............+..+.........+.........+.....+........+....+...+.
+....+.........
    ....+.........+.....+....+..........+..+.+
...................................
    ............+...............+...............................+
.............++
    ++++++++++++++++++++++++++++++++++++++++++++++++*
    [emoyle@elysium:~]$
```

Since the process does take some time to complete, the pattern of dots, plusses, and stars is shown as a "progress indicator," so we know that the process isn't hung while the lengthy operation transpires. Once we've obtained the parameter file, we can now call the gendsa command to generate a DSA key just as we generated an RSA key. We'll use almost exactly the same syntax, except that instead of specifying the modulus bits, we'll specify instead the path to the parameters file like so:

```
[emoyle@elysium:~]$ openssl gendsa -out .dsakey -aes128 .dsaparams
Generating DSA key, 1024 bits
Enter PEM pass phrase:
Verifying - Enter PEM pass phrase:
[emoyle@elysium:~]$
```

Once we've created the file in this way, we should have a file containing something similar to the following:

```
[emoyle@elysium:~]$ cat .dsakey
-----BEGIN DSA PRIVATE KEY-----
Proc-Type: 4,ENCRYPTED
DEK-Info: AES-128-CBC,BAB943EE639D69F4DA7BAE41F94D86EB
9Iwb4bguohNMC2vLAscOs/ZzUM25FouYzwmWrwWGVqSauPR384lSPQuHFHdhi2w+
cyZDFa/Y2JZbMzYW9o2iOpsEroi587OaAJcI9DImPlv9YozPf2Ybs/hQg6j/CKxh
TiqeJuNzwRZE3T+NEsPqNvUVbJaXW+F6AA/jSOZKDOOKCsGeowTcR8DwR3TjOU9z
gJ/LxAXEX3ofi6AcjnarQOktLF6eTsfPCoT1vVml8GNPrer8zj+9hFJpHOJ2s66f
2/p2/KvO4QwgOiFkyGXaHhN5Wln6hl4EFGypp4f+eO7OTxJH3+QgdrMVvUVaENZe
uZBLV6hyzvrbHEdOBne62h/TtwbTvPbNjsEMycjd24YbHx38bAT5+38JVE9sKMxO
HSLo9zYHJI1JPxvBgYwztDEoMTRos1gmjoZOOJGY5npRvQKx44BzWA7mp/cHfLYg
boAOM1sD7BPSmeeNujkOU3pN3WQ8TQGaqRkCJhoOjeqDORqR/qgrO2Fv1Qd8bEVL
I7k2CHuNazyVfrzrxiPab2NiLP6BJNen6gOLYafqLxQGKNJb31NfZngStGLU4WrF
ZaGUbb2wvbda/KlCOH+U4g==
-----END DSA PRIVATE KEY-----
[emoyle@elysium:~]$
```

Even if we encrypt the contents of the file with a password or passphrase that only we know, it helps to ensure that only we have access to the key from a permissions perspective; we'll probably want to ensure that only we are able to view the contents of the files we've created:

```
[emoyle@elysium:~]$ ls -a | grep '[.].sakey' | xargs -t chmod 600
chmod 600 .dsakey .rsakey
[emoyle@elysium:~]$ ls -la | grep '[.].sakey'
-rw-------    1 emoyle   other         751 Apr 11 21:23 .dsakey
-rw-------    1 emoyle   other         986 Apr 11 21:02 .rsakey
[emoyle@elysium:~]$
```

Actually, it's debatable as to whether we want to retain the write permission ourselves, but for now, we'll assume we do. Having done this, we now have key files we can use for encryption or for the creation of digital signatures.

7.7.1.2 Creating Command-Line Signatures

To generate a signature of a file, we will again use the `dgst` command we discussed in dealing with the command-line creation of message digests. We will specify the file to be signed in the same way as we specified it in our digest usage, but this time, we will add the `–sign` flag in combination with our key file to inform the utility we wish to create a digital signature. If we are using RSA, we can use pretty much any of the supported message digest algorithms, but if we are using DSA, we'll have to specify the "dss1" algorithm or else we will get an error. Considering this, usage is a snap:

```
    [emoyle@elysium:~]$ openssl dgst -hex -dss1 -sign .dsakey \
    --> openssl-0.9.7g.tar.gz
    Enter pass phrase for .dsakey:
    DSA(openssl-0.9.7g.tar.gz)=
302c02147b3ffac3541750dc9264fdfd14fe3cfa9cb30bc60214
    217ab6c142716f9ef93f777443065c21b17ca6e7
    [emoyle@elysium:~]$
```

or if we want to sign with RSA:

```
    [emoyle@elysium:~]$ openssl dgst -hex -sha1 -sign .rsakey \
    --> openssl-0.9.7g.tar.gz
    Enter pass phrase for .rsakey:
    SHA1(openssl-0.9.7g.tar.gz)=
9fa7d499eb3c9dc617d6161afe1d6a2cbfd5722c7eb683778d1
    6b7773a8958c294c17ad68061aab78736c994f87e84a7eee3d4f64b71f178fe
550bfb1c3d7eb1626
    97cd72661f98e8e4cb75153bb39fdcc9e2fac77842225100633810 3c4de3c46e
0503698dd25f3791
```

```
6ffda6523bd0229d243af5ac0f370f0078e388df6a307
[emoyle@elysium:~]$
```

In this case, signing is the easy part. We're just using the -hex parameter here to make the output readable; however, in practice, most of the time, we'll want to leave that parameter off in order to verify the signature later. If we do not want to encode the signature data, we would just leave the -hex option off the usage string, which will cause the data to be printed to stdout using binary encoding only.

7.7.1.3 Command-Line Public Key Extraction

Before we can verify any signatures we produce in this way, we'll need to render the public half of our signing key into a format that others can pick up and use for the verification process. To do this, we will use the rsa and dsa commands, which are used (among other things) to manipulate rsa and dsa keys such as allowing extraction of only the public key information from a private key file. For example, to output only the public information from the rsa key we created before, we would use the following command string:

```
[emoyle@elysium:~]$ openssl rsa -in .rsakey -pubout -out .rsapubkey
Enter pass phrase for .rsakey:
writing RSA key
[emoyle@elysium:~]$
```

The -out option instructs the utility to create a file called .rsapubkey that contains the public key information. The contents of the file would appear similar to the following:

```
[emoyle@elysium:~]$ cat .rsapubkey
-----BEGIN PUBLIC KEY-----
MIGfMA0GCSqGSIb3DQEBAQUAA4GNADCBiQKBgQDG5j6AtK3jpvLEjg3Kz9nG43DU
F8XG3rE9u5o0EWG/RQbis3hUbvXZu+eRJno5vsIy+M2eMWAMR39o1sT/IWtK5BGz
HX0dbdxm+qTLUIBoFnTjGWA4bj7nC1uPsIdn/XebUKgeL09bfrKSwmuHAfYY/41F
BANRp0YRrV1ynL09PQIDAQAB
-----END PUBLIC KEY-----
[emoyle@elysium:~]$
```

The same usage applies for DSA:

```
[emoyle@elysium:~]$ openssl dsa -in .dsakey -pubout -out .dsapubkey
read DSA key
Enter PEM pass phrase:
writing DSA key
[emoyle@elysium:~]$
```

Again, the output is similar:

```
[emoyle@elysium:~]$ cat .dsapubkey
-----BEGIN PUBLIC KEY-----
MIIBtjCCASsGByqGSM44BAEwggEeAoGBAMkc9CoSfjyjbVeVBeBImeGO/4G4/jPb
V+ytesnmnl5utrWQr58sVCpZVKnXmH6M3OOhFdOosGfiRKXPr3k6bIopiqr+9c/V
KHkSUWqSL2vtoTtczrfrJ9APGZogi2JdN/GHOwPub+GtutLiOtxqYl+2rPIfGlNX
H4FqBECJnkBfAhUAhnPj9sOze5H9aY+MHXaIIivyhyUCgYAsODIHyEjvfcaucu/O
SSZ88/xaaMNgobxuf2nwVpugnMi8cYtJCdsl1ZhOSMa+E57Oob7SlX3TdYZcbTlt
Io5dPYnhhju5QGhG29+7ZARMsmylKFp3rB4XcXVRghIPo/GzFdRy4VUF+67i5auG
HQ7QKgZtCsYHdA1pGRlbtL51OgOBhAACgYAXJd75Jjt1JPqtXcKtYAHGalQBASK6
8Vk2O4kTtZnXlEGUV3o4tVO8sQMVoPf+BuoRgEGwoxHhrTzr6wY7XBAMqfCJ8tjA
bNuLZnM3b+9NeqoiF4llh9rIEymYwp/Vjif93W1BhpIbhENVzxhiCfDQPzdcQLG5
Xvhp8FNPZyYy9A==
-----END PUBLIC KEY-----
[emoyle@elysium:~]$
```

Note that in the case of the public key, we are not concerned with file permissions as we were with the private key file.

7.7.1.4 Command-Line Signature Verification

Verification of the signature also takes place using the `dgst` command, just as was the case with signing. We specify the `–verify` flag in combination with the location of a file containing the public key of the signer, and the `–signature` flag specifying the location of a signature file containing the previously generated signature. We must also specify the signing algorithm that was used to effect the signature using the appropriate flag. The usage is identical for RSA and DSA; the only change between the two is the digest algorithm type. To verify a file, we will need to make sure that the signature data is in a format the utility can understand (binary format, for example). For example, we could create the signature of an arbitrary file and place it in a signature file like so:

```
[emoyle@elysium:~]$ openssl dgst -dss1 -sign .dsakey \
--> openssl-0.9.7g.tar.gz > openssl-0.9.7g.tar.gz.dsasig
Enter pass phrase for .dsakey:
[emoyle@elysium:~]$
```

or, using RSA, like so:

```
[emoyle@elysium:~]$ openssl dgst -sha1 -sign .rsakey \
--> openssl-0.9.7g.tar.gz > openssl-0.9.7g.tar.gz.rsasig
Enter pass phrase for .rsakey:
[emoyle@elysium:~]$
```

To verify these signature files, we would use the verification flags to specify the location of the corresponding public key and the location of the signature files for the file we wish to verify; for DSA:

```
[emoyle@elysium:~]$ openssl dgst -dss1 -verify .dsapubkey \
--> -signature openssl-0.9.7g.tar.gz.dsasig openssl-0.9.7g.tar.gz
Verified OK
[emoyle@elysium:~]$
```

or for RSA:

```
[emoyle@elysium:~]$ openssl dgst -sha1 -verify .rsapubkey \
--> -signature openssl-0.9.7g.tar.gz.rsasig openssl-0.9.7g.tar.gz
Verified OK
[emoyle@elysium:~]$
```

Using this methodology, we can implement functionality to sign backup files, sign data going across a network, add both encryption and signatures to files, and numerous other security functionalities.

7.7.2 Using Digital Signatures Programmatically

Of course, as useful as the command-line interface is, sometimes we will need to access the API programmatically. The mechanism for doing so is a bit more complicated than some of the functionality we've used so far, so in preparation to undertake this challenge, we should familiarize ourselves ahead of time with the routines we are going to use in the signing and verification process. From a high level, we are again going to call the EVP API, this time using the signing and verification routines provided therein according to steps: initialize, update, and finalize. However, in addition, we'll need to use a few ancillary key-manipulation functions, since the key structures we have been using up until now have been in the form of buffers, and these functions require keys of a different type. By now, we should be used to working with this API since we've used it for almost every piece of functionality we have yet made use of.

7.7.2.1 Signing Data

As before, we will start by explaining the signature process in the absence of key creation; in fact, without key manipulation, the use of the signing API is almost identical to message digest functionality (with the exception that we need to supply a key during the final call). To review the steps from a high level, in order to sign, we will use the following high-level approach:

1. **High-level initialization:** Initialization of the library's internal state will take place at this time.

2. **Signature initialization**: Initialization of the particular signature "instance" we will be using will take place at this time.
3. **Iterative signing update**: We will pass our data through the digest a buffer at a time. We will likely want to break larger data blocks into smaller "chunks," which we will operate on a piece at a time.
4. **Signature finalization**: We will need to instruct the signature API that we are done using it and that the last "chunk" of data has been reached.
5. **High-level cleanup**: At this time, any constructs that were created will be freed/released.

We've probably seen these steps enough times by now that we can intuit how the steps will operate in practice before we even explicitly apply them at a lower level of abstraction. However, to be thorough, the following describes how the functions we will use map to these steps:

High-level initialization steps: Declare a variable of type `EVP_MD_CTX` to use for storing the "digest context," which in turn is used by the signing functionality—this context consists of the internal resources and variables associated with a particular operation. Call `EVP_MD_CTX_init()`to initialize the "EVP context."

Digest initialization steps: Call `EVP_SignInit_ex()` to bind the appropriate implementation and algorithm to the context we supply.

Iterative digest update steps: Iteratively call `EVP_SignUpdate()` one or more times, passing in the buffer that is being hashed in piecemeal fashion.

Digest finalization steps: Call `EVP_SignFinal_ex()` to "finalize" the digest operation and apply the signature to the digest.

High-level cleanup steps: Clean up the resources and state used the by the library internally by calling `EVP_MD_CTX_cleanup()`.

The functions referred to in these steps are described in detail as follows:

`EVP_MD_CTX_init()`: We saw this function once before during our use of message digests; because a message digest is used by the signing API internally, this function is used to create the "context" struct that will hold the internal state of the signing operation. The return is void, so there is no differentiation between success and failure.

`EVP_SignInit_ex()`: As usual, we will use this function to bind the appropriate algorithm and algorithm implementation to the context object. The function returns 0 (failure) or nonzero (success). The function accepts a context pointer (`struct EVP_MD_CTX*`) as input, a message digest algorithm pointer (`struct EVP_MD*`), and an implementation, which (unless we are using specialized hardware) will usually be `NULL`.

`EVP_SignUpdate()`: We will call this function one or more times to iteratively pass all the data we wish to sign "through" the signing process. We will want to send the data through in a "buffer by buffer" fashion. By calling this routine more than once for a particular operation, we can separate large buffers or perform incremental operations on noncontiguous data locations (such as files). The function returns 0 (failure) or nonzero (success). According to evp.h, this function has the following signature:

```
int EVP_SignUpdate(EVP_MD_CTX *ctx, const void *d, size_t cnt);
```

The function accepts the following parameters:

ctx: The context that should be used for the current operation.

d: The data over which to compute the digest.

cnt: The size of d in bytes.

`EVP_SignFinal()`: We will call this function once we have passed all the data we wish to sign through the algorithm using the previous call. This function will perform the actual signature and pass back to us a buffer containing the completed signature for the data we've specified. The function returns 0 (failure) or nonzero (success). According to evp.h, this function has the following signature:

```
int EVP_SignFinal(EVP_MD_CTX *ctx,unsigned char *sig,unsigned int *s,
EVP_PKEY *pkey);
```

The function accepts the following parameters:

ctx: The context that should be used for the current operation.

sig: An output buffer of sufficient size to hold the signature we wish to create.

s: A pointer to an unsigned integer that will be updated by the function to indicate the amount of data stored in the `sig` parameter.

pkey: The private key we wish to sign the data with.

`EVP_MD_CTX_cleanup()`: Used to release any internal structures in use by the message digest portion of the signature context. The function returns 0 (failure) or nonzero (success), and takes only one argument: the context that is to be released.

Putting these routines in context, and leaving out the details of key manipulation for the time being, usage is no more difficult than straight message digest functionality:

```
char * message = "This is the message.";
//generate and init the context
EVP_MD_CTX signCtx;
EVP_MD_CTX_init(&signCtx);
//bind digest
int result = EVP_SignInit_ex(&signCtx,
    EVP_sha1(), NULL);
if(!result) {
    bomb_out();
}
//pass data through
result = EVP_SignUpdate(&signCtx,
    message, strlen(message));
if(!result) {
    bomb_out();
}
//leaving out key details for now
EVP_PKEY * privateKey = GetTheKey();
char signature[256];
unsigned int sigLen = 0;
//finalize
result = EVP_SignFinal(&signCtx,
        (unsigned char*)signature,
        &sigLen,
        privateKey);
//deallocate and cleanup
FreeTheKey(privateKey);
EVP_MD_CTX_cleanup(&signCtx);
```

The same usage would also apply for DSA. In the case of DSA, we would merely replace the `EVP_sha1()` parameter to the corresponding DSA digest algorithm: `EVP_dss1()`. The selection of digest "locks us in" to the public key cryptography that will be applied: dss1 corresponds to SHA-1 + DSA, every other message digest uses RSA.

7.7.2.2 Key Manipulation (Key Generation and Conversion)

To fill in the missing sections from the previous sample usage, we will need to populate the functions `GetTheKey()` and `FreeTheKey()`, which were left undefined during the example. We started the discussion of the programmatic signing API by saying that there was quite a bit more complexity in the API than in previous portions of the API we've covered; however, the sample usage does not appear much more complex (and it isn't). The majority of the additional complexity we were referring to comes in during this portion of the discussion: namely, the creation, generation, storage, and manipulation of the underlying key structures that are used within the

API. There are a number of routines within OpenSSL designed to assist in key storage, key generation, key encoding, and so on that are slightly more complex to use than some of the other basic functionality we've covered.

To sign anything, we'll first need to generate keys that our application can use, we will then need to share the public half of the key pairs we generate with other parties, and we will need to translate the keys from whatever format they happen to be stored in into structures the library can use internally. Looking again at the `EVP_SignFinal()` call, we notice that the function expects to receive a structure of type `EVP_PKEY *`, which corresponds to a private key to which our application has access. First, we'll look at the functions we have access to that allow us to perform operations on values of this type (defined in evp.h):

`EVP_PKEY_new()`: Allocate and initialize a new `EVP_PKEY` struct.

`EVP_PKEY_free()`: Release a previously allocated `EVP_PKEY` struct.

`EVP_PKEY_assign()`: Assign data (key values) to a previously allocated EVP_PKEY struct.

There are, additionally, macros supplied by the library such as `EVP_PKEY_assign_RSA()` and `EVP_PKEY_assign_DSA()` that we can use to assign key values of a particular type directly from the output from certain key generation functions. There are, in addition to these, a number of other `PKEY` functions, but for the majority of our purposes, these will suffice.

Key generation is most easily performed using the algorithm-specific key generation functions correlating to the algorithm we wish to sign with. For example, to generate an RSA key, the `RSA_generate_key()` function (defined in rsa.h) will allow us to do so using a specified modulus size, a specified public exponent, and a pointer to a callback function that will be called during the key generation process (allowing us to implement a status meter or perform other operations while key generation is in process). According to rsa.h, the function has the following signature:

```
RSA *RSA_generate_key(int num, unsigned long e,
    void (*callback)(int,int,void *), void *cb_arg);
```

For the majority of our usage, we can readily specify NULL to the last two arguments. Additionally, the second parameter, the public exponent, can be easily mapped to one of the public exponent constants defined in rsa.h; for example, we can readily use RSA_F4 for the prime value "65537." One thing we will notice from this function, however, is that the return value (the `RSA*` containing the key values) is not of an appropriate type to immediately supply to `EVP_SignFinal()`. Namely, it is not of type EVP_PKEY*. To convert it to the appropriate type, we will need to pass it to a macro like EVP_PKEY_assign_RSA() in order for the key to be used by the API we discussed. For example, if we wanted to generate a new key and immediately use it for signing, we could implement the missing `GetTheKey()` function (the function that we left out of the previous usage) as follows:

```
EVP_PKEY* GetTheKey() {
    RSA *rsa=NULL;
    rsa=RSA_generate_key(1024,RSA_F4,NULL,NULL);
    EVP_PKEY * pkey;
    pkey = EVP_PKEY_new();
    EVP_PKEY_assign_RSA(pkey, rsa);
    return pkey;
}
```

Of course, we will need to free the resources we've allocated when we're done with the key as follows:

```
void FreeTheKey(EVP_PKEY* key) {
    EVP_PKEY_free(key);
}
```

7.7.2.3 Key Manipulation (Storing Keys on the Filesystem)

In this case, we create a new key that we can use for signing and delete it after use; however, on the downside, once the application goes away, nobody will be able to verify the signatures we create. In practice, we will want to create public/private key pairs and use them for an indeterminate amount of time. We'll want to generate the keys once, read them in multiple times (e.g., from the filesystem), and export the corresponding public key to other applications that might want to validate the signatures we create. Exporting and importing the keys can be a bit tricky; there are quite a few routines available for writing the keys to and reading the keys from the filesystem, and for converting the keys to various other structures and types. As you can see in pem.h, there are many manipulation routines we can use to write and read public and private keys from a file (or any other stream). However, given the large number of functions available, we are only going to cover the most common usage: specifically, writing/reading the keys to a file, and low-level serialization of the keys to a string. With these two tools, we can implement most of the functionality our applications will need, and (using the serialized key string) if need be, we can implement other non-OpenSSL methods for manipulating the key if we should so desire.

The basic usage for writing either of these structures to the disk is via the following functions:

`PEM_write_PUBKEY()`: This function writes a public key to a file. The function returns 0 (error) or nonzero (success). According to pem.h, this function has the following signature:

```
int PEM_write_PUBKEY(FILE *fp, EVP_PKEY *x);
```

The following are the arguments to this function:

fp: file pointer (`FILE*`) usually generated with `fopen()` or a similar file open call.

x: The structure containing the public key that will be written.

`PEM_write_ PrivateKey()`: This function writes a private key to a file, applying encryption to it (optionally) during the process. The function returns 0 (error) or nonzero (success). According to pem.h, this function has the following signature:

```
int PEM_write_PrivateKey(FILE *fp, EVP_PKEY *x,
                const EVP_CIPHER *enc
                unsigned char *kstr, int klen,
                pem_password_cb *cb, void *u);
```

We have the option of specifying key bytes to the encipherment algorithm, or specifying a password that will be used for encryption and decryption. The following are the arguments to this function:

fp: A file pointer (`FILE*`) usually generated with `fopen()` or a similar file open call.

x: The structure containing the private key that will be written.

enc: A pointer to an `EVP_CIPHER*` instance that will be used to apply cryptography to the key. If `NULL` is specified, no encryption will be used.

kstr: The string containing the key bytes.

klen: The length of the key supplied in kstr.

cb: A callback function used to obtain the password.

u: A password used to protect the private key; will only be used if kstr and klen are `NULL`.

Adding, for example, the ability to export key data to our previous example would yield usage similar to the following:

```
if(!KeyExists) {
    try {

        //gen the key, as per normal
        RSA *rsa=NULL;
        rsa=RSA_generate_key(1024,RSA_F4,NULL,NULL);
        if(!rsa) { throw -1; };
```

```
            EVP_PKEY * pkey;
            pkey = EVP_PKEY_new();
            EVP_PKEY_assign_RSA(pkey, rsa);

            //export private key with password (sample here)
            FILE * stream = fopen("rsa.key", "w+");
            int result = PEM_write_PrivateKey(stream,
                pkey,
                EVP_aes_128_cbc(),
                NULL,
                NULL,
                NULL,
                “A Robust Password”);
            fclose(stream);
            if(!result) { throw -1; }

            //export public key (no password)
            stream = fopen("rsapub.key", "w+");
            result = PEM_write_PUBKEY(stream,
                pkey);
            fclose(stream);
            if(!result) { throw -1; };
            return pkey;
        } catch(int) {
            ERR_load_crypto_strings();
            ERR_print_errors_fp(stdout);
            ERR_free_strings();
            bomb_out();
        }
    } else {
```

Loading the file uses the corresponding functions available in pem.h, namely: `PEM_read_PUBKEY()` and `PEM_read_PrivateKey()`. Note, however, that we will need to resolve at runtime the encryption algorithms used to perform the protection of the private key; as it was during the runtime-resolution of symmetric cipher names in our applications, it is equally important that we prepare the library to resolve the algorithm names by including a call to `OpenSSL_add_all_algorithms()`. The following describes their usage in depth:

`PEM_read_PUBKEY()`: This function reads a public key from a file. The function returns 0 (error) or nonzero (success). According to pem.h, this function has the signature:

```
EVP_PKEY *PEM_read_PUBKEY(FILE *fp, EVP_PKEY **x,
                pem_password_cb *cb, void *u);
```

The following are the arguments to this function:

fp: A file pointer (`FILE*`) usually generated with `fopen()` or a similar file open call.

x: The structure containing the public key that will be written. By indicating `NULL` in this parameter, the function will allocate a new structure for us.

cb: A password callback function (`NULL`).

u: `NULL`.

`PEM_read_PrivateKey()`: This function reads a private key from a file. The function returns 0 (error) or nonzero (success). According to pem.h, this function has the signature:

```
EVP_PKEY *PEM_read_PrivateKey(FILE *fp, EVP_PKEY **x,
                pem_password_cb *cb, void *u);
```

fp: A file pointer (`FILE*`) usually generated with `fopen()` or a similar file open call.

x: The structure containing the public key that will be written. By indicating `NULL` in this parameter, the function will allocate a new structure for us.

cb: A password callback function; we can either implement a callback function to obtain the password or merely specify it in the next parameter.

u: The password used to encrypt the private key bytes during the save operation.

Completing the other half of the "else" statement we created in the last example (key export), the following would read in the private and public key files we created and construct key objects from them:

```
} else {
    try {
        OpenSSL_add_all_algorithms();
        FILE * stream = fopen("rsa.key", "r");
        EVP_PKEY* pkey = PEM_read_PrivateKey(stream,
            NULL,
            NULL,
            "A Robust Password");
        fclose(stream);
        if(!pkey) { throw -1; }
```

```
            stream = fopen("rsapub.key", "r");
            EVP_PKEY * pubKey = PEM_read_PUBKEY(stream,
                NULL, NULL, NULL);
            fclose(stream);
            if(!pubKey) { throw -1; };
            return pkey;
        } catch(int) {
            ERR_load_crypto_strings();
            ERR_print_errors_fp(stdout);
            ERR_free_strings();
            bomb_out();
        }
    }
```

There is, of course, "more than one way to butter toast." Dozens of functions not covered in this chapter allow a developer to serialize public and private keys to the filesystem using internal OpenSSL I/O abstractions (e.g., the BIO API), and functions that serialize particular types of keys rather than opaque key types (e.g., RSA/DSA/DH). We're not going to cover those here; we're just covering one fairly simple usage—other techniques can be examined and experimented with if a developer so chooses.

7.7.2.4 Key Manipulation (Binary Serialization)

Of course, there are times when we will want to save the key value, but we won't necessarily want to put the structure onto the filesystem. In these cases, we can use the same internal serialization functions the library uses for implementation—the file export functionality. The functions for serializing a key into a contiguous binary structure and deserializing a binary structure into a structure usable by the library are:

- `i2d_PublicKey()` for serialization of a public key to a buffer.
- `d2i_PublicKey()` for deserialization of the public key to a structure.
- `i2d_PrivateKey()` for serialization of a private key to a buffer.
- `d2i_PrivateKey()` for deserialization of the private key to a structure.

These functions all perform the same way; the "i2d" functions take as input the structure we want to convert (such as a public or private key), and populate an internal buffer with the value. They also *update* the pointer we supply with the end of the buffer, so in a typical usage scenario, we will need to reset the pointer to where it was before we called the function. The "d2i" functions convert a byte string to the appropriate type of buffer we'll be using. Since usage is identical for public and private keys, we'll just go ahead and illustrate sample usage for the `id2_PublicKey` and `d2i_PublicKey` rather than going through all the permutations:

```
//serialize
int pubKeyLen = i2d_PublicKey(pkey, NULL);
unsigned char * keyBuf = new unsigned char[pubKeyLen];
pubKeyLen = i2d_PublicKey(pkey, &keyBuf);
keyBuf -= pubKeyLen;
//deserialize
EVP_PKEY * newKey = d2i_PublicKey(EVP_PKEY_RSA,
    NULL, //allocate new key for us
    &keyBuf, pubKeyLen);
//clean up
EVP_PKEY_free(newKey);
delete keyBuf;
```

7.8 ASYMMETRIC ENCRYPTION

The last of the low-level encryption functionality we will cover before moving into secure communications deals with using the command-line interface and the programmatic API to encrypt data (for privacy) using asymmetric encryption. In approaching the topic, however, it is useful to discuss a few different types of usage according to *what* we are trying to do. For example, are we writing an application that needs to use RSA at a very low level for compatibility with an existing application (will we be encrypting symmetric keys, small blocks of data for some purpose that does not have to do with the exchange of large amount of data)? Or do we have a broader goal of wishing to share arbitrary data structures with a number of different individuals using public key cryptography? This question is important to answer early, since there are a few different ways to interact with the API: low-level RSA operation or a higher level "sealing" mechanism whereby we can symmetrically encrypt a large amount of data but use RSA as the mechanism to transport that data. Although we'll look at approaches to do both those tasks, we'll concentrate much more on the higher level "seal" approach rather than the lower level functionality (since the need to use the lower level functionality will be much more remote than the higher level interfaces).

7.8.1 Asymmetric Encryption on the Command Line

Contrary to what we might expect, OpenSSL does support RSA from the command line; however, it is most unlikely that we will find the need to encrypt data for privacy using the routines supported there. We will not spend much time on the usage of this functionality, other than to mention the existence of it, draw a very broad brush of usage, and move on to the C API. The command for working with low-level RSA operations from the command line is `rsautl`; these are the RSA utility commands that allow us to encrypt, sign, and decrypt data, and so on at a very low level. From a functionality perspective, the usage is intuitive and the functionality thorough:

```
Usage: rsautl [options]
-in file        input file
-out file       output file
-inkey file     input key
-keyform arg    private key format - default PEM
-pubin          input is an RSA public
-certin         input is a certificate carrying an RSA public key
-ssl            use SSL v2 padding
-raw            use no padding
-pkcs           use PKCS#1 v1.5 padding (default)
-oaep           use PKCS#1 OAEP
-sign           sign with private key
-verify         verify with public key
-encrypt        encrypt with public key
-decrypt        decrypt with private key
-hexdump        hex dump output
-engine e       use engine e, possibly a hardware device.
-passin arg     pass phrase source
```

From among these arguments, we would use the –`encrypt` flag for the encryption process and –`decrypt` for the decryption process. We will need to specify the input key file (in our case, .rsapubkey), and we will need to use the –`pubin` flag to inform the utility that we just have an RSA public key and no corresponding private key. We can use the –`hexdump` flag to make the data more readable if we like, although a binary representation is much more versatile with respect to usage. Encrypting a value using these flags would proceed as follows:

```
    [emoyle@elysium:~]$  echo "RSA Command Line Encrypt" | \
    --> openssl rsautl -pubin -inkey .rsapubkey -encrypt -hexdump
    0000 - 77 28 d9 f8 f3 7a 15 87-41 b0 36 84 61 c3 b4 dd
w(...z..A.6.a...
    0010 - ea ac 39 75 a4 75 d9 04-1e 7e 98 53 eb 46 dc 96
..9u.u...~.S.F..
    0020 - fd 82 80 e6 3a bf 93 ff-fe de 56 8d d3 e7 24 08
....:.....V...$.
    0030 - a2 c6 3a 01 5c c1 32 be-a1 06 17 8d b2 60 99 e9
..:.\.2......`..
    0040 - fd fe b7 40 72 d2 ab fd-3b c7 8c c5 15 02 8a 71
...@r...;......q
    0050 - 3c 5f ff 95 a8 38 ae e3-1a b5 83 f5 f7 4e 71 85
<_...8.......Nq.
```

```
    0060 - 8d 8d 1a 49 72 0b 54 f6-3d 01 4f d7 a0 66 31 a6
...Ir.T.=.O..f1.
    0070 - 4f 8e ec 85 9f 50 db 52-b7 d0 3c 64 ea 86 04 35
O....P.R..<d...5
    [emoyle@elysium:~]$
```

7.8.2 Asymmetric Encryption via "Seal"

Some libraries such as OpenSSL make available to us a "seal"-ing functionality that we can use to encrypt data. As explained, most often in practical usage of asymmetric encryption for privacy, we will want to avoid encrypting large amounts of data with the asymmetric algorithm. Instead, ideally we will want to encrypt the bulk of the data with a symmetric algorithm and then encrypt the symmetric key with the public key—a useful technique. Some libraries assist in automating the process by supplying us with an API that we can use to perform this process at a high level. OpenSSL is such a library and makes available this functionality via the EVP API. The calls we'll be making to perform this should be familiar by now, as they almost exactly mirror symmetric encryption. The only difference between this and symmetric encryption is the extra parameters in the initialization call. Skipping the high-level description of the calls, since we've seen them quite a bit already in this section and they remain the same in this usage, the usage steps to make use of this functionality are as follows:

1. **High-level initialization steps:** Declare a variable of type `EVP_CIPHER_CTX` to use for storing the "cipher context" or the internal resources and variables associated with a particular cipher operation. Call `EVP_CIPHER_CTX_init()`to initialize the "EVP context."
2. **Sealing initialization steps:** Call `EVP_SealInit()` to bind the created context to a random key, a random IV, and the algorithm we specify. Additionally, supply a public key that will be used to encrypt the resultant symmetric key.
3. **Iterative seal update steps:** Iteratively call `EVP_SealUpdate()` one or more times, passing in the plaintext buffer that is to be sealed in piecemeal fashion.
4. **Seal finalization steps:** Call `EVP_SealFinal()` to "finalize" the cipher-specific encryption operation, performing any padding that may need to transpire at this time. Once padding has been completed, asymmetric cryptography will be applied.
5. **High-level cleanup steps:** Clean up the resources and state used the by the library internally by calling `EVP_CIPHER_CTX_cleanup()`.

All of the calls are identical to symmetric encryption, with the exception of the seal initialization call. Therefore, we will include at this time only a description of that function and refer the reader back to the symmetric cryptography EVP API discussion for information about using the other functions:

`EVP_SealInit()`: This function will bind a symmetric cipher to the context we specify; additionally, it will generate a random key for that algorithm and a random IV, informing us of the results of each random value. We will need to specify one or more public keys to use in the asymmetric operation, and will need to provide output buffers to receive the results of the random key/IV generation. Note that this function allows for sealing for more than one individual at a time; this can lead to some additional complexity in calling it, but makes development easier when multiple recipients are required for a sealed artifact. According to evp.h, this function has the signature:

```
int EVP_SealInit(EVP_CIPHER_CTX *ctx, const EVP_CIPHER *type,
                 unsigned char **ek, int *ekl, unsigned char *iv,
                 EVP_PKEY **pubk, int npubk);
```

The function returns 0 (failure) or nonzero (success). The following are descriptions of the required parameters:

ctx: The context we created to which the cipher and key(s) will be bound.

type: The symmetric cipher used to perform the operation; this will correspond to a call such as `EVP_aes_128_cbc()`, which populates an `EVP_CIPHER *` struct.

ek: An array of pointers to buffers; there will be one key generated for each public key we supply; as such, we need to have one entry in the buffer array for each of those keys. Each entry in the array should be big enough to handle the size of the output key values; Note that since the keys will be encrypted with the public key, we will likely want to determine output size dynamically and ahead of time using the `EVP_PKEY_size()` routine as highlighted in the user documentation.

ekl: An array of integers that will be updated with the actual size in bytes of the random keys generated after encryption under the context of the public key(s).

iv: The initialization vector used for this encryption.

pubk: An array of public keys; public keys should correspond to the entities that will need to decrypt and use the data.

npubk: The number of entries in the pubk array.

Given that we will not be called upon to implement this functionality often, we've left specific usage out of the inline text of this chapter for brevity. There are, as always, samples on the companion CD-ROM (/Examples/Chapter 7/EVP/Seal) that a developer can use for reference.

7.8.3 Asymmetric Decryption via "Open"

The opposite of "seal" is "open" according to OpenSSL EVP nomenclature; in short, any data that has been "sealed" using the functions described in the previous section can be readily "unsealed" (opened) using the same EVP API. From a usage perspective, we will use a cipher context as we did with sealing, and will initialize it in the same way. However, this time we will make calls to `EVP_OpenInit()`, `EVP_OpenUpdate()`, and `EVP_OpenFinal()`. Again, the only difference between the encryption calls and the open calls are in the usage of the first function (`EVP_OpenInit()`). Since our usage of this functionality is likely to be limited and the mechanics of usage are mostly equivalent to that of symmetric ciphers, we're only going to discuss the modified call (`EVP_OpenInit()`) in detail in this section:

`EVP_OpenInit()`: This function will use a supplied RSA public key for decryption of a symmetric key in accordance with the cipher type we specify. The resultant decrypted key, in combination with an IV that we specify, will be bound to the cipher context. The function returns 0 (failure) or nonzero (success). According to evp.h, the function has the signature:

```
int EVP_OpenInit(EVP_CIPHER_CTX *ctx,EVP_CIPHER *type,
                 unsigned char *ek,
                           int ekl,unsigned char *iv,
                 EVP_PKEY *priv);
```

The following are descriptions of the required parameters:

ctx: The context we created to which the cipher and key(s) will be bound.

type: The symmetric cipher used to perform the decryption operation; this will correspond to a call such as `EVP_aes_128_cbc()` or any other call that creates a struct of a useable type.

ek: The encrypted key as a buffer.

ekl: The length in bytes of the key buffer.

iv: The initialization vector to be bound to the context.

priv: The private key that will be used to decrypt the key.

7.9 SECURE COMMUNICATIONS

The strength of the OpenSSL library is, unquestionably, the implementation of SSL/TLS it provides. The C API to the secure socket functionality is intuitive and powerful, and there even exists a command-line interface to SSL sockets (like netcat, but over SSL). The library supports server sockets and client sockets, and comes preenabled with a large number of X.509 CA certificates, which makes working with SSL a snap from a user's point of view.

7.9.1 Secure Communications from the Command Line

By far, one of the "coolest" features of OpenSSL is the command-line secure socket support. Those developers who have used the versatile "netcat" utility to send and receive data over sockets via the command line will immediately recognize the usefulness of having such a utility. Use of the functionality is straightforward, and it allows us to rapidly write shell scripts or batch files that can connect to a remote machine and gather information, or to set up a socket that will listen for inbound SSL connections and respond to them as we like. This function is implemented via the ubiquitous "openssl" command-line utility, and to make use of the client portion of this functionality, we merely use the `s_client` command. Usage information for `s_client` is as follows and may seem intimidating at first, but it really isn't, as we will explain:

```
    usage: s_client args
     -host host     - use -connect instead
     -port port     - use -connect instead
     -connect host:port - who to connect to (default is localhost:4433)
     -verify arg    - turn on peer certificate verification
     -cert arg      - certificate file to use, PEM format assumed
     -key arg       - Private key file to use, PEM format assumed, in
cert file if
                      not specified but cert file is.
     -CApath arg    - PEM format directory of CA's
     -CAfile arg    - PEM format file of CA's
     -reconnect     - Drop and re-make the connection with the same
Session-ID
     -pause         - sleep(1) after each read(2) and write(2) system
call
     -showcerts     - show all certificates in the chain
     -debug         - extra output
     -msg           - Show protocol messages
     -nbio_test     - more ssl protocol testing
     -state         - print the 'ssl' states
     -nbio          - Run with non-blocking IO
     -crlf          - convert LF from terminal into CRLF
     -quiet         - no s_client output
     -ign_eof       - ignore input eof (default when -quiet)
     -ssl2          - just use SSLv2
     -ssl3          - just use SSLv3
```

```
-tls1          - just use TLSv1
-no_tls1/-no_ssl3/-no_ssl2 - turn off that protocol
-bugs          - Switch on all SSL implementation bug workarounds
-serverpref    - Use server's cipher preferences (only SSLv2)
-cipher        - preferred cipher to use, use the 'openssl ciphers'
                 command to see what is available
-starttls prot - use the STARTTLS command before starting TLS
                 for those protocols that support it, where
                 'prot' defines which one to assume.  Currently,
                 only "smtp" and "pop3" are supported.
-engine id     - Initialise and use the specified engine
-rand file:file:...
```

Granted, this is a long list of arguments. However, most of the time, we can connect to an SSL server using only a few switches. First, in using `s_client`, we will need to specify the –`connect` flag and give a host and port for the client to connect to. If we just want to establish a connection and we don't much care about the security of that connection, that's all we need to specify. For example, we could connect to an arbitrary SSL-enabled Web site just using that single switch:

```
[emoyle@elysium:~]$ openssl s_client -connect www.microsoft.com:443 \
--> | more
depth=2 /CN=Microsoft Internet Authority
verify error:num=20:unable to get local issuer certificate
verify return:0
CONNECTED(00000004)
---
```

In practice, however, this is usually undesirable, given that we'll want to make sure the certificate of the remote site is issued by a CA we trust. To make sure this is validated, we'll want to specify a path to a directory containing CA certificates or to a single file containing multiple CA certificates. Assuming we have a directory with PEM-encoded CA certificates that we can use for validation, we can just use the –`CApath` flag followed by the location of those certificates like so:

```
    [emoyle@elysium:~/openssl-0.9.7g]$ openssl s_client -CApath
./certs/ \
    --> -connect www.verisign.com:443
    CONNECTED(00000004)
    depth=2 /C=US/O=VeriSign, Inc./OU=Class 3 Public Primary
Certification Authority
    verify return:1
    depth=1 /O=VeriSign Trust Network/OU=VeriSign, Inc./OU=VeriSign
International Se
```

```
    rver CA - Class 3/OU=www.verisign.com/CPS Incorp.by Ref. LIABILITY
LTD.(c)97 Ver
    iSign
    verify return:1
    depth=0 /C=US/ST=California/L=Mountain View/O=VeriSign,
Inc./OU=Production Servi
    ces/OU=Terms of use at www.verisign.com/rpa (c)00/CN=www.verisign.com
    verify return:1
    [...]
```

To "stifle" output on stdout (so we can use the functionality in a script, for example), we would specify the `–quiet` flag.

From a server perspective, implementation is also fairly easy to use at a basic level; the server version of the SSL socket command-line functionality is `s_server`, and it is equally functional as the `s_client` utility. To make use of it, we would call the openssl command-line utility and specify the `s_server` argument. The usage instructions are too voluminous to list inline in this chapter (they would take up almost two full pages of text), but we won't let that scare us away. The important thing to note about the server side of the connection, however, is that either we will need a server certificate to make use of the functionality, or if we're in a hurry, we can implement it using an anonymous "no certificate" flag (which will use anonymous Diffie-Hellman for key exchange). In general, it only takes an hour or two to get a certificate from a test CA or from a certificate server in a typical enterprise so it's useful to consider obtaining and using an actual certificate rather than "mocking it up." For the purposes of demonstration, the following illustrates how to use the `–nocert` flag to set up a command-line server connection:

```
[emoyle@elysium:~/openssl-0.9.7g]$ openssl s_server -accept 4444 \
-nocert
Using default temp DH parameters
ACCEPT
```

Scripts that illustrate how to install a completed certificate are included on the companion CD-ROM (/Examples/Chapter 7/Certs) under the examples for this section. Once we have a certificate and corresponding private key to use for the server side of the session, we will use the `–cert` and `–key` flags to provide `s_server` with the location of our certificate and private key, respectively. However, for most common usage, we will probably not need to build a Web server, so we can consult the additional reference material if we're doing something more challenging, but leave it out of the detailed instructions.

7.9.2 Programmatic Secure Sockets

Establishing sockets connectivity using OpenSSL is similar to the process we would use if we were using the Berkeley sockets API. We must perform a few steps ahead of time, of course, and we'll need to implement different platform configuration procedures depending on the side of the connection we wish to implement (server side or client side). However, for the most part, we can use OpenSSL in a manner very similar to the way we would do any other sockets programming.

7.9.2.1 Client Side: Connecting to an SSL Server

From a high level, the methodology to create a default socket connection to an SSL server is as follows:

1. **Initialize the library:** Call the appropriate functions to instantiate and initialize any internal structures used by the library.
2. **Instantiate a new SSL context:** Call the functions needed to construct an SSL communication context.
3. **Create the socket:** Create a Berkeley socket that will be used for the underlying transport. Bind the socket to the SSL context.
4. **Check the certificate validity:** Ensure that we are connecting to the appropriate party.
5. **Read/Write operations:** Read and write from the socket using the appropriate functions.
6. **Close the socket:** Indicate to the library that the connection is at a close.
7. **Release the library:** Call the appropriate function to free the internal resources of the library.

Mapping these high -level steps to actual functions within the API, we get the following updated steps:

1. **Library initialization:** Call `SSL_library_init()`.
2. **Context creation:** Call `SSL_CTX_new()` and specify a `SSL_METHOD` to govern protocol version support.
3. **Create the transport:** Create an underlying socket to be used as the transport for the SSL session. The easiest way to do this is with a combination of the Berkeley socket() call and the OpenSSL function `BIO_new_socket()`. Bind the context to a particular input/output channel using `SSL_new()`. The socket must then be bound to the SSL input/output channel using `SSL_set_bio()`. When complete, call `SSL_connect()`.
4. **Check certificate:** Use `SSL_get_peer_certificate()` to obtain the remote server's certificate for comparison and compare it with the hostname we

intended to connect to. Checking the CN is a little complicated, so it's best to just cut and paste that part from the sample code or from usage examples provided on the OpenSSL Web site.

5. **Read/Write operations:** Call `SSL_read()` to read and `SSL_write` to write to the socket.
6. **Close the socket:** Call `SSL_shutdown()` to close the socket and free the connection.
7. **Release the library:** Call `SSL_CTX_free()` to release the context.

Since these functions are relatively easy to use, each taking only one or two parameters at most, we can probably skip a detailed function-by-function breakdown and let the usage do the talking. As such, the following sample usage implements the preceding steps, providing everything we need for a secure communication pathway with a remote peer:

```
//initialize
SSL_library_init();

//create a new method allowing for all versions of the protocol
SSL_METHOD * method = SSLv23_client_method();
//bind method to context
SSL_CTX * ctx = SSL_CTX_new(method);
//create the socket
SOCKET mySocket = get_socket();
BIO* bio = BIO_new_socket(mySocket,BIO_NOCLOSE);
//we will need to set where the CA file(s) is/are located
//for verification to work
set_certificate_options();
SSL * ssl = SSL_new(ctx);
SSL_set_bio(ssl, bio, bio);
int result = SSL_connect(ssl);
if(!result) {
    //can't connect, bomb out
}
//check the certificate
result = SSL_get_verify_result(ssl);
if(result !=X509_V_OK) {
    //can't verify, bomb out
    bomb_out();
}
//check cert for validity
X509 * remote_cert = SSL_get_peer_certificate(ssl);
char theCommonName[1024];
```

```
    X509_NAME_get_text_by_NID(
        X509_get_subject_name(remote_cert),
        NID_commonName, theCommonName,
        sizeof(theCommonName));
    bool differs = true;
#ifdef WIN32
    if(!stricmp(hostname, theCommonName)) {
        differs = false;
    }
#else
    if(!strcasecmp(hostname, theCommmonName)) {
        differs = false;
    }
#endif
    X509_free(remote_cert);
    if(differs) {
        //not the expected CN, bomb out
        bomb_out();
    }
    //read and write on the socket
    SSL_shutdown(ssl);  //send socket shutdown
    SSL_CTX_free(ctx);
```

Of course, in practice we would not want to do everything inline as shown; we'd be better off wrapping the functionality in an `SSLSocket` or similar class or creating our own higher level socket API, since there are a number of routines required. In addition, since the details of creating Berkeley sockets can vary according to our platform, we've left the specifics out of the sample usage. Given the conditional compilation required to support both Winsock and Berkeley sockets, we would probably want to either concentrate on the platform we're running on, or create abstract classes for that functionality as well. However, just so we have a compiling and running example, we could assume that a typical implementation might look something like the following in the Unix (Berkeley sockets) world:

```
struct sockaddr_in socketaddr;
socketaddr.sin_family=AF_INET;
socketaddr.sin_addr.s_addr=inet_addr("www.microsoft.com");
socketaddr.sin_port=443;
SOCKET mySocket = socket(AF_INET, SOCK_STREAM, 0);
```

ON THE CD

Note that there are examples of using both the Winsock2 API and the Berkeley API on the companion CD-ROM (/Examples/Chapter 7/Sockets/Windows and /Examples/Chapter 7/Sockets/Berkeley, respectively).

7.9.2.2 Server Side: Accepting SSL Connections

Fortunately for us, a large number of the methods required for server support are the same as required for client support. Most of the time, simple usage scenarios won't include heavy-hitting SSL server functionality like building a Web server, supporting little-used cipher suites, or any other highly complicated functionality. Therefore, we'll limit our discussion to how the API differs from the client-side API, and we'll refer the reader interested in more complicated SSL server applications to the material contained on the companion CD-ROM (/Examples/Chapter 7/Sockets/Server). The calls we will make will not change much, the only difference is that we will wait until we have received a connection in the server's `accept()` loop to bind the BIO to the socket. In addition, we don't have to do any checking of certificate validity in the case of server sockets. To implement the server-side of the communication, all we need do is perform the library initialization routines, `bind()` to a local port, run a traditional `accept()` loop, and place the resultant connected socket (returned from `accept()`) into an OpenSSL bio structure just as we did with client sockets. After that is completed, we can immediately read and write to the SSL socket using `SSL_read()` and `SSL_write()`. Given the already-voluminous length of this chapter, and given that a typical usage scenario will likely not require the implementation of server sockets, we will leave the usage for this out of the chapter text. However, there is a sample of a simple server application on the companion CD-ROM included in the sample material for this chapter.

7.10 ENDNOTES

1. *www.openssl.org/docs/apps/openssl.html*
2. *www.openssl.org/docs/crypto/RAND_egd.html#*
3. *http://egd.sourceforge.net/*
4. *www.aet.tu-cottbus.de/personen/jaenicke/postfix_tls/prngd.html*
5. As of the time of this writing, the documentation for the HMAC API has not yet been updated to include specifically the changes made for the engine API. However, developers should be aware that previous versions of this call had four parameters rather than five, thus leading to the apparent inconsistency in the online OpenSSL documentation.
6. Note that the E value referred to is the "public exponent" discussed previously.

8 Developing with CAPI

In This Chapter

- Chapter Goal
- Preparing the Environment
- CryptoAPI versus .NET Security Classes
- Symmetric Encryption and Decryption with .NET
- Symmetric Encryption and Decryption with CryptoAPI
- Message Digests with .NET
- Message Digests with CryptoAPI
- Signing Data with .NET
- Signing Data with CryptoAPI
- Random Number Generation with .NET
- Random Number Generation with CryptoAPI
- SSL Sockets with .NET
- SSL Sockets with WinInet and SSPI
- Endnotes

Microsoft has provided a robust cryptographic API (CAPI) that we can use when we are writing applications targeted toward the Windows platform. CAPI uses a provider-style architecture in much the same way JCA does to segregate cryptographic interfaces from cryptographic implementations. The goal of using this architecture is to allow Microsoft or third-party implementers of cryptography to install and remove their cryptographic functionality from the operating system with minimal impact on the applications on that platform. These providers may serve a number of purposes. They may, for example, supply support for particular cryptographic hardware such as accelerators or HSM, support algorithms that are not available in the default CSPs, or be designed to comply with particular standards, regulations, or certification requirements. For the most part, unless we are going to be using a specialized accelerator, HSM, or other hardware, we will not require the addition of new CSPs to write the majority of our applications.

8.1 CHAPTER GOAL

Microsoft has made available a number of information-rich articles through the MSDN (Microsoft Developer Network) Library that include a complete CAPI function reference, sample code, training, technical articles, and so forth. The goal of this chapter is not to replace any of that; instead, here we attempt to consolidate and summarize that material. The Microsoft documentation is being continually updated, improved, and extended to address new features and new functionality, so developers are encouraged to investigate the material available there in addition to the material here. In other words, this material is just a starting point, a "window" into what can be done using CAPI as a framework. Innumerable features of CAPI are not discussed here, so just because we don't cover something, don't assume it can't be done.

8.2 PREPARING THE ENVIRONMENT

There are a number of ways to implement and integrate with CAPI depending on the language we are using and the type of functionality we need to use. We can use CAPI through the functions provided through the Platform SDK (in the same manner we would access any of the other Windows API), use functionality supplied through CAPICOM (a COM interface to the core CAPI architecture), or use the .NET framework class library to access the cryptographic routines in the `System.Security.Cryptography` namespace. To prepare our platform to use these technologies, we need one of three things:

- An application development environment configured to make use of the functions supplied within the Platform SDK
- An application development environment capable of using COM automation components
- An application development environment capable of making use of the .NET framework

Since both CAPI and the .NET cryptography classes are Microsoft technologies, all of what we discuss in this chapter relates specifically to Microsoft Windows development. As such, we're going to assume that developers reading this are probably using a development tool in the Visual Studio family (e.g., Visual C++, Visual C#, Visual Basic, etc.), or another tool that is already configured to build Windows applications (such as a tool that is already configured to locate the appropriate files from the platform SDK). If this is the case, no further preparation of the environment is required. In other words, any tool that can develop Windows applications can also build CAPI applications (e.g., in a C context, `wincrypt.h`, which contains the majority of the definitions for CAPI functionality, is included directly by the Platform SDK's main header file `windows.h`). Therefore, you can leap right in to the business of building applications with CAPI. It should be noted, however, that to use some of the more recent functional improvements available in the library (e.g., AES functionality), we may need to update the version of the platform SDK—the SDK can be updated via the Microsoft Platform SDK Web site.[1]

8.3 CRYPTOAPI VERSUS .NET SECURITY CLASSES

Before we delve into the specifics of cryptography as per Microsoft's implementation, we need to get a few definitions out of the way. As used within this section, the term *CryptoAPI* or *CAPI* refers specifically to the Cryptographic Application Programming Interface. This is functionality exposed through the Microsoft Platform SDK for the purposes of allowing Windows applications to make use of operating system security services. Historically, this API was introduced in Windows NT 4.0 and OSR 2 of Microsoft Windows 95[2] and has been built upon since that time. The easiest way to make use of the functionality is through the same mechanism as we would any other Platform SDK service. In C/C++ environments, for example, we can dynamically link against the appropriate .dll objects that contain the functionality and call the appropriate functions, or we can statically link against the supplied .lib files provided in the SDK distribution. In other environments, such as Visual Basic, we can dynamically link the appropriate shared object and use the functionality provided to use within the platform itself. Within the past few years, Microsoft has made available additional security functionality within the .NET framework to streamline the process of writing security functionality. Within the context of these chapters, we refer to this functionality as the .NET Security Classes, specifically the functionality offered via the `System.Security.Cryptography` namespace. In discussing these various approaches, it should explicitly be stated that the Platform SDK is *not* the easiest way to get our job done. Rather, using the .NET framework is much simpler, provides the same (or extended) functionality, and will enable us to complete our development goals faster in most circumstances. We'll see the extent to which this is true as we move through this chapter.

In almost every circumstance, working with the .NET classes is far preferable to working with CAPI given both the flexibility and ease of use. What might take 100 lines of CAPI code to accomplish can generally be done in a fraction of that time using .NET. There are times, however, when we will have no choice but to use CAPI; for example, if we are building client support into a legacy client/server application. Additionally, we might wish to optimize performance and thus avoid the use of managed code, or we might find it difficult to use the semantics of the .NET C++ managed extensions and prefer writing to the CAPI instead. No matter what the impetus is, we cannot assume that use of .NET will apply in all circumstances. Given that we will be covering both APIs, we've organized this chapter by task rather than by API, and within each task, we've covered the easier to use .NET framework first and the more difficult to use CAPI functions afterward. This is to present the "easier to use" material first, and only once that's out of the way to cover the more difficult material. We anticipate that the "easier" material will be targeted first by a developer with limited time, and only if that approach is inaccessible will a developer consider a more complicated or "bulkier" CAPI approach.

8.3.1 CAPICOM: An Alternative Interface

CAPICOM is a COM interface to the CryptoAPI. CAPICOM provides some limited visibility into the rich CryptoAPI through automation and thereby allows visibility into cryptographic functionality from scripting environments such as JScript and VBScript. Historically, CAPICOM was used in environments like IIS ASP scripting where CAPI functionality was required, but calling the low-level platform SDK functions was either impractical or impracticable. As a brief overview, CAPICOM is an ActiveX control (capicom.dll) that was registered with the system and allowed scripting developers to use signing, verification, encryption, and decryption functionality. However, in today's world, CAPICOM is of limited usefulness for a few reasons. Primarily, the purpose of CAPICOM is to render cryptographic functionality accessible to scripting developers; this purpose has been obviated by the functionality in the .NET SDK. Additionally, even if we preferred CAPICOM for whatever reason (perhaps we are already familiar with the API and would prefer using it rather than learning the .NET API), the functionality within CAPICOM is limited to a highly reduced subset of the encryption and signing functionality available both through .NET and the CryptoAPI. For example, the CAPICOM symmetric encryption interface supports only the following algorithms:

- RC2
- RC4
- DES
- Triple-DES

Other symmetric algorithms (e.g., AES) are not supported. Since there is rarely a case when we would prefer to use a limited complicated API when a simpler, cleaner, and more functional API is available in all the same circumstances (i.e., .NET), we will not be going into CAPICOM much (if at all) in this chapter. While there are some CAPICOM examples on the companion CD-ROM (/Examples/Chapter 8/CAPICOM) included for the sake of completeness, we ask that a developer question seriously its use before committing to a design that relies upon it.

8.4 SYMMETRIC ENCRYPTION AND DECRYPTION WITH .NET

Encryption and decryption, in Microsoft's .NET methodology, takes place predominantly by means of streams; more specifically, by attaching an instance of a special type of stream called a *CryptoStream* to a more traditional stream like a MemoryStream or a file. As we write data to the CryptoStream or read data from it, the encryption or decryption takes place. To generate the CryptoStream, first, we will instantiate a *service provider* that implements that algorithm we are interested in using, and we will subsequently attach that service provider, in combination with the appropriate key, to the CryptoStream. Put together, these two tasks are extremely simple to use and incredibly powerful.

8.4.1 Using CryptoStream

Since the `CryptoStream` class is so powerful, it deserves special recognition and enhanced explanation before we go too far into how it is used for symmetric cryptography. `CryptoStream` is the mechanism we will use time and time again to bind a regular "run of the mill" stream (such as the stream classes found in `System.IO`) to classes that implement the `ICryptoTransform` interface. In programming with .NET, you're probably already familiar with streams, the interface that .NET provides for writing and reading to sockets, files, and memory in an abstract way. We've probably used file streams (`System.IO.FileStream`), for example, to write data to the filesystem, or memory streams (`System.IO.MemoryStream`) to write data to a static buffer. We've probably written code like the following C# code that uses streams in a "traditional" way:

```
    System.IO.FileStream fStream = new System.IO.FileStream
("fstream.txt",
    System.IO.FileMode.Create);
    fStream.Write(dataBuffer, 0, dataBuffer.Length);
    fStream.Close();
```

However, by instantiating a `CryptoStream` instance, we can apply anything that implements a cryptographic transformation (through the `ICryptoTransform` interface) to data passing through the stream. What makes this so incredibly powerful is that almost all of the functionality for encrypting data, generating hashes, computing MACs, and so forth, implements the `CryptoStream` interface. This means that we can seamlessly apply cryptography to any data stream, or we can chain cryptographic functions together to perform incredibly complex functionality with relatively little code. For example, we could couple a `CryptoStream` containing a symmetric algorithm with one that produces a hash, and simultaneously generate a hash of the data while we encrypt it. The only thing we have to worry about is the order in which we construct the streams and tie them to each other (e.g., we might want to ensure that the plaintext of a file is hashed before we encrypt it). In any event, we will use the CryptoStream class repeatedly throughout this section to perform various cryptographic tasks, so it helps to become familiar with it up front.

To make use of the encryption functionality, first we will need to locate the appropriate service provider that maps to the algorithm we wish to use. As of the time of this writing, the default service providers available are:

`RijndaelManaged`: A service provider implementation of the Rijndael algorithm. Note that Rijndael is the algorithm upon which AES is based; in other words, don't let the name fool you: use of Rijndael with a key-length specified in the AES will provide equivalent functionality.

`TripleDESCryptoServiceProvider`: A service provider implementation of Triple-DES.

`DESCryptoServiceProvider`: A service provider implementation of DES.

`RC2CryptoServiceProvider`: A service provider implementation of RC2.

The specific process for using the encryption functionality entails binding a key and (if needed, an IV) to the algorithm. Once we have done so, we can attach the implementation to a CryptoStream using the `CreateEncryptor ()` method to obtain a reference to an object implementing the `ICryptoTransform` interface (an interface that does cryptography on a block-by-block basis). By contrast, if we wish to decrypt data, we would call the `CreateDecryptor` method. In short, the `CreateEncryptor()` and `CreateDecryptor()` methods of our algorithm's service provider will generate for us the appropriate object to supply to the CryptoStream constructor during instantiation.

Laid out more specifically, the following steps are all that are required to generate a CryptoStream to encrypt data:

1. Instantiate a service provider of the appropriate algorithm type. As of the time of this writing, the algorithms for which service providers exist are DES, Triple-DES, Rijndael (AES), and RC2, all accessible through service provider classes.
2. Call the `CreateEncryptor()` method with the appropriate key and IV (if required) of the service provider to obtain a reference to an `ICryptoTransform` instance. If we do not specify a key and IV at this time, new ones will be created for us from random data.
3. Bind the resultant object to a CryptoStream by specifying it during the call to the CryptoStream constructor.
4. Write to the CryptoStream to apply encryption to the plaintext using the `Write()` method. Write takes a buffer array, an "offset" (where in the buffer to start writing), and a length as its arguments.
5. Close the stream when done.

Let's see these steps in action using C# to encrypt some data. The following code implements the preceding steps and includes some appropriate data-transformation classes (e.g., to render the plaintext string into a byte array in order to write it to the CryptoStream):

```
    String plainText = "This is the plaintext.";
    ASCIIEncoding toAscii = new ASCIIEncoding();
    System.IO.MemoryStream memStream = new
System.IO.MemoryStream(256);
    RijndaelManaged myR = new RijndaelManaged();
    CryptoStream cryptStream = new CryptoStream(memStream,
        myR.CreateEncryptor(), CryptoStreamMode.Write);
    byte[] asciiPlainText = toAscii.GetBytes(plainText.ToCharArray());
    cryptStream.Write(asciiPlainText, 0, asciiPlainText.Length);
    cryptStream.Flush()
    cryptStream.Close();
```

Performing the same operations in any other managed language is almost identical, be it Visual Basic, J#, or even C++. The next example demonstrates the same functionality in C++, but before doing so, we should briefly mention that this book uses the updated C++/CLI syntax for C++ rather than the MC++ syntax that was used in early releases of managed C++. This might seem a bit confusing for those developers who aren't used to the "revamped" syntax, but the few C++ examples listed in this section should not pose much of a problem for those still ramping up on the new syntax. The following note lays out some of the key differences that we're drawing on to allow developers familiar with MC++ to read and understand the examples as presented.

Note about C++/CLI: This chapter uses the relatively new C++/CLI syntax for managed C++ rather than MC++; for the scope of these examples, only the following features are directly relevant:

- *C++/CLI uses the managed reference "cap" punctuator (^) rather than the MC++ pointer "star" punctuator (*) for referenced types. Whereas with MC++ we would instantiate a managed type using the same or similar syntax to traditional object instantiation, C++/CLI uses a slightly modified instantiation syntax to differentiate managed from unmanaged types.*
- *C++/CLI uses the* `gcnew` *operator rather than* `new` *where appropriate for managed type instantiation. MC++ created __gc pointers using the traditional* `new` *operator, which was confusing and no longer allowed under the new syntax; the* `gcnew` *operator allows differentiation between managed (garbage collected) and unmanaged objects.*

- *Array behavior is somewhat different; the stdcli::language namespace allows the creation of arrays using the updated* `array<type>^` *syntax for managed arrays. Note that this requires importation of the appropriate namespace such as a line specifying "*`using namespace stdcli::language;`*" at the beginning of the page.*

We've chosen to use the newer syntax throughout this section, as it allows less confusion between managed and unmanaged types, and in an attempt to "future proof" the examples for longer duration. Therefore, the following would generate the CryptoStream in managed C++ the same way we did in C# earlier:

```
using namespace System;
using namespace System::Security::Cryptography;
using namespace System::IO;
using namespace System::Text;
int _tmain()
{
    System::String^ plainText = "Plaintext";
    ASCIIEncoding^ toAscii = gcnew ASCIIEncoding();
    RijndaelManaged^ myR = gcnew RijndaelManaged();
    MemoryStream^ memStream = gcnew MemoryStream(256);
    CryptoStream^ cryptStream = gcnew CryptoStream(memStream,
        myR->CreateEncryptor(), CryptoStreamMode::Write);
}
```

That's all there is to it! Decryption is just as simple; instead of using the method `CreateEncryptor()`, we use `CreateDecryptor()`. Since we can't rely on the implementation to create a new key and IV for us when decrypting, we'll have to bind the key and IV as appropriate when decrypting, but other than that, the majority of the steps remain the same. Described in depth, the steps for decrypting using a symmetric algorithm are as follows:

1. Instantiate a service provider of the appropriate algorithm type.
2. Call the `CreateDecryptor()` method with the appropriate key and IV of the service provider to obtain a reference to an `ICryptoTransform` instance.
3. Bind the resultant object to a CryptoStream by specifying it during the call to the CryptoStream constructor.
4. Use the CryptoStream to decrypt the ciphertext.
5. Close the stream when done.

The following generates a CryptoStream that can be used for the decryption of the ciphertext generated in the previous example:

```
byte[] block = memStream.ToArray();
System.IO.MemoryStream outStream = new System.IO.MemoryStream();
CryptoStream decryptStream = new CryptoStream(outStream,
    myR.CreateDecryptor(), CryptoStreamMode.Write);
decryptStream.Write(block, 0, block.Length);
decryptStream.Flush();
decryptStream.Close();
```

At the end of this sample routine, the MemoryStream referred to by `outStream` will contain the plaintext that was originally specified in the original encryption.

8.4.2 Keys and Key Generation

Of course, in an actual .NET implementation scenario, we will usually need to do more than just work in the context of a single service provider. In the examples cited previously, sticking to a single service provider allowed us to avoid discussion of key generation while we looked instead at how the mechanics of the encryption calls work. In other words, we leveraged the fact that the `myR` object (our instance of RijndaelManaged) had a random key and IV bound to it—since we did not specify values for either of these parameters, the underlying implementation generated random values for each. In the context of a real-life application, we will find this "default secure key" functionality incredibly useful, but it does not encompass the whole of the functionality we will draw on day to day. In real life, we will likely be forced to "remember" keys from session to session, derive keys from user passwords, store keys, read in key bytes from legacy structures, and so forth. All of these cases are seamlessly handled by the Cryptography classes.

Each service provider contains properties that are used to set the IV and key values, intuitively named the "IV" property and the "Key" property. At any time, we can generate a new key or IV within a service provider class by calling the `GenerateKey()` or `GenerateIV()` methods, respectively, which will cause new random values to be generated. In other words, these methods will generate a new random key or IV as specified and bind it to the appropriate property within the service provider implementation. We can "extract" a key or IV value from a service provider class by referencing the property within the service provider, retrieving the value as a byte array, or we can set the key or IV to a new value by setting the property to a value we specify. All of this is fairly intuitive and can be done in a single line of code. For example, to set a byte array equal to the value of the key used for encryption in our previous example, we would merely author code similar to the following:

```
byte[] theKey = myR.Key;
```

It can't get any simpler than that. To set the value to something else, we would merely set the `myR.Key` property on the left of the assignment, and the target value on the right.

Alternatively, we can explicitly set a `CryptoStream` to use a particular key and IV during the call to `CreateEncryptor()` or `CreateDecryptor()`. Both of these methods are overloaded to have signatures `CreateEncryptor(byte[] key, byte[] IV)` and `CreateDecryptor(byte[] key, byte[] IV)`. Each of these methods provides a handy way for us to specify the appropriate key and IV at the time we create our stream. If we wish to preserve a key or IV value between sessions, all we need do is copy the internal value to a byte array in our application and subsequently save the contents of that byte array. If we need to send the key to another locality, we can employ a number of different strategies such as encryption of that key with an asymmetric key, encryption of the key with a different one (perhaps one derived from a password), and so on.

8.4.3 Password-Based Key Derivation

In many cases, we might want to derive a key from a user-supplied password. The default methodology for doing this as supplied by the .NET cryptography classes is a wrapper around the CryptoAPI methodology for performing this task (`CryptDeriveKey()`, discussed later in this section) that is fairly easy to use. The specific class required to derive a key that can be used in our applications from a supplied password is `PasswordDeriveBytes`. To use this class, all we need do is instantiate it and call the `CryptDeriveKey()` method supplied within the class itself. `CryptDeriveKey` requires four parameters to return a key; the C# method signature is listed as follows:

```
public byte[] CryptDeriveKey(
   string algname,
   string alghashname,
   int keySize,
   byte[] rgbIV
);
```

The input parameters are as follows:

`Algname`: The name of the symmetric encryption algorithm that will be used as part of the key derivation process. This can be DES (passed as a string such as "DES"), Triple-DES (string "TripleDES"), or RC2 (string "RC2").[3] Currently, AES is (unfortunately) not supported.

`Alghashname`: The name of the message digest algorithm that will be used as part of the key derivation process. This can be MD5 (passed as a string such as "MD5"), SHA (string "SHA"), or SHA-1 (string "SHA1")[4].

`Keysize`: The size, in bits, of the desired resultant key.

`rgbIV`: The IV to use for the key-derivation process; note that this is separate and distinct from any IV that will be used within our application for the encryption of data. The IV should be "remembered" by our application since we will need to use it again if we intend to regenerate this key at a later time.

In creating the `PasswordDeriveBytes` object, we'll need to specify the password as a `byte[]` array and a salt as a `byte[]` array. The salt value is optional, but will increase the difficulty of dictionary-type attacks against the password. To demonstrate usage, we are going to leave out the salt, but our null value could be replaced with a value supplied on a user-by-user basis within your application or with a randomly generated value stored with any text encrypted with the password-derived key. Basic usage to generate a 128-bit key is as follows:

```
    PasswordDeriveBytes pdb = new PasswordDeriveBytes("A Robust
Password", null);
    byte[] pdbIV = new byte[] { 0x1, 0x2, 0x3, 0x4, 0x5, 0x6, 0x7, 0x8 };
    byte[] pdbKey = pdb.CryptDeriveKey("RC2", "SHA1", 128, pdbIV);
```

Note that since the `CryptDeriveKey` method is calling the underlying CryptoAPI `CryptDeriveKey` function, the usage is confined to the same constraints enumerated in the "Password-Based Key Derivation" section of the CryptoAPI usage section in this chapter.

8.5 SYMMETRIC ENCRYPTION AND DECRYPTION WITH CRYPTOAPI

CAPI, like every other facet of the Microsoft Windows API, has evolved quite a bit since its inception and initial release in Microsoft Windows NT 4.0. There have been quite a few iterations of the security functionality, and now with the advent of the .NET framework, access to cryptographic functions has become even simpler and much more powerful. Within this section, we'll review both methods of interacting with the security feature-set, both for developers working in a traditional C/C++ context and those working in a .NET context. To start the discussion, we'll review the basics of using CAPI through the default platform SDK interface. To make use of CAPI, there is some terminology we should become acquainted with first, as it will be used repeatedly throughout our tasks of building secure applications:

Cryptographic Service Providers (CSPs): Cryptographic functionality within CAPI is, as stated previously, implemented through a provider architecture (similar to Java's JCA). The underlying cryptographic algorithms are implemented within various CSPs, and we, as users of those algorithms, need to understand that every piece of functionality we make use of will take place within the context of CSP and will use functionality implemented within that CSP. As such, almost all of the functions we call to use cryptographic functionality will require as input a handle to a CSP with an appropriate implementation.

Key containers: It is not always possible or desirable to separate the cryptographic functionality implemented by a CSP from the keys that will be used by that functionality. For example, if we intend to use a hardware key storage device (HSM), we might never wish to have the keys leave that storage device, and instead generate, store, and use the keys only within the context of the hardware device. To provide an abstract interface to the cryptographic functionality in both hardware and software situations (no matter the underlying implementation), CAPI requires that we obtain a reference to a *key container* in our use of cryptographic functionality. A key container is a protected region within the CSP used for secure storage, usually secure storage of keys. Key containers are named, allowing multiple applications to use the same CSP, and each has its own key container it can use. Under most circumstances, to make use of cryptographic functionality, we will need to use keys that are located within this secure storage region.

8.5.1 Obtaining a Handle to a CSP

The first step in making use of the cryptographic functionality is to generate a handle to a CSP and key container, which is done through use of the `CryptAcquireContext` function. The handle we obtain from this function will be used by all subsequent CAPI calls, so it is important to familiarize ourselves with the call early in the process. The function returns a `BOOL` (Boolean) indicating success or failure. It accepts as input a pointer to the handle value we wish to obtain, the name of the key container we wish to retrieve, the name of the CSP we wish to use, a constant delineating the provider type, and one of a few "flags" that provide instruction as to how the function should behave. More detail on the input values is provided here:

Context handle: Supplied to the function as input, the handle pointed to by this value will be modified by the function to refer to a handle to the requested CSP.

Container name: In calling the `CryptAcquireContext` function, we must specifically instruct the CSP which key container we wish to bind to the context we're requesting. A CSP can have multiple key containers, and our application can make use of multiple containers, each with a different name, to help segregate modules, components, or classes. If this value is not specified (i.e., if the pointer is null), a default container name is used. Although much of the sample code supplied by Microsoft uses the default container, it is not recommended that we do this in most situations (doing so can bring about functional issues such as keys being overwritten or otherwise destroyed by other applications).

Provider name: In situations in which we require a specific provider (e.g., when we wish to ensure that we use a hardware CSP), we can explicitly request it by name. If we do not specify a value here, a default provider of the type specified in the next parameter will be used. Unless we are targeting a particular CSP (e.g., a hardware provider), this value is not required.

Provider type: A constant specifying the functional requirements of the CSP we wish to obtain a handle to; the type of provider used will vary depending on the task we wish to perform. Some provider types indicate "general purpose" functionality and some specify particular functionality. For example, if we wish to use a general-purpose CSP that supports AES, we could request a provider of type PROV_RSA_AES. If we only need functionality to implement digital signatures using RSA or DSS, we could request a provider of type PROV_RSA_SIG or PROV_DSS, respectively. These "types" are all constants defined in the Microsoft literature (enumerated in `wincrypt.h` in the Platform SDK).

Flags: Also defined in `wincrypt.h`, one of several flags can be passed to this call:

`CRYPT_VERIFYCONTEXT`: This specifies that private keys will not be required (e.g., the CSP will only be used in a verify context for which access to non-public keys will not be required). If this flag is set, the container name must be null.

`CRYPT_NEWKEYSET`: Generates a new key container under the name specified.

`CRYPT_MACHINE_KEYSET`: Specifies that the keys should be bound to the machine rather than to the profile of the current user. This flag is of primary importance if we are writing a service or other application that runs outside of a user session (such as ISAPI filters or extensions that run inside a service).

`CRYPT_DELETEKEYSET`: Delete the key container specified by the name supplied in the container name variable.

`CRYPT_SILENT`: Do not display any type of UI to the user. Some CSPs will inform the user of key generation activity and/or key usage activity by displaying a dialog box or application window. Use of this flag turns off that functionality.

Note that the use of this function implies that a given application that wishes to store keys must create a valid key container first. Should a key container be requested by name without an application first having created a key container, the `CryptAcquireContext` function will return `FALSE` (indicating error), and `GetLastError()` will return the value `NTE_BAD_KEYSET`. A useful strategy is to call the `CryptAcquireContext` function twice, the first time checking for the NTE_BAD_KEYSET error condition and recalling CryptAcquireContext with the CRYPT_NEWKEYSET parameter in such a case. If we request a context in this way, we must destroy it once we are done using it with a corresponding call to CryptReleaseContext.

8.5.1.1 Account Considerations

Most of the time, the CSPs supplied by default in the OS will store key containers within the profile of the current user. This does not necessarily mean the user that is currently logged on to the system, but refers instead to the user context within which the application is running. This can be problematic if we are writing a service, writing applications that impersonate a number of different users, and so forth. If we are writing an application of this type (e.g., one that requires a particular key to be used inside a service or one where we cannot anticipate under which user context we will be running), we need to consider instantiating the key container appropriately (e.g., through the use of the CRYPT_MACHINE_KEYSET flag in the call to CryptAcquireContext() to bind the keys to a machine rather than a user). Foreknowledge of this can prevent some rather difficult to isolate debugging issues later in our application development, so it helps to spell this out explicitly before we start the development process.

8.5.1.2 Algorithm Identifier Constants

To use symmetric cryptography under CAPI, first we must decide what algorithm we are interested in using. Once we have selected a symmetric algorithm, we should familiarize ourselves with the *algorithm identifier constant* that maps to it. Next, we will need to determine what CSP we require for that algorithm to be available. Finally, we will have to review and understand the appropriate key size for that algorithm. Defined in wincrypt.h, the algorithm identifiers are constants that we will need to supply to the library both in generating keys and initializing the library to perform encryption operations. The following are a few examples of algorithm identifiers as defined in wincrypt.h. Note that this list also includes some of the noteworthy asymmetric encryption constants, hashing constants, symmetric encryption constants, and so forth.

- Message digests:
  CALG_MD2
  CALG_MD4
  CALG_MD5
  CALG_SHA
  CALG_SHA1
  CALG_MAC

- Signing:
  `CALG_RSA_SIGN`
  `CALG_DSS_SIGN`
  `CALG_NO_SIGN`
- Symmetric encryption:
  `CALG_DES`
  `CALG_3DES_112`
  `CALG_3DES`
  `CALG_DESX`
  `CALG_RC2`
  `CALG_RC4`
  `CALG_RC5`
  `CALG_AES_128`
  `CALG_AES_192`
  `CALG_AES_256`
  `CALG_AES`
  `CALG_SHA_256`
  `CALG_SHA_384`
  `CALG_SHA_512`

These are just a handful of what's defined. Obviously, we won't be using all the algorithm constants in our applications. Of those in the list, CALG_AES (and the more-specific AES identifiers) and CALG_3DES will be the symmetric encryption candidates we will most often use.

Important Note about CALG_AES: as of the time of this writing, there are platform restrictions with respect to where CALG_AES can be used. Specifically, CALG_AES is not available on Microsoft Windows 2000 or Microsoft Windows NT 4.0. As a workaround for situations where AES is a requirement, the .NET class System.Security.Cryptography.RijndaelManaged can be used on these platforms provided they are configured to support the .NET framework. Therefore, if we are targeting a version of Windows on which AES is not supported through CryptoAPI, we will need to use a different library, use a different algorithm, or use .NET.

8.5.2 Using `CryptEncrypt()`

The core of the CryptoAPI encryption functionality for symmetric encryption is available through the `CryptEncrypt` routine. This function is defined in `wincrypt.h`, and to make use of it, our library will have to link with `advapi32.lib` (done by default in new projects using Visual Studio). The function signature is as follows as per MSDN[5]:

```
BOOL WINAPI CryptEncrypt(
  HCRYPTKEY hKey,
  HCRYPTHASH hHash,
  BOOL Final,
  DWORD dwFlags,
  BYTE* pbData,
  DWORD* pdwDataLen,
  DWORD dwBufLen
);
```

Usage is not exactly intuitive, since some of the values serve as both input and output; therefore, let's explain the meaning of the parameters in detail:

hKey: will be a handle to the key we wish to use for this encryption operation. We will need to use one of the many key manipulation functions provided to us in the library in order to obtain a key in an appropriate format to be supplied to this routine. In the next section, we'll talk about mechanisms for using a key in this manner.

hHash: is an optional handle to a hashing algorithm should we require or desire one. If we wanted, for example, to simultaneously compute a hash of our plaintext while encryption the data, we could obtain a performance benefit by computing both transformations at the same time. We will not be using this parameter within the sample code in this chapter.

Final: will instruct the underlying implementation as to whether this is the final iteration of `CryptEncrypt()`. In using `CryptEncrypt()`, we may iteratively call the function a number of times with a subset of the total data we wish to encrypt. This is useful, for example, if we wish to encrypt a large file or if we are encrypting data on a socket. Specifying that a given block is the "final" block allows the underlying implementation to apply padding to any odd-sized blocks we may have supplied to the algorithm and allows the implementation to depopulate any internal state that has been set up for chaining blocks together (e.g., with CBC mode of a block cipher).

dwFlags: is mostly unused with the exception of overriding the default padding methodology in certain asymmetric encryption contexts. Most of our usage will leave this value empty. A full list of values is contained in the MSDN usage instructions for this call either on the MSDN library or on the Microsoft Web site.

pbData: will contain the buffer we wish to encrypt and will be used by the implementation to store the encrypted text. *Note that this implies that our plaintext data will be overwritten.* The buffer supplied should be of a size large enough to contain the ciphertext output and any padding. This routine does not automatically maintain any internal plaintext buffers to handle odd-sized data; as such, the data we supply must be a multiple of the block size for the algorithm we are using unless the `Final` flag is set.

`pdwDataLen:` should contain the size of the plaintext data pointed to by `pbData` as input to the function; this is *not* necessarily the size of the buffer but the size of the valid data contained in the buffer. The function will set this variable internally to be the size of the output data. *This implies that the value we supply will be overwritten.* As stated previously, the data we supply must be a multiple of the block size for the algorithm we are using unless the `Final` flag is set.

`dwBufLen:` is the size in bytes of the buffer that is pointed to by `pbData`; this is the amount of space allocated for the buffer, not the size of the input data.

To use this function, we'll have to "tee" a few things up before we can make the call. Specifically, aside from setting up the appropriate input/output buffer and obtaining a context, we will need to obtain a valid reference to a key that can be supplied to the routine for performing the encryption. We can do this one of a few different ways using functions available in the SDK:

- Use `CryptGenKey` to obtain a new random symmetric session key.
- Use `CryptImportKey` to import existing key bytes into a key structure.
- Use `CryptDeriveKey` to generate a new key from hashed data such as a password.

Each of these functions and the associated usage are explained in the following subsections.

8.5.3 Generating a New Session Key Using `CryptGenKey()`

To generate a new random symmetric key, we will use the `CryptGenKey()` function. Note that although this same function is used to generate both asymmetric and symmetric keys, the usage we discuss here applies only to symmetric key generation. According to MSDN, the following is the function signature for `CryptGenKey`:

```
BOOL WINAPI CryptGenKey(
  HCRYPTPROV hProv,
  ALG_ID Algid,
  DWORD dwFlags,
  HCRYPTKEY* phKey
);
```

Usage is easy: `hProv` is the handle to the context, `Algid` is the algorithm identifier that corresponds to the symmetric algorithm for which we desire to generate a key, `dwFlags` is one of a few "behavior-controlling" flags that govern the behavior of the underlying CSP, and `phKey` is the output where the new key will be stored. Since this function is used to generate both symmetric and asymmetric keys, not all of the flags will be appropriate for our usage addressing symmetric algorithms. We'll list them all for the sake of completeness, but note that only the symmetric-key generation flags are appropriate. The following flags are available for use, but most of the time, we will limit our selection to the first two:

CRYPT_EXPORTABLE: Denotes that the key can be exported from the CSP. Within most usage scenarios, we should set this flag in the context of symmetric session keys. If we do not, only our application in its current context will be able to access the keys.

CRYPT_USER_PROTECTED: Denotes that the key is "protected" by the user. The specific behavior of this protection will vary from CSP to CSP, but in general, it means that a user is presented with a dialog box questioning if the user wishes to allow or disallow access.

CRYPT_ARCHIVABLE: Allows the key to be exported upon initial creation, but not exported after an initial call has been made to `CryptDestroyKey()` or the handle is otherwise closed.

CRYPT_CREATE_SALT: Specifies that a key should contain a corresponding salt value; this functionality is useful only with 40-bit keys, and is therefore not within the scope of our usage.

CRYPT_NO_SALT: Specifies that a 40-bit key should not contain a corresponding salt value; not within the scope of our discussion.

CRYPT_PREGEN: Specifies that the context is a DSS or Diffie-Hellman initial key generation. This is not in the scope of our usage for symmetric key generation.

Most of the time, we'll only use the first few flags for the majority of situations we will encounter in new-application situations. Legacy code situations are another matter, however—we might come across legacy code that uses the 40-bit key specific salt parameters under those situations.

8.5.4 Usage Example: Encryption

Putting the previous discussions on context acquisition, buffer encryption, and session key generation together, the following usage example demonstrates how to instantiate a CSP, generate a random session key, and encrypt a buffer containing arbitrary plaintext:

```
#include <string.h>
#include <windows.h>
#include <iostream.h>
```

```
void main() {
try {
    HCRYPTPROV hProv;

    BOOL didItWork = CryptAcquireContext(&hProv, //provider handle
        "myContainer",  //container name
        NULL, //no provider name, use default
        PROV_RSA_AES, // AES provider for updated algorithms
        NULL); //no flags

    if(!didItWork) {
        if(GetLastError()==NTE_BAD_KEYSET) {

            //same as above, only use CRYPT_NEWKEYSET to
            //try to create a new container
            didItWork = CryptAcquireContext(&hProv,
 "myContainer",
                NULL, PROV_RSA_AES,
                CRYPT_NEWKEYSET); //new key flag

            if(!didItWork) {
                throw GetLastError();
            }
        } else {
            throw GetLastError();
        }
    }
    HCRYPTKEY myKey = 0;

    didItWork = CryptGenKey(hProv, //provider handle
        CALG_AES_128, //algorithm for key generation
        CRYPT_EXPORTABLE, //can export the key
        &myKey); //key handle

    if(!didItWork) {
        throw GetLastError();
    }

    const char * plaintext = "PlainText.";
    unsigned char buffer[256];
    unsigned long strSize = strlen(plaintext)+1;
    memcpy(buffer, plaintext, strlen(plaintext)+1);
```

```
    didItWork = CryptEncrypt(
mykey, //key handle.  specifies algorithm
        NULL, //no hashing algorithm for AES
        TRUE, //only one iteration, so it is final
        NULL, //no flags
        buffer, //input buffer
        &strSize, //length of input, length of output
        sizeof(buffer)); //size of buffer

    if(!didItWork) {
        throw GetLastError();
    }

    //clean up
    CryptDestroyKey(myKey);
    CryptReleaseContext(hProv, NULL);

} catch (DWORD error) {
    char msgbuffer[1024];
    FormatMessage(
    FORMAT_MESSAGE_FROM_SYSTEM, NULL, error,
    MAKELANGID(LANG_NEUTRAL, SUBLANG_DEFAULT),
    msgbuffer, sizeof(msgbuffer), NULL );
    cerr << msgbuffer << endl << flush;
}
}
```

We don't have to only use AES, and we can iteratively call `CryptEncrypt()` with more data if we like, only specifying that the process is "final" on the last block. Once we are done encrypting our data, we'll need to save the session key somewhere and read it back in at a later time to decrypt the data. This is usually done by "exporting" the key using the `CryptExportKey()` function and reading it back in again with `CryptImportKey()`.

8.5.5 Importing and Exporting Session Keys

When we create a session key using `CryptGenKey()` as we did in the previous section, most of the time, we'll want to save the key for later use. Before we call `CryptDestroyKey()` and overwrite the contents of the key currently in use, we want to use a function like `CryptExportKey()` to make sure we serialize the key into a portable structure for later use. Later, we can read back in the key from the structure generated by using `CryptImportKey()`. These functions provide quite a bit of functionality in addition to merely rendering the key portable, such as the facility to protect the contents of the session keys by encrypting them under the context of a "key exchange key." Actually, it is quite difficult to obtain the plaintext value of a symmetric session key using the default Microsoft-supplied CSPs. In other words, by default we cannot export a secret symmetric session key without providing a handle to a new key under which it is to be encrypted. We can encrypt the session key under the context of a symmetric key or an asymmetric key-exchange key; the most commonly used methodology is to use an asymmetric key for this purpose. Although we haven't yet reached the section of this chapter dealing with asymmetric cryptography, we'll discuss exporting session keys using a key-exchange key at this time, both because it is appropriate to the discussion, and because the majority of the cryptographic functionality will take place "under the hood" and hence does not require our intervention.

This functionality (encrypting the key under another key for safe transportation) is a bit more complicated than some of the other material we've covered so far. However, since it is our primary method for storing session keys between sessions, we'll need to wade through it. From a high level, the goal is to use a public key associated with a user account on the system (or the machine itself) to encrypt the symmetric key during export. Later, a user with access to the corresponding key-exchange private key can decrypt the exported session key, import it, and use the session key to decrypt data. It is important to note that the user context is very important here. If we are running under the context of a service, and we created our context by calling `CryptAcquireContext()` with `CRYPT_MACHINE_KEYSET`, we need to be aware of this if we decide to share keys among other applications that are not in the same context. In short, since the key-exchange key is associated with an *account*, we'll need to consider this when we wish to reimport the key and use it.

Since the procedure here is a little complex, it helps to outline ahead of time the exact steps associated with what we're going to do:

1. Ensure we have a key-exchange key to use for exporting and importing session keys. Generate a new key-exchange key if we do not already have one in the container we're using.
2. Obtain a handle to the key-exchange key to supply to `CryptExportKey()` and `CryptImportKey()`.
3. Use the key-exchange key handle with `CryptExportKey()` to export the symmetric session key.
4. Use the key-exchange key handle with `CryptImportKey()` to import the symmetric session key.

The first step is to make sure a key-exchange key exists within the current context. This is done using the same function we used to create the session key, `CryptGenKey()`. The only difference is that this time instead of specifying a symmetric algorithm to create a session key, we'll be specifying `AT_KEYEXCHANGE`. Since the goal is to allow the key-exchange key to persist between sessions, we only need to do this once the first time we want to export a key, and of course we'll need to free the resources associated with the key by calling `CryptDestroyKey()` when we're finished using it. The usage to do this is as follows:

```
HCRYPTKEY userKey;
didItWork = CryptGenKey(hProv,
    AT_KEYEXCHANGE,
    NULL,
    &userKey);
```

This operation will take a few seconds to complete, so it's important that we plan for this appropriately in our application (such as doing it ahead of time during application startup). Once we've created the key, we can use the CAPI function `CryptGetUserKey()`to obtain a handle to the appropriate user key-exchange key. This sounds difficult, but it really isn't. To call `CryptGetUserKey()`, all we need do is specify the context handle (which we used when generating our session key), a flag specifying `AT_KEYEXCHANGE` (meaning that we're interested in the key exchange key), and a place to store the key that will be obtained. We'll use this same function in other contexts later, but we'll reserve the rest of that discussion once we've covered asymmetric cryptography using CryptoAPI. The usage for this is as follows:

```
didItWork = CryptGetUserKey(hProv,
    AT_KEYEXCHANGE,
    &userKey);
```

So now, we've prepared everything we need to actually get the job of exporting the session key done. As stated, we will use the function `CryptExportKey()` to render the key portable; according to MSDN, the function signature for `CryptExportKey()` is as follows[6]:

```
BOOL WINAPI CryptExportKey(
```

- `HCRYPTKEY hKey,`
- `HCRYPTKEY hExpKey,`
- `DWORD dwBlobType,`
- `DWORD dwFlags,`
- `BYTE* pbData,`
- `DWORD* pdwDataLen`
- `);`

There is a lot we can do with this function; however, to keep the waters from getting cloudy at this point, we're just going to address the simplest possible use-case and reserve a more detailed discussion of key exporting for later in this chapter. The function returns TRUE or FALSE indicating success or failure. Looking at only the subset of functionality to export a key as an unprotected buffer, the following values are appropriate inputs and outputs to this function:

hKey: The handle to the key we wish to export.

hExpKey: Used for protecting the key (protection is optional).

dwBlobType: Governs the type of structure into which the key will be placed.

dwFlags: Parameters specifying additional behavior during export. For the purposes of exporting session keys, this parameter will be either null or CRYPT_DESTROYKEY to indicate that we wish the key to be destroyed after exportation.

pbData: A pointer to the buffer that will be used to hold the exported key "blob" (structure). If we specify a null pointer, the function will only compute the number of required bytes to store the structure (storing the value in **pdwDataLen**).

pdwDataLen: The size of the buffer pointed to by **pbData**. If we specified null for **pbData**, this value will contain the minimum number of bytes required to store the key.

Subsequently, we can import the key back in from the structure using the CryptImportKey() function. According to MSDN, this function has the following signature:

```
BOOL WINAPI CryptImportKey(
  HCRYPTPROV hProv,
  BYTE* pbData,
  DWORD dwDataLen,
  HCRYPTKEY hPubKey,
  DWORD dwFlags,
  HCRYPTKEY* phKey
);
```

As with most CAPI functions, the function returns TRUE or FALSE to indicate success or failure; additionally, the parameters are as follows:

hProv: A handle to the context into which we intend to import the key.

pbData: A pointer to a buffer that contains the serialized structure previously retrieved from CryptExportKey().

dwDataLen: The length of the buffer pointed to by pbData.

hPubKey: Any key that was used to protect the value during export. For the purposes of this discussion, this parameter will be zero to indicate that it has not been protected.

dwFlags: Flags governing the import behavior. For our purposes in this discussion, we will use `CRYPT_EXPORTABLE` if we intend to export the key again, or zero to indicate no flags.

phKey: The output key handle that will be generated for us containing the usable key handle. Note that this handle must be released with `CryptDestroyKey()` when we are done with it.

From a usage perspective, using these functions in this limited capacity is forthright, and is demonstrated here:

```
//get the key exchange key
didItWork = CryptGetUserKey(hProv,
    AT_KEYEXCHANGE,
    &userKey);
if(!didItWork) {
    throw GetLastError();
}

DWORD keyBufferSize = 0;
//first, obtain the size required for the key
//buffer by calling it with null ptr for
//buffer
didItWork = CryptExportKey(myKey,
    userKey,
    SIMPLEBLOB,
    NULL,
    0,
    & keyBufferSize);
if(!didItWork) {
    throw GetLastError();
}
//allocate storage buffer
unsigned char * keyBuffer = new unsigned char[keyBufferSize];

//we've made our buffer the right size,
//now do the actual export
didItWork = CryptExportKey(myKey,
    userKey,
    SIMPLEBLOB,
    NULL,
```

```
        keyBuffer,
        & keyBufferSize);
    if(!didItWork) {
        throw GetLastError();
    }

    CryptDestroyKey(myKey);

    //later, import the key
    didItWork = CryptImportKey(hProv, keyBuffer,
        keyBufferSize, userKey, NULL, &myKey);
    if(!didItWork) {
        throw GetLastError();
    }

    //free resources
    delete keyBuffer;
    CryptDestroyKey(myKey);
    CryptDestroyKey(userKey);
    CryptReleaseContext(hProv, NULL);
```

8.6 MESSAGE DIGESTS WITH .NET

While symmetric encryption using the .NET classes was incredibly easy to effect, use of message digest functionality is even easier. .NET contains a number of hash algorithm implementations, each of which is ultimately derived from the base class `HashAlgorithm`. To generate a message digest, we merely instantiate an object of the appropriate message digest class and call the `ComputeHash()` method. This method will pass back to us a byte array containing the hash of the input data. As of now, the message digest (hash) algorithms are implemented as service providers through the classes listed in Table 8.1.

TABLE 8.1 Service Provider Classes

Algorithm	Class
SHA-1	SHA1CryptoServiceProvider
MD5	MD5CryptoServiceProvider
SHA-256	SHA256Managed
SHA-384	SHA384Managed
SHA-512	SHA512Managed

It should be noted that the `ComputeHash()` methods of these service providers are overloaded to accept varying types of input depending on use. For example, they will accept a byte array, a stream (e.g., to compute the hash of a large file), or a portion of a byte array (accepting a byte array, an offset, and a length).

For example, if we wanted to compute an SHA-256 hash of a message, we could implement code similar to the following (demonstrated in C#):

```
//create our service provider
SHA256Managed sha = new SHA256Managed();

//encode the text as an ASCII byte array
string text = "This is the message to hash";
ASCIIEncoding toAscii = new ASCIIEncoding();
byte[] bText = toAscii.GetBytes(text) ;

//generate the digest
byte[] myhash = sha.ComputeHash(bText);
```

It's as simple as that; upon running this code snippet, the byte array "myhash" will contain the message digest of the input text. If we wanted to use another algorithm, we would merely substitute the appropriate algorithm's class during the instantiation process. The following code demonstrates using MD5 to compute a hash, this time in Visual Basic:

```
    //Create service provider
    Dim myMD5 As New System.Security.Cryptography.
MD5CryptoServiceProvider()
    Dim toHash As New String("this is the message to hash")
    Dim toAscii As New System.Text.ASCIIEncoding()

    //get message as byte array
    Dim toHashAscii As Byte() = toAscii.GetBytes(toHash)
    //perform hash
    Dim hashCode As Byte() = myMD5.ComputeHash(toHashAscii)
```

8.6.1 MAC Functionality with .NET

In addition to creating a simple hash of an input, we can easily compute a MAC of given input data by adding a key and using another subclass of `HashAlgorithm`, `KeyedHashAlgorithm`. To use this functionality, we will instantiate an instance of the service provider that matches the MAC algorithm we want. During instantiation of the MAC service provider, we can choose to specify a key, or we can have the implementation generate a new random key for us by using the default constructor.

With a few exceptions, the majority of hashing functions implemented via a service provider have an HMAC counterpart in 2.0 of the .NET Framework. Since some of that functionality has yet to be thoroughly advertised in the instructional material, it's useful to use the namespace browser in your development environment to see what's implemented (MSDN only has instructions for `HMACSHA1` and `MACTripleDES` listed at this time, although other algorithms are clearly available and usable). After we have instantiated an object of the appropriate type of service provider, we will again create a `CryptoStream`, but this time we will bind it with our MAC-ing service provider instead of an encryption service provider as we did with symmetric encryption. We will send our data through the stream, and in so doing cause the MAC to be applied. Once we have sent the data through the stream, we close it by calling the `Close()` method, and may then obtain the MAC value by extracting the `Hash` property of the service provider. The following C# code demonstrates this usage in action:

```
HMACSHA256 myHMAC = new HMACSHA256();
CryptoStream hmacStream = new CryptoStream(System.IO.Stream.Null,
        myHMAC, CryptoStreamMode.Write);
string text = "This is the message to hash";
ASCIIEncoding toAscii = new ASCIIEncoding();
byte[] bText = toAscii.GetBytes(text);
hmacStream.Write(bText, 0, bText.Length);
hmacStream.Close();
byte[] myMac = myHMAC.Hash;
```

Just as we can get and set the `Key` property in symmetric encryption service providers, we can also get and set the `Key` property in our MAC service providers. This allows us to save the key for later use or to share a key between applications.

In the previous example, we pointed the `CryptoStream` to a Null stream (`System.IO.Stream.Null`). A very useful way to use this class is to point it to a extant stream such as a file or memory stream. By doing so, the underlying implementation will write the data to the stream in linear fashion (e.g., as we write to it) and append the MAC when we close the associated stream. In this way, we can easily append a MAC to any data we are sending down a stream just by running it through a `CryptoStream` serially during the process.

8.7 MESSAGE DIGESTS WITH CRYPTOAPI

To compute a hash of data using CAPI via the Platform SDK, our usage will center on the `CryptCreateHash()`, `CryptHashData()`, and `CryptGetHashParam()` functions. These three functions used together allow us to instantiate a hash object, use that hash object to calculate the hash of data supplied, and then ultimately retrieve the hash value. We will use the first function to generate a handle to a hash object, and the second function to iteratively pass the data through the hash function. According to MSDN, the following is the function signature for `CryptCreateHash()`:

```
BOOL WINAPI CryptCreateHash(
  HCRYPTPROV hProv,
  ALG_ID Algid,
  HCRYPTKEY hKey,
  DWORD dwFlags,
  HCRYPTHASH* phHash
);
```

To use the function, we will need a context handle obtained by calling `CryptAcquireContext()`, we will need the algorithm identifier constant that maps to the hashing function we wish to perform, we can optionally specify a key for MAC generation, and we will specify a pointer where the handle to the newly created hash object will be placed. The constants we can use for the ALG_ID are:

```
CALG_MD2
CALG_MD5
CALG_SHA
CALG_SHA1
```

Once we have generated the hash object, we will then iteratively call `CryptHashData()` to supply the data we wish to hash. The function signature for `CryptHashData()` is:

```
BOOL WINAPI CryptHashData(
  HCRYPTHASH hHash,
  BYTE* pbData,
  DWORD dwDataLen,
  DWORD dwFlags
);
```

In calling this function, we will always specify 0 for the flags parameter, the handle to the hash object created in the previous call to `CryptCreateHash()`, and we will specify the buffer we wish to hash and the corresponding length of the buffer. We can call this function any number of times to add data; for example, if we have a large file we wish to pass in to the function in chunks rather than as one large buffer. Once we have submitted the last of the data to the hash object using this function, we will obtain the results of the hash by calling `CryptGetHashParam()`. Per MSDN, the function signature for this is:

```
BOOL WINAPI CryptGetHashParam(
  HCRYPTHASH hHash,
  DWORD dwParam,
  BYTE* pbData,
  DWORD* pdwDataLen,
  DWORD dwFlags
);
```

As input, we will pass the handle to the hash object, the value `HP_HASHVAL` in the `dwParam` field, a buffer of sufficient size to accommodate the hash value, the length of that buffer, and 0 for the flags. Once we've done this, we cannot supply any more data to `CryptHashData()`.

The following sample code demonstrates using these functions to generate a hash of an arbitrary buffer containing some test data (note that this example presumes you have already established a context):

```
HCRYPTHASH pHash = 0;

//create the hash object
didItWork = CryptCreateHash(hProv,CALG_SHA1, NULL, 0, &pHash);
if(!didItWork) {
    throw GetLastError();
}
const char * toHash = "This is the data to hash.";

//do the work one or more times
didItWork = CryptHashData(pHash, (unsigned char*)toHash,
strlen(toHash)+1, 0);
if(!didItWork) {
    throw GetLastError();
}

//retrieve the hash value
unsigned char hash[20];
DWORD hashSize = sizeof(hash);
didItWork = CryptGetHashParam(pHash, HP_HASHVAL, hash, &hashSize, 0);
if(!didItWork) {
    throw GetLastError();
}

//free the hash object
CryptDestroyHash(pHash);
```

Although we might find it a little counter-intuitive to call three (or more) functions to get a single hash value, the functions are used both for retrieving a hash value directly and for more complex purposes such as creating a keyed hash or signing data. Let's look in the next section at how these same functions could be used to create a MAC over some input data.

8.7.1 MAC Functionality with CryptoAPI

To generate a MAC instead of a message digest, the process is very similar to the previous example of generating a hash. We will call all the same functions, but instead of using a digest algorithm identifier in our call to `CryptCreateHash()`, we will specify `CALG_HMAC` or `CALG_MAC` and we will pass a key as well. Although it is counter-intuitive, in generating the key to use for our HMAC, we will generate the key using the same algorithm constants as if we were generating a symmetric session key of the same (or longer) length. The MSDN documentation recommends using any symmetric key, and seeing as how the requisite key size for HMAC is 160 bits, we'll use a symmetric key that is 160 bits or longer—in this example, a 192-bit AES key. Once we have generated a key, we'll need to inform CAPI that we intend to use HMAC in our hash by calling `CryptSetHashParam()` and telling it that we intend to use HMAC through the `dwFlags` parameter and we want to use SHA1 by using the `HMAC_INFO` struct. We'll want to zero out the entirety of the `HMAC_INFO` struct with the exception of the algorithm we want to use for the HMAC. This might sound a little confusing, but in the context of usage, it's not that difficult to understand:

```
HCRYPTHASH pHash = 0;
HCRYPTKEY hashKey = 0;

//create a key to use for HMAC
didItWork = CryptGenKey(hProv, CALG_AES_192,
    CRYPT_EXPORTABLE, &hashKey);
if(!didItWork) {
    throw GetLastError();
}

//create the hash object
didItWork = CryptCreateHash(hProv,CALG_HMAC, hashKey, 0, &pHash);
if(!didItWork) {
    throw GetLastError();
}

//generate and zero out the struct
HMAC_INFO hmacInfo;
memset(&hmacInfo, 0x0, sizeof(hmacInfo));
//set the algorithm type to use
```

```
    hmacInfo.HashAlgid = CALG_SHA1;

    //bind the parameters to the hash
    didItWork = CryptSetHashParam(pHash, HP_HMAC_INFO,
(BYTE*)&hmacInfo, 0);
    if(!didItWork) {
        throw GetLastError();
    }

    const char * toHash = "This is the data to hash.";

    //do the work one or more times
    didItWork = CryptHashData(pHash, (unsigned char*)toHash,
strlen(toHash)+1, 0);
    if(!didItWork) {
        throw GetLastError();
    }

    //retrieve the hash value
    unsigned char hash[20];
    memset(hash, 0x0, sizeof(hash));
    DWORD hashSize = sizeof(hash);
    didItWork = CryptGetHashParam(pHash, HP_HASHVAL, hash, &hashSize, 0);
    if(!didItWork) {
        throw GetLastError();
    }
```

This is obviously more difficult than using the .NET classes (plus, the .NET classes let us use more secure algorithms like SHA-256), but if we are not in a position to use .NET, this CAPI code will get the job done.

8.8 SIGNING DATA WITH .NET

Just as we saw symmetric algorithms encapsulated in service provider classes, asymmetric cryptographic such as RSA and DSA are also likewise encapsulated. Specifically, RSA is encapsulated in the `RSACryptoServiceProvider` class, and DSA is encapsulated in the `DSACryptoServiceProvider` class. These classes support both encryption for privacy and signing. Just as keys are "automagically" created when we create a new instance of a symmetric encryption service provider, the same is true of the asymmetric cryptographic classes. This is true no matter if we are working with DSA or RSA.

Once we have obtained a new instance of the service provider class, we can immediately use the instance to sign data by calling the `SignData()` method. If we intend to use DSA, we'll call the method directly specifying the data to sign as a string or buffer. If we use RSA, we'll need to specify both the data and the hashing algorithm, since unlike the DSS (the signature specification of which DSA is a part), a specific hashing algorithm isn't called for. To specify the hashing algorithm, we can use a string (indicating the name of the hashing algorithm), the type of the hashing algorithm, or an instance of the hashing algorithm (by passing in a reference to a message digest service provider). Deciding which of these parameters to pass is a matter of style, but in most cases, an instance is easiest and less error prone. The underlying implementation of the `SignData()` method will create a hash of the data we supply (either a byte buffer or a stream), and will then subsequently sign the hash automatically for us. For example, to create a new RSA service provider and use the randomly generated new keys to generate a signature of a file on the disk, we would author code similar to the following C# example:

```
    RSACryptoServiceProvider myRSA = new RSACryptoServiceProvider();
    System.IO.FileStream fStream = new
System.IO.FileStream("c:\\new.txt",
        System.IO.FileMode.Open);
    byte[] theSig = myRSA.SignData(fStream,
        new SHA1CryptoServiceProvider());
```

The code in this sample would read in the contents of the stream pointed to (in this case, the contents of a test file on the filesystem), sign it, and return the signature. If we'd rather specify a buffer rather than a stream in our call to perform the signature, we could do that as well. For example, the following Visual J# code demonstrates using DSA to sign a `ubyte[]` array rather than a stream:

```
DSACryptoServiceProvider myDSA = new DSACryptoServiceProvider();
String toSign = new String("This is the data to sign");
ASCIIEncoding toAscii = new ASCIIEncoding();
ubyte[] signBuf = toAscii.GetBytes(toSign);
ubyte[] sig = myDSA.SignData(signBuf);
```

We do not have to sign and hash the data all in one step. Instead, we could perform the same procedure by breaking it in two steps: first by hashing the data using an instance of a message digest service provider, and then by signing the hash using the `SignHash()` method. However, since we can just specify a stream as input into the `SignData()` method, if we intend to simply sign the data (with applying specific signature formatting), it is often easiest to perform the whole procedure in one quick step using `SignData()`.

To verify a signature at a later time, we need an instance of a service provider that has the public verification key bound to it. Assuming for the moment that we are going to use the same instance of the service provider object we used to generate the signature (since the public key is already bound to it), verification can be easily demonstrated. We would merely call the `VerifyData()` method or `VerifyHash()` to do so. When performing the signature, we had the option to separate the hashing of the data from the creation of the signature, which we didn't do because we could just pass the whole stream into the signing process and thus read the contents of the stream, hash those contents, and sign the hash all in one quick step. However, since we do not have the option of handing anything to the `VerifyData()` method other than a byte array (at least not in the current versions of the SDK), it is often desirable to compute a hash of a stream first and then use the `VerifyHash()` method to determine if the signature is valid. If we do have the data as a byte array, we can use `VerifyData()` instead of going through the extra step. No matter if we decide to verify the data using the `VerifyData()` method or verify the hash using the `VerifyHash()` method, the input arguments are (more or less) the same. We would specify first the corresponding data to be verified (or hash of that data) as a `byte[]` array, a string indicating what algorithm was used to originally generate the hash (e.g., "SHA1"), and the contents of the previously generated signature. `VerifyData()` and `VerifyHash()` both return a Boolean value specifying if the signature is valid—true for valid, false for invalid.

If we wanted to introduce verification to the previous RSA example to demonstrate usage, doing so would be easy. Although, note that since we are working with file streams, we will need to "rewind" (i.e., seek to offset 0 from the beginning of the stream) to make sure the contents of the entire file are reread during the hash generation process:

```
    RSACryptoServiceProvider myRSA = new RSACryptoServiceProvider();
    System.IO.FileStream fStream = new
System.IO.FileStream("c:\\new.txt",
        System.IO.FileMode.Open);
    byte[] theSig = myRSA.SignData(fStream,
        new SHA1CryptoServiceProvider());

    //now get the hash to verify
    SHA1CryptoServiceProvider mySHA = new SHA1CryptoServiceProvider();
    fStream.Seek(0, System.IO.SeekOrigin.Begin);
    byte[] theHash = mySHA.ComputeHash(fStream);

    bool isValid = myRSA.VerifyHash(theHash,
        "SHA1", theSig);
```

Of course, more often than not, we won't have the option of using the same instance of a service provider class for both verification and signature. Therefore, we need a mechanism to bind key information (both private and public) to an instance to make use of this functionality in any real way.

8.8.1 Exporting and Importing Keys

Both RSACryptoServiceProvider and DSACryptoServiceProvider have methods for exporting and importing key information. The primary methods for exporting and importing key information directly are ExportParameters() and ImportParameters(), respectively. ExportParameters() allows us to export either public key only or both private and public key information from a given instance of a service provider class (either RSA or DSA). The ExportParameters() function takes a Boolean value as an argument specifying whether to include the private key in the export information; in calling it, we will specify false to obtain only public key information, or true to obtain both private and public keys. The results of this export will be stored either in an RSAParameters structure or in a DSAParameters structure depending on the type of algorithm we're using. Coupled with native .NET serialization concepts, this methodology is incredibly simple to use. For example, if we wanted to serialize the internal state of an RSACryptoServiceProvider instance into a key file, we could do this easily by using an instance of a BinaryFormatter. Given the verbosity of referring to this class explicitly, we'll assume we've put a "using" call like the following before we refer to it:

```
using System.Runtime.Serialization.Formatters.Binary;
```

Now that we can refer implicitly to the BinaryFormatter class, we could write code like the following to serialize our key data from a running RSA or DSA service provider instance:

```
    //create the instance
    RSACryptoServiceProvider myRSA = new RSACryptoServiceProvider();

    //create a binary formatter and bind it to a stream
    BinaryFormatter binF = new BinaryFormatter();
    System.IO.FileStream keyFile = new
System.IO.FileStream("c:\\key.dat",
                    System.IO.FileMode.Create);

    //serialize the keys into the file
    binF.Serialize(keyFile, myRSA.ExportParameters(true));

    keyFile.Close();
```

Later, we'll need to import the RSAParameters or DSAParameters back into the service provider class to verify signature or to create new signatures using the same key. Doing that is easy as well using the `ImportParameters()` method. `ImportParameters()` takes only one argument, consisting of the previously saved parameters. For example, code like the following does this:

```
RSACryptoServiceProvider newRSA = new RSACryptoServiceProvider();
newRSA.ImportParameters((RSAParameters)binF.Deserialize(
    keyFile, null));
```

Obviously, we want to use discretion with how we approach the saving of the private key information. We might want, for example, to implement a system that encrypts the private key information using a symmetric algorithm (using a password derived key or an application key) by means of a `CryptoStream` during the serialization process depending on the type of application we're writing. In .NET, the ease of use of the functionality allows us to concentrate on the important challenges like "where to store the key" rather than the details of the key export mechanics.

8.8.2 Signature Formats

Using the `SignData()` method is the most direct way to create a hash and a resultant signature. However, in many applications, we must ensure interoperability with other products or that signatures generated by our application conform to a particular standard. To meet those goals, we will need to introduce two new classes to the equation: specifically, the base classes `AsymmetricSignatureFormatter` and `AsymmetricSignatureDeformatter`. The subclasses of these two base classes allow us to impose rules on how a signature is represented and the format that is used to generate the final resultant output. We can use the following formatters to represent signatures in the current iterations of the .NET framework:

- `DSASignatureFormatter` (DSA)
- `RSAPKCS1SignatureFormatter` (RSA)

The `DSASignatureFormatter` will ensure that the signatures we generate comply with the signature format required by the DSS, and the `RSAPKCS1SignatureFormatter` will ensure that the signatures comply with PKCS #1, version 1.5. To use a signature formatter, we merely instantiate the type of formatter we intend to use in our application, bind the appropriate message digest algorithm to it through the `SetHashAlgorithm()` method, and then call the `CreateSignature()` method, specifying the hash value we wish to use for the signature process. The following C# example demonstrates how this would be effected using RSA to generate a PKCS #1 signature:

```
    //new service provider bound to signature format
    RSACryptoServiceProvider myRSA = new RSACryptoServiceProvider();
    RSAPKCS1SignatureFormatter signFormat = new
RSAPKCS1SignatureFormatter(myRSA);

    //bind appropriate hash algorithm
    signFormat.SetHashAlgorithm("SHA1");

    SHA1CryptoServiceProvider mySHA = new SHA1CryptoServiceProvider();
    System.IO.FileStream toSign = new System.IO.FileStream("c:\\new.txt",
        System.IO.FileMode.Open);
    byte[] hash = mySHA.ComputeHash(toSign);

    //sign the hash and create signature
    byte[] theSig = signFormat.CreateSignature(hash);
```

Checking the signature is just as easy, only instead of using the "formatter," we'll use the corresponding "deformatter." In calling the deformatter, we'll start by using the `SetHashAlgorithm()` method to set the appropriate message digest algorithm that was used to create the signature, and subsequently we will call the `VerifySignature()` method to check the validity of the signature. The following code demonstrates using an instance of `RSAPKCS1SignatureDeformatter` to check the validity of the signature generated in the previous sample:

```
//create new deformatter
//create new deformatter
RSAPKCS1SignatureDeformatter formatVerify = new
    RSAPKCS1SignatureDeformatter(myRSA);

//bind hash algorithm
formatVerify.SetHashAlgorithm("SHA1");

//verify
bool isValid = formatVerify.VerifySignature(hash, theSig);
formatVerify = new
    RSAPKCS1SignatureDeformatter(myRSA);

//bind hash algorithm
formatVerify.SetHashAlgorithm("SHA1");

//verify
bool isValid = formatVerify.VerifySignature(hash, theSig);
```

Creation of a signature compliant with the DSA is just as easy as the creation of the PKCS #1 signatures in the previous samples. For example, the following Visual Basic code demonstrates how we would create a signature using a formatter and verify it using a deformatter using the DSA rather than PKCS #1:

```
'Create new asymmetric provider
Dim myDSA As New DSACryptoServiceProvider()

'bind provider to the formatter and deformatter
Dim sigFormat As New DSASignatureFormatter(myDSA)
Dim verifyFormat As New DSASignatureDeformatter(myDSA)

'create hashing provider
Dim mySHA As New SHA1CryptoServiceProvider()

'buffer to sign
Dim toSign As New String("This is the text to sign")
Dim toAscii As New System.Text.ASCIIEncoding()

'set formatters to the right hashing algorithm
sigFormat.SetHashAlgorithm("SHA1")
verifyFormat.SetHashAlgorithm("SHA1")

'hash the text and create the signature
Dim theHash As Byte() = mySHA.ComputeHash(toAscii.GetBytes(toSign))
Dim theSignature As Byte() = sigFormat.CreateSignature(theHash)

'verify
Dim isValid As Boolean = verifyFormat.VerifySignature(theHash,
theSignature)
```

This mechanism, using signature "formatters" to sign data and using a corresponding signature "deformatter" to verify the signature, is extremely powerful and easy to use.

8.9 SIGNING DATA WITH CRYPTOAPI

CAPI provides signature functionality as well. The mechanisms provided by CAPI for signing are complicated and difficult to use, but they do provide enormous versatility to the developer (versatility that is not accessible in the current .NET Cryptography classes). There are a few ways to sign using the CryptoAPI-supplied functions; the "lowest level" of these functions, which we will discuss first, does not incorporate hashing and signing into a single call. In other words, the creation of the digest from the message and the application of asymmetric cryptography to the digest are two discrete steps. First, we will create a digest of the message as we did earlier in this chapter, and then we will apply the signature to that hash by calling a new function, `CryptSignHash()`.

8.9.1 Signing a Hash with CAPI

According to MSDN, the following is the signature for this function:

```
BOOL WINAPI CryptSignHash(
  HCRYPTHASH hHash,
  DWORD dwKeySpec,
  LPCTSTR sDescription,
  DWORD dwFlags,
  BYTE* pbSignature,
  DWORD* pdwSigLen
);
```

The arguments to this function are as follows:

`hHash`: The handle to the hash object created through previous calls to `CryptCreateHash()` containing the hashed data generated with `CryptHashData()`.

`dwKeySpec`:– A `DWORD` indicating which key in the user's key container to use for the signature: as of this time, this can either be `AT_KEYEXCHANGE` or `AT_SIGNATURE`.

`sDescription`: Must be `NULL`.

`dwFlags`: Flags indicating how the signature is to be applied. Use this flag to indicate if the OID (object identifier) of the hashing algorithm should *not* be placed in the signature (`CRYPT_NOHASHOID`), or if the signature will be generated according to FIPS 186-2 (`CRYPT_X931_FORMAT`). If no flag is set, the OID will be placed in the signature as per PKCS #7.[7]

`pbSignature`: The buffer to hold the output signature value. If this value is null, the function will merely indicate the minimum resultant buffer size instead of computing the actual signature.

`pdwSigLen`: A pointer to a `DWORD` indicating the amount of data allocated for the signature buffer and used internally by the function to store the actual amount of data used within that buffer.

Use of this function to generate a signature presupposes that a key of the appropriate type is located within the key container associated with the hash object; if there is no key of the appropriate type (e.g., `AT_SIGNATURE`), this call will fail. If we do not have a key already, we will need to write code similar to the following to generate one:

```
HCRYPTKEY theSigningKey;
didItWork = CryptGenKey(hProv, AT_SIGNATURE, NULL, &theSigningKey);
if(!didItWork) {
    throw GetLastError();
}
CryptDestroyKey(theSigningKey);
```

Once we have generated a key, code similar to the following will allow us to generate a signature given a hash:

```
    //determine size
    DWORD sigLen = 0;
    didItWork = CryptSignHash(pHash, AT_SIGNATURE, NULL, NULL, NULL,
&sigLen);
    if(!didItWork) {
        throw GetLastError();
    }

    //generate the signature
    unsigned char * sig = new unsigned char[sigLen];
    didItWork = CryptSignHash(pHash, AT_SIGNATURE, NULL, NULL, sig,
&sigLen);
    if(!didItWork) {
    throw GetLastError();
    }
    delete sig;
```

This example makes use of this function to provide the size of the resultant signature buffer first and then the actual performing of the signing process once that buffer has been automatically generated. Once we are done using the hash, we will need to destroy it just as we would if we had created the hash object for the purpose of a message digest. This could be done such as:

```
CryptDestroyHash(pHash);
```

8.9.2 Verifying a Hash with CAPI

The verification of signatures using a similar process is possible as well. As with signing, we will first obtain a hash of the data using the message digest functions outlined earlier in the chapter, and we will then use the SDK function `CryptVerify Signature()` to ensure the signature is correct and valid. According to MSDN, the function signature of `CryptVerifySignature()` is as follows:

```
BOOL WINAPI CryptVerifySignature(
  HCRYPTHASH hHash,
  BYTE* pbSignature,
  DWORD dwSigLen,
  HCRYPTKEY hPubKey,
  LPCTSTR sDescription,
  DWORD dwFlags
);
```

The following are the parameters to this function:

hHash: The hash algorithm object that was used to recompute the hash of the data that was signed.

pbSignature: The buffer containing the signature bytes.

dwSigLen: The length of the signature.

sDescription: Unused. This parameter must be null.

dwFlags: The same flag value that was set when the signature was created.

Of course, necessitated by this function is acquisition of an appropriate key object containing the public key that corresponds to the private key originally used to create the signature. A brief discussion of how this key is to be obtained is warranted before we delve into the specifics of how to call the verification function.

8.9.2.1 Obtaining the Verification Public Key

Since the verification process presupposes that the caller has access to the public key, we will need to account for this in our applications. In practice, this means that our applications calling this routine will need to use the same key context as was originally used to create the signature, or specifically import the public key for the verification process. If we are using the same key context, we can use a function like `CryptGetUserKey()` to retrieve the private/public key pair of type `AT_SIGNATURE`. Recalling our previous discussions of keys, we've seen this function used in the past under other circumstances; for example, to make session keys available between applications that do not share the same context. Use of this function for acquisition of the signing key proceeds in much the same way it did for key exchange keys. However, this time, instead of specifying `AT_KEYEXCHANGE` as the type of key we wish to obtain a handle to, we will specify `AT_SIGNATURE` as we wish to obtain the signing key. Sample usage is as follows:

```
HCRYPTKEY userKey;
didItWork = CryptGetUserKey(hProv, AT_SIGNATURE,
    &userKey);
if(!didItWork) {
```

```
        throw GetLastError();
    }
```

However, if we do not have the luxury of using the same context (which will be most real-life scenarios), we'll need to specifically make the public key available to applications that will need to verify signatures. One way we can do this is by using the `CryptExportKey()` function that we covered in our dealings with the sharing of session keys. However, this usage requires that we use the `CryptExportKey()` function in a somewhat different way from when we used it previously. Recalling our previous examination of this function, we were required to specify a key exchange key that would be used to protect the key contents after exportation as part of the process of rendering the session key portable. However, in this context, the key we need is only the public data—since it is by definition public, it would not make sense to require any protection of the underlying key data. Since we do not need to supplementally protect the key contents, our usage does not require the specification of an additional key, so we can leave any references to an additional key out of our call entirely. Therefore, in making use of the exportation functionality to make the public key "generally available," we would call the `CryptExportKey()` in a manner similar to the following:

```
//export the key for later signature verification
DWORD pubDataLen = 0;
unsigned char* pubKeyData = 0;

//find out how big our buffer needs to be
didItWork = CryptExportKey(userKey, NULL, PUBLICKEYBLOB,
    NULL, pubKeyData, &pubDataLen);
if(!didItWork) {
    throw GetLastError();
}

//allocate data of the right size
pubKeyData = new unsigned char[pubDataLen];

//export the key
didItWork = CryptExportKey(userKey, NULL, PUBLICKEYBLOB,
    NULL, pubKeyData, &pubDataLen);
if(!didItWork) {
    throw GetLastError();
}
```

Once we have exported the key, we can import it in preparation for our call to `CryptVerifySignature()`. Importation operates in a straightforward manner just as we would do with a shared session key:

```
HCRYPTKEY userKey;
didItWork = CryptGetUserKey(hProv, AT_SIGNATURE,
    &userKey);
if(!didItWork) {
    throw GetLastError();
}
```

Importing the key in this way, we can now go about calling the signature verification function, specifying the appropriate public key when called upon to do so. Of course, no matter how we obtain the key object, we must remember to free it when we are done with our cryptographic operations through a call to `CryptDestroyKey()`:

```
CryptDestroyKey(userKey);
```

8.9.2.2 Performing the Verification

Once we have a valid key handle to use and we have generated a hash of the data we wish to validate, all we need do is call the signature verification function outlined earlier. The function will return `TRUE` if the signature is valid, and `FALSE` both in the event that the signature is not valid and an error occurs that prevents the signature from being validated. The value of `GetLastError()` will vary depending on the reason for which the signature verification failed; the most common error condition is `NTE_BAD_SIGNATURE`, which arises due to an invalid or incorrectly formatted signature.

```
didItWork = CryptVerifySignature(pHash, sig, sigLen, importedKey,
                                 NULL, 0);
if(!didItWork) {
    if(GetLastError() == NTE_BAD_SIGNATURE) {
        //likely that the signature was invalid
    }
    throw GetLastError();
}
```

And that's the whole process! We can directly incorporate the signing and verification functions into applications that need to use it.

8.10 RANDOM NUMBER GENERATION WITH .NET

Unlike some of the other libraries covered in detail throughout the latter portions of this book, we will not often need to explicitly generate random numbers for cryptographic purposes when using the Microsoft-supplied libraries. As such, we haven't needed to specifically address random number generation in this section at all. In fact, the typical situations in which we would need to use random numbers (signatures using DSA, symmetric key generation, etc.) are all abstracted from us to the point that we do not need to incorporate random number generation directly at any point during any of the usage we've covered so far. However, there are other circumstances within our applications where we might need to gain access to cryptographically robust random numbers, and both the .NET SDK and the CryptoAPI provide easy-to-use mechanisms for gaining access to these numbers. We might, for example, require random number generation to seed another library, or we might need random numbers within our application itself (for purposes completely unrelated to the application's security features). In this case, we can rapidly and easily draw upon the functionality for random number generation built into the Microsoft libraries.

Similar to the rest of the security functionality, obtaining random bytes using the .NET SDK is significantly easier than it is to get to them through CAPI. To obtain the random values, all we need to do is make use of a new class that we have not yet addressed throughout our discussions: `System.Security.Cryptography.RNGCryptoServiceProvider`. This is a service provider class just the way that all the other functionality related to signing/digests/symmetric cryptography took the form of service providers. Creating an instance of this service provider class and calling the `GetBytes()` method located within that class will allow us to entirely fill any supplied `byte[]` array with random numbers of cryptographic quality. We will not need to seed the generator or perform any other RNG-specific initialization of any kind other than direct instantiation. As such, the usage is straightforward and intuitive; using J# to demonstrate, the following sample code fills a `ubyte[]` array with random data using an instance of `RNGCryptoServiceProvider`:

```
RNGCryptoServiceProvider rng = new RNGCryptoServiceProvider();
ubyte[] myRandom = new ubyte[256];
rng.GetBytes(myRandom);
```

The same usage applies for any other language we might be working in. For example, the following C++ code does the same thing as the previous example:

```
RNGCryptoServiceProvider^ rng = gcnew RNGCryptoServiceProvider();
array<Byte>^ myRandom = gcnew array<Byte>(256);
rng->GetBytes(myRandom);
```

Note that this second example requires the importation of the stdcli::language namespace to make use of the `array` keyword.

8.11 RANDOM NUMBER GENERATION WITH CRYPTOAPI

`CryptGenRandom()` is a function provided by CAPI to generate random bytes using the internal mechanisms that CAPI itself uses to drive symmetric and asymmetric key generation, signature processes, and numerous other functionality that presupposes randomness information. As with the .NET cryptography classes, the circumstances under which we would need to use this functionality are limited, as the random number generation facility used for session key generation, asymmetric key generation, signatures, and so forth is all done internal to the library. However, if our application requires random numbers for some other purpose ancillary to the cryptographic operation of CAPI itself, the function `CryptGenRandom()` is provided for our use.

`CryptGenRandom()` is straightforward to use. Basically, all we need to supply is a context handle (obtained through a call to `CryptAcquireContext()`), a buffer used to store output random data, and a length indicating how much data we wish to obtain from the library. The following example demonstrates how to fill a random buffer with random data in much the same way we did with the .NET cryptography classes outlined in the previous section:

```
    unsigned char randomBuffer[256];
    didItWork = CryptGenRandom(hProv, sizeof(randomBuffer),
randomBuffer);
    if(!didItWork) {
        throw GetLastError();
    }
```

Of course, we will need to appropriately release the context when we are done with it just as we would with any other cryptographic functionality. Including the creation of the context and subsequent release of that context, the following demonstrates how we would generate the random data in context:

```
HCRYPTPROV hProv;

try {
//acquire the context
BOOL didItWork = CryptAcquireContext(&hProv, //provider handle
    "myContainer",  //container name
    NULL, //no provider name, use default
    PROV_RSA_AES, // AES provider for updated algorithms
    NULL); //no flags

if(!didItWork) {
    if(GetLastError()==NTE_BAD_KEYSET) {
```

```
            //same as above, only use CRYPT_NEWKEYSET to
            //try to create a new container
            didItWork = CryptAcquireContext(&hProv, "myContainer",
                NULL, PROV_RSA_AES,
                CRYPT_NEWKEYSET); //new key flag

            if(!didItWork) {
                throw GetLastError();
            }
        } else {
            throw GetLastError();
        }
    }

    //generate the randomness
    unsigned char randomBuffer[256];
    didItWork = CryptGenRandom(hProv, sizeof(randomBuffer),
randomBuffer);
    if(!didItWork) {
        throw GetLastError();
    }

    //release the context
    CryptReleaseContext(hProv, 0);

    //handle error conditions
    } catch (DWORD error) {
        char msgbuffer[1024];
        FormatMessage(
            FORMAT_MESSAGE_FROM_SYSTEM, NULL, error,
            MAKELANGID(LANG_NEUTRAL, SUBLANG_DEFAULT),
            msgbuffer, sizeof(msgbuffer), NULL );
            cerr << msgbuffer << endl << flush;
    }

    }
```

Some of the other libraries covered by this book have significantly more complicated usage for this same functionality. The brevity of obtaining random data using the .NET API (or the "relative" brevity of using CAPI), coupled with the fact that no additional seeding of the generator is required, allows a convenient way to obtain random numbers, including a good random seed for other libraries if we so desire.

8.12 SSL SOCKETS WITH .NET

The real strength of the .NET framework lies in its capability to allow access to Web services. While we will not always be working with Web services in our applications, the underlying engine built into the .NET API to handle these types of requests is a very powerful mechanism we can use for any HTTP (or other socket) transactions. Unquestionably, the easiest way to implement secure network connectivity using .NET is by leveraging the inherent HTTP (over SSL) capabilities of the framework. When working with HTTP, creating secure sockets is a snap, as SSL is "built in" to the default `System.Net.WebRequest` and `System.Net.WebResponse` classes. Instead of specifying a "vanilla" address in our instantiation of the `WebRequest`, we would specify an SSL-protected URL and the implementation will "take care of the rest." Many developers will already be familiar with these classes and will not require further explanation; however, for developers who have not used these objects, a brief explanation is in order. While we don't have time to cover everything about HTTP and how it works in this section, we'll just breeze through the high-level concepts, since networking with .NET is much easier at an "HTTP level" than at a "TCP level."

The .NET WebRequest class encapsulates everything having to do with making an HTTP request; in other words, when we connect to a Web server to obtain data, our browser makes a human-readable HTTP request on our behalf. As an example, that request might look like the following:

```
    GET / HTTP/1.0
    Accept: */*
    Accept-Language: en-us
    Pragma: no-cache
    User-Agent: Mozilla/4.0 (compatible; MSIE 6.0; Windows NT 5.1; SV1;
.NET CLR 1.1.4322; .NET CLR 2.0.40607)
    Host: www.google.com
    Proxy-Connection: Keep-Alive
```

The process of making this request, including the underlying opening of sockets, establishment of connection to the server, formatting of the request headers, and so on is all handled for us by the `WebRequest` class. As a result of the request, the server prepares an HTTP response containing the data that was specified by the request. The response might look like:

```
HTTP/1.0 200 OK
Cache-Control: private
Content-Type: text/html
Server: GWS/2.1
Date: Thu, 21 Apr 2005 14:45:50 GMT
```

```
Connection: Close
....data
```

This resultant data, including the process of reading from the socket, interpreting the response, and so on is handled by the `WebResponse` object. Making use of these classes requires only the briefest of code; for example, to establish a new SSL request using the .NET framework:

```
    String toConnectTo = "https://www.microsoft.com/";
    System.Net.WebRequest myRequest =
System.Net.WebRequest.Create(toConnectTo);
    System.Net.WebResponse myResponse = myRequest.GetResponse();
```

This sample creates a socket connection to Microsoft's SSL Web site and retrieves the response body. By using this code, the request made would appear simply as:

```
GET / HTTP/1.1
Host: www.microsoft.com
```

To manipulate any aspect of the request, we would manipulate the appropriate property within the request object prior to making the response. In this example, all the details of manipulating the socket are handled for us internally to the class. Note that the underlying implementation of these classes will obtain information from the "LAN Settings" controls box as set in Internet Explorer to determine proxy configuration.

The response from the Web server will be encapsulated in the `WebResponse` object that we obtain from calling `GetResponse()`. We can then retrieve the response as a stream using the `WebResponse.GetResponseStream()`, or we can access information about the response by using the properties associated with the object (e.g., obtaining the content length by using the `ContentLength` property).

Of course, we can't always assume that we are going to need to use HTTP alone in our applications. Unfortunately, the .NET framework does not provide a lower level SSL socket methodology such as that provided by OpenSSL (e.g., something analogous to the `SSLSocket` and `SSLServerSocket` functionality we'll see in the Java usage examples). In the event that we require lower level SSL socket interaction, there are third-party components that can be purchased or freely downloaded to provide similar abstractions (e.g., the Mentalis open source SSL socket library, or the for-purchase DART PowerTCP SSL Sockets for .NET library[8]). Alternatively, if we require SSL functionality only to facilitate intercomponent interaction (in other words, to assist in getting our components to talk to each other), one solution we can implement is to use the "remoting" capability for interobject communication in .NET. Remoting is a .NET remote access methodology allowing for intercomponent interaction, which cannot be given a full treatment within the confines of this chapter. However, suffice it to say that the `HTTPChannel` methodology (using SOAP as a transport) will allow for remote invocation and communication in a manner that is compatible with SSL.

ON THE CD

Examples of a remotable type and host process are included on the companion CD-ROM (/Examples/Chapter 8/dotnet_remoteable). Additionally, MSDN provides detailed step-by-step instructions on how to author and enable components that communicate with each other in the section of the .NET framework dealing with remoting.[9]

Of course, if none of these methodologies meets our needs, there's no rule saying that we need to stay within the context of the managed framework. In other words, if our application cannot use HTTP over SSL, is not satisfied by using the remotable functionality, and we cannot install third-party components, we can always use the inherent SSL features of Win32 covered in the next section through the .NET supplied `PInvoke` nonmanaged invocation mechanism. `PInvoke` allows us to obtain access to any of the underlying platform APIs, including the SSPI and WinInet interfaces, which will be covered in the next section. It should be stated, though, that the situations under which we will need to do this are limited, and SSPI is not the easiest interface to use, so a call to OpenSSL rather than SSPI using `PInvoke` is something to consider.

8.13 SSL SOCKETS WITH WININET AND SSPI

ON THE CD

Similar to the SSL functionality provided in .NET, using the Platform SDK, we can establish SSL connectivity "the easy way" (WinInet) or "the hard way" (SSPI), but we can only use the "easy way" when we're using HTTP. Actually, that deserves a bit of clarification: neither of these approaches is "easy." WinInet is complicated to use, and SSPI is even more complicated than that; a useful approach if we require SSL functionality from inside a Windows application is to *use another library*. This may sound like a drastic position to take; after all, we don't want to build in dependencies to more than one library if we don't have to. However, as we'll see as we move through this subsection, SSL using either approach is extremely difficult and requires extremely verbose code. Use of these calls will almost certainly slow your development time more than using a library like OpenSSL, JCE, .NET WebRequest classes, add-on libraries for .NET, or just about anything else. Understandably, there are situations in which we cannot avoid using these calls, but it should be stressed highly that we've found these calls difficult to make and they've slowed our development time in the past. However, if a developer is already fluent in using WinInet, his or her mileage will obviously vary from ours.

So, to select an approach for how to conduct secure communications in our applications, we need to choose between WinInet (if we're using HTTP) and the SSPI if we're using lower level socket functionality. We're probably already slightly familiar with WinInet if we've done much Windows development: WinInet is the default API provided to us for the purposes of establishing remote connectivity, particularly HTTP and FTP functionality. WinInet supports SSL "out of the box" and can be used to establish SSL connections directly. Since we can only use WinInet for a limited set of protocols (i.e., HTTP, FTP, or Gopher), we're limited to HTTP over SSL. SSPI, our other choice, stands for *Security Support Provider Interface*, and while it allows arbitrary data to be sent back and forth over secured sockets, it is complicated and extremely difficult to use, so we'll want to use that as a "path of last resort." It bears saying again given the complexity of usage: if we're using Windows and we want to rapidly author an application that makes use of SSL and we're considering using SSPI, we might be well served to take a moment and ask ourselves if we have the option of installing and using OpenSSL for our socket connectivity to make the process a little easier. However, we'll discuss how to use the interface in the event that using another library is not an option. Note that our goal here is not to cover any of this material in depth—we want to quickly and rapidly get secure communication into our software. If we are writing a more complicated application such as a Web server, SSL accelerator, or any other application where socket connectivity (and secure socket connectivity) will be the main focus of our application, obviously we'll want to delve into these APIs much more than the limited coverage provided in this book.

8.13.1 SSL via WinInet

The steps required to use WinInet to do this are as follows:

1. Use the function `InternetAttemptConnect()` to ensure an Internet connection is established (enabling, if required, any dial-up activity that must take place).
2. (Optionally) use the function `InternetCheckConnection()` to ensure a connection is present. Since this function uses "ping" (ICMP Echo) to determine the connection state, and ping is both slow and unreliable, it is often desirable to leave this call out and assume the Internet connection is already established.
3. Use `InternetOpen()` to acquire the handle that will be used by subsequent functions.
4. Use `InternetConnect()` to establish the appropriate protocol type we are interested in (HTTP).

5. Use `HttpOpenRequest()` to create the HTTP request and bind the appropriate verb, version, agent, and other headers to the request.
6. Use `HttpSendRequest()` to send the actual request and retrieve the server response.
7. Use `HttpQueryInfo()` to retrieve information about the server response.
8. Use `InternetReadFile()` to read the response.
9. Use `InternetCloseHandle()` to free any resources associated with the open connection.

This is the process to establish an HTTP connection to a server. The underlying OS will differentiate between SSL and non-SSL HTTP, so provided we supply the appropriate data in our arguments, we can be assured of a secure transaction. Some of these functions require quite a few arguments, so we'll go through each of the functions in more detail before demonstrating simple usage; hang on, because there are quite a few calls required, each of which has a number of usage options.

8.13.1.1 Function Details in Usage Order

`InternetAttemptConnect()`: This function takes no arguments and returns `TRUE/FALSE`, indicating if the operation was successful.

`InternetOpen()`: This function will return a handle to us that we will use in subsequent ISAPI functions. According to MSDN, the function signature is as follows:

```
HINTERNET InternetOpen(
  LPCTSTR lpszAgent,
  DWORD dwAccessType,
  LPCTSTR lpszProxyName,
  LPCTSTR lpszProxyBypass,
  DWORD dwFlags
);
```

The parameters to this function are as follows:

`lpszAgent`: This will contain the user agent in HTTP transactions.

`dwAccessType`: The "access type" identifying how and where the implementation will receive proxy information. This parameter must be specified and must be one of:

`INTERNET_OPEN_TYPE_DIRECT`: Direct connection, no proxy.

`INTERNET_OPEN_TYPE_PRECONFIG`: Retrieve configuration information from the registry.

`INTERNET_OPEN_TYPE_PRECONFIG_WITH_NO_AUTOPROXY`: Same as the previous value with the exception that it will not run any startup files such as Internet Setup (.ins) or JScript (.js) initialization files.

INTERNET_OPEN_TYPE_PROXY: Uses the proxy information supplied in this function for all requests unless the hostname specified for the request is contained within a supplied proxy bypass list.

lpszProxyName: The hostname (or address) of the proxy server (if any). Unless we are going to specifically indicate the use of a proxy in the "access type" parameter, this value can be null.

lpszProxyBypass: A list of hostnames that will not be proxied; this value should be null unless we specifically indicated use of a proxy in the previous arguments.

dwFlags: A `DWORD` indicating option behavior for the socket, such as asynchronous communication (`INTERNET_FLAG_ASYNC`), or load only from the local cache (`INTERNET_FLAG_FROM_CACHE`).

InternetConnect(): This is a complicated function with quite a few arguments; however, for the purposes of establishing only HTTP connections, the arguments are relatively unchanging. According to MSDN, the following is the function signature for `InternetConnect()`:

```
HINTERNET InternetConnect(
  HINTERNET hInternet,
  LPCTSTR lpszServerName,
  INTERNET_PORT nServerPort,
  LPCTSTR lpszUsername,
  LPCTSTR lpszPassword,
  DWORD dwService,
  DWORD dwFlags,
  DWORD_PTR dwContext
);
```

The parameters are as follows:

hInternet: The handle we obtained in the call to `InternetOpen()`.

lpszServerName: The hostname (or IP address) of the server we wish to connect to.

nServerPort: The port we wish to connect to. For our purposes (since we are mostly interested in SSL connectivity), this value will most often be `INTERNET_DEFAULT_HTTPS_PORT` to indicate port 443. Note that if we wish to specify a nonstandard port, we will do so in this parameter.

lpszUsername: The username to be used for HTTP authentication (if any). For anonymous access or another authentication vehicle besides HTTP authentication, this parameter should be null.

lpszPassword: The password corresponding to the username. If no username is to be used or for a blank password, this value should be null.

dwService: The service type constant; for our purposes this will always be INTERNET_SERVICE_HTTP.

dwContext: Application-specific context value that is used during callbacks.

HttpOpenRequest(): This will be used to prepare a particular request to the server; the signature, as per MSDN, is as follows:

```
HINTERNET HttpOpenRequest(
  HINTERNET hConnect,
  LPCTSTR lpszVerb,
  LPCTSTR lpszObjectName,
  LPCTSTR lpszVersion,
  LPCTSTR lpszReferer,
  LPCTSTR* lpszAcceptTypes,
  DWORD dwFlags,
  DWORD_PTR dwContext
);
```

The parameters to this function are as follows:

hConnect: The handle we obtained from InternetConnect().

lpszVerb: The "verb" for our request; this maps to one of the standard HTTP verbs such as "GET," "POST," "HEAD," etc.

lpszObjectName: The name of the object we are requesting; this is usually a filename for our purposes.

lpszVersion: The HTTP version; leaving this as null, the HTTP 1.1 version string will be used (i.e., "HTTP/1.1").

lpszReferer: The HTTP "Referrer" header value. We can usually use an empty string here, since a referrer is rarely required and in most contexts, we won't be implementing Web surfing capability in our applications at this level.

lpszAcceptTypes: The HTTP "Accept" header value. If this is NULL, the server will leave the header value empty.

dwFlags: Behavioral flags related to how the request will be handled; specified in this value are quite a number of options specifying how to handle redirects, how to govern cache behavior, etc. For our purposes, we must always set the INTERNET_FLAG_SECURE flag specifying that SSL will be used. Optionally, we can specify INTERNET_FLAG_IGNORE_REDIRECT_TO_HTTP to prevent HTTPS pages redirecting to HTTP pages. Other useful flags for an SSL context are INTERNET_FLAG_IGNORE_CERT_DATE_INVALID to override invalid dates in digital certificates (such as a certificate having expired), and INTERNET_FLAG_IGNORE_CERT_CN_INVALID to ignore a wrong "CN" ("common name," usually meaning FQDN in an HTTP context) on the remote server certificate.

`dwContext`: The application-specific context value for callbacks.

`HttpSendRequest()`: Sends the request to the server. The signature is as follows:

```
BOOL HttpSendRequest(
  HINTERNET hRequest,
  LPCTSTR lpszHeaders,
  DWORD dwHeadersLength,
  LPVOID lpOptional,
  DWORD dwOptionalLength
);
```

The following are the parameter details for this operation:

`hRequest`: The request handle generated in `HTTPOpenRequest()`.

`lpszHeaders`: Any additional header values to send. Usually, this will be NULL.

`dwHeadersLength`: The length of the string specified in the previous parameter.

`lpOptional`: Optional data sent after the headers. This would be the HTTP body for `PUT` and `POST` operations.

`dwOptionalLength`: Length of the optional data in the previous parameter.

`HttpQueryInfo(`: Obtain information about the result status of an HTTP operation. The signature is as follows:

```
BOOL HttpQueryInfo(
  HINTERNET hRequest,
  DWORD dwInfoLevel,
  LPVOID lpvBuffer,
  LPDWORD lpdwBufferLength,
  LPDWORD lpdwIndex
);
```

The parameters are as follows:

`hRequest`: The handle to the request we are interested in obtaining information about.

`dwInfoLevel`: What we wish to find out about; although a wide range of information can be requested, most often we are interested in `HTTP_QUERY_STATUS_CODE` to determine the response code from the server.

`lpvBuffer`: The buffer in which the informational output will be stored. If this parameter is null, the minimum size of the buffer required will be placed in `lpdwBufferLength`.

`lpdwBufferLength`: A pointer to a `DWORD` indicating the size of the buffer pointed to by `lpvBuffer`. Note that this value will be modified by the function to point to the actual size of the buffer used.

`lpdwIndex`: A zero-based index value for determining which of multiple values (e.g., if there are two headers of the same name).

`InternetReadFile()`: Read the server response. The function is called in a manner almost identical to the SDK `ReadFile()` function. The signature of this function is as follows:

```
BOOL InternetReadFile(
  HINTERNET hFile,
  LPVOID lpBuffer,
  DWORD dwNumberOfBytesToRead,
  LPDWORD lpdwNumberOfBytesRead
);
```

The parameters are as follows:

`hFile`: The handle returned from `HTTPOpenRequest()`.

`lpBuffer`: The output buffer in which the response data will be stored.

`dwNumberOfBytesToRead`: How much data should be read.

`lpdwNumberOfBytesRead`: How much data was actually read. Will be zero if no more data is available.

`InternetCloseHandle()`: Close the handle and free any remaining resources. This must be called for the handle created by `HTTPOpenRequest()`, the one created by `InternetConnect()` and the handle created by `InternetOpen()`. The function takes only one parameter: the handle to be closed.

8.13.1.2 Simple Usage Example

Obviously, these functions are extremely complicated and difficult to use given the number of parameters required, the number of functions, and the number of handles that we must keep track of. Note that to compile and run the sample, we will need to include <wininet.h> in our source and link against wininet.lib during linkage. The following is a very simple usage scenario that uses SSL to obtain data from the default Microsoft secure site; it is not a brief example, but the whole source has been included for clarity:

```
#include <windows.h>
#include <iostream.h>
#include <wininet.h>

void PrintError(DWORD error) {
    char msgbuffer[1024];
```

```
        FormatMessage(
        FORMAT_MESSAGE_FROM_SYSTEM, NULL, error,
        MAKELANGID(LANG_NEUTRAL, SUBLANG_DEFAULT),
        msgbuffer, sizeof(msgbuffer), NULL );
        cerr << msgbuffer << endl << flush;
    }

    void bomb_out() {
        exit(-1);
    }

    void check(BOOL returnVal) {
        if(!returnVal) {
            DWORD error = GetLastError();
            PrintError(error);
            bomb_out();
        }
    }

    void main() {

        DWORD result = InternetAttemptConnect(0);
        if(result != ERROR_SUCCESS) {
            PrintError(result);
            bomb_out();
        }

        HINTERNET hNet = InternetOpen("My User Agent", //bogus User-Agent
            INTERNET_OPEN_TYPE_DIRECT, //use direct connection
            NULL, //no proxy
            NULL, //no proxy bypass
            0); //no flags

        if(!hNet) { check(false); } //fail and print message

        HINTERNET hConnect = InternetConnect(hNet,
            "www.microsoft.com",
            INTERNET_DEFAULT_HTTPS_PORT,
            "", //no username
            "", //no password
            INTERNET_SERVICE_HTTP,
            0, //no flags
            0); //no context
```

```
if(!hNet) { check(false); } //fail and print message

HINTERNET hRequest = HttpOpenRequest(hConnect,
    "GET",
    "", //default page
    NULL, //default version
    NULL, //no refer
    NULL, //no accept types
    INTERNET_FLAG_SECURE, //secure flag
    0); //no context

if(!hNet) { check(false); } //fail and print message

check(HttpSendRequest(hRequest,
    NULL, //no additional headers
    0, //for above
    NULL, //no content
    0)); //for above

DWORD queryLen = 0;
char returnString[256];
queryLen = sizeof(returnString);
check(HttpQueryInfo(hRequest,
    HTTP_QUERY_STATUS_CODE, //what did the server say?
    returnString,
    & queryLen, //length of query
    0)); //position zero

//at this point, we could ensure that the response is
//"200", but we'll assume that we're interested no
//matter what the response value is
bool moreToRead = true;
while(moreToRead) {
    queryLen = 0;
    check(InternetReadFile(hRequest,
        returnString,
        sizeof(returnString),
        &queryLen));
    if(queryLen == 0) {
        moreToRead = false;
    } else {
        cout << returnString;
    }
}
```

```
        cout << flush;
        InternetCloseHandle(hRequest);
        InternetCloseHandle(hConnect);
        InternetCloseHandle(hNet);

    }
```

As stated earlier, this is not the easiest way to support SSL connectivity, but it will work and does not require that we install anything additional on the system. If given the choice between .NET managed code and this older API, we'd do well to consider using the .NET SDK to perform this type of request.

8.13.2 SSL via SSPI

To close out this topic, we're left with the SSPI. As stated previously, SSPI stands for Security Support Provider Interface, and is a pathway made available to us to use the same SSL functionality as is used internally to Windows. SChannel is the "Secure Channel" functionality provided by Windows. SChannel is used, for example, by Internet Explorer to implement the secure sockets functionality inherent in the browser and is accessible through a complicated API that we can leverage to implement secure sockets in our code. SSPI is not bound to any particular protocol, so we don't have to limit ourselves to HTTP for the application layer in making use of SSL, and it is not bound to a particular transport provider, so we can segregate the underlying socket implementation from the encryption and decryption of data. We don't see this very flexible approach to the same degree in any of the libraries. However, this flexibility comes at the expense of simplicity, for SSPI is extremely difficult to use correctly given the large numbers of parameters that must be supplied to the various functions. On the plus side, most of the functions look scarier than they are; quite a few parameters are used in other non-SChannel contexts and therefore must always be null in our usage.

Getting into the specifics of usage, it should first be stated clearly that *since the SSPI is not bound to any particular transport mechanism, we will need to employ a transport mechanism independently from the SSPI code.* In other words, we might choose to use Berkeley sockets as an underlying transport mechanism via the Winsock API, or something like the `System.Net.Sockets.Socket` Berkeley socket implementation within the managed framework as the transport. Either way, we'll need to create and use the socket API independent from the secure channel. Aside from the basic socket functionality that we'll use to get our example code to work, it should be explicitly stated that the nuances of the various socket APIs in Windows are outside the scope of this book, so we won't be covering them in detail. The time required to give a fair treatment to these APIs would not allow for a thorough enough discussion in the limited space available. That's not to say, however, that there aren't a number of excellent resources available that will help the developer understand them; as always, we've tried to make sufficient references available to help in your development tasks in the "references" section of this chapter's material.

We've divided this section into two parts, client tasks and server tasks, and attempted to show how they would interact in the typical SSL context. We'll go through the client-side tasks first, and then through the server-side tasks. We've elected to leave a usage sample out of the inline chapter text, as the source code required to perform either a client-side or server-side session is extremely complex. However, that material is on the companion CD-ROM (/Examples/Chapter 8/SSPI) for readers to peruse at leisure.

ON THE CD

8.13.2.1 SSPI Client-Side Connection

The following steps are required for an SSL client using SSPI:

1. Use `AcquireCredentialsHandle()` to obtain a handle to the credentials of the current user or another user.
2. Iteratively call `InitializeSecurityContext()` to generate a context-establishment token and send the result to the server. If needed (if the function returns `SEC_I_CONTINUE_NEEDED`), we will need to use the `CompleteAuthToken()` function to ensure a usable token is created. As long as tokens need to be generated and sent to the server, we must iteratively do so by calling `InitializeSecurityContext()` and `CompleteAuthToken()`. The number of required tokens will vary depending on factors associated with the connection, such as if mutual authentication is to be used. Once the context is fully established, the routine will return `SEC_E_OK`.
3. Once the context is established, we can send and receive data. In sending data, we will first need to call `EncryptMessage()` and send the *resultant encrypted message only*; in received data, we should call `DecryptMessage()`to perform our application processing.
4. Upon completion of the transaction and when we are ready to close the socket, we will call `DeleteSecurityContext()` to free the structures we generated during context creation.
5. Call `FreeCredentialsHandle()` on the handle generated in the call to `AcquireCredentialsHandle()`.
6. Obviously, the vague number of times that we will need to call `InitializeSecurityContext()` would complicate our development tasks in and of itself. However, development is further complicated by the large number of parameters that need to be supplied to these functions. The following details the functions that are used for client-side session establishment and data transfer:

`AcquireCredentialsHandle()`: This function is called at the beginning of session establishment. According to MSDN, this function has the following signature:

```
SECURITY_STATUS SEC_Entry AcquireCredentialsHandle(
  SEC_CHAR* pszPrincipal,
  SEC_CHAR* pszPackage,
  ULONG fCredentialUse,
  PLUID pvLogonID,
  PVOID pAuthData,
  SEC_GET_KEY_FN pGetKeyFn,
  PVOID pvGetKeyArgument,
  PCredHandle phCredential,
  PTimeStamp ptsExpiry
);
```

The parameters are as follows:

`pszPrincipal`: Unused in s/channel; value must be `NULL`.

`pszPackage`: The package name that will be used. Use `UNISP_NAME` (defined in schannel.h) for the "unified" provider, or the name of a particular provider (such as the results of a call to `EnumerateSecurityPackages()`), or as defined in schannel.h.

`fCredentialUse`: Can be either `SECPKG_CRED_OUTBOUND` or `SECPKG_CRED_INBOUND`. For our purposes (e.g., client only), this will be `SECPKG_CRED_OUTBOUND`.

`pvLogonID`: Not used, must be `NULL`.

`pAuthData`: Authentication structure; since we're using SChannel, if we don't elect to use `NULL` (forcing default authentication credentials), we'll need to specify a structure of type `SCHANNEL_CRED`.

`pGetKeyFn`: Not used, must be `NULL`.

`pvGetKeyArgument`: Not used, must be `NULL`.

`phCredential`: A pointer to a `CredHandle` that will receive the output handle.

`ptsExpiry`: A pointer to the timestamp indicating when the credential will expire.

`InitializeSecurityContext()`: This function is called at the beginning of session establishment. According to MSDN, this function has the following signature:

```
SECURITY_STATUS SEC_Entry InitializeSecurityContext (
  PCredHandle phCredential,
  PCtxtHandle phContext,
  SEC_CHAR* pszTargetName,
  ULONG fContextReq,
```

```
        ULONG Reserved1,
        ULONG TargetDataRep,
        PSecBufferDesc pInput,
        ULONG Reserved2,
        PCtxtHandle phNewContext,
        PSecBufferDesc pOutput,
        PULONG pfContextAttr,
        PTimeStamp ptsExpiry
    );
```

The parameters are as follows:

phCredential: The handle returned from `AcquireCredentialsHandle()`.

phContext: The first time this is called, the value is `NULL`. During the iterative loop required to establish the connection, the value should be updated with the results of the previous call's output in `phNewContext`.

pszTargetName: The name that should match the CN on the certificate of the remote server.

fContextReq: Bit flags that can be used to govern behavior of the operation. The possible values are:

- **ISC_REQ_ALLOCATE_MEMORY**: Allocate buffers for us. If we do this, we'll need to call `FreeContextBuffer()` when we're done using the allocated buffer.
- **ISC_REQ_CONFIDENTIALITY**: Encrypt messages; by selecting this, we'll have to call `EncryptMessage()` before we send the data.
- **ISC_REQ_CONNECTION**: According to MSDN, "security context will not handle formatting messages," meaning the onus is on us to make sure messages are properly formatted if we select this.
- **ISC_REQ_EXTENDED_ERROR**: Inform the server of error status.
- **ISC_REQ_INTEGRITY**: Sign the data.
- **ISC_REQ_MANUAL_CRED_VALIDATION**: Indicates that we wish to validate the server credential manually; otherwise, the underlying implementation will do it for us.
- **ISC_REQ_MUTUAL_AUTH**: Use mutual authentication.
- **ISC_REQ_REPLAY_DETECT**: Use replay detection.
- **ISC_REQ_SEQUENCE_DETECT**: Detect messages out of sequence.
- **ISC_REQ_STREAM**: Support streams.
- **ISC_REQ_USE_SUPPLIED_CREDS**: Do not attempt to automatically generate credentials (use supplied credentials only).

Reserved1: Reserved, must be zero.

TargetDataRep: Unused, must be zero.

pInput: A pointer to a SecBufferDesc structure; the first time the function is called, this must be NULL. Subsequent calls should contain the value received from the server and an empty buffer of type SECBUFFER_EMPTY with two data members set to zero (pvBuffer and cbBuffer).

Reserved2: Reserved, must be zero.

phNewContext: On the first call, this value is populated with the resultant new context handle; on subsequent calls, specify NULL.

pOutput: A pointer to a SecBufferDesc structure that will contain the function output.

pfContextAttr: Output bit flags describing the context.

ptsExpiry: Output value describing the expiration time of the context.

CompleteAuthToken(): Used to complete an authentication token. According to MSDN, this function has the following signature:

```
SECURITY_STATUS SEC_Entry CompleteAuthToken(
  PCtxtHandle phContext,
  PSecBufferDesc pToken
);
```

The parameters are as follows:

phContext: The context generated via InitializeSecurityContext().

pToken: The output token value.

EncryptMessage(): Used to prepare messages to be sent between peers. According to MSDN, this function has the following signature:

```
SECURITY_STATUS SEC_Entry EncryptMessage(
  PCtxtHandle phContext,
  ULONG fQOP,
  PSecBufferDesc pMessage,
  ULONG MessageSeqNo
);
```

The parameters are as follows:

phContext: The context generated via InitializeSecurityContext().

fQOP: Package-specific flags; only choice for SChannel is SECQOP_WRAP_OOB_DATA for OOB (out of band) data.

pMessage: A pointer to a SecBufferDesc that contains the message to be encrypted; upon calling the function, the plaintext contents will be overwritten with the encrypted contents.

MessageSeqNo: Must be zero.

`DecryptMessage()`: Used to prepare messages received between peers. According to MSDN, this function has the following signature:

```
SECURITY_STATUS SEC_Entry DecryptMessage(
  PCtxtHandle phContext,
  PSecBufferDesc pMessage,
  ULONG MessageSeqNo,
  PULONG pfQOP
);
```

The parameters are as follows:

`phContext`: The context generated via `InitializeSecurityContext()`.

`pMessage`: A pointer to a `SecBufferDesc` that contains the message to be decrypted; upon calling the function, the encrypted contents will be overwritten with the plaintext contents.

`MessageSeqNo`: Must be zero.

`fQOP`: Package-specific flags; not used and must be `NULL`.

`DeleteSecurityContext()`: Used to free resources allocated during the call to `InitializeSecurityContext()`. The only parameter is the context to be deleted.

`FreeCredentialsHandle()`: Used to free resources allocated during the call to `AcquireCredentialHandle()`: The only parameter is the handle to be deleted.

8.13.2.2 SSPI Server-Side Connection

The server side of an SSPI connection is similar to the client side, with only a few differences. Context establishment is similar, only we'll be calling the other side of the context generation function `AcceptSecurityContext()` rather than `InitializeSecurityContext()`. However, the methodology is very similar in how we call it. The following outlines the server-side procedure for establishing a secure connection; this time from the server point of view:

1. Use `AcquireCredentialsHandle()` to obtain a handle to the credentials of the current user or another user.
2. Iteratively call `AcceptSecurityContext()` in combination with `CompleteAuthToken()` if required to establish the server-side context.
3. Once the context is established, we can send and receive data. In sending data, we will first need to call `EncryptMessage()` and send the *resultant encrypted message only*; in received data, we should call `DecryptMessage()` in order to perform our application processing.
4. Upon completion of the transaction and when we are ready to close the socket, we will call `DeleteSecurityContext()` to free the structures we generated during context creation.

5. Call `FreeCredentialsHandle()` on the handle generated in the call to `AcquireCredentialsHandle()`.

The following details the functions that are used for server-side session establishment and data transfer that are *not* covered in the function descriptions for client session establishment. There is only one function that applies to server-side connections, but does not apply to client-side connections:

`AcceptSecurityContext()`: Analogous to `InitializeSecurityContext()`, this function is iteratively called by the server during session establishment. As per MSDN, the function signature is:

```
SECURITY_STATUS SEC_Entry AcceptSecurityContext(
  PCredHandle phCredential,
  PCtxtHandle phContext,
  PSecBufferDesc pInput,
  ULONG fContextReq,
  PCtxtHandle phNewContext,
  PSecBufferDesc pOutput,
  PULONG pfContextAttr,
  PTimeStamp ptsTimeStamp
);
```

The parameters are as follows:

`phCredential`: The credential handle received from `AcquireCredentialsHandle()`.

`phContext`: A pointer to a `CtxtHandle`; during the first call to this function, the value is `NULL`. On subsequent calls, the value is updated with the results of the previous calls.

`pInput`: Pointer to a `SecBufferDesc` struct that contains the value generated by the client and passed to the server. The second buffer member of the struct must be empty.

`fContextReq`: Bit flags that specify attributes of the connection; the valid flags are:

`ASC_REQ_ALLOCATE_MEMORY`: Allocate buffers for us. If we do this, we'll need to call `FreeContextBuffer()` when we're done using the allocated buffer.

`ASC_REQ_CONFIDENTIALITY`: Encrypt messages; by selecting this, we'll have to call `EncryptMessage()` before we send the data.

`ASC_REQ_CONNECTION`: According to MSDN, "security context will not handle formatting messages," meaning the onus is on us to make sure messages are properly formatted if we select this.

`ASC_REQ_EXTENDED_ERROR`: Inform the client of error status.

`ASC_REQ_MUTUAL_AUTH`: Force mutual authentication.

- **ASC_REQ_REPLAY_DETECT:** Use replay detection.
- **ASC_REQ_SEQUENCE_DETECT:** Detect messages out of sequence.
- **ASC_REQ_STREAM:** Support streams.

phNewContext: On the first call, this value is populated with the resultant new context handle; on subsequent calls, specify NULL.

pOutput: A pointer to a SecBufferDesc structure that will contain the function output.

pfContextAttr: Output bit flags describing the context.

ptsTimeStamp: Output value describing the expiration time of the context.

As we discussed earlier, providing a full usage scenario inline with the text is difficult due to the large amount of software required to implement either a client or a server using the SSPI. However, we would direct interested readers who wish to debug the code and see it in action to the companion CD-ROM SSPI example, where they will find additional resources to help them use these features (/Examples/Chapter 8/SSPI and /Examples/Chapter 8/SSPI_Wrapper). Additionally, there are some helpful MSDN and other Internet references that will help the developer in using this material.

ON THE CD

8.14 ENDNOTES

1. *www.microsoft.com/msdownload/platformsdk/sdkupdate/*
2. *http://msdn.microsoft.com/library/default.asp?url=/library/en-us/win9x/append_2zjd.asp*
3. *http://blogs.msdn.com/shawnfa/archive/2004/04/14/113514.aspx*
4. *http://blogs.msdn.com/shawnfa/archive/2004/04/14/113514.aspx*
5. *http://msdn.microsoft.com/library/default.asp?url=/library/en-us/seccrypto/security/cryptencrypt.asp*
6. *http://msdn.microsoft.com/library/default.asp?url=/library/en-us/seccrypto/security/cryptexportkey.asp*
7. *http://msdn.microsoft.com/library/default.asp?url=/library/en-us/seccrypto/security/cryptsignhash.asp*
8. *www.dart.com/tcpdotnet.asp*
9. *http://msdn.microsoft.com/library/default.asp?url=/library/en-us/cpguide/html/cpconbuildingbasicnetremotingapplication.asp*

9 Developing with JCA/JCE

In This Chapter

- Chapter Goal
- Preparing the Environment
- Encryption and Decryption—"Low-Level" Techniques
- Encryption and Decryption—"High Level" Techniques
- Signing and Verifying Data
- Advanced Techniques
- Summary
- Endnotes

JCA stands for "Java Security Architecture" and JCE stands for "Java Security Extensions." JCA was introduced in JDK 1.1 and provides the overarching framework for the development of cryptography in Java; the JCE extends the functionality of the JCA to supply the additional cryptographic functionality that we'll need to perform common security tasks.

The JCA uses a "provider" model as the core principal of its design in a manner similar to CAPI. From a "fifty thousand foot" level, the API provides a general pattern of cryptographic functionality that should work in an abstract way. The runtime environment allows access to those abstract descriptions by allowing a caller to request a specific implementation of that functionality in a loosely coupled, "late binding" way. Using the behavioral "template," numerous individuals can write "providers" that implement specific portions of the functionality the API designers abstractly described. As a specific example of how this principle works in practice, we can look at how the JCA approaches the concept of "ciphers." JCA supplies the developer with an abstract description of how an encipherment algorithm should behave, and outlines a "universal" interface to that behavior by means of an abstract class—the Cipher class. In other words, the JCA developers have defined a "contract" for how ciphers should behave. For example, they've decided that all ciphers should be able to encrypt data (as the functionality to encrypt is something that can be said to be universal among encipherment algorithms), and specified that anything claiming to be a cipher should implement encryption functionality through the same calling methodology. The runtime environment then accepts requests by applications for something that implements this functionality and receives an implementation of it dynamically at runtime.

Using the provider design principal in this way does a few things. First and foremost, it allows an application developer to use any symmetric or asymmetric cipher without having to spend time worrying about the implementation details of the algorithm he or she is working with (since the same interface will apply no matter which provider is supplying the implementation). In other words, designers of applications can write their applications to the defined interface without foreknowledge of the particular encipherment algorithms that will be used by the application or their implementations. Instead, developers write to the interface, and (depending on how and where they intend to release their product) deployment personnel ensure that only providers who meet the appropriate deployment-related criteria (such as standards/regulatory compliance, export requirements, customer security policy, etc.) are in the pool of available providers. As we can see, this is an extremely powerful mechanism, because it allows developers to refrain from implementing "customization" code within their own code; instead, they can just write the application and leave the selection of the underlying implementation to the runtime environment in use.

So, keeping in mind that the JCA uses a provider model, let's look at the overall JCA architecture in more depth to see exactly how the pieces fit together. Then, we'll take an in-depth tour through the API and see the classes/methods in action we'll use to develop our applications.

9.1 CHAPTER GOAL

It is not the goal of this chapter to replace any of the already excellent documentation supplied by Sun in their descriptions of the JCE/JCA API. In fact, Sun has done an excellent job of providing reference materials that outline every method, class, and argument to a very high degree of specificity. In addition, the documentation provides some useful guidance for getting up and running, installing new providers, and provides some helpful sample code as well. However, it is often helpful to walk through complicated material in a step-by-step fashion. As anyone who has ever been overwhelmed with too much information knows, being presented with every method signature of every class and accompanying textual descriptions can sometimes be more confusing than helpful. In the same way an English dictionary is more useful to someone who already speaks English than someone who does not, a compendium describing the API in all its specifics is a useful reference, but sometimes we need a guide rather than a reference—in other words, we need a way to get started. This chapter attempts to provide one possible method of understanding the API to the developer; we attempt to concentrate on the things we'll use most of the time, and mention some of the more infrequently occurring features of the API.

This chapter is intended to provide the bare minimum required to sit down and start working. We've done our best to create a rapid learning path to the functionality that will be used most often, and deemphasize rarely used material, material that can be done an easier way, or material that is of only academic interest. It is not our intention to rehash or replace the Sun documentation, so where the reader will be better served by referring to the Sun docs, we say so. This chapter assumes that the reader is comfortable with rudimentary Java development. Specifically, we assume the reader knows how to author and compile Java source, how to run some type of Java software (applications, applets, or servlets), is familiar with the syntax of the Java language, and we anticipate that the developer has a reasonable understanding of Java primitives and the core library.

9.1.1 Engines

At the highest levels of the JCA API are the "engine" classes; with very few exceptions, we will interact almost entirely with the engine portion of the API without knowing or caring about anything going on at a lower level. In a nutshell, an engine class represents all the interfaces associated with performing a cryptographic operation at an abstract level (i.e., without an actual implementation of that functionality). It is useless without an underlying implementation that supplies the functionality and behavior in question, but we'll get to that more in a minute. As an example of engine classes, we've talked time and again about the primitive cryptographic functionality such as message digests and digital signatures; within the Java API, these abstract concepts are represented with corresponding engine classes. To further specify this example, two classes the API provides us with are `MessageDigest` and `Signature`, which wrap the underlying implementations of message digest functionality and signature functionality, respectively. These examples are contained within the underlying provider and are (for the most part) opaque to the developer. Figure 9.1 illustrates the cryptographic primitives and the corresponding engine implementation in the Java API.

Cryptographic Primitive	Engine Class
Hashing (Message Digests)	java.security.MessageDigest
MAC (Keyed Hash)	javax.crypto.Mac
PRNG (Random Number Generation)	java.security.SecureRandom
Key Generation (Symmetric)	javax.crypto.KeyGenerator
Signature	java.security.Signature
Symmetric Encryption	javax.crypto.Cipher
Key Exchange	javax.crypto.KeyAgreement

FIGURE 9.1 Cryptographic engine classes.

For the most part, all engine classes behave the same way within the JCE with respect to instantiation. To instantiate an engine class, we will typically use a static `getInstance()` method within the engine class to request that the runtime supply us with a reference to a specific implementation instance. We'll go through this in more detail in subsequent explanations and examples, but it is useful to note that we can always control where the Java environment obtains the implementation from by specifying a target provider in our request. For example, we might wish to create a secure random source; to do so, we will use the engine class `SecureRandom`. Since `SecureRandom` is an engine class and we use all engine classes the same way, we can call `SecureRandom.getInstance()` to obtain a reference. If we are fine with the default PRNG algorithm and we don't have a provider preference, we can leave the provider unspecified in our request for an implementation. The call to request that instance would look something like the following:

```
SecureRandom rand = SecureRandom.getInstance();
```

If we wanted to specify a particular algorithm for random number generation (but we still don't have a particular preference for provider), we could request the particular algorithm as well:

```
SecureRandom rand = SecureRandom.getInstance("SHA1PRNG");
```

Finally, if we wanted to specify a particular provider, we can do that by indicating the provider we like (either by reference or by name) after supplying the algorithm. Note that if we are going to specify the provider, we also have to be specific about the algorithm we intend to use within the engine class—this is required since the algorithm information is required in situations where a provider is specified. An example would be:

```
SecureRandom rand = SecureRandom.getInstance("SHA1PRNG", "SUN");
```

As specified, the default provider is "SUN" (here specified in the second argument). If we were to use a different provider, we would need to replace this string with the name of the other provider.

9.1.2 Representations of Primitives

For the most part, all the primitives we've covered throughout this book are available to the developer in an abstract form within the JCA. Specifically, the following are valid classes:

```
MessageDigest
Cipher
SecureRandom
Signature
Key
Mac
KeyGenerator
```

Ideally, developers reading this list will have some familiarity with the purpose (if not the use) of all the preceding engine classes. One can correctly intuit, for example, that the `Cipher` class will contain the requisite functionality for manipulating ciphers (both symmetric and asymmetric), whereas `MessageDigest` will contain the requisite functionality for message digest creation. Note that the engine classes do not extend to algorithm selection, as we can and will request particular algorithms by name in the call to `getInstance()`.

9.1.3 Providers

The number and character of providers available on a particular system may vary according to the role of that system and the characteristics of the applications deployed on that machine. Let's talk a little bit about the provider that will be on (almost) every system, and about why (and how) we might go about changing providers to something other than the default.

9.1.3.1 The Default Provider

Sun provides a default provider for us to use for developing our cryptographic functionality; for quite a number of contexts, we will not need to install additional providers to develop our applications. Following is the primary cryptographic functionality supplied by the default provider.

A number of symmetric ciphers, including:

- RC4/ARCFOUR
- AES
- TripleDES
- DES
- Blowfish =
- RC2
- RC5
- RSA (for signing as per PKCS #1)
- Password-Based Encryption (key derivation + symmetric algorithm) according to PKCS #5.

A number of hashing algorithms available for HMAC or computing message digests, including:

- SHA-1
- MD5

Note that the functionality provided by the default provider is thorough and will encompass a large percentage of the work we will need to do with cryptography. However, there are cases where we might need to extend or expand beyond the default provider. We'll look at how other providers can extend the functionality available to our applications, some of the main choices for doing so, and how to obtain and install those other providers.

9.1.3.2 Commercial Providers

Numerous vendors provide commercial JCE provider implementations. These providers add value by providing additional support options, additional platform coverage, enhancing the performance of the underlying implementation, or by providing compliance with additional standards (both industry and regulatory standards). Typically, these providers attempt to expand upon the functionality (or remediate a limitation) of the default provider. For example, the default JCE cryptographic provider(s) are not FIPS 140-2 certified; in a government context, a government entity may wish to purchase a commercial provider that is FIPS certified with regard to this standard to gain the acceptance of their accreditation personnel. Although mentioned earlier in this book, it bears repeating that the BSAFE toolkit supplies such a provider as part of its Crypto-J and SSL-J product offerings. These commercial providers significantly expand on the functionality of the default provider in one way or another, and can be combined in a number of ways to add features to the applications we write. Although not an exhaustive list, the following commercial providers are useful for us to note:

IAIK providers: The IAIK (Institute for Applied Information Processing and Communication) provides a commercial JCE implementation for the purposes of building on the functionality of the Sun default provider, providing support options for the implementation, and for compliance/certification with standards (e.g., common criteria). Further details are available from the IAIK Web site at *http://jce.iaik.tugraz.at/*.

Wedgetail Communications: Wedgetail (*www.wedgetail.com*) offers a commercial implementation of a JCE provider. This implementation offers expanded functionality (such as support for algorithms and modes of operation not included in the SUN provider), and professional support for the implementation.

RSA Crypto-J (part of the B/SAFE toolkit): As mentioned earlier in this book, RSA's own BSAFE offering provides a JCE provider as part of its suite. This provider offers extended implementation of cryptographic algorithms, additional modes of operation, professional support, and FIPS 140-1 certification.

9.1.3.3 Free Providers

A number of providers are available free of charge as open source, freeware, or free offerings from commercial vendors. Typically, these offerings attempt to provide additional functionality over and above the default Sun provider, or extend the Java cryptographic platform to other platforms not supported by Sun. Some free providers of note include:

Assembla JCE Provider for Microsoft Key store: This provider allows integration between keys created and stored in Microsoft CAPI (e.g., associated with an account in NT/2000/XP). Support is also offered by Assembla, but comes with additional cost.

BouncyCastle: The "Legion of the Bouncy Castle" provides an open source JCE provider implementation that extends and expands upon the cryptographic functionality included in the default Sun provider. The quantity and flexibility of cryptographic algorithms supplied by the Bouncy Castle provider are quite extensive.

IBM: IBM offers security functionality through the IBM implementation of the JDK. IBM's JDK offering supports additional platforms over and above those offered by Sun (e.g., Linux on supported IBM hardware).

9.2 PREPARING THE ENVIRONMENT

Before we can dig in and start developing with the JCA, we need to make sure our environment is structured appropriately, and is configured in such a way that we are ready to start writing, compiling, and running applications. The good news is that for the most part, if you are developing with Java, you are ready to develop with the JCA. For those who aren't already developing with Java, we'll briefly run through the steps they need in order to start (or at least to make sure all the examples in this book compile and run). Developers who already have a Java development environment they are comfortable with may skip to the next section and not feel that they've missed anything.

9.2.1 Installing J2SE (or J2EE/J2ME)

To compile and run the examples in this book, you'll need a Java compiler and a Java Runtime Environment (JRE) that contains the necessary cryptographic providers and other support libraries required for our cryptographic applications to run. Obtaining and installing a recent (after 1.4) JDK will satisfy both these requirements. For example, as of the time of this writing, J2SE 5.0 JDK contains all of the required material. This can be downloaded from Sun at *http://java.sun.com*.

For example, to install the necessary files on an UltraSparc running Solaris 9:

1. Go to the Sun Web site and follow the links to download the Sun J2SE 5.0 JDK for the Solaris/Sparc platform (the name of the file is "jdk-1_5_0-solaris-sparc.sh"). Note that we want to choose the 64-bit or 32-bit version as appropriate for our platform.
2. Grant the .sh file the executable permission if needed (i.e., chmod +x).
3. Execute the .sh file.
4. Accept the license agreement.
5. The installer will create the jdk1.5.0 directory structure, including all the appropriate tools and utilities required to support the examples in this book.
6. Link the appropriate executables (e.g., /bin/java, /usr/local/bin/javac, or any others for your environment) to those in the distribution, or ensure that the executables supplied with the distribution are in your environment's PATH.

To install the appropriate Java framework on a Windows machine, we would go to the Sun Web site, follow the links for the J2SE 5.0 JDK, and select the Windows install (offline or online). We would then follow the installation instructions presented to us on the screen to configure the environment. The installer will place the JDK files in the appropriate directory and will make the appropriate environmental configuration changes required.

9.2.2 Installing "Unlimited" Cryptography

Due to import restrictions in certain countries, the default Sun Java Runtime Environment is configured to allow "strong but limited" cryptography from the JCE. "Strong but limited" means that the algorithms that can be used are "strong" (i.e., RSA, Triple-DES, etc. are all available for use), but the key sizes have some restrictions built in (e.g., key sizes in algorithms that support a variable key length have an artificially created fixed "ceiling"). The precise ceiling values are robust (and the values are spelled out explicitly in the default_local.policy file contained within the local_policy.jar file in <java-home>/lib/security), but some of the providers we've covered in this book require that the unlimited cryptography policy files be installed for successful operation. (If you don't have them, you'll get exceptions stating that you have an invalid key size.) By default, the JRE limits the key sizes in this way through the security policy files that ship with the JRE. However, these policy files can be overridden through the installation of policy files made available by Sun that provide the unlimited functionality.

To install the unlimited policy files, we will want to download and install the "Unlimited Strength Jurisdiction Policy Files" from Sun (*http://java.sun.com/products/jce/index-14.html#UnlimitedDownload*). This download will contain two .jar files, which we will want to (ultimately) move to <java-home>/lib/security/ (where <java-home> is the installation locality of the java root directory. This will vary according to platform; for reference, the java executable and the keytool executable are typically installed in <java-home>/bin/). It is always a good idea to make a copy of the policy files currently residing in the <java-home>/lib/security/ directory before we overwrite them with these new files, in case we wish to revert to the strong (but limited) policy at a later time (e.g., for platform testing).

Installing the new policy is straightforward. Following are the complete steps (with illustrations for the Windows platform) to demonstrate how this is done:

1. Navigate to the "downloads" section of the J2SE Development Kit portion of the Sun Web site. For J2SE 5.0, this is *http://java.sun.com/j2se/1.5.0/download.jsp*.
2. Under the heading "Other Downloads," select the entry "Java Cryptography Extension (JCE) Unlimited Strength Jurisdiction Policy Files 5.0" shown in Figure 9.2.
3. Download the associated .zip file, place it somewhere convenient, and open it (newer versions of Windows can open .zip files seamlessly; users of older platforms may need to download a zip viewer utility before decompressing the files). Inside the file, you will see a directory called "jce," and within that are four files. The ones we are interested in are the two jar files.

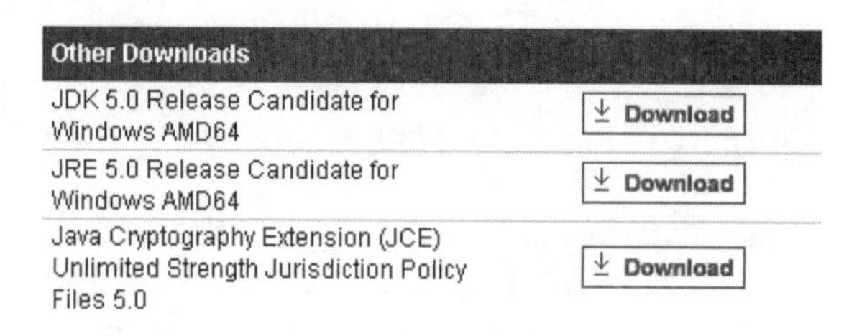

FIGURE 9.2 Obtaining Unlimited Strength Policy Files.

4. Navigate to the directory where the jdk is installed, and under the subdirectory jre/lib/security, locate and make a copy of the two files listed there. The default contents of the directory are shown in Figure 9.3.

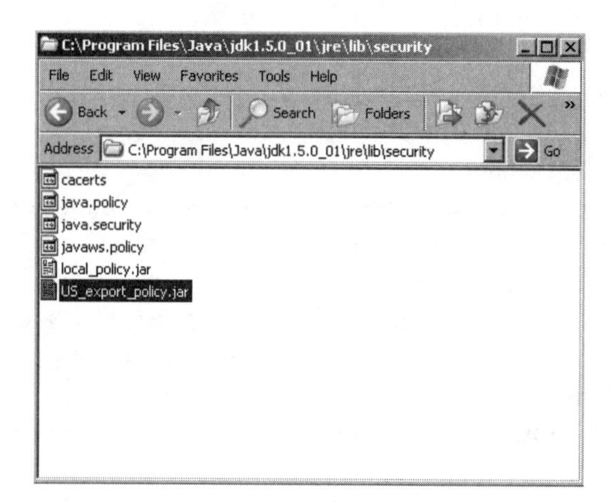

FIGURE 9.3 Contents of the Security Directory.

5. Make copies of the two .jar files that are contained within that directory, and move the files from the download file into the directory to replace the old files. This is demonstrated in Figure 9.4.

That's it! We're now ready to make use of "unlimited" cryptography.

9.2.3 Installing Additional Providers

If the default provider does not meet the needs of our application, we will need to select and install a provider that does. Installation of a new provider is relatively

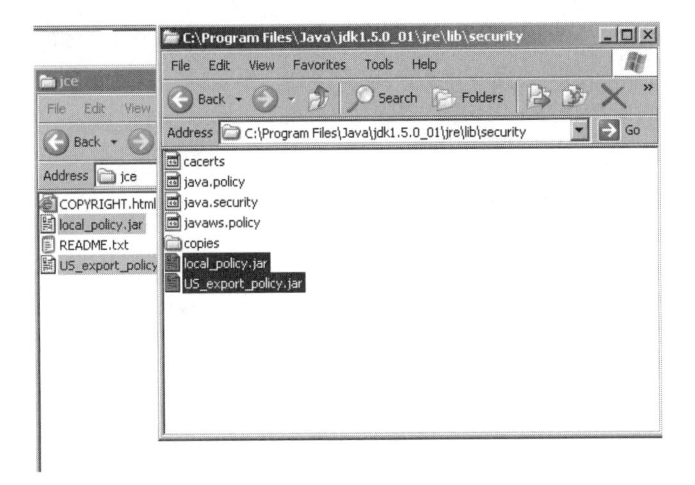

FIGURE 9.4 Update policy archives.

straightforward and can be done in one of two ways: static or dynamic registration. Although we'll go through both methods, we'll often find static registration the easiest methodology to employ in most circumstances since it can be done in one shot and doesn't require us to add any lines to our software.

9.2.3.1 Static Registration

To statically register a JCE provider, there are two straightforward steps we'll need to undertake. First, we need to obtain the .jar file containing the provider and place it somewhere where it can be found by the JRE. Although the J2SE documentation tells us that we can put the provider .jar anywhere in the CLASSPATH, we'll find that most of the time, it's easiest to just drop the .jar file in <java-home>/lib/ext/. Next, we'll need to make sure we "inform" the JRE that a new provider is accessible to the system. We do this by adding an entry to the <java-home>/lib/security/ java.security text file indicating the relative priority of the new provider. This sounds a bit confusing, but is actually rather simple; java.security contains a number of provider entries in the format security.provider.*number*, where *number* is the priority order of the providers (the lower the number, the higher the priority). We'll want to keep the Sun providers that come with our JRE first in the list (since doing otherwise can cause erratic behavior in some unexpected places), and add the new one to the end of the list. As an example, let's add a new provider (in this example, the BouncyCastle provider) to a default installation of the J2SE 1.5.0 SDK on a machine running Sun Solaris 9:

1. First, let's assume the .jar file is already located in the appropriate directory; using the example machine (assuming the JDK has been installed in /usr), we would put it in /usr/jdk1.5.0/jre/lib/ext. If we wanted to install the BouncyCastle provider, for example, we would want to make sure the appropriate .jar file (e.g., bcprov-jdk15-125.jar) is present in that directory. Let's do that now:

```
[emoyle@elysium:/usr/jdk1.5.0/jre/lib/ext]$ ls -la | grep bcprov
-rw-r--r--   1 root   staff     935999 Nov 12 15:32 bcprov-jdk15-
125.jar
```

2. Next, we'll want to add the provider to the list of providers recognized by the runtime environment. We'll do this by locating the provider list in the appropriate file and adding the new one to that list. In our example, we would want to open the file /usr/jdk1.5.0/jre/lib/security/java.security and find the following section of text:

```
security.provider.1=sun.security.pkcs11.SunPKCS11
${java.home}/lib/security/sunpkcs11-solaris.cfg
security.provider.2=sun.security.provider.Sun
security.provider.3=sun.security.rsa.SunRsaSign
security.provider.4=com.sun.net.ssl.internal.ssl.Provider
security.provider.5=com.sun.crypto.provider.SunJCE
security.provider.6=sun.security.jgss.SunProvider
security.provider.7=com.sun.security.sasl.Provider
```

Figure 9.5 demonstrates what this file looks like before editing.

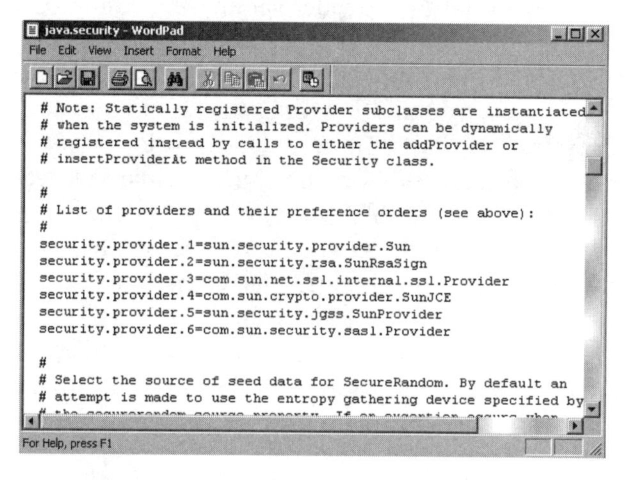

FIGURE 9.5 java.security: changes required.

1. To add our new provider, we'll want to add a new line specifying the provider we wish to add to the end of the list. In this example, "8" is at the end of the list of Sun installed providers and is "free" (i.e., it is not already occupied by another provider). Therefore, let's add the following line and save the file:

```
security.provider.8=org.bouncycastle.jce.provider.
BouncyCastleProvider
```

2. On a Windows machine, Figure 9.6 demonstrates the addition of this new provider. Since we have different default installed providers on the Windows platform than we did on the Solaris platform, we'll use the priority value of 7 instead of 8, which we used in the previous example.

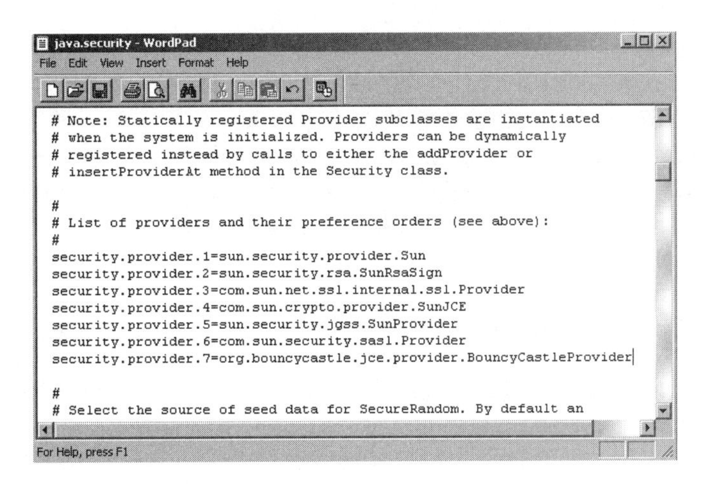

FIGURE 9.6 java.security: adding a new provider.

We've now installed a new provider. If there are additional providers we want to install, we can just go ahead and drop those in at this time as well.

9.2.3.2 Dynamic Registration

As mentioned, we do not have to statically install new providers. We may often find this the simplest and most direct way to do so, but there is another way in case this method is not available to us or convenient in the context of our application. We can use the Java API itself to add new providers to the provider pool by calling the static `addProvider()` method within `java.security.Security`. If the provider has not been statically added to the system, this is a useful method to add the provider to the provider pool during program execution. As we did with static registration, let's go ahead and use this method to add the BouncyCastle provider to a system running Sun Solaris 9. We'll use the same system as before, so the BouncyCastle provider is still located in the /usr/jdk1.5.0/jre/lib/ext directory, although there are no references to the provider in the java.security file. Note that we could put the provider anywhere in the classpath and retain the same results.

To dynamically register the provider, we'll need to dynamically register it in every program we write. The following code will allow us to do this:

```
import java.security.Security;
import org.bouncycastle.jce.provider.BouncyCastleProvider;
public class Main {
        public static void main(String argv[]) throws Exception {
                java.security.Security.addProvider(new
                        BouncyCastleProvider());
    }
}
```

This code doesn't do anything other than add the provider and make it available for use in the program. Now, we can go ahead and request that provider from the runtime when instantiating an engine class just as we would if the provider was statically registered. More information on the `addProvider()` method can be found in the Java API documentation; since we will not often use this method, we won't cover it in additional detail here. If we attempt to explicitly reference a provider by name and it is not present, the following will occur at *runtime*:

```
Exception in thread "main" java.security.NoSuchProviderException: No
such provider: yellow
        at javax.crypto.Cipher.getInstance(DashoA12275)
        at EncryptStream.main(EncryptStream.java:21)
```

In other words, the runtime will throw a `NoSuchProviderException`. A useful technique in situations where we have a preferred provider is to look for the preferred provider by name, catch `NoSuchProviderException`, and retry with another nonpreferred provider if it is not available. Note the related exception `NoSuchAlgorithmException` if we specify an algorithm that does not exist:

```
Exception in thread "main" java.security.NoSuchAlgorithmException:
Cannot find any provider supporting AESSS
        at javax.crypto.Cipher.getInstance(DashoA12275)
        at EncryptStream.main(EncryptStream.java:21)
```

9.3 ENCRYPTION AND DECRYPTION–"LOW-LEVEL" TECHNIQUES

Now that we know a little about the API we're going to be using, and we know a bit about how to customize the Java interpreted environment to accommodate our security needs, how do we go about writing software that uses this cryptographic functionality? In terms of actually doing work, we first need to evaluate the context in which we'll be writing the software, and we'll tailor the approach to that context. In the upcoming sections, we'll concentrate primarily on three types of examples: cryptography in Java applications, applets, and servlets. We'll try to keep the examples relevant and easy to implement; nobody knows ahead of time the challenges that will be faced by every developer in every situation, but a few things occur more often than others do. We'll try to zero in on those things that happen more often than not.

9.3.1 Symmetric Encryption and Decryption

The Java API provider does not provide a low-level interface quite as flexible as some of the other libraries and techniques we've been discussing. Unlike some of the other platforms, there is less of a differentiation in the Java platform between the "higher level API" and the "lower level API." Let's take a moment to contrast this with our discussions around the CAPI API. In looking at CAPI, the high level is incredibly abstract, involving one or two lines of code (e.g., with CAPICOM) to perform amazingly complex operations, while requiring (at an SDK level) very complex structures and pages of accompanying source code. Java is quite the opposite. The JCE constructs are all much higher level than any other corresponding API[1]. This is not as negative as it would seem on the surface; to the contrary, the developers of the Java API have done quite a good job of isolating the developer from complexity while not significantly reducing the flexibility of what can be done with their tools. We'll go through some of the more complicated ways we can use the API to achieve the same level of control over the operations we have in other libraries. However, suffice it to say at this point that we can often avoid some of the more code-intensive and confusing steps we would need to perform if we were writing to another library.

9.3.1.1 Symmetric Encryption–Instantiating a Cipher Object

The lowest level API available to us in the JCE provides opaque access to cryptographic encryption primitives on an algorithm-by-algorithm basis. At that level, all we'll need to do in preparation for performing our encryption is decide what algorithm to use and obtain a key. Next, we can optionally decide what padding mechanism and cipher mode we want to use as well—or we can leave those details to the library and use the default values for these. Each algorithm, padding methodology, and mode of operation corresponds to a static string that will be recognized by the provider pool to locate the data "transformation" you wish to perform.

Since each provider implements its own list of supported transformations (and corresponding identification strings), the list of algorithms, modes, and padding supported by a given provider should be reviewed to ensure the providers in use match the requirements of the application. Once we have determined that our design is supported by the providers installed (or obtained and installed a provider that does support our design), we will then make note of the identification strings used by the provider to identify the algorithm, padding, and mode of the cipher we wish to use. If we like, we can request that the default values for mode and padding be used; this means that at a minimum we must determine the algorithm constant that identifies the algorithm we wish to use within our application.

Once we decide what algorithm we wish to use, and we know the appropriate constant value to specify in our request, we will need to use the static method `getInstance()` in `javax.crypto.Cipher` to obtain an instance that corresponds to the functionality we require. The request to obtain the Cipher instance (i.e., the input parameter to the `getInstance()` call) is a string in the format `<algorithm>/<mode>/<padding>`, where `<algorithm>`, `<mode>`, and `<padding>` are the string constants mapping to the transformations they represent. This can sound confusing at first, so let's go through an example; this process makes a great deal more sense when we see it applied versus written down. For example, if our application design required us to use the AES algorithm in CBC mode and we wanted to use the padding mechanism specified in PKCS #5 (all solid choices), we would look at the following list of constants in the Java API documentation to find out the constant identification string for the AES algorithm:

- AES
- ARCFOUR/RC4
- Blowfish
- DES
- DESede (note that this refers to Triple-DES ("ede" refers to a common mode of Triple-DES operation, "encrypt, decrypt, encrypt")
- ECIES (Elliptic Curve Integrated Encryption Scheme)
- RC2
- RC4
- RC5

Looking at this list, note that the string "AES" maps to the AES algorithm, and so would need to be supplied to the `getInstance()` method. Next, we want to pick the algorithm mode we wish to use from the list of supported modes:

- CBC
- CFB
- ECB
- OFB
- PCBC (Propagating Cipher Block Chaining)

Our application design specified CBC, since it is robust, commonly used, and ubiquitously supported. We'll go ahead and note that the string for CBC mode is "CBC." Next, we want to select the padding mechanism[2] from the available choices. Again, our choices are:

- ISO10126Padding
- PKCS5Padding
- SSL3Padding

We'll select PKCS5Padding for our example again, since it's called for in our design (again, it's robust and commonly implemented). Putting all three values together, and putting our string in `<algorithm>/<mode>/<padding>` format using the constants we've located, we get the string `AES/CBC/PKCS5Padding`. Therefore, this is the string we'll want to supply verbatim to the `getInstance()` call of the `Cipher` class. Most of the time, for our purposes, we will want to implement AES for new applications, PKCS5 padding, and CBC mode. This is by no means a requirement, but is probably a good choice for a new application, as it uses a current, active, strong standard cipher (AES) in a strong and common mode (CBC) with the most common type of padding (PKCS5).

Now that we know what string to use during the instantiation process, we can go ahead and obtain an instance of the appropriate `Cipher`. The procedure for doing the actual `Cipher` instantiation is as follows:

1. Import `javax.crypto.Cipher` into the class where we'll use the encryption functionality.

In current versions of the J2SE, the default providers supplied by Sun provide a `Cipher` that meets this description, so we do not need to install any additional providers to get a cipher that matches our prerequisites. If we are using an old version that does not contain AES, we will need to select a different algorithm, use another provider that does incorporate the functionality, or upgrade the version of the JRE we're using. It is important to note that we can still compile the code even if the string we specify does not map to a valid transformation. This can lead to some hard-to-find bugs at times, so we'll want to make sure the transformation we request is available on our development, test, and production platforms. In fact, it's often helpful to look at what kind of error message is generated by the application if the underlying provider is of an incorrect version to assist in debugging should this occur.

2. Use the static method `getInstance()` in `javax.crypto.Cipher`, specifying "AES/CBC/PKCS5Padding" as the algorithm, mode, and padding that we would like used.
3. Therefore, to generate a Cipher instance, we would want to first include in our application code something similar to the following:

```
javax.crypto.Cipher enc =
javax.crypto.Cipher.getInstance("AES/CBC/PKCS5Padding");
```

4. A line like this will generate a new cipher object instance that can now be coupled with an encryption key and used to perform encryption and decryption operations.

9.3.1.2 Symmetric Encryption–Using the Cipher Object to Encrypt

Now that we've prepared an instance of the appropriate type, let's go ahead and actually encrypt and decrypt some data with it. Once an instance is obtained, there are three steps involved in encrypting or decrypting data:

1. **Initialization of the cipher (`init`):** At this time, we will also specify the "operating mode" of the cipher ("operating mode" should not be confused with the "mode of operation" we specified in our call to `getInstance()`). The operating mode will be one of two values for generic data encryption/decryption operations (`ENCRYPT_MODE` or `DECRYPT_MODE`). Additionally, at this time, the key that will be used for encryption or decryption operations will be specified.
2. **(Optional) Updating the cipher with all the "nonterminating" data (`update`):** This may sound confusing, but "nonterminating" in this context means anything up to (but not including) the last block of data; more specifically, one or more blocks of zero or more bytes comprised of data that is to be encrypted by our application. Since the block sizes are variable, updating is an optional step provided for convenience and performance reasons (such as if a developer wishes to encrypt a large file that is impractical to read in all at once, or wishes to encrypt data on a socket a piece at a time).
3. **Notification to the cipher that the final block of data has been submitted for encryption (`doFinal`):** The API has been designed in such as way as to require explicit notification of "finality" to the underlying implementation—this allows the underlying implementation to know when to add any required padding. This method signals the termination of an encipher (or decipher) operation.

The methods of `javax.crypto.Cipher` corresponding to the preceding steps are `init()`, `update()`, and `doFinal()`, respectively. The `init()` method is responsible for collecting any and all data required for the cipher to operate, with the exception of the requisite input values such as the plaintext bytes. For example, keys (and other information) related to what mode the algorithm should operate in (encrypt or decrypt mode), algorithm-specific initialization information, and so on are all specified at the time of initialization. The `update` method (the calling of which is optional) may be used iteratively as needed to encrypt portions of data and to retrieve the intermediate results of the encryption. At the conclusion of the operation, `doFinal()` is called to obtain the concluding portion of encrypted data, including any padding that needs to be applied to the output.

We'll get to the specifics of the `Key` class later in this chapter when we delve into the generating, storing, and manipulating of keys. However, for now we can (correctly) assume that `Key` is an opaque type required by the encipherment process. Therefore, the encryption and decryption code presented here presupposes the existence of a variable `theKey`, which (at this time) will remain undefined to reduce the complexity of the example.

Looking at the steps we've outlined already, code similar to the following will encrypt the test data we specify:

```
javax.crypto.Cipher enc =

javax.crypto.Cipher.getInstance("AES/CBC/PKCS5Padding");
enc.init(enc.ENCRYPT_MODE, theKey);
enc.update(intermediateData);
outBuffer = enc.doFinal(finalData);
```

Using the same conventions, code similar to the following will decrypt data:

```
javax.crypto.Cipher dec =

javax.crypto.Cipher.getInstance("AES/CBC/PKCS5Padding");
dec.init(DECRYPT_MODE, theKey);
dec.update(intermediateEncryptedData);
plainText = dec.doFinal(finalEncryptedData);
```

9.1.3.3 Avoiding Common Problems

There are a few things we should take note of at this time. In general, we will need to make sure we successfully initialize a `Cipher` instance before we can do any sort of encryption or decryption. Therefore, we should be aware of a few things that can go wrong at the initialization stage so we can avoid them.

The following describes some of the exceptions we might encounter from the JCE. Most of the time they will arise during the debugging process, as they are both usage errors that we usually cannot recover from at runtime. If we encounter them during the debugging process, we'll probably want to go back and implement the recommendations described under each.

`BadPaddingException`

Most of the examples in this book use some type of padding in the algorithm selection. If we elect not to use padding and we are using a block cipher, we need to make sure we do not attempt to encrypt data that is not a multiple of the block size, or if we do, that we pad it appropriately first. If we fail to manually pad appropriately and we have specified the instantiation of a block cipher (contained in the opaque `Cipher` instance) that will not pad for us, we will want to catch and handle exceptions of this type. Most of the time, this type of exception will manifest itself as a `BadPaddingException` during subsequent encryption or decryption operations. If this occurs during encryption, we can either elect to have the Java implementation pad for us (this is the easiest way provided we do not need to conform to a particular padding methodology), or review our manual padding implementation to make sure we are padding appropriately.

`InvalidStateException`

At this step, we may develop complicated classes designed to handle various initialization and encryption asynchronously. In other words, we might build functionality that erroneously assumes that appropriate initialization of the cipher has been effected but in actuality, it has not. Most of the time, calling methods out of order or using an uninitialized `Cipher` will result in an `InvalidStateException` during a subsequent operation. In the event we encounter this during our development process, we will want to review our software to make sure we are using an appropriately initialized `Cipher` instance.

9.3.2 Asymmetric Encryption (Not Including Signing)—Using a Cipher to Encrypt Asymmetrically

As discussed in previous sections, there are only a few times when we will wish to undertake encryption of data (for privacy) ourselves using an asymmetric algorithm. For example, there might be times when we are integrating with proprietary protocols (and therefore where we can't use a higher level interface to use for performing the requisite tasks). In any event, some JCE providers allow us to use the `Cipher` interface described earlier to perform asymmetric encryption operations. Note that later in this chapter, we will be reviewing some "higher level" (easier) ways to accomplish large portions of the functionality that asymmetric encryption (for privacy) has historically been used for (such as wrapping a symmetric key). For most purposes, these higher level APIs will be more desirable since they are easier to use, easier to debug, and maintain compliance with industry standards. That being said, let's take a moment to review in the event our applications will require us to perform an asymmetric operation in this way.

9.3.2.1 Asymmetric Encryption Prerequisites

Not all providers allow us to directly make use of the RSA algorithm via the `Cipher` engine class. For example, many providers do not allow us to make a call such as this:

```
Cipher myRSACipher = Cipher.getInstance("RSA");
```

Perhaps most importantly, the Sun default provider did not historically allow this call to take place. In versions up to 1.5.0 (released while this book was being authored), a call such as the preceding one listed would result in an `Exception` such as this:

```
Exception in thread "main" java.security.NoSuchAlgorithmException:
Cannot find any provider supporting RSA
            at javax.crypto.Cipher.getInstance(DashoA6275)
```

However, as of now (versions post 1.5.0), calls to `Cipher.getInstance()` specifying an algorithm identifier string of "RSA" (or something more specific including mode and padding) will retrieve a valid `Cipher` instance that can be used for cryptographic operations. It should be explicitly stated that the situations in which we would want to use this interface are rare. Our two most common uses of asymmetric crypto—key wrapping and signing—exist in JCA within *different* interfaces and are therefore usually inappropriate contexts for a `Cipher` instance of type RSA.

9.3.2.2 Asymmetric Encryption–Usage

If we continue to ignore anything related to keys, we find that the API for encipherment using an asymmetric algorithm is identical to encipherment using a symmetric algorithm. Therefore, if we replace `AES` with `RSA` in our previous examples, we will produce valid code. Making a modification such as that and adjusting for differences in the required initialization, the following code will compile and execute without error under J2SE SDK 1.5.0. (Note that the variable `pair` is undefined here—we'll get to it in our subsequent discussions relating to keys, but for now we'll assume it is a valid reference to a structure containing the key pair.)

```
Cipher rsa = Cipher.getInstance("RSA");
          rsa.init(Cipher.ENCRYPT_MODE, pair.getPublic());
          byte[] plain = new String("testing").getBytes();
          byte[] out = rsa.doFinal(plain);
```

9.3.3 Message Digests

We've seen message digests in a variety of contexts; they provide very useful functionality in a number of situations and are able to process a large amount of information quickly. The typical message digest API is incremental in the same way that encipherment is. "Incremental" in this context means that since we may need to supply a large volume of input, we will need to iteratively "update" the data we provide to the library through repeated calls into the same routine.

9.3.3.1 Message Digests–Instantiating a `MessageDigest` Object

As we might expect, creating a message digest starts in a manner similar to all other engine classes in that we are going to start the process by making a request for an instance. In this case, the instance we are going to request is located in the package `java.security.MessageDigest`. As with `javax.crypto.Cipher`, the appropriate method within `MessageDigest` we are going to call is `getInstance()`, and like `Cipher`, each provider will have a static list of string constants we will use to refer to a particular message digest algorithm. In the default provider supplied by Sun, the following message digest algorithms are present and implemented:

- MD2
- MD5
- SHA-1
- SHA-256
- SHA-384
- SHA-512

The following will create an instance of a `MessageDigest` object encapsulating the SHA-1 algorithm:

```
java.security.MessageDigest md =
java.security.MessageDigest.getInstance("SHA-1");
```

The newly created `MessageDigest` object is now ready for use. Let's go ahead and use it to create a `MessageDigest` value from some sample text.

9.3.3.2 Using the `MessageDigest` Object

There are two steps involved in creating a `MessageDigest` from a given piece of data:

1. **(Optional) Call the `update()` method of `MessageDigest`:** Note that this is an iterative call that will contain the nonterminal bytes of the message to be digested. The final block is the terminating zero or more bytes of the mes-

sage. This method is not required and is therefore provided for both performance and usability reasons to the developer.

2. **Call the `digest()` method within the `MessageDigest` class**: Note that this will conclude the digest operation, so all bytes from the message should be supplied to the digest instance using update before this call is made.

Code similar to the following can be used to create a `MessageDigest` from a given message:

```
java.security.MessageDigest md =
    java.security.MessageDigest.getInstance("SHA-1");
md.update(firstPartofMessage); //demo of optional update call
byte theDigest[] = md.digest();
```

ON THE CD

Some examples of using the `MessageDigest` routines for real-life applications are provided on the companion CD-ROM (/Examples/Chapter 9/Digests).

9.3.4 Creating and Storing Keys

Java provides some very useful functionality for key generation (both symmetric and asymmetric). Of particular import and note is that key generation for asymmetric algorithms and symmetric algorithms occur in almost exactly the same way and by calling almost exactly the same methods. We'll go through what the methods are in detail in just a minute; we just want to note at this time that Java makes these methods accessible to use for the developer.

9.3.4.1 About `SecureRandom`

As we've seen in other libraries, before we can talk about key generation, we need to talk about secure random data generation. `SecureRandom` is an engine class that provides (intuitively) a secure pseudo-random number source to the caller. Periodically, we will be called on to instantiate a `SecureRandom` instance (particularly during operations that generate cryptographic keys). It should be noted that since this is an engine class, the methodology for instantiating a `SecureRandom` instance is (again) through the use of the `getInstance()` static method contained within the `SecureRandom` class. The developers of the API, however, have made available a default constructor that will retrieve the first PRNG implementation it comes across in the provider pool. "The first implementation" will be the implementation associated with the highest priority provider in the provider pool that contains a PRNG implementation (therefore, it will usually be the default Sun provider). This random number generator does not (fortunately for us) require seeding prior to use, so we can go ahead and instantiate it and start getting random data from it.

9.3.4.2 Creating Session Keys and Other Random Symmetric Keys

The `KeyGenerator` class is used for the creation of all symmetric keys. It requires little initialization prior to use within our application and takes only a few lines of code. It does, however, require a robust source of randomness to function. In keeping with obtaining "strong" random numbers, we'll want to use the `SecureRandom` class as our randomness source, since it will provide the strength we need to generate keys. We'll go about creating a random source as per the instructions in the previous section, and couple that to the key generation process. Here is a quick overview of the steps required to generate symmetric keys:

1. Create a random source that can be used by the key generator for any required randomness (this is optional and will be done for us if we do not specify a random source).
2. Use the method `getInstance()` in the `KeyGenerator` class to obtain a new instance. Input to this method should be the string constant corresponding to the algorithm we wish to create a key for (e.g., AES).
3. Initialize the `KeyGenerator` by supplying the random source to the `KeyGenerator`.
4. Perform the key generation procedure by calling the `generateKey()` method of `KeyGenerator` with no arguments.

Code similar to the following would be used to create a new key for the AES algorithm. Note that in this example, we're presuming the requisite classes from `javax.crypto` and `java.security` are already imported. This can be accomplished by including the statements `import javax.crypto.*;` and `import java.security.*` at the beginning of the source file:

```
SecureRandom random = new SecureRandom();
KeyGenerator keyGen = KeyGenerator.getInstance("AES");
keyGen.init(random);
Key myKey = keyGen.generateKey();  //generate AES key
```

The default key size is 128 bits, although we can explicitly request the provider to provide other key values (provided we have installed the unlimited cryptography policy files) by using the `init()` overloads that take a key size. For example, we could substitute the following call instead of the `init()` call used earlier to create a 256-bit key:

```
keyGen.init(256, random);
```

9.3.4.3 Avoiding Common Problems

Following are some of the most common problems that can happen during the key generation process.

InvalidKeyException

`InvalidKeyException` can occur in a few circumstances; in this section, we'll talk about the most likely cause during automatic key generation. If a key is created for one cipher and we attempt to use it in a different (incompatible) cipher, the interpretive environment will prevent us from doing so. Additionally, if we attempt to use a key that is too big for the policy installed on the system (see the section "Installing 'Unlimited' Cryptography"), we would get an exception of this type. If we do get this exception, we should go back and make sure our environment is appropriately set up (in that we have the appropriate "unlimited" policy files installed) and we are using the key in an appropriate algorithm.

9.3.4.4 Manual Creation of Symmetric Keys (Supplying the Key Directly)

Oftentimes, we don't have the luxury of creating new, strong symmetric keys for our applications. For example, we might have a preexisting transaction set up with another entity where we are forced to share a symmetric key between them and ourselves. Authoring an application where we have to incorporate preexisting keys is arguably not an ideal situation, but legacy systems are the hard reality of the modern business environment. In situations in which we can't create new keys using the methodology described previously, we might have to use a mechanism where a static value needs to be supplied that will form the key bytes for our application. To do this, let's look at two classes provided by the API to do this: Key Specifications and Key Factories.

Key Specification Classes

The Java API requires that we use the `Key` class in combination with a `Cipher` to produce encrypted (or decrypted) output. However, the `Key` class, as an opaque representation of the key data, does not provide the developer with the ability to specify what the key bytes are at time of creation. Therefore, we will require a mechanism whereby we can transparently represent keys—where we can manipulate the key data directly and tell the API what we would like the key bytes to be. Java provides this functionality through the use of key specifications.

The Java API documentation tells us that a "key specification" is a transparent representation of a key that can be used by the developer to manipulate key data in a number of ways. However, a key specification cannot just be created and used by itself; it needs to be used in combination with a `KeyFactory` (we'll cover this in just a minute) to transform a key specification into a `Key` used as input to a `Cipher`. However, to accomplish the most common task, creating a key from known bytes, there is a shortcut provided to us by the API developers. This shortcut provides the easiest and most expedient method of creating a new `SecretKey` instance in a format useable by a `Cipher` from existing key bytes. Namely, we create an instance of the high-level SecretKeySpec class using the SecretKeySpec(keyData, algorithmString). SecretKeySpec implements the SecretKey interface, which makes the SecretKeySpec useful as input to a Cipher. Put another way, since SecretKeySpec implements SecretKey, any SecretKeySpec we create is also a valid SecretKey. As an example, the following would create SecretKeySpec (and transitively, a SecretKey) from existing key bytes:

```
byte[] keyData = new String("1234567890ABCDEF").getBytes();
javax.crypto.spec.SecretKeySpec keySpec = new
        javax.crypto.spec.SecretKeySpec(keyData, "AES");
```

Note that here we are creating a 128-bit AES key. Obviously, there are a few problems with this approach. First, in a real situation we would *never* want to hardcode the key into the source. Hardcoding a key is always an undesirable practice in any language, but it is a particularly bad idea in Java, as bytecode is not difficult to decompile. In addition, in a real-life scenario, we wouldn't want to use the bytes and not "purge" the buffer when we're done with it; instead, in most cases, we'll want to zero the buffer after use. However, it is instructive to leave the example free of "ancillary" code such as reading the key from the filesystem or storage device, extracting it from any protection features, purging the key buffer, and so forth, because it highlights the key creation code itself and illustrates the point that the key data as supplied to the SecretKeySpec constructor can be arbitrary.

Key Factories

Another way to produce a key from existing bytes is to use a "key factory." A key factory, as described earlier, is used to transform a Key into a KeySpec (and the reverse, a KeySpec into a Key). As stated earlier, by far the easiest way in a symmetric key context to instantiate a Key instance with particular key bytes is to use a SecretKeySpec; however, this is not the only way to do so. If we are using an algorithm that contains parameter information in addition to the key, we can use a KeyFactory for this purpose instead; we can also use the KeyFactory methodology according to personal preference or to suit the design of our application. It is useful for the developer to become familiar with this technique, as key factories are also used for instantiation operations on nonsymmetric keys such as RSA and DSA.

To create a key from static data using this approach, here are the steps to follow:

1. Instantiate a KeySpec of the appropriate type and populate it with the appropriate data we wish our key to contain. The easiest way to populate the KeySpec with the appropriate data is to use the constructor that allows us to specify key bytes at the time of instantiation.

2. Use the `getInstance()` method in `javax.crypto.SecretKeyFactory` to obtain a reference to a factory that will transform a `KeySpec` into a `Key`. The call to `getInstance()` should include the algorithm constant string identifying the algorithm corresponding to the type of key we wish to use.
3. Use the `generateSecret()` method of `KeyFactory` to get a `Key` instance corresponding to the `KeySpec` we supply in the method call.

In case the steps as described seem confusing, let's go through an example to demonstrate how this works. We'll be using a Triple-DES `KeySpec` in this case to create a key that can be subsequently used for Triple-DES operation:

```
 byte[] keyData = new String("1234567890ABCDEF1234567890ABCDEF"
        ).getBytes(); //overlong buffer explained below
DESedeKeySpec tripleDesKeySpec = new DESedeKeySpec(keyData);
SecretKeyFactory secrets = SecretKeyFactory.getInstance(
                    "DESede");
SecretKey secretKey = secrets.generateSecret(tripleDesKeySpec);
```

In doing this, two shortcuts should immediately be pointed out. First, we have again hardcoded the key bytes into the application contrary to acceptable security practices. Additionally, we've supplied an overly long key to the `KeySpec` to illustrate how the `KeySpec` will truncate the key bits we have supplied to make an acceptable key. In this example, only the first 24 bytes of the key data are incorporated into the `Key` information, and the rest are discarded. For the sake of brevity, we've again left out the "purging" of the key bytes after use. The key we generate can then be used in our call to the `init()` method of the cipher as demonstrated in our earlier examples using session keys.

9.3.4.5 Asymmetric Key Generation (Generating a Key Pair for DSA or RSA)

Generating an asymmetric key can be done in one of two ways; essentially, there's an "abstract" way and a "lower level" way. The high-level method is most expedient in all cases except those in which require integration with legacy code or have "highly intrusive" security requirements (meaning that our key generation procedures have to use specific parameters that don't happen to be the default for our JCE cryptographic providers). If we merely want to generate an asymmetric key and we don't have any requirement that the key be generated with any specific parameters (e.g., specific DSA integer values, specific values for the RSA public exponent, etc.), then creation of an asymmetric key pair is simplified (note again that this will be most cases). Briefly, we will use the `KeyPairGenerator` (analogous to the `KeyGenerator` we used when creating symmetric keys) initialized with a random number source. The methods and classes we will call will be almost identical to those we called during the symmetric key initialization, with the exception that they are specifically constructed to operate on `KeyPair(s)` rather than a `Key` alone. Briefly, here are the steps for key pair generation:

1. Instantiate and initialize a secure random number generator (this is optional and will be done for us automatically if we do not specifically do so).
2. Instantiate a `KeyPairGenerator` instance by calling the static method `getInstance()` of `KeyPairGenerator`. Note that we will want to use the algorithm standard identification constant (e.g., RSA or DSA) during our call to retrieve an instance.
3. Initialize the `KeyPairGenerator` by telling it the key size in bits of output keys and specifying the random number source that will be used during the key generation operation.
4. Generate the key pair through the `generateKeyPair()` method. For example, to generate a DSA key using the default parameters, we would write code similar to the following:

```
SecureRandom rand = new SecureRandom();
KeyPairGenerator keyGen = KeyPairGenerator.getInstance("DSA");
keyGen.initialize(1024, rand);
KeyPair keyPair = keyGen.generateKeyPair();
```

9.3.4.6 Asymmetric Key Generation with Specific Parameters (Using Specific Nondefault Values)

If we wish to generate a key that does use particular parameters, we can do so using the same `KeyPairGenerator` we used in the last section; however, we need to add a few things to it for the key pair generation process. It should be noted that most of the time, we neither need or want to change the parameter values from their defaults unless we are in one of two situations: if we are working in an environment that has very specific policy in and around key generation procedures (such as particular constants that must be used and so forth), or we are integrating with a legacy application. In either event, if we can, we'll want to avoid having to specify these values, as it increases the complexity of the key generation procedure somewhat. If we are in a situation in which we can't get around specifying any of these parameters, the procedure is the same, except that we will wish to instantiate and populate an instance of an `AlgorithmParameterSpec` of the appropriate type. If we are using RSA, we will want to create an `RSAKeyGenParameterSpec` (which implements `AlgorithmParameterSpec`), and if we are using DSA, we will want to create a `DSAParameterSpec` (which also implements `AlgorithmParameterSpec`). These classes allow us to control the key generation parameters, setting them to values other than the defaults.

Given that we want to manipulate some of the key generation parameters in our key generation, here are the steps outlined with specificity:

1. Instantiate and initialize a secure random number generator (this is optional and will be done for us automatically if we do not specifically do so).
2. Instantiate a `KeyPairGenerator` instance by calling the static method `getInstance()` of `KeyPairGenerator`. Note that we will wish to use the algorithm standard identification constant during our call to retrieve an instance.
3. Instantiate an appropriate `AlgorithmParameterSpec` and set the values we wish to manipulate.
4. Initialize the `KeyPairGenerator` by telling it the key size of output keys and specifying the random number source that will be used during the key generation operation.
5. Generate the key pair through the `generateKeyPair()` method.

For example, if we need to use an RSA public exponent of "3" rather than the default value of "65537" (perhaps for backward compatibility with legacy code), we could use code similar to the following:

```
SecureRandom rand = new SecureRandom();
KeyPairGenerator keyGen = KeyPairGenerator.getInstance("RSA");
java.security.spec.RSAKeyGenParameterSpec rsaSpec =
                 new java.security.spec.RSAKeyGenParameterSpec(
                1024, new java.math.BigInteger("3"));
keyGen.initialize(rsaSpec, rand);
KeyPair keyPair = keyGen.generateKeyPair();
```

Note that in creating the `RSAKeyGenParameterSpec`, the exponent data is of type `BigInteger` rather than `Integer`. Therefore, we must use an appropriate `BigInteger` constructor (here the decimal string representation "3") rather than just specifying the `Integer` literal 3. Again, note that this process is still much easier to use than some of the other libraries we're covering, even though it has grown in complexity somewhat when compared to the default case. We can use the key generation parameters to change the public exponent value, the key "modulus bits" (size), DSA integer values, and so on.

9.3.4.7 Manual Creation of Asymmetric Keys (Supplying Asymmetric Keys Directly)

We will not often have to do this, but in situations in which we wish to be backwardly compatible with existing applications, we may have to explicitly supply the asymmetric key data to an application we are writing. This will happen much more often with higher level constructs such as X.509 digital certificates (for which there are easier methods to import covered later in this chapter), but it may sometimes happen with proprietary applications that incorporate asymmetric cryptography. The case where we would need to specifically represent an asymmetric key is unlikely to occur in an "encryption for privacy" context (it is more likely to occur in the case of signing and verifying). However, in the event we are replacing a legacy system and we are unable to change the key for that application, we may be called upon to do this. For the interests of thoroughness, we will cover this here, but since doing this is likely to be an infrequent occurrence, we'll spend limited time and space on the example code and outlining the steps.

Basically, the population of the key with the appropriate data will take place in a manner similar to that employed for symmetric key population (with explicitly defined data) described earlier in this chapter. Since in this example, we're concerned with encryption for privacy, note that we do not have to supply the private key, but only the public half of the key data. As was the case with symmetric keys, we will instantiate a `KeySpec` of the appropriate type and will populate that `KeySpec` with the value we wish the key to have. We will then create a `KeyFactory` class (note that this is `KeyFactory` as opposed to the `SecretKeyFactory` we used while generating symmetric keys), which we will use to perform the actual transmutation. Here is an example of this in action:

```
//we just want to obtain the public key
RSAPublicKeySpec rsapubspec = new RSAPublicKeySpec(modulus,
                                                   publicExponent);
KeyFactory myKeyFactory = KeyFactory.getInstance("RSA");
PublicKey myPublicKey = myKeyFactory.generatePublic(rsapubspec);
Cipher cipher = Cipher.getInstance("RSA");
cipher.init(cipher.ENCRYPT_MODE, myPublicKey);
```

The cipher can now be used to encrypt data. Note that to use this example, we will need to import the packages `java.math.BigInteger`, `java.security.spec.*`, `java.security.*`, and `javax.crypto.*`. In this example, the variables `modulus` should contain the modulus of the public key, and `publicExponent` should contain the public exponent that was used in the public key. The specifics of obtaining this information will vary according to the format that was used in the software we are importing from, and therefore a description of the methods for obtaining that information is outside the scope of this book. However, almost all libraries will contain a method to extract this information, and proprietary (nonlibrary) encryption code that does this can likely be inspected to determine the values to supply for appropriate functionality in the previous example.

9.3.5 Password-Based Encryption (Initializing a Cipher from Password Values)

We've saved password-based key derivation (as the Sun documentation calls it, "PBE") until now, because (as we've seen in previous libraries) implementation of this concept is rarely easy or painless. Java is no exception: to successfully derive a key from a password, there are a number of additional steps that we'll need to undertake before we can do so. Reading through the Sun documentation on the subject of PBE can be a daunting task for a developer not extensively familiar with the jargon (and with the Java cryptography API). Therefore, since there are a number of new classes involved, and there are some security issues present if we do this wrong, let's make sure we go through the problem carefully first before actually looking at the steps in order, or go through some sample code.

Warning! *The Sun documentation provides a stern warning for developers about how to obtain the password and store it internal to the application. It tells us that using* `java.lang.String` *for storage of the password is dangerous because we cannot clear the memory once we are done with it. We'll want to treat the password with the same sensitivity (or more sensitivity) as we would key data. However, there is an additional challenge with passwords in that we might be tempted to store the password data (at least transiently) in a* `java.lang.String`*; we really shouldn't do this since it makes purging the memory difficult (Java strings cannot be overwritten). Therefore, we will wish to use a byte or char array for storing the password, and we will want to make sure we overwrite or "zeroize" that buffer when we're done performing our cryptographic operations.*

9.3.5.1 Additional Classes

In addition to the classes we've used already for encryption, we will need to incorporate the `PBEKeySpec` and `PBEParameterSpec` classes to use password-based key derivation according to PKCS #5. Following is a short description of those classes and what they're used for:

`PBEParameterSpec`: The `PBEParameterSpec` is used to specify two values that are required by PKCS #5: "iteration count" and "salt." Without going into an extreme amount of detail, these two values are used by the key derivation function to strengthen the keys that are derived from the password (e.g., in brute force searches). We will specify values for these fields during the instantiation of the `PBEParameterSpec`, prior to initialization of the cipher. For those developers reading these chapters out of order, we'll want to follow the recommendations of PKCS #5 in selecting values for both salt and iteration count. PKCS #5 recommends a number greater than 1000 (lower numbers have slightly better performance) for iteration count, and a random salt value of at least 8 octets.

As long as the values are greater than these minimum recommended values, we can use pretty much use any value for both.

PBEKeySpec: This class will hold the password we've collected from the user and will be used in combination with a SecretKeyFactory (an instance of which was generated using one of the PBE algorithm identification constants). The PBE algorithm constants are in the format PBEWith<hash>and<cipher>, where <hash> is one of the supported digest algorithms, and <cipher> is one of the supported symmetric encryption algorithms.[3] Obviously, we will want to use similar guidelines during the selection of algorithms for password-based key derivation as we would for any other part of the application.

Having laid out the new classes we'll need to employ in performing PBE operations, let's go through the steps in detail.

1. Import javax.crypto.spec.*, javax.crypto.*, and java.security.*.
2. Generate random information for use as the salt value.
3. Instantiate a new PBEParameterSpec and specifying salt and iteration count during construction.
4. Instantiate a new instance of PBEKeySpec using the password supplied by the user.
5. Obtain an instance of a SecretKeyFactory using SecretKeyFactory.getInstance() and supplying the appropriate PBE algorithm constant for PBE.
6. Call the generateSecret() method of the SecretKeyFactory obtained in the previous step, specifying the PBEKeySpec containing the password.
7. Obtain an instance of Cipher using Cipher.getInstance() and supplying the same algorithm constant string as used to generate the key.
8. Initialize the cipher using the key and the PBEParameterSpec containing the salt and iteration count value.

In performing these operations, we would author code similar to the following:

```
SecureRandom rand = new SecureRandom();
byte[] salt = new byte[8];
rand.nextBytes(salt);
PBEParameterSpec parameterSpec = new PBEParameterSpec(
                salt, 1024);
PBEKeySpec myKeySpec = new PBEKeySpec(getPassword());
SecretKeyFactory keyFactory = SecretKeyFactory.getInstance(
                                "PBEWithMD5andDES");
SecretKey myKey = keyFactory.generateSecret(myKeySpec);
```

```
Cipher myCipher = Cipher.getInstance("PBEWithMD5andDES");
myCipher.init(Cipher.ENCRYPT_MODE, myKey, parameterSpec);
```

Note that although `PBEWithMD5andDES` is provided to us by Sun, in many cases we will wish to expand the provider pool to include support for additional algorithms beyond MD5 and DES in cases where we wish to employ password-based key derivation.

9.4 ENCRYPTION AND DECRYPTION—"HIGH LEVEL" TECHNIQUES

The previous APIs we've covered are classified as "low level" because (for the most part) they require us to be aware of the encryption primitives directly (including specifics about those primitives). However, Java provides additional mechanisms to approach security problems at a higher level. This section will address non-"primitive-centric" methodologies for performing some of these tasks. Most of the time, we will find it desirable to use a higher level API for this purpose rather than a lower level one (since less code is involved, debugging is easier, and the APIs are "friendlier"). Therefore, without further ado, let's look at some of these APIs and what they can offer us.

9.4.1 Cipher Input and Output Streams (How to Quickly Encrypt or Decrypt a File, Byte Array, or Other Stream)

The easiest way to encrypt something like a file (or a network connection or anything else in Java that can be represented as an `InputStream` or `OutputStream`) is through the use of the `CipherInputStream` and `CipherOutputStream` classes. As the names suggest, these classes can be attached to other streams and used to encrypt large amounts of data as it passes through the stream. They are very simple to use, and greatly simplify the process of encryption and decryption. The steps involved to use an input (or output) stream are as follows:

1. Instantiate the appropriate `Cipher` instance that will be used for the bulk encryption of data.
2. Attach the `Cipher` to the `CipherInputStream` (or `CipherOutputStream` as appropriate).
3. Use the `read()` (or `write()`) method to "push" the data through the stream (causing it to be operated on by the cryptography along the way).

For example, to encrypt the contents of data that we write to a file, we would use code similar to the following:

```
FileOutputStream fs = new FileOutputStream("out.enc");
Cipher cipher = Cipher.getInstance("AES");
cipher.init(cipher.ENCRYPT_MODE, myKey);
CipherOutputStream out = new CipherOutputStream(fs, cipher);
out.write(new String("Testing").getBytes());
out.flush();
out.close();
```

Note that in this example, we used an undefined value `myKey` during the initialization of the `Cipher`. This is done for brevity, but in context, a developer would precede this example code with key creation code in his or her usage as appropriate. Note also that just as encrypted data can be written out to a file using `CipherOutputStream`, `CipherInputStream` could be initialized in an identical manner (specifying the cipher and associated input stream in the call to the constructor) to read the data out again from the file. This is an extremely powerful concept and allows us to implement functionality such as file encryption in a manner of minutes rather than hours.

9.4.1.1 Stream Example

To demonstrate the power of this concept, let's quickly implement a file encryption utility. We'll keep the example short and sweet: we'll accept a command-line argument of a file and we'll product an encrypted version of that file in the same directory. The following example demonstrates this:

```
import java.io.*;
import javax.crypto.*;
import java.security.*;
public class EncryptStream {
public static void main(String argv[]) throws Exception {
        if(argv.length == 0) {
                System.err.println("Usage: EncryptStream <file>");
                System.exit(-1);
        }
    //create the new streams
        FileOutputStream fOut = new
FileOutputStream(argv[0].concat(".enc"));
        FileInputStream fIn = new FileInputStream(argv[0]);
      //create random key for encryption
        KeyGenerator keyGen = KeyGenerator.getInstance("AES");
        keyGen.init(new SecureRandom());
        Key myKey = keyGen.generateKey();
        //prime the cipher
```

```
  Cipher cipher = Cipher.getInstance("AES");
        cipher.init(cipher.ENCRYPT_MODE, myKey);
        CipherOutputStream encOut = new CipherOutputStream(fOut,
cipher);
       //read loop for encryption of the file
        int numRead = 0;
        do {
                byte[] buf = new byte[1024];
                numRead = fIn.read(buf);
                if(numRead > 0) {
                        encOut.write(buf, 0, numRead);
                }
        } while (numRead != -1);
        encOut.flush();
        encOut.close();
        fIn.close();
        fOut.close();
}
```

Obviously, this isn't the prettiest implementation or the most useful, but it's not bad for something we can rapidly write to encrypt a file.

9.4.2 Sealed Objects (Quickly Encrypting Serialized Objects)

Another option we can use in some circumstances is the concept of "sealing" an object. This concept applies to instances where we are working with objects that implement the `Serializable` interface and can thus readily be represented as a string by "packaging" the internal state, tokenizing it, and rendering it into a binary (hence storable) format. In working with Java, one of the most powerful techniques available to us is serialization, and from an implementation perspective, a very powerful feature is the ability to add encryption to the already serialized data during this process using the "Sealed Object" concept supplied to us in the API. In dealing with objects that have been serialized in this way, we can overlay application of encipherment to the serialized structure and thereby render the object "sealed." In other words, serialization enables an object to be saved as a string; encrypting that resultant string causes the object to be "sealed." There are only two steps involved, so let's go through them from a usage standpoint:

1. Instantiate and initialize a `Cipher` instance (setting appropriate keys and choosing an appropriate algorithm).
2. Instantiate a `SealedObject`, specifying the `Cipher` we wish to use during construction.

And that's it! At the end of this, we'll have a tidy, fully secured object that protects its own internal state from unauthorized access. Putting these steps into action, to rapidly protect an object during the serialization process (perhaps an object that has sensitive internal state), we would write code similar to the following (we'll use a `Hashtable` to illustrate the point):

```
Hashtable myHashTable = new Hashtable();
myHashTable.put("aString", "theString");
Cipher cipher = Cipher.getInstance("AES");
cipher.init(cipher.ENCRYPT_MODE, myKey);
SealedObject sealedHT = new SealedObject(myHashTable, cipher);
```

Note that we'll need to import `java.util.Hashtable`, `javax.crypto.*`, and `java.security.*` (or only the requisite classes from those packages if we prefer) for the preceding code to compile. In addition, we've left the variable `myKey` undefined, as the key specifics of the key we intend to use will vary according to the usage (and since it simplifies the example).

9.4.3 Wrapping Keys (Safely Transporting Keys and Creating "Master" Keys)

If we wish to safely transport, save, or send a key across an insecure medium, one way the JCE makes this easier for us to do so is by supplying the key wrapping functionality provided to us via the `Cipher` implementation. "Wrapping" a key implies that we will be applying cryptography to the key to extract it from the cipher and render it safe for transport. The Sun documentation around this principle is a little confusing, so let's look at situations in which this concept would be particularly useful:

- When we wish to use individual symmetric keys for a large number of entities (e.g., files), but wish all these symmetric keys to be encrypted under one "master" user key (or an escrow key, etc.).
- When we wish to securely extract a key from a hardware device for use at a later time.

These situations can all be effected by manually employing other functionality already described in this chapter (e.g., serializing key state as a `SealedObject`). However, `Cipher`'s `wrap` and `unwrap` capability makes this both easier to use (arguably) and more versatile in situations in which we want to support both hardware and software implementations. Obviously, using the wrapping functionality implies a broader context through which this would be useful, so examples of usage without the context will appear a bit contrived. However, to demonstrate usage, note the following (contrived) example of wrapping a Triple-DES key with AES:

```
Cipher wrapper = Cipher.getInstance("AES");
SecretKeySpec toWrap = new SecretKeySpec(keyData, "DESede");
KeyGenerator keyGen = KeyGenerator.getInstance("AES");
keyGen.init(rand);
Key myKey = keyGen.generateKey();
wrapper.init(wrapper.WRAP_MODE, myKey);
byte[] theKey = wrapper.wrap(toWrap);
```

To unwrap the previously wrapped key, we just call the corresponding `unwrap()` method, specifying `PRIVATE_KEY`, `SECRET_KEY`, or `PUBLIC_KEY` in doing so. For example:

```
wrapper.init(wrapper.UNWRAP_MODE, myKey);
Key newKey = wrapper.unwrap(theKey, "DESede",
            wrapper.SECRET_KEY);
```

9.5 SIGNING AND VERIFYING DATA

As is the case with a number of the APIs we have seen throughout this book, the use of the signature and verification portions of the API in the JCE are roughly analogous to the encryption (for privacy) functionality in the same library. Rather than use the `Cipher` engine class we discussed earlier in this chapter, when we wish to calculate signatures of a string of text, we will use the `Signature` engine class. The `Signature` class is used for both the creation and verification of digital signatures.

9.5.1 Creating Signatures Using the `Signature` Class

Recalling the use of `Cipher`, we first initialized the `Cipher` (telling it whether we were going to encrypt or decrypt and supplying the key), and we then (optionally) iteratively called `update()` supplying the data we wished to encrypt. In our use of `Cipher`, when we were done supplying additional material for encipherment, we then informed the `Cipher` that we were finished updating the input and we "pulled the trigger" on the encryption operation by supplying the last block of data. From the standpoint of high-level steps, the use of the `Signature` class is not much different; the steps to initialize the `Signature` are somewhat different from encipherment (note also that signing and verifying are different during the initialization process). In other words, the specific method calls are different in name, but analogous in function.

To get a bit more specific, here are the steps for creating a signature (signing) using the `Signature` class:

1. Use the `Signature.getInstance()` method to request an instance of the `Signature` engine class. As with `Cipher` (and all other engine classes), we'll need to supply the appropriate algorithm identification string and (optionally) provider identification string if we have a particular requirement in those areas. (We can also specify a reference to a provider rather than the static identifier string if we are dynamically loading a provider.)
2. We will then initialize the `Signature` by using the `initSign()` method and specifying the private key that will be used to perform the signature when making the call. More specifically, we will need to instantiate and populate an instance of `PrivateKey` that contains the key data for use in the signing process—this `PrivateKey` instance will be bound to the `Signature` instance at this time.
3. Iteratively call `update()`, specifying the data we wish to sign. Note that we need to call this method at least once—the final methods for "pulling the trigger" on the signature (e.g., `sign()` and `verify()`) do not give us a method signature that allows us to supply data during the final call, so we will need to specify all of our data before that time.
4. Finally, we will call `sign()` to calculate the final signature value.

For example, if we wished to sign data, we would write code similar to the following; leaving out the specifics of key generation, this code generates a signature of the supplied plaintext:

```
//give ourselves some bogus data to sign
byte[] myBytes = new String("ABCDEFG").getBytes();
Signature sign = Signature.getInstance("RSA");
sign.initSign(privateKey);
sign.update(myBytes);
byte[] mySig = sign.sign();
```

9.5.2 Verifying Signatures Using the `Signature` Class

Similar to the creation of signatures, the `Signature` class can be used to verify signatures. Note, however, that the method for initialization of the `Signature` in the case of verification is different. Additionally, instead of calling `sign()` as we did when creating signatures, we will call a different method (`verify()`). For completeness, here are the steps involved in verifying a signature using the `Signature` class:

1. Use the `Signature.getInstance()` method to request an instance of `Signature`. As input to this call, we'll need to supply the appropriate algorithm identification string and (optionally) provider identification string (or reference).

2. We will then initialize the `Signature` for verification by using the `initVerify()` method and specifying the public key corresponding to the private key that produced the signature. Note that we can supply the key either as a `PublicKey` instance or as a `Certificate` instance (we'll cover the `Certificate` class and certificate manipulation later in this chapter, but it is useful to note that we can supply one if need be to the verification process).
3. Iteratively call `update()`, specifying the data we wish to verify.
4. Finally, we will call `verify()` to determine final verification of the data supplied; the call to `verify()` will also contain the signature we wish to validate against.

For example, if we wish to verify data, we would write code similar to the following (again, this leaves out the details of instantiating the key):

```
Signature sig = Signature.getInstance("RSA");
sig.initVerify(publicKey);
sig.update(theDataThatWasSigned);
boolean isGood = sig.verify(theSigData);
```

It is useful to note in the preceding code that one of two things will happen as a result of an invalid signature; if the underlying library can understand the format of the signature, a determination will be made as to its validity and a true/false value returned. In other words, if the result is determined to not be a matching signature value for the signed message, a negative result will be returned from the `verify()` method. However, another common outcome of this method is that the `verify()` method will throw an exception of type `SignatureException`. If we merely specify arbitrary data for the signature, this is the most likely result since the data will not be formatted/encoded properly for the verification to take place. An exception condition also indicates that the signature is invalid (since it cannot be understood by the underlying library as a signature) and should be handled by software implementing this type of functionality. Given that this is the case, it is often helpful to enclose the call to `verify()` in a try/catch block and handle any `SignatureException` in a manner similar to a negative result from the method. For example:

```
boolean isValid = false;
try {
isValid = sig.verify(theSigData);
} catch (SignatureException e) {
    isValid = false;
}
```

9.5.3 Obtaining Public Keys from X.509 Certificates

As we've seen with other APIs, most of the time, our public keys will come to us in the format of an X.509 public key certificate (or more accurately, as part of an X.509 certificate). X.509 certificates are difficult to parse natively, and the developers of the JCE have recognized the inherent difficulty in manipulating certificates and have therefore made certificates more accessible to the Java developer by supplying an easy-to-use certificate management interface as part of the `java.security` package. The package `java.security.cert` contains a number of classes we can use for the manipulation of public key certificates. The methods we will employ most often, however, are those associated with obtaining public key information from a certificate body (note, however, that as we just outlined, we don't have to extract the key from the certificate to perform a signature verification). The whole procedure is a little complicated, so we'll break the process down into steps as we have with other techniques, but first we'll talk a little about the new classes we'll require for this procedure.

`Certificate`: A `Certificate` object will contain the methods required to perform operations on and get information about X.509 public key certificates.

`CertificateFactory`: The `CertificateFactory` class will enable us to take an `InputStream` containing an encoded certificate and render a `Certificate` object.

To obtain public key information from a certificate, we will first need to instantiate a `CertificateFactory` through the use of `CertificateFactory.getInstance()`. There are a number of things we can do with X.509 certificates, and a number of places where their use can help us build security functionality. However, in all cases, the primary purpose of the certificate is to map a key to an entity and render that key portable. Therefore, to use a certificate for its most basic purpose, let's go through the steps required to obtain a public key from a certificate and use it to verify a signature. This example is a little contrived, since we could just use the certificate itself in our call to `Signature::initVerify()`; however, it is useful to demonstrate the functionality:

1. Instantiate a `CertificateFactory` using `CertificateFactory.getInstance()` and specifying "X.509" as the certificate type static identifier string.
2. Use the `CertificateFactory.generateCertificate()` method, specifying a reference to an `InputStream` containing the X.509 certificate in DER encoded Base64 format. The return value will be an object of type `Certificate`.
3. Call `Certificate.getPublicKey()` to obtain the public key in a format suitable for use in verification of signatures.

As we can see, the steps required to manipulate certificates are abstract and intuitive. Note, though, that the contents of the certificate cannot be manipulated within the software; for example, we would not be able to change the expiration date or issue date since these values are set by the CA and are not modifiable. It should be noted as well that the `CertificateFactory` functionality expects to read the certificate in Base64 DER encoded format. This is a common format and can be exported from most browsers, servers, and other applications as such. While this is a common method for representing certificates, it certainly is not the only way, and we may need to convert the certificate format to one of those formats understood by the JCA prior to use.

9.6 ADVANCED TECHNIQUES

As with all the APIs covered in this book, a few "advanced techniques" put a large amount of the security functionality together to create much more advanced sets of functionality. Java in general, and the JCE in particular, have a number of easy-to-use structures that facilitate the creation of security functionality. In this section, we'll go into secure network connectivity, the key exchange API, and key storage; this functionality continues in the vein of the rest of the library by providing powerful tools to the developer while requiring minimal code to make them.

9.6.1 Key Storage with a `KeyStore` (Storing Keys the Easy Way)

One very useful property of the Java JCE API is the availability of a simple, easy-to-use "armored" key storage locality. Note that we've made the point repeatedly throughout this book that the engineer's view of cryptography will most of the time be about key management. In the Java world, we have some robust tools to assist us in that endeavor; this functionality is implemented specifically through a concept known as "keystores." We'll go through how to use keystores as an "easy way" to assist with secure key management, but since we'll also need keystores when we discuss SSL, we'll go through how to store server and client SSL authentication certificates as well.

A keystore can be thought of as a trusted "vault-like" repository for keys and other information. The keystore authenticates applications (and users) that attempt to access it through a password, which is used internally by the keystore to encrypt itself during serialization operations and decrypt itself during loading operations. Using a methodology of this type has a number of advantages in both security (e.g., additional protection for keys while they are at rest on the filesystem) and convenience (e.g., keys can be stored in the keystore and architects/developers can concern themselves less with the implementation of key storage procedures and more with the development of application security procedures). We have a few interfaces to application keystores, but the primary one is through the use of the `keytool` application bundled with our Java distribution.

9.6.2 Manipulating KeyStores with the keytool Console Utility

The keytool utility allows us to create new keystores and manipulate existing keystores from the command line. Although Java does not provide a limit to the amount of keystores that can be created, most of the time it is more convenient to create one keystore and use it to hold the majority of an application's keys. Having just one is much more manageable than having more than one. Note that this does not mean that if a particular application demands another one that we should feel any restrictions associated with creating more; we're just saying that in most cases, it's easier and more manageable to manipulate just one keystore.

Running the keytool without argument produces the following help output:

```
Eden:~ emoyle$ keytool
keytool usage:
-certreq      [-v] [-alias <alias>] [-sigalg <sigalg>]
              [-file <csr_file>] [-keypass <keypass>]
              [-keystore <keystore>] [-storepass <storepass>]
              [-storetype <storetype>] [-provider <provider_class_name>]
...
-delete       [-v] -alias <alias>
              [-keystore <keystore>] [-storepass <storepass>]
              [-storetype <storetype>] [-provider <provider_class_name>]
...
-export       [-v] [-rfc] [-alias <alias>] [-file <cert_file>]
              [-keystore <keystore>] [-storepass <storepass>]
              [-storetype <storetype>] [-provider <provider_class_name>]
...
-genkey       [-v] [-alias <alias>] [-keyalg <keyalg>]
              [-keysize <keysize>] [-sigalg <sigalg>]
              [-dname <dname>] [-validity <valDays>]
              [-keypass <keypass>] [-keystore <keystore>]
              [-storepass <storepass>] [-storetype <storetype>]
              [-provider <provider_class_name>] ...
-help
-identitydb   [-v] [-file <idb_file>] [-keystore <keystore>]
              [-storepass <storepass>] [-storetype <storetype>]
              [-provider <provider_class_name>] ...
-import       [-v] [-noprompt] [-trustcacerts] [-alias <alias>]
              [-file <cert_file>] [-keypass <keypass>]
              [-keystore <keystore>] [-storepass <storepass>]
              [-storetype <storetype>] [-provider <provider_class_name>]
...
-keyclone     [-v] [-alias <alias>] -dest <dest_alias>
              [-keypass <keypass>] [-new <new_keypass>]
              [-keystore <keystore>] [-storepass <storepass>]
```

```
              [-storetype <storetype>] [-provider <provider_class_name>]
...
-keypasswd    [-v] [-alias <alias>]
              [-keypass <old_keypass>] [-new <new_keypass>]
              [-keystore <keystore>] [-storepass <storepass>]
              [-storetype <storetype>] [-provider <provider_class_name>]
...
-list         [-v | -rfc] [-alias <alias>]
              [-keystore <keystore>] [-storepass <storepass>]
              [-storetype <storetype>] [-provider <provider_class_name>]
...
-printcert    [-v] [-file <cert_file>]
-selfcert     [-v] [-alias <alias>] [-sigalg <sigalg>]
              [-dname <dname>] [-validity <valDays>]
              [-keypass <keypass>] [-keystore <keystore>]
              [-storepass <storepass>] [-storetype <storetype>]
              [-provider <provider_class_name>] ...
-storepasswd [-v] [-new <new_storepass>]
              [-keystore <keystore>] [-storepass <storepass>]
              [-storetype <storetype>] [-provider <provider_class_name>]
```

This list of features appears daunting, and the options (and suboptions) appear complex. However, for the most part, we will only use a few of these options with any regularity:

-genkey: The `genkey` option, as we can probably guess, instructs the `keytool` that we'll be generating a new key. This is used, for example, as a preliminary part of generating a new certificate. When creating a new key in this way, we'll want to specify an algorithm using the –`keyalg` flag (usually, we'll specify RSA). We'll also want to specify a keystore "alias" using the –`alias` flag (a name that we'll use to refer to the keystore), and the keystore name using the –`keystore` flag. The keystore name will be the file that will be used for storing the key.

Generating a new key according to this process yields the following:

```
Eden:~ emoyle$ keytool -genkey -keyalg rsa -keystore my.keystore -alias
newkeystore
Enter keystore password:  A Robust Password
What is your first and last name?
  [Unknown]:  Ed Moyle
What is the name of your organizational unit?
  [Unknown]:  Development
What is the name of your organization?
  [Unknown]:  Security Curve
```

```
What is the name of your City or Locality?
  [Unknown]:  Amherst
What is the name of your State or Province?
  [Unknown]:  New Hampshire
What is the two-letter country code for this unit?
  [Unknown]:  US
Is CN=Ed Moyle, OU=Development, O=Security Curve, L=Amherst, ST=New
Hampshire, C=US correct?
  [no]:  yes
Enter key password for <newkeystore>
        (RETURN if same as keystore password):
Eden:~ emoyle$
```

In this example, we've created the new keystore and stored it in a file called "my.keystore," which will be created in the current working directory.

`-list`: This command, intuitively enough, lists keys in the keystore. We would use this command to see the status of any keys that are contained in the store. We would need to specify the name of the keystore during usage using the `–keystore` flag. Doing this on the keystore we just made yields the following:

```
Eden:~ emoyle$ keytool -list -keystore my.keystore
Enter keystore password:  A Robust Password
Keystore type: jks
Keystore provider: SUN
Your keystore contains 1 entry
newkeystore, Dec 10, 2004, keyEntry,
Certificate fingerprint (MD5):
D4:BA:23:0F:F4:E7:FD:F7:89:B5:73:EA:14:C8:97:2C
Eden:~ emoyle$
```

Note that performing the `list` operation does not print the key pair in its entirety, but just provides us the fingerprint or unique representation that can be used to identify the certificate as one among many.

`-certreq`: Using a self-signed certificate is all well and good for testing, but in a production scenario, we would most likely wish to have an internal or commercial CA issue our certificates. For us to generate a Certificate Signing Request (CSR), we will need to include the public key that is contained in our store. To do this, we use this option, specifying the alias and keystore using the appropriate flags. Running this command, we get the following:

```
Eden:~ emoyle$ keytool -certreq -alias newkeystore -keystore
my.keystore
```

```
Enter keystore password:  A Robust Password
-----BEGIN NEW CERTIFICATE REQUEST-----
MIIBuTCCASICAQAweTELMAkGA1UEBhMCVVMxFjAUBgNVBAgTDU5ldyBIYW1wc2hpcmUxEDA
OBgNV
BAcTBOFtaGVyc3QxFzAVBgNVBAoTDlNlY3VyaXR5IEN1cnZlMRQwEgYDVQQLEwtEZXZlbG9
wbWVu
dDERMA8GA1UEAxMIRWQgTW95bGUwgZ8wDQYJKoZIhvcNAQEBBQADgY0AMIGJAoGBAOcUy46
cBNCE
rFOoTwZmKHN35uux1ONOLUcDdEcXOWCO4tKy+3WhfR9nsiPIGOHVt23+n273WuLDBtGhXNa
AZ7wU
7Abpl2pXdqxkpExGGTTwS2Qg35jfMkoXe3MdpgK7Fimy2OPmCZJv4nCiE19RL3dLhiGiIKW
1x6qe
LsWCImsXAgMBAAGgADANBgkqhkiG9w0BAQQFAAOBgQDBTNC2OwL/3/hwSIW9a52Q6fJOhW9
BTI3Y
rtnh2r4If0lkq2wPM92LuP11KG4MLEmNGTVCr7zp7+OTiDDiUjc8uPeyvA1CbNMKPI/bdRB
o5+GW
cOzTtwrWRv8yOHflg2I5lU9ONJbac7pC17fHUOCAaomOypfqXQODLmNkbL3EbQ==
-----END NEW CERTIFICATE REQUEST-----
Eden:~ emoyle$
```

`-import`: When we receive a response from the CA, we will need to associate that response (the created certificate) with the key entry in our database. To do so, we use the `import` flag, specifying the response from the CA by using the `–file` flag (and specifying the file containing the signed certificate), and supplying the appropriate alias (using the `–alias` flag) and the keystore locality (using the `–keystore` flag). It is important to note that the issued certificate must be in a format the keytool utility can understand; this can either be a binary representation of the data (DER encoded), or Base64 encoded text. If we use printable text, we need to make sure the input does not contain any extraneous lines or characters. For example, if we receive the certificate in an email, we must not have the email headers or any other body included (even trailing whitespace at the end of the file can interfere with the import operation). Using the tool to import an issued certificate and corresponding certificate chain (including the issuing CA's certificate) is demonstrated as follows:

```
Eden:~ emoyle$ keytool -import -alias newkeystore -keystore my.keystore
-file cert.txt
Enter keystore password:  A Robust Password
Top-level certificate in reply:
Owner: CN=Security Curve CA, DC=securitycurve, DC=com
Issuer: CN=Security Curve CA, DC=securitycurve, DC=com
Serial number: 79d6ba79bb83a4914bfd7c78078b274c
Valid from: Mon Apr 04 13:51:41 EDT 2005 until: Sun Apr 04 14:00:27 EDT
2010
```

```
Certificate fingerprints:
         MD5:  7F:B2:7C:3B:43:BD:C3:C5:BF:4E:74:79:DA:C6:C6:42
         SHA1:
C7:02:9C:C2:47:AA:1D:3F:00:9E:82:4B:0B:0A:31:D0:4D:94:0B:9B...
is not trusted. Install reply anyway? [no]:  yes
Certificate reply was installed in keystore
```

-printcert: When retrieving a reply from a CA, it is often useful to validate the incoming response to ensure it can be read in by the `keytool` utility, and that the response contains the correct certificate. To accomplish both these things, we can instruct `keytool` to print the details of the certificate contained in a response using the `-printcert` flag. The usage is as follows:

```
Eden:~ emoyle$ keytool -printcert -file cert.txt
Certificate[1]:
Owner: CN=Ed Moyle, OU=Development, O=Security Curve, L=Amherst, ST=New
Hampshire, C=US
Issuer: CN=Security Curve CA, DC=securitycurve, DC=com
Serial number: 152c0907000000000002
Valid from: Mon Apr 04 15:34:11 EDT 2005 until: Tue Apr 04 15:44:11 EDT
2006
Certificate fingerprints:
         MD5:  41:6F:14:96:B9:70:17:AC:D8:28:D8:61:5A:5F:C9:D5
         SHA1:
92:84:49:0B:E2:60:F8:91:D4:6F:97:B1:A3:0A:B9:2E:5D:AE:73:DF
Certificate[2]:
Owner: CN=Security Curve CA, DC=securitycurve, DC=com
Issuer: CN=Security Curve CA, DC=securitycurve, DC=com
Serial number: 79d6ba79bb83a4914bfd7c78078b274c
Valid from: Mon Apr 04 13:51:41 EDT 2005 until: Sun Apr 04 14:00:27 EDT
2010
Certificate fingerprints:
         MD5:  7F:B2:7C:3B:43:BD:C3:C5:BF:4E:74:79:DA:C6:C6:42
         SHA1:
C7:02:9C:C2:47:AA:1D:3F:00:9E:82:4B:0B:0A:31:D0:4D:94:0B:9B
```

Numerous other options are supported by the `keytool` utility as well. We encourage the developer to play around with the `keytool` utility to explore the powerful features that are provided. At the bare minimum, however, we will need to know how to request and install certificates into a keystore to allow us to use server SSL sockets in the next section, and the mutual authentication features of SSL (e.g., client authentication).

9.6.3 Manipulating Keystores Programmatically

Since we will need to select keystores to load at runtime through a programmatic interface, we will also need to be accustomed to using the keystore programmatic API. This API is implemented as an engine class, and therefore the specifics of instantiating one proceed according to the rules we've already covered with respect to engine classes. Specifically, we'll want to use the `getInstance()` call and specify the type of keystore (usually JKS) and the provider when doing so.

Most of the time, we'll be loading keystores that we've created using the `keytool` command-line utility (this is not always the case—more on that in a minute). In most cases, keystores need to be explicitly "loaded" from the filesystem; Java provides a `load()` method for specifically this purpose, and in using it, we'll need to specify a `FileInputStream` and keystore password in the call to `load()`. Note that we will want to take pains to prevent any unauthorized access to the password (so we'll want to scrub the memory when we're done with it).

The `KeyStore` API is very powerful. We can use it to explicitly load keys and certificates for use in SSL sessions, but a particularly powerful way to use keystores is for the secure storage of secret keys our application will use. This feature should not be overlooked when designing new applications. We can store anything that is of type `Key` in the keystore as long as we associate it with an alias for later retrieval. The following code dynamically loads a keystore (the same one we created in the previous section) and prepares it for use:

```
KeyStore store = KeyStore.getInstance("JKS");
FileInputStream fileIS = new FileInputStream("my.keystore");
ks.load(fileIS, new String("A Robust Password").toCharArray());
```

We can now insert new keys into it using the `setKeyEntry()` method, and extract keys from it using the corresponding `getKey()` method.

9.6.4 SSL

As with the rest of the libraries covered in this book, the SSL API provided by the Java cryptographic API mirrors the underlying sockets API. However, in the case of Java sockets, we are already very abstracted from the traditional and ubiquitous Berkeley API; the java socket constructs are incredibly powerful and highly "automated." The SSL functionality is no different; in fact, a developer can (under most circumstances) "cut and paste" existing socket code (with the exception of the construction of the socket) into an SSL-aware application and have it work without modification!

9.6.4.1 SSL Clients

Those familiar with the Java socket API will immediately recognize the almost transparent manner in which SSL is overlaid on top of the Java `Socket` (and `Server`

Socket) API. In fact, we were quite serious when we said that in order to take arbitrary client socket functionality and render it into SSL functionality, most of the time we will only require a few additional lines of code. More specifically, in the majority of cases, to add SSL to existing socket functionality, we can do it with one new line of code and a change to one of the existing lines.

It should be said that even though the underlying interface to the SSL Socket API is not difficult to use, it *is* a little different from the "engine classes" we're probably used to working with by now. We don't have a getInstance() method as we would with a pure cryptographic engine class. Instead, we'll be using the functionality within the Socket API, and specifying the type of sockets we wish to use—in this case, type SSLSocket.

Specifically, let's investigate in more depth how to create an SSL socket; there are only two steps required to do so:

1. Instantiate an instance of an SSLSocketFactory using the method SSLSocket Factory.getDefault() to retrieve the default SSLSocketFactory.
2. Use the createSocket() method to create an SSLSocket pointing to the host and port we specify while making this call.

That's it; after the second step, we can directly send and receive information to and from the server we've connected to with confidence that the communication channel is encrypted with SSL. We will need to import javax.net.SocketFactory, javax.net.ssl.SSLSocketFactory, and java.net.Socket to compile and use these constructs:

```
SocketFactory fact = SSLSocketFactory.getDefault();
Socket s = fact.createSocket("127.0.0.1", 443);
```

The preceding code seamlessly and transparently generates a socket instance (in this instance, a connection to the localhost via the loopback address on port 443) that we can now use to send and receive SSL encrypted data.

9.6.4.2 SSL Servers

In much the same way that SSL client sockets are created, we can also transparently introduce SSL functionality to the server side of a socket connection. The following steps will allow us to do this:

1. Instantiate an instance of an SSLServerSocketFactory using the method SSLServerSocketFactory.getDefault() to retrieve the default SSLServer SocketFactory.
2. Use the createServerSocket() method to create an SSLServerSocket listening on the port that we specify while making this call.

Just as the previous example, we need to import or explicitly reference the appropriate classes from `javax.net.ssl`, and `javax.net` to use the functionality. Having done so, the following code would perform this functionality:

```
ServerSocketFactory servfact = SSLServerSocketFactory.
    getDefault();
ServerSocket server = servfact.createServerSocket( 443);
```

It should be noted that all the properties of server sockets that are true in non-SSL sockets are true in SSL sockets as well. For example, if we are going to create a socket listening on the standard SSL port (443), we would need to be a root/administrative user. These restrictions that are true in regular sockets programming are equally true when dealing with the SSL portion of the socket API. There's an important caveat associated with SSL sockets programming in Java that should be explicitly mentioned at this time: use of SSL as you may remember implies the use of a digital certificate for either the server alone (in the case of server authentication) or the client (in the case of client authentication). Specifying a keystore containing a certificate is not difficult for the developer, but will require knowledge of a few other classes in addition to the `KeyManager` class already covered.

This may be a little confusing to see it outlined in this way, but the usage should make much more sense once we see it in practice. Therefore, we'll go through the new classes in a cursory manner.

SSLContext

If we are creating server sockets that will be used to conduct any type of SSL communication, or client sockets that will use mutual authentication, we will need to make use of this class. This class allows us to control some of the lower level details associated with creating SSL-aware sockets (both client and server). Most of the time, we will use it to bind specific properties (such as certification information and key material) to the underlying `SSLServerSocketFactory` that will be used for creating our `ServerSocket`(s). To use a specific certificate and a specific key for that certificate in our application, we will need to use the `getServerSocketFactory()` method in this class to obtain the `SSLServerSocketFactory` that will be bound to the certificate and private key we wish to use. This may sound complicated, but there's really just one call that we'll need to make to do this. Also, during initialization of the `SSLContext`, when calling the `init()` method, we may optionally supply one or more `KeyManager` instances, one or more `TrustManager` instances to the class, and/or a source of random numbers. `KeyManager` instances will allow us to bind keystores and certificates to the connection (e.g., our server certificate). `TrustManager` instances will allow us to manipulate the trust decisions made on the `Socket` (e.g., which CAs are trusted and which aren't). Either of these parameters can be null, in which case the default values will be used. Additionally, the random number generator can be null, in which case the default will be used.

KeyManagerFactory

To instruct the `SSLContext` about which keys and certificates we want it to use during the SSL negotiation, we will need to take our `KeyManager` and present it to the `SSLContext` in a format it understands. We do this through the use of the `KeyManagerFactory` class. With this class as well, the usage may sound complicated, but it's only a matter of calling one method within the class to perform the required functionality.

Including an additional required import (`javax.net.ssl.*`), the following code would take our example `KeyManager` and prepare it for use with `SSLServerSockets`:

```
KeyStore store = KeyStore.getInstance("JKS");
FileInputStream fileIS = new FileInputStream("my.keystore");
store.load(fileIS, robustPassword);
KeyManagerFactory kmfactory = KeyManagerFactory.getInstance(
            "SunX509");
kmfactory.init(store, robustPassword);
SSLContext context = SSLContext.getInstance("TLS");
//specifying null for default TrustManager and randomness
context.init(kmfactory.getKeyManagers(), null, null);
SSLServerSocketFactory sslserverfactory =
                                  context.getServerSocketFactory();
```

Now, new `SSLServerSockets` that are created from the new factory will use the keys we've specified.

9.6.4.3 Controlling Negotiated CipherSuites

Those developers who need to change the default suite of ciphers used by the JCE (e.g., those developers in a U.S. government context who are required to adhere to FIPS-compliant operating mode) will need to ensure that non-FIPS algorithms are removed from the supported lists so they will not be negotiated as part of the normal SSL session-establishment process. This is usually done during the configuration of the runtime environment (e.g., by installing a FIPS-compliant service provider). However, should a developer wish to use a more "hands on" approach, functionality exists within the API to do so. Specifically, `SSLSocket()` and `SSLServerSocket()` implement the following methods that allow finer-grain control over the ciphersuites that can be negotiated during a connection:

Method `getEnabledCipherSuites()`: Returns a list of strings containing the standard names of the ciphersuites that are currently enabled.

Method `getSupportedCipherSuites()`: Returns a list of strings containing the standard names of the ciphersuites that are supported (but not necessarily enabled) by the runtime environment.

Method `setEnabledCipherSuites()`: Takes as input a list of strings that will be flagged as "enabled" and ready for negotiation by the client or the server.

For example, to obtain and print a list of supported ciphersuites on a listening SSL socket, we could implement code similar to the following:

```
ServerSocketFactory fact = SSLServerSocketFactory.getDefault();
        ServerSocket s = fact.createServerSocket(4433);
        String[] suites =
((SSLServerSocket)s).getSupportedCipherSuites();
        for(int i = 0; i < suites.length; i++) {
                System.out.println(suites[i]);
        }
```

The output of this code would be the following list of supported cipher strings:

```
SSL_RSA_WITH_RC4_128_MD5
SSL_RSA_WITH_RC4_128_SHA
TLS_RSA_WITH_AES_128_CBC_SHA
TLS_DHE_RSA_WITH_AES_128_CBC_SHA
TLS_DHE_DSS_WITH_AES_128_CBC_SHA
SSL_RSA_WITH_3DES_EDE_CBC_SHA
SSL_DHE_RSA_WITH_3DES_EDE_CBC_SHA
SSL_DHE_DSS_WITH_3DES_EDE_CBC_SHA
SSL_RSA_WITH_DES_CBC_SHA
SSL_DHE_RSA_WITH_DES_CBC_SHA
SSL_DHE_DSS_WITH_DES_CBC_SHA
SSL_RSA_EXPORT_WITH_RC4_40_MD5
SSL_RSA_EXPORT_WITH_DES40_CBC_SHA
SSL_DHE_RSA_EXPORT_WITH_DES40_CBC_SHA
SSL_DHE_DSS_EXPORT_WITH_DES40_CBC_SHA
SSL_RSA_WITH_NULL_MD5
SSL_RSA_WITH_NULL_SHA
SSL_DH_anon_WITH_RC4_128_MD5
TLS_DH_anon_WITH_AES_128_CBC_SHA
SSL_DH_anon_WITH_3DES_EDE_CBC_SHA
SSL_DH_anon_WITH_DES_CBC_SHA
SSL_DH_anon_EXPORT_WITH_RC4_40_MD5
SSL_DH_anon_EXPORT_WITH_DES40_CBC_SHA
```

If we wished to modify which of the supported protocols are available to the socket, we would merely call `setEnabledCipherSuites()` with an array containing the appropriate string values corresponding to the cipher suites we want to include.

The same type of control is provided over versions of the TLS/SSL specification as well. For the sake of completeness, these methods are outlined here:

Method `getEnabledProtocols()`: This method returns a list of strings containing the standard names of the protocol versions that are flagged as enabled (and thus usable).

Method `getSupportedProtocols()`: Returns a list of strings containing the standard names of the protocol versions that are supported (but not necessarily enabled) by the runtime environment.

Method `setEnabledProtocols()`: Takes as input a list of strings that will be flagged as "enabled" and thus available for use by the application.

For example, if we wish to determine which of the available SSL/TLS protocols are enabled, we could write code similar to the following:

```
ServerSocketFactory fact = SSLServerSocketFactory.getDefault();
        ServerSocket s = fact.createServerSocket(4433);
        String[] suites = ((SSLServerSocket)s).getEnabledProtocols();
        for(int i = 0; i < suites.length; i++) {
                System.out.println(suites[i]);
        }
```

The output for this would be similar to the following:

```
SSLv2Hello
SSLv3
TLSv1
```

If we wanted to change which versions of the protocols are enabled, we would merely call `setEnabledProtocols()` with an array of string values corresponding to the protocol versions we wish to support.

9.6.5 Key Agreement

For the sake of completeness, we felt that a thorough explanation of this topic should at least mention the key agreement API provided by Java. However, it should be stated that this API includes some concepts that we haven't covered in as much detail, and the techniques discussed can be effected using other, more familiar primitives. However, should the need arise, we do not want to leave the developer unprepared for situations in which either backward compatibility or lack of foresight on our part leaves the developer without awareness of this functionality. Therefore, what follows is an overview of how to use the Java cryptographic API for Diffie-Hellman Key agreement. As we've outlined, Diffie-Hellman is often used to communicate a symmetric key between two parties where neither party has advance knowledge of the key. We're going to speed through this material to at least get the developer started with using this methodology, but since this section is, by design, "rapidly covered," we recommend that a developer wishing to use Diffie-Hellman in a production scenario augment this material with the documentation from Sun.

Before we can use Diffie-Hellman for key exchange, we will need to generate the Diffie-Hellman parameters through a mechanism similar to the generation of DSA parameters. Specifically, we'll use the `AlgorithmParameterGenerator` class to generate the values we need. Note that this process can be time and CPU intensive, so it is useful to do this once and reuse the resultant values. Although the Sun documentation creates delineation between the parameter generation and the usage, for the sake of brevity, we're going to include the parameter generation in the requisite usage steps outlined here:

1. Obtain an instance to a `AlgorithmParameterGenerator` using the `getInstance()` method and specifying the static string "DH" to indicate that we wish to generate Diffie-Hellman parameters.
2. Initialize the `AlgorithmParameterGenerator` by calling the `init()` method and specifying the key size we wish to use.
3. Generate the parameters by calling the `generateParameters()` method in the `AlgorithmParameterGenerator` class (this process might look familiar, since we did similar steps for our usage of DSA in previous sections).
4. Obtain an instance of a `KeyPairGenerator` using the `getInstance()` method and specifying "DH," indicating that we wish to obtain a Diffie-Hellman key generator.
5. Create a `DHParameterSpec` including the values we created during the parameter generation process.
6. Initialize the `KeyPairGenerator` specifying the parameter spec created in the previous step.
7. Call the `generateKeypair()` method of the `KeyPairGenerator` to create a public and private key for use in the key agreement.
8. Obtain the public key from the other party and send our public key to the other party.
9. Obtain a reference to a `KeyAgreement` object using the `getInstance()` method and specifying the static string "DH" to indicate that we are using Diffie-Hellman key agreement.

10. Initialize the `KeyAgreement` object using the private key obtained from the key pair generation process.
11. Use the `doPhase()` method of the `KeyAgreement` object to allow the key generation to proceed, and specify "`true`" in the second parameter to inform the object that this is the last phase.
12. Call `generateSecret()`, specifying the algorithm for which we are doing the key agreement (e.g., "AES").

These steps appear daunting, and are more difficult to use than some of the other facets of the API we've covered. Rather than listing the example code here to put it into context, we've included some examples on the companion CD-ROM (/Examples/Chapter 9/Key Exchange/) of this concept in action (including two peers that will exchange keys). Since this API is more difficult to understand (and probably of less usefulness than some of the other material), we've endeavored to provide that example code in as "cut and paste"-able a manner as possible.

9.7 SUMMARY

We've looked throughout this chapter at some of the ways Java provides security functionality to the developer. As any language, Java can exist in many forms: servlets, applications, applets, and plenty of other contexts. Hopefully, the material in this section is useful in all those contexts; within this section, we've tried to remain "context agnostic" with respect to the particulars of the Java environment you're working in by using routines that are applicable across a variety of contexts. However, on the companion CD-ROM, you'll find a few more examples that are not divorced from the context and include the ancillary servlet, application (Examples/Chapter 9/Servlet/), or applet (Examples/Chapter 9/Applet/) code to function within the specific context within which a developer is working.

9.8 ENDNOTES

1. A possible exception to this would be to look at certain portions of the .NET API in isolation from the rest of the Microsoft CAPI functionality.
2. Note that there is an additional padding methodology (OAEPWith<digest> And<mgf>Padding) that makes sense only in an asymmetric context; therefore, it is not included in this section but included in other contexts.
3. The examples given in the Sun documentation are `PBEWithMD5AndDES` and `PBEWithHmacSHA1AndDESede` (note that it does not appear that Sun has actually implemented the latter).

10 Developing with BSAFE

In This Chapter

The RSA BSAFE product has a long and proud history; it was in use to build industrial-strength cryptographic functionality years before the other libraries in this book were even started. The reasons for this long-term success of BSAFE are clear: BSAFE offers a range of functionality, flexibility, and control not seen in any of the other libraries. While the RSA developers have come up with a very useful API that abstracts that control when we don't want to concern ourselves, it is always there for us to use if we desire. We'll see as we get into the usage that given this flexibility and control, there is a good reason why BSAFE is the only library covered in this book that we have to explicitly pay for.

10.1 CHAPTER GOAL

This chapter is not designed to replace the excellent documentation supplied by RSA in their BSAFE suite of products. RSA has supplied (quite literally) thousands of pages of reference documentation that thoroughly describe every function supplied within the toolkit; in addition, RSA provides a number of example applications that demonstrate the toolkit features in action from a functional perspective. Instead of trying to replace that documentation, this chapter is designed to augment it by giving the developer both a "starting place" and a comfort level with using the RSA toolkit in a number of security development situations. In other words, the goal is to give developers a rapid learning path so they are able to start planning (and writing) their application without needing to locate their proposed usage within the RSA documentation.

10.2 BSAFE OVERVIEW

BSAFE is an extremely comprehensive suite of utilities that allows a developer to implement cryptographic functionality in a number of common languages and on a number of common platforms. Some of the components within the BSAFE API were historically distinct from each other, but have since been integrated into a coherent toolset. For our purposes, we are considering the BSAFE toolkit to be:

RSA BSAFE Cert-C: Cryptographic functionality in C related specifically to X.509 digital certificates.

RSA BSAFE Cert-J: Cryptographic functionality in Java related specifically to X.509 digital certificates.

RSA BSAFE Crypto-C: Generic cryptographic functionality implemented in C.

RSA BSAFE Crypto-J: Generic cryptographic functionality implemented in Java.

RSA BSAFE SSL-C: Secure Sockets Layer (SSL/TLS) functionality implemented in C.

RSA BSAFE SSL-J: Secure Sockets Layer (SSL/TLS) functionality implemented in Java.

RSA BSAFE Secure WS-C: Web services security library implemented in C.

RSA BSAFE Secure WS-J: Web services security library implemented in Java.

These individual subcomponents are more or less distinct and separate from each other. For example, if one wishes to implement functionality entirely in Java, one would not require any of the C components (in fact, developers would never even need to install any portion of these toolkits on their system). Likewise, if a developer were not implementing SSL functionality, he or she would not need to install the SSL portions of the toolkits to develop cryptographic components. Unlike the CAPI and the JCE (but like OpenSSL), the RSA library needs to be installed and the environment appropriately configured to make use of the functionality. We'll walk a developer through customization of the environment and installation of the products in more detail in just a moment.

In laying out the specifics of the BSAFE APIs within this chapter, we've had to make a few decisions about which portion of the API to cover (since a great deal of functionality is exposed through these APIs), and the scope of the API is quite broad. In doing so, we've elected to concentrate primarily on the C APIs; note that the Java API has two interfaces—one independent of the JCA, and one that is written as a JCA provider. As the Java section of this book is equally applicable to the RSA Java provider as it is to the default Sun provider, we feel that limiting discussion of the RSA API in this way is not performing a disservice to the developer reading this book. In addition to concentrating on the C API, we've also chosen to concentrate primarily on the cryptographic routines and the SSL portions of the functionality (leaving out a large body of the certificate-related functionality). This is not to say that we will not deal with certificates in this section—quite the contrary. However, the very powerful and exhaustive treatment that certificates receive at the hands of the BSAFE developers far exceeds the usage-centric scope of this book. In general, anything and everything that one could possibly wish to do with certificates is exposed through the BSAFE API; in fact, building a commercial Certificate Authority (CA) is quite within the capabilities of RSA's toolkit. Since we are not (most likely) interested in building a commercial CA, and we are most often concerned with usage of certificates that enable us to write application software, a large portion of the RSA BSAFE certificate API is not covered within this chapter.

10.3 OVERVIEW OF BSAFE CRYPTO-C

The architecture of BSAFE Crypto-C (at least the internal mechanics of its architecture) is almost completely hidden from the developer. The API presents a consistent usage façade that conceals the underlying mechanics of the implementation and "universalizes" the calls we need to make to leverage the cryptography. From the caller's point of view, there are a few "global concepts" we need to keep in mind when developing any applications with BSAFE; specifically, algorithm choosers and surrender functions. We will see these two concepts at work in every BSAFE application we write, so it is imperative that we understand what they're for and how they work before we attempt to use them.

10.3.1 Algorithm Choosers

An *algorithm chooser* is a construct provided by RSA that allows a developer to isolate the portions of the API that will be used ahead of time, list those algorithms (and other functionalities), and link in from the static library what is required by the application. The algorithm chooser allows us to specify *algorithm methods* (AMs) within it. Each algorithm method corresponds to a subset of the whole cryptographic functionality available to us. Some of the algorithm methods are very specific, delineating the use of a particular algorithm with a particular key size, for example, whereas others are more general (such as corresponding to an algorithm using a variety of key lengths). Since Crypto-C is distributed as a static .lib file, this construct allows a developer to control the size of the final executable image(s) produced by allowing the linker to bring in only the appropriate functionality from the library that will be directly used within the application. Therefore, as we design our applications, we'll want to make note of the algorithms we select so we can create a chooser that incorporates only the functionality we are going to use. Moreover, should we desire to do so, we can create more than one chooser if we like to segregate functionality within our own code base, meaning that we can always add more cryptographic routines later and not have to worry about modifying a single "global" chooser somewhere else in our application.

10.3.2 Surrender Functions

In the majority of calls into the BSAFE API, we have the option of supplying a *surrender function* as part of the call. A surrender function is a pointer to a function that will be called back by the Crypto-C API. More precisely, "time-consuming" cryptographic calls (such as RSA key generation or other long operations) allow us to specify a function pointer (the *surrender function*) that will be periodically called by the BSAFE API during "slow to complete" operations. Providing this functionality allows the developer to implement, either in the presence or absence of threading, status-reporting mechanisms such as progress meters, progress bars, spinning cursors, hourglasses, and other methods to visually indicate to the user that the operation is in progress. Additionally, the surrender function can be used to implement functionality, allowing a user to halt or abandon an operation that is taking an unusually long time to complete.

While the surrender concept is particularly useful for implementing functionality like progress meters and counters, it should be noted that it does not take the place of threading in certain situations. For example, if we are authoring a user interface, rather than using a UI thread for completion of a cryptographic operation (and therefore "seizing" the UI during the cryptography), it is always a useful idea to spawn a new thread in which to perform the cryptography (and thus allow time-critical or user-centric items like GUI screens, sockets, and so forth free to respond to stimulus during the cryptographic operations). In a pinch, such as if our platform does not support threading and we require a mechanism to update/refresh a UI window, we can use the surrender function as a place to do those updates, but note that this can lead to "choppy" UI behavior. Examples of ways to implement a UI progress counter using the Crypto-C surrender context mechanism while inside a non-UI thread are included on the companion CD-ROM(/Examples/Chapter 10/Surrender), but will not be used specifically within the usage examples in this section.

ON THE CD

10.3.3 Crypto-C Function Concepts

The functions provided to us by the Crypto-C API all have (more or less) the same overall structure. As we move through the API, we'll find that the typical procedure will entail the following steps:

1. Instantiation of algorithm, key, and other required structures
2. Initialization of algorithm, key, and other structures
3. Initialization of cryptographic operation
4. (Optional) Update of cryptographic operation
5. Conclusion of cryptographic operation
6. Freeing/destruction of required structures

State information associated with algorithms and keys are stored in "objects" (structs) that we as developers will specifically instantiate prior to use (usually via an explicit call to a creation function). We'll also need to specifically free any of this state information using the API when we are concluded with our operations (again through an explicit call to a destruction function). The following functions and declarations are typically used in the following order to perform a given operation:
Instantiation of a chooser containing the appropriate algorithm methods.

1. Call `B_CreateAlgorithmObject()` to instantiate the appropriate algorithm object and set up any internal data structures required by the library.
2. Call `B_CreateKeyObject()` (if a key is required) to instantiate the internal key-specific data structures required by the library.
3. Call `B_SetKeyInfo()` (if a key is required) to initialize the key and bind any required key data to the key object.
4. Call `B_SetAlgorithmInfo()` to initialize the algorithm and bind any required algorithm data to the algorithm object.
5. Cryptographic or other operation—this can entail encryption, signing, or any other API contained in the library. Note that these will have specific function names that vary from operation to operation. This step entails a sequence of Init, Update, and Final, with the update step being iteratively called with any data that needs to be processed.

6. Call `B_DestroyKeyObject()` (if a key is required) to free key-specific resources.
7. Call `B_DestoryAlgorithmObject()` to free algorithm-specific resources.

This same sequence will be used for almost anything we wish to do with the API, so it bears getting familiar with early. In fact, the BSAFE developers have done a very good job in taking a large amount of varied and seemingly disparate functionality and making it available through a common "universal" API.

10.4 OVERVIEW OF BSAFE CRYPTO-J

Crypto-J can operate in a number of ways. The most common modes of operation are to make calls through the JCE-standard interfaces (after installing Crypto-J as a new provider), but there is a non-JCE API as well for those developers who seek additional functionality or are for whatever reason uncomfortable with the JCE. The Java cryptographic API supplied by BSAFE has been purposefully designed by RSA to be very similar to the JCE when *not* used as a JCE provider and cleanly insertable into the JCE provider pool when installed as a JCE provider. Since this book is all about simplicity, we are going to assume that a developer writing in Java will prefer portability over and above any extra "niceties" offered by the Crypto-J API. In other words, since this book is about offering developers a confusion-free path to doing their job, we'll assume that one way of doing the "Java cryptography" task is enough. In particular, the same support and compliance (e.g., FIPS) benefits of Crypto-J are present to the developer in either mode when working with Crypto-J, so we can simplify the task of writing to BSAFE tremendously by focusing only on the JCE API. In fairness to the RSA toolkit, it should be noted that the alternative API supplied by RSA in this toolkit is *not* superfluous—it can be more convenient to use the non-JCE API, and it provides more precision control over the cryptographic operations to the developer. However, it does come with the drawbacks of not being portable to other providers and requiring the developer to learn an additional API over and above that of the JCE (or the BSAFE C API, for that matter).

10.4.1 Using BSAFE Crypto-J

For the most part, the decision to use Crypto-J versus using JCE with the built-in Sun cryptographic provider will not impact the application developer to any great degree from a functional perspective; this is true in both the case of the developer using Crypto-J as a JCE provider and those writing to the API directly. In other words, application designers may wish to use the RSA toolkit for reasons of available support, regulatory requirements, or support for cryptographic algorithms not available in the built-in Sun provider, but they can meet all these objectives while using the same API (JCE) with which they are already comfortable. The developer who wishes to install and use Crypto-J as a JCE provider should refer to Chapter 9 (particularly instructions on installing new providers) as well as the usage examples to see how the BSAFE JCE provider is used and installed. It should be noted that if developers wish to maintain a level of FIPS compliance, they must install the FIPS-compliant version of the toolkit for the particular platform they are writing for and not a non-FIPS-compliant one. Additionally, care should be taken when using the static `getInstance()` method of the overlying JCE engine class (this is described in more detail in Chapter 9) to request the BSAFE provider directly. This can be done by using the appropriate static identifier string for the library as the second parameter to the `getInstance()` call; the provider implementation string for RSA Crypto-J is "JsafeJCE," so this is the value we would specify when making that call. Specifically, while a call such as `Cipher.getInstance("AES")` would obtain the default AES implementation (the Sun provider unless we've explicitly reconfigured it), a call such as `Cipher.getInstance` ("AES," "JsafeJCE") would use the RSA provider to obtain the AES implementation.

10.5 IMPORTANT CRYPTO-C SAFETY CONSIDERATIONS

A developer must plan for a number of things when using BSAFE that can be disastrous in the final application if not accounted for. Specifically, there are quite a few times when we, the callers, are expected to supply key information, plaintext values, random seeds, and other "confidential" values to the library. As we can intuit, none of these values is explicitly cleared or "zeroized" for us after they are used if we are using regular heap- or stack-based buffers in making the calls. Some of the other libraries we've dealt with mitigated this for us in some way (by allowing us to make sure the keys cannot be extracted in an unsafe way, or providing classes that explicitly handle the safe destruction of the data for us). However, Crypto-C does not provide any inherent "memory zeroization" in an automatic fashion outside the library; additionally, the RSA-supplied sample code that provides demonstrations of how to go about using the API does not detail with any great degree of specificity where/how this should be done. In discussing where/how the developer can add functionality to clear sensitive buffers, the developer making use of the BSAFE API is particularly encouraged to review the material outlined in Chapter 6 of this book detailing easy and portable ways to do this without introducing additional coding overhead. However, if a developer prefers, explicit zeroization of the buffers can be implemented readily through other mechanisms. This book will attempt to point out situations in which memory should be purged after use to make sure developers are prepared when they encounter these circumstances.

Once the developer has selected a strategy to use when zeroizing sensitive information, the application code should be examined for situations in which sensitive information is used. The most common situation in which we will wish to make sure sensitive memory is purged is when we are dealing with buffers that have been dynamically allocated (i.e., buffers that are allocated on the heap using a call like `malloc()` or the operator `new`). Note that this does not imply that stack-based buffers are "safe" (they are not), just that the amount of time residual information is likely to remain un-overwritten is likely to be shorter on the stack versus the heap. In general, it is easiest if we treat any memory (stack or heap memory) containing sensitive data as potentially at risk (and therefore should be purged when usage is complete).

10.6 SETTING UP CRYPTO-C

Setting up our environment to use Crypto-C is not difficult, but does require that we do a few things to get off and running. We will need to install the toolkit; this step should be self-evident. To do this, we merely run the installation executable and specify the location where we wish the installer to place the files. This directory will contain everything we need, including (most notably) the static libraries for the platforms we're installing on and the associated include files that will allow us to compile new applications. This section details how to customize your projects/makefiles to use these include files (headers), and how to specify to the linker that you will be including a static library to link against to resolve symbols associated with the cryptographic routines.

10.6.1 Finding and Including the Appropriate Files

Once we've installed the Crypto-C libraries, we will need to update new projects to ensure the compiler is able to find the Crypto-C headers and the linker is able to find and link against the appropriate static libraries for our platform. To use the Crypto-C toolkits (and any of the additional RSA functionality that rests upon it), we'll need to make sure the following are true:

- The *compiler* is able to find the requisite *header* files accompanying the Crypto-C toolkit.
- The *linker* is able to find the requisite *library* files accompanying the Crypto-C toolkit.
- We have supplied suitable memory-management routines for use by the Crypto-C library.

Although specific instructions for how to use particular compilers and/or development environments is outside the scope of this book, we'll be presenting information on how to incorporate the include files and library files into specific environments to give developers a "leg up" on compiling the examples in this book (since providing this information might prove useful as a level set). Following are more specific instructions on how to configure projects to use the BSAFE library in particular development environments and on particular platforms.

10.6.1.1 Setting Additional Include Directories

Installed with the RSA Crypto-C product is a directory `\include` that contains all the include files we'll need to compile BSAFE aware applications. The exact location of this directory will vary depending on the version of BSAFE we are using, the platform we're using, and choices made during the installation process. Unless the directory structure has been modified subsequent to installation of the product, the include directory will be located in `<BSAFE_ROOT>/<platform_package_name>/include`, where `<BSAFE_ROOT>` is the full path used by the BSAFE install at the time of installation, and `<platform_package_name>` is the package name used by BSAFE on the platform we are using (of course, the path separator should be updated to match the separator for the platform in question). Here are a few examples of include directory location using the 6.1.2.1 version of the BSAFE Crypto-C product:

- On a Windows system where the installation locality is `C:\Program Files\RSA BSAFE Crypto-C\6.1.2.1\`, the include directory would be `C:\Program Files\RSA BSAFE Crypto-C\6.1.2.1\win32pkg\include\`.
- On a Solaris system where the installation locality is `/usr/bsafe/`, the include directory is located in `/usr/bsafe/cryptoc6121/include/`.

We'll get to more specific compiler instructions in a moment, but it is useful to call out at this time exactly where these files will reside on these common platforms.

10.6.1.2 Linking with Additional Libraries

In addition to supplying the include files mentioned in the previous section, BSAFE supplies library files that contain the cryptographic functionality. We will need to link our object files against these files and we will need to configure the linker so it can find the library files. The BSAFE library files will be installed to `<BSAFE_ROOT>/<platform_package_name>/lib/<architecture>/`, where `<BSAFE_ROOT>` is the full path used by the BSAFE install at the time of installation, `<platform_package_name>` is the BSAFE package name on the platform we are using, and `<architecture>` corresponds to the hardware portion of the platform we're using. The following examples demonstrate the locations of the libraries on the same example platforms used previously using version 6.1.2.1 of the BSAFE product:

- On a Windows system where the installation locality is: `C:\Program Files\RSA BSAFE Crypto-C\6.1.2.1\`, the library files associated with the 32-bit Intel architecture would be located in the directory `C:\Program Files\RSA BSAFE`

Crypto-C\6.1.2.1\win32pkg\lib\ia32\. (Note that ia32 is the "single threaded" library, ia32mt is "multithreaded statically linked with C libraries," and ia32md is "multithreaded dynamically linked with CRT." We will need to ensure that we select the appropriate library to match both the characteristics of our application and the model we've selected for building our application.)

- On a Solaris Ultra-Sparc system where the installation locality is /usr/bsafe/, the library files would be located in /usr/bsafe/cryptoc6121/lib/sparcv8/.

10.6.1.3 Required Memory, Buffer, and String Manipulation Routines

The BSAFE library requires that we supply a few platform-specific manipulation routines to make use of the library. These routines are of the form T_<routine>, where <routine> is the routine that needs to be supplied. The "sample" file tstdlib.c is supplied by RSA as a "demonstration" of how to implement these functions. Although supplied "only as a demonstration," it is often easiest for a developer to include this file directly in any projects that will make use of the Crypto-C libraries. Alternatively, we can implement them ourselves and reuse our implementation in any project in which we will use BSAFE. The BSAFE example provided in Chapter 4 illustrates one implementation of those functions (usually just a wrapper around the buffer manipulation functions), and we've reproduced some additional examples on the companion CD-ROM (/Examples/Chapter 10/Buffers).

ON THE CD

10.6.2 Microsoft Developer Studio

For the purposes of this book, we've made some choices about which development platforms we will target for our toolkit demonstrations. For our examples on the Microsoft platform, we will employ the ubiquitous Microsoft Developer Studio to demonstrate (since Microsoft Developer Studio is the most widely used commercial development environment for the Microsoft operating system platform). We'll use a couple of different versions of this IDE to use an environment with which the developer is comfortable. Insofar as customization of the environment goes, developers will need to make the decision as to whether they will globally modify the environment to support BSAFE (a change they will only have to do once), or update each new project on a "project by project" basis to include the additional BSAFE files. As we've done with other APIs covered earlier in this book, we will update each project first to incorporate the appropriate settings for simplicity. Using a project-by-project approach is useful because it reduces the compile/link time somewhat for other projects that do not use the toolkit, and it is fairly easy to do once we understand it. Doing this for new projects will become "second nature" and will help make our projects "portable" to be compiled on machines that do not have our same global compiler/linker settings. We'll also briefly run through how to globally configure the projects, but in general, we'll probably want to only modify the projects, since this makes our project more portable and reduces confusion when attempting to compile a project on a machine that does not have the same settings.

To configure the environment for Microsoft Developer Studio, we'll use Microsoft Visual C++ 6.0 and Microsoft Visual C++ 2005 as example environments.

10.6.2.1 Microsoft Visual Studio 6

In selecting a target IDE to use, we've elected to use a somewhat older version of the Developer Studio, and one "bleeding edge" version of the tool. Looking at the Visual Studio environment, we'll want to update the project settings so the BSAFE include files and library files are found by the compiler and linker, respectively. To do this, we'll want to add the directory containing the BSAFE include files in our project's Additional Include Directories located in the Project Settings property pane under the C++ tab. Here are step-by-step instructions to add that directory to a new project:

1. From a new or existing project, select the Project menu item and select Settings from the drop-down menu. Figure 10.1 shows the resulting project screen that will be shown in doing so.

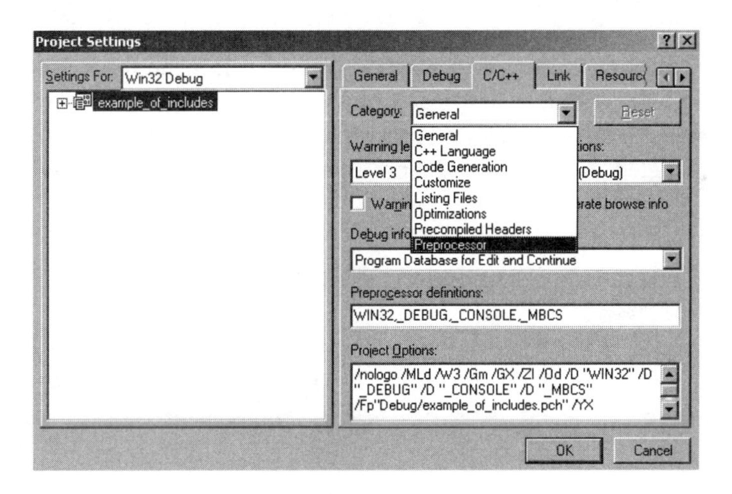

FIGURE 10.1 Project Settings screen.

2. From the C/C++ tab, select the Category drop-down list box and select the Preprocessor list item.
3. Under Additional Include Directories, specify the directory containing the BSAFE include (e.g., header) files. Figure 10.2 shows the project changes incorporated and the new include files ready for use.

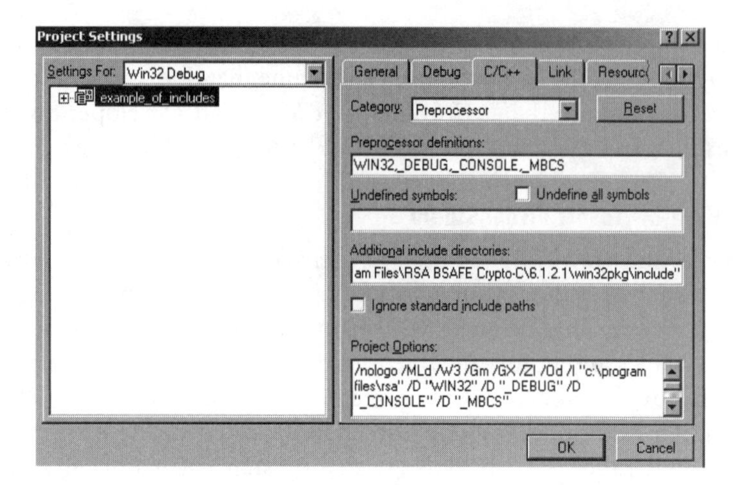

FIGURE 10.2 Adding include directories.

That completes the incorporation of the additional include directories into the project; now, we'll go ahead and add the libraries:

1. From the Project property pane, select the Link tab.
2. In the Category drop-down list box, select the Input list item as shown in Figure 10.3.
3. Add the library files appropriate for your architecture to the edit box labeled "Object/library modules" (library files should be separated by spaces).

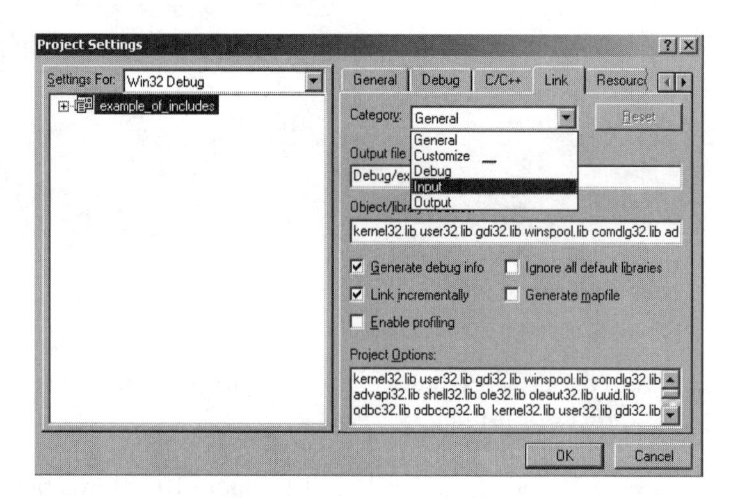

FIGURE 10.3 Update input settings.

4. Add the directory containing the library files referenced earlier to the edit box labeled "Additional library path." When complete, you will have similar entries filled in as demonstrated in Figure 10.4.

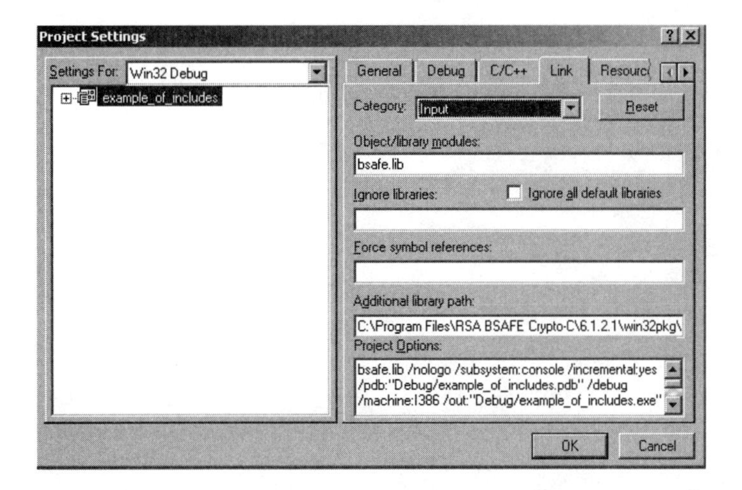

FIGURE 10.4 Add library files.

Once these steps are complete, we can click OK on the project Properties pane and proceed to add the file we've created containing the memory manipulations routines to the project. Having done this, we are ready to incorporate BSAFE Crypto-C functionality into our projects without additional modification.

Microsoft Visual C++ 2005–Additional Include Directories

For those developers using Visual C++ 2005, the steps for updating the project are similar to those followed with previous versions. First, we'll make sure the compiler is able to find the headers required by BSAFE:

1. With our project open (either a newly created project or an existing project), select the Project menu item and the Properties menu item from the bottom of the drop-down menu. This yields a dialog similar to the one displayed in Figure 10.5.
2. From the tree-control on the left side of the resulting property pane, select the C/C++ subitem (note that by default, we'll need to have a C++ or C file in our project to see this menu item).
3. In the space labeled "Additional Include Directories," specify the directory containing the BSAFE include (e.g., header) files (see Figure 10.6).

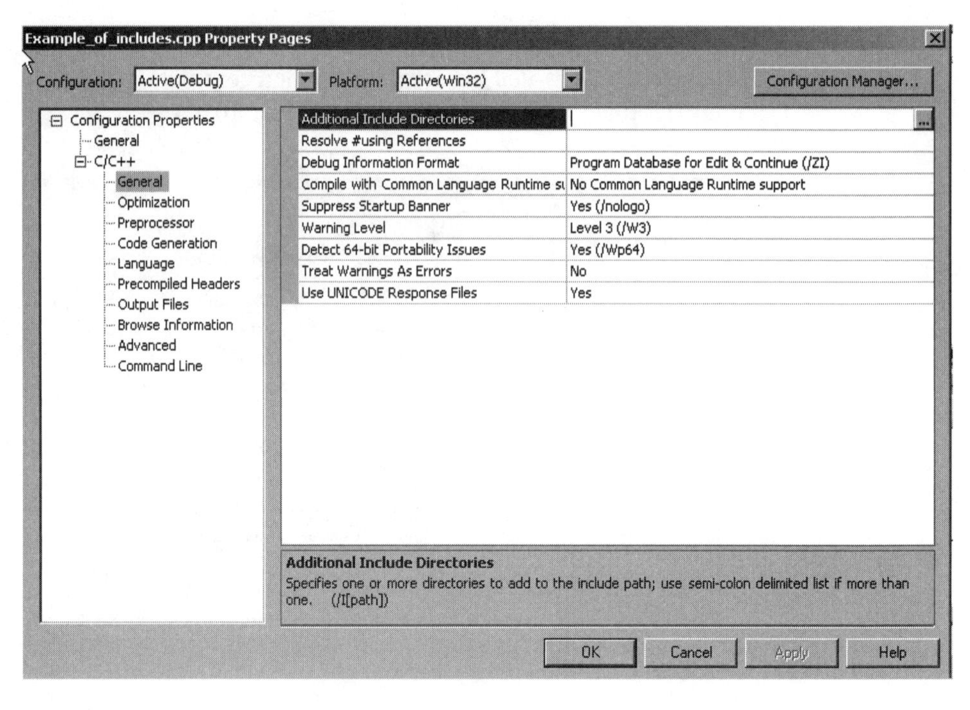

FIGURE 10.5 Project Settings screen.

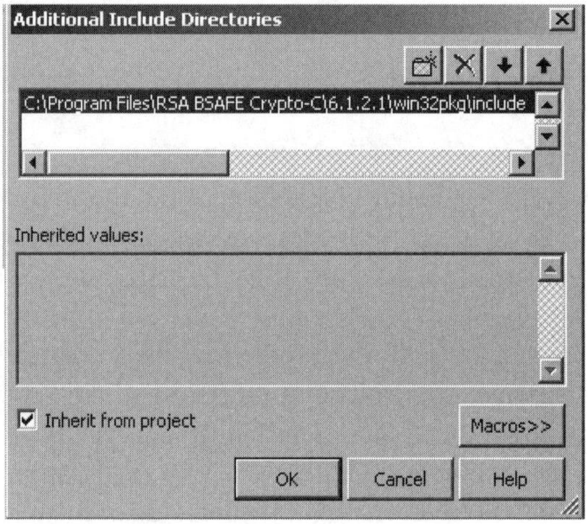

Additional Include Directories
C:\Program Files\RSA BSAFE Crypto-C\6.1.2.1\win32pkg\include
Inherited values:
Inherit from project
Macros>>
OK Cancel Help

FIGURE 10.6 Update include directories.

This will incorporate the additional include directories into the project (see Figure 10.7).

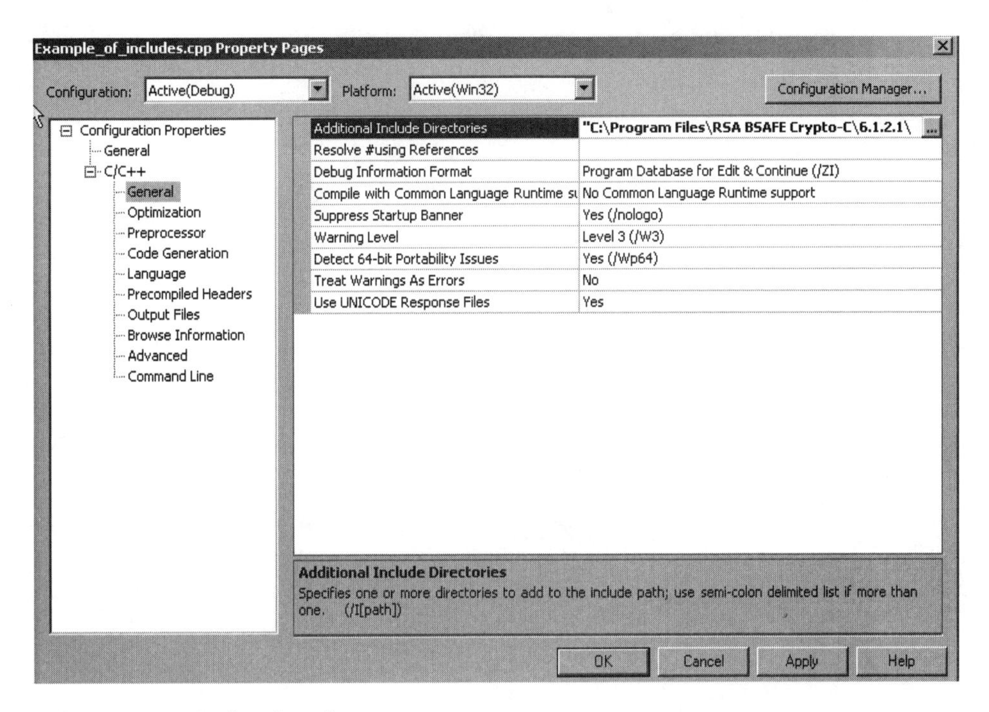

FIGURE 10.7 Updated settings.

And now for the libraries:

1. From the Project property pane, expand the Linker subitem using the left-hand tree control. The enumeration of this item and the subsequent screen are shown in Figure 10.8.
2. Under the expanded Linker subitems, select the General item.
3. In the space labeled "Additional Library Directories," navigate to the directory containing the single-threaded, multithreaded static, or multithreaded dynamic version of the library as appropriate. This dialog is shown in Figure 10.9.
4. Under the expanded Linker subitems, select the Input item.
5. In the space labeled "Additional Dependencies," specify the library files shipped with the BSAFE API (e.g., bsafe.lib and sec32ipi.lib for Crypto-C). This dialog is shown in Figure 10.10.

Once these steps are complete, we can click OK on the project Properties pane and proceed to add the file we've created containing the memory manipulations routines to the project. Figure 10.11 shows the property pane with the additional library directory and the new library added to the project.

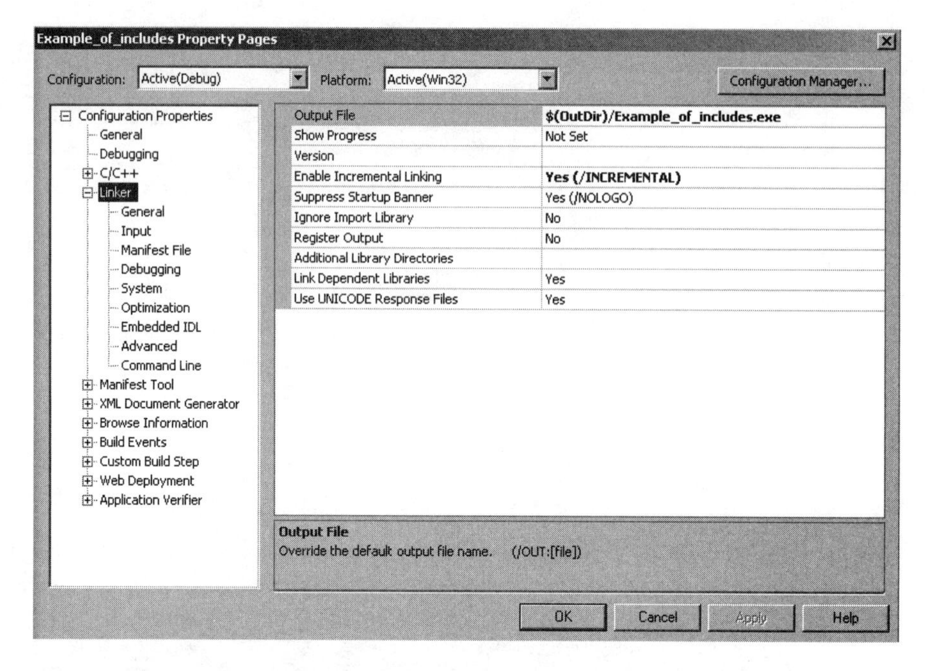

FIGURE 10.8 Update Linker settings.

FIGURE 10.9 Select runtime threading.

Having done this, we are ready to incorporate BSAFE Crypto-C functionality into our projects.

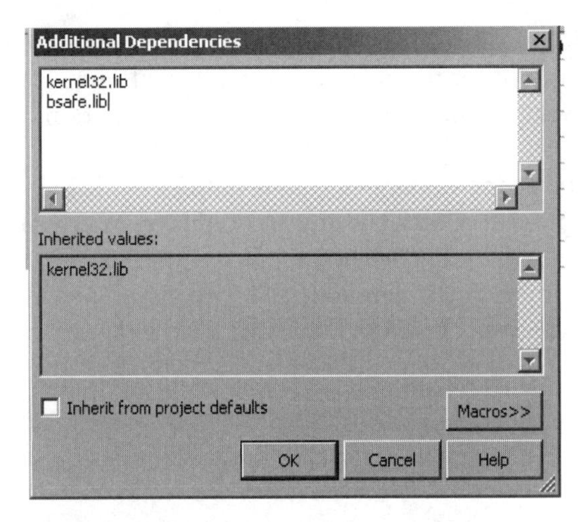

FIGURE 10.10 Add libraries to linkage.

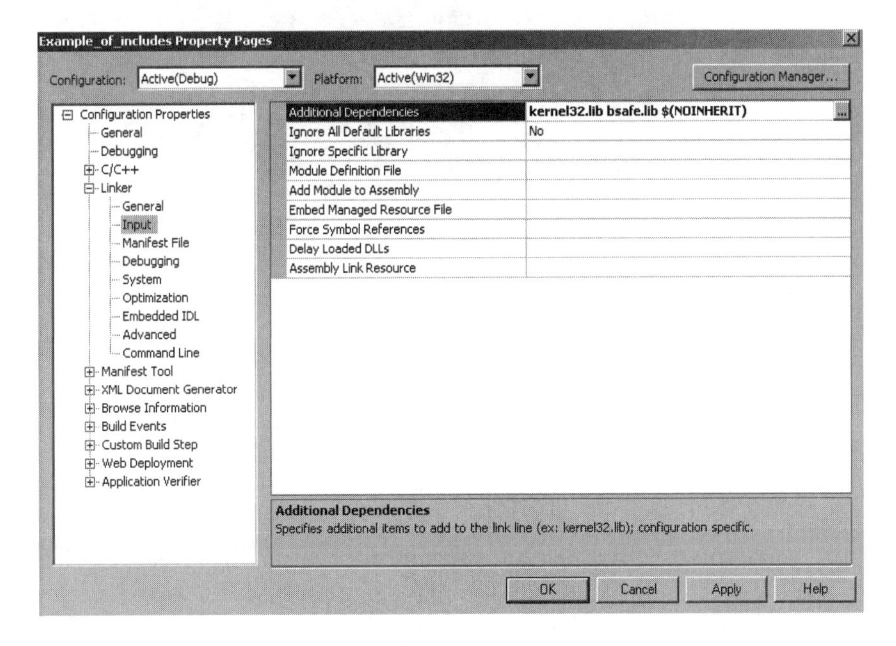

FIGURE 10.11 New library added.

10.6.3 Setting the Global Includes and Libraries

As mentioned earlier, under most circumstances, we'll refrain from modifying the global developer studio environment to automatically find our includes and libraries.

For the sake of completeness, however, we've included some steps on how to use this approach as well (in the case, for example, that numerous projects will be written by one developer and project-by-project configuration of includes and libraries is burdensome).

To modify the developer studio settings to include the BSAFE includes, the following procedure outlines how to do this on Microsoft Developer Studio 6:

1. From the main window, select the "Tools" menu, and select "Options." The screen shown in Figure 10.12 will appear.

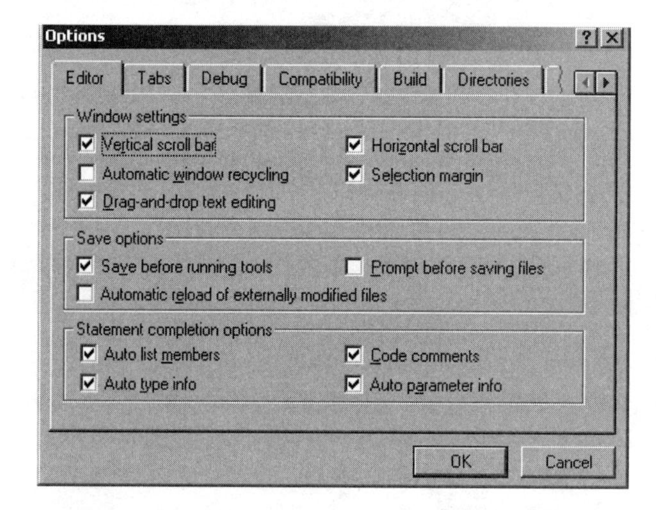

FIGURE 10.12 Options menu.

2. From the resulting dialog box, select the Directories tab and modify both "Include files" and "Library files" to contain the BSAFE directories for the products we've targeted. These settings are shown in Figure 10.13.

We will still need to update the libraries within the project explicitly, but we've set the path to find them without having to specify additional directories.

The steps for VC 2005 are similar:

1. From the "Tools" menu, select "Options." You will be shown the screen depicted in Figure 10.14.
2. Under Project and Solutions, navigate to Visual C++ Directories. Set both "Include files" and "Library files" to incorporate the directories for the RSA projects we're targeting. This dialog is shown in Figure 10.15.

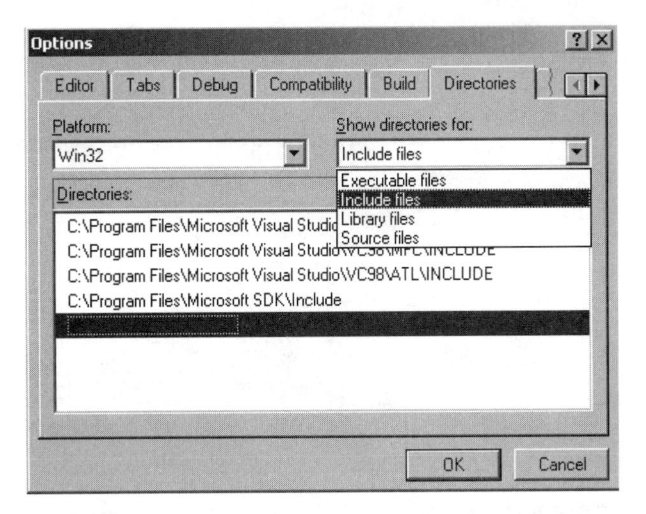

FIGURE 10.13 Adding library and include directories.

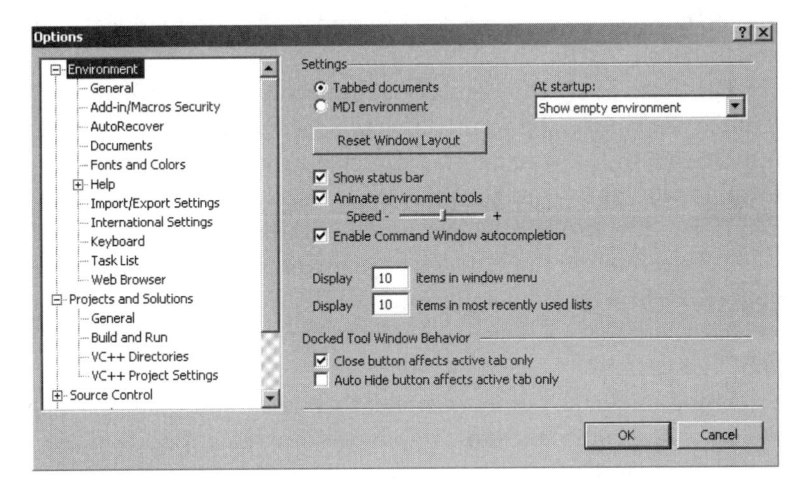

FIGURE 10.14 Options menu.

And that's it! We'll still need to specify the library file in our projects, but we won't have to update the additional directories every time for each new project we do.

10.6.4 Other Platforms Using cc, gcc, or g++

It is arguably somewhat easier for users of a command-line interface (either entered directly from the command line or through a makefile) to incorporate the additional library files and include (header) files into their programs (since they do not

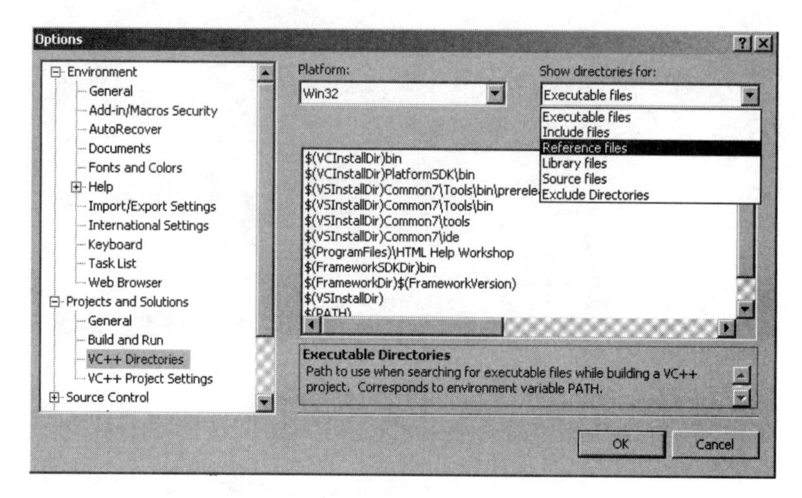

FIGURE 10.15 Adding library and include directories.

have to navigate screens, but can just update the commands they use for compiling and linking).

For those of us who regularly compile on these platforms, we're already quite familiar with using the `-I` directive to specify that we are going to bring in additional header files from another directory. Additionally, we may already be comfortable with the `-L` linker directive, which specifies that we will be including additional directories in which to find libraries. Once we specify these two things, we only need to use the `-l` flag on the linker to specify to the compiler that we are going to be bringing in new libraries. We'll just include the base library name in our `-l` usage, and the linker will append the appropriate extension and prefix (usually "lib") for us.

Using gcc (or any other compiler that uses traditional cc syntax), we would use the following commands to compile and link an application that uses the BSAFE library (remember that we've installed BSAFE in `/usr/bsafe/`):

```
    [emoyle@elysium:~/usebsafe]$ g++ -c -
I/usr/bsafe/cryptoc6121/include main.cpp
    [emoyle@elysium:~/usebsafe]$ g++ -omain main.o -
L/usr/bsafe/cryptoc6121/lib/sparcv8 -lbsafe -static
```

In this example, we've pointed the compiler to the location of the include files using the `-I` flag; we've also adjusted the included library files through the `-L` directive, which allows us (in combination with the `-l` directive) to reference the BSAFE library file (libbsafe.a) in this example.

10.7 PREPARING OTHER RSA TOOLS FOR USE

In the same way we set up the Crypto-C functionality, we'll need to add any additional portions of the BSAFE functionality we intend to use to the project in just the same way. All of the C API's supplied by RSA come with appropriate libraries and headers that we should incorporate into our development environment in the same way we've incorporated the material described earlier, depending on which libs our application requires.

10.8 ENCRYPTING AND DECRYPTING

Without a doubt, the strength of the RSA library is in the fine-grain control provided to the developer during general-purpose cryptographic operations. This library provides more control in the form of algorithm options, programmatic functionality, and so on than any of the other libraries we've covered (OpenSSL is close and rapidly gaining). In other words, the BSAFE authors were extremely careful to ensure that the library is "broad" in that all the functionality potentially required by a caller is available should he or she need it. Most often, we will not need to exercise this control, but it is nice to know it is there if we need it.

Given the fine-grain control of cryptographic operations within BSAFE, developers approaching the RSA library expecting to find high-level APIs with only a few customization options will be sorely disappointed; this is not the library's strength nor is it something within the library developers' design goals. Note that this is by no means a criticism of the functionality provided by RSA. However, we felt that an explanation of the lack of a "high-level techniques" section was owed to the developers who have noticed the uniform format across the rest of the book and have therefore noted that this chapter differs from the others in that it does not provide a delineation between high- and low-level techniques. In other words, most of the description in this chapter is of lower level APIs rather than higher level ones.

10.8.1 Symmetric Encryption and Decryption

BSAFE, as we've stated earlier, is designed to "leave nothing to chance" and is balanced heavily on the side of control in the control/brevity tradeoff. As such, we as developers are provided a number of places where we interact with the library. Before we go into specifics of how to use the symmetric encryption functionality targeted in this section, there are a few concepts that we will use in other contexts over and above symmetric encryption (but are required for symmetric encryption as well): algorithm objects, algorithm identifiers, key objects, and key identifiers.

10.8.1.1 Algorithm Objects

Algorithm objects are structs explicitly created by the application developer that are used by the BSAFE API to contain state information associated with a particular cryptographic operation. The algorithm object is created using the Crypto-C function `B_CreateAlgorithmObject()`. This call will create an artifact (an algorithm object) that is a pointer into memory owned and managed by the library. We don't really have to concern ourselves with the specifics of how the library manages internal state information, so we can look at this object as an opaque artifact. We will use this object in our calls to the underlying library to specify which algorithm "context" (instance) we wish to perform an operation on. In this way, we can have numerous cryptographic operations going on in parallel, and we will differentiate among them by specifying this object in our calls to the library.

10.8.1.2 Algorithm Identifiers

An *algorithm identifier*, or AI, is a constant that specifies to the BSAFE library which algorithm is to be used. These algorithm identifiers are specific, and there may be numerous AIs for each algorithm. For example, the following four are all AES algorithm identifiers (there are over 20 different AES algorithm identifiers—these are just the most pertinent to standard usage), reflecting various key sizes and modes used with AES:

- `AI_AES_CBCPad`
- `AI_AES128_CBCPad`
- `AI_AES_ECB`
- `AI_AES128_ECB`

It isn't practical to list all the algorithm identifiers here. The AIs corresponding to symmetric encryption operations (not including other types of cryptographic operations) that will be used by this book in examples context are:

`AI_AES_CBCPad`: AI specifying AES in CBC mode with padding applied; the AI does not specify a key length, so any of 128, 192, or 256 bits can be used.

`AI_DES_EDE_CBCPad_IV8`: AI specifying Triple-DES in CBC mode with an IV (initialization vector) of 8 bytes.

These two combinations of ciphers and modes are useful for the majority of situations we will encounter in developing new applications. We will always need to remember that backward compatibility can and will be a factor in application design. However, for symmetric encryption choices, these are probably the best bet since they are recommended by NIST for use in commercial and government contexts, and give acceptable performance on modern hardware. Included with the BSAFE documentation is an exhaustive list of all the AIs included in the library; developers who require a particular algorithm not discussed in this book (for backward compatibility or any other reason) are encouraged to consult the RSA documentation for reference. If another AI should be selected, the usage will remain the same as that described in this book within a given category (e.g., usage of the DES algorithm would be nearly identical to Triple-DES).

10.8.1.3 Key Objects

Just as we will create and destroy algorithm objects that contain state information associated with a particular algorithm we are using, we will also create and destroy key objects that are used internally by the BSAFE object to hold state information associated with the key. For example, if we are using DES, the key object would contain information such as if parity adjustment has been or should be performed on the key. This key object is similar in nature to an algorithm object, being explicitly created through a call to `B_CreateKeyObject()` and explicitly destroyed through a call to `B_DestroyKeyObject()`. Just as we didn't need to understand how the algorithm objects work internally, we don't need to understand how key objects work internally. We can view this as an opaque structure that merely indicates to the library which key is to be used with which operation.

10.8.1.4 Key Identifiers

Just as algorithms have AIs that are used to uniquely identify algorithms and modes, keys have KIs (*key identifiers*) that specify properties about the key (primarily key length, although a KI may also specify an algorithm when particular algorithms must have specific key properties). For the purposes of symmetric encryption (as with AIs, this does not include other cryptographic operations), the following KI types will be used:

`KI_Item`: Identifies that the KI is of type "Item"; in BSAFE parlance, an "Item" is a struct containing both a length and an associated buffer.

`KI_DES24Strong`: Specifies that the key is a 24-byte DES key (i.e., 192-bit for Triple-DES) and will be checked against known weak keys and have appropriate parity adjustment applied prior to use.

10.8.1.5 Symmetric Encryption–Steps

Some developers might argue that the BSAFE library is more complex than other libraries covered in this book; it is certainly true that performing a given operation takes more lines of code using the BSAFE API versus any of the other APIs. We've already noted the precision that comes with this "complexity"; however, another way to look at the tradeoff is to say that what we sacrifice in terms of concise expression is made up for in universality of the API. It can certainly be said that the steps required to encrypt and decrypt data are significantly more in number than in other APIs. It is also accurate to say that the steps required to symmetrically encrypt data are universal across all the algorithms supported and that the same steps apply for almost any other cryptographic operation we wish to perform. Rather than spend more time describing the process in the abstract, let's look at some specific usage to illustrate the point. To start this process, the following are the steps required to encrypt a piece of data:

1. Create an algorithm chooser (this can be static or within the scope of the function/method that will use the cryptographic functionality) containing the algorithms we intend to use in our application. Most of the time, we'll want to use `AM_AES_CBC_ENCRYPT`.
2. Declare our algorithm and key variables, setting them to null pointers (ideally using the RSA supplied `NULL_PTR`) in the process.
3. Call `B_CreateAlgorithmObject()` to create and initialize the algorithm "object" (state information struct).
4. Call `B_CreateKeyObject()` to create and initialize the key "object" (state information struct).
5. Call `B_SetAlgorithmInfo()`, specifying the appropriate AI corresponding to the encryption algorithm we intend to use. At this time, we will also specify a random initialization vector to be used (when using a mode that requires an IV).
6. Call `B_SetKeyInfo()`, specifying an appropriate KI corresponding to the type of key we wish to use.
7. Manually populate the members of the key object struct to contain the values corresponding to the length and data of the key we wish to use.
8. Call `B_EncryptInit()` to bind the key, algorithm chooser, and surrender context (if any) to the encryption functionality.
9. Optionally, call `B_EncryptUpdate()`, specifying incremental portions of the data that is to be encrypted (note that this call is provided for convenience and performance reasons—if the data to be encrypted is small, this step may be omitted).
10. Call `B_EncryptFinal()`, specifying the last of the data to be encrypted.
11. Call `B_DestroyAlgorithmObject()` to free any resources associated with the algorithm.
12. Call `B_DestroyKeyObject()` to free any resources associated with the key.

Granted, these steps are more involved than the other libraries we've covered. However, they only have to be learned once in order to understand almost all of the

Crypto-C API usage. Rather than immediately supplying the sample code to put these steps in context, there is one point we need to address before we can do so; namely, we need to talk about initialization vectors and how/why we need to obtain them.

10.8.1.6 Random Initialization Vectors

Unlike some of the other libraries we've seen, Crypto-C requires us to manually supply a random IV for symmetric algorithms that will be operated in CBC mode (and other modes that require an IV). Block ciphers used in CBC mode always require an IV (the IV used in conjunction with the feedback register is what defines CBC mode). Some of the libraries we've covered automatically handle the generation of an IV for us, but this particular library does not. Therefore, we will need to generate an IV ourselves (and use it appropriately) when we wish to use Crypto-C block ciphers in CBC mode.

Generating an IV is straightforward. A useful way to generate an IV is to use a randomly generated value supplied to the algorithm object as part of the call to `B_SetAlgorithmInfo()`. Note that we will want to ensure that we transmit the IV along with the data, since it will be required to decrypt the data later. Later in this chapter, we'll discuss and demonstrate the use of pseudo-random number generation algorithms within BSAFE, and we'll see how we can leverage these to produce randomly generated IVs. For now, however, we'll use "demonstration" (and thereby "unsafe") values for the IV (e.g., all zeros in the source in the next section). Note that we're just using the unsafe value for demonstration purposes, and that production applications should use a random value. However, since we're covering symmetric cryptography first (and we haven't discussed random number generation yet), we'll have to wait a bit before we can introduce that in practice.

10.8.1.7 Example Code

If we were to take steps enumerated before our IV digression and write code that implements them, we would generate code similar to the following (note that the whole source listing [including #includes, the application's main, etc.] is presented here due to the complexity of the example). After the example is presented, we'll walk through the calls in detail to make sure the developer understands the steps involved:

```
#include "bsafe.h"
#include <malloc.h>
#include <memory.h>
#include <stdlib.h>
#include <stdio.h>
#include <string.h>
```

```
class RSA_Exception {
public:
    RSA_Exception(int errorCode) {
        this->errorCode = errorCode;
    }
    int getErrorCode() {
        return errorCode;
    }
private:
    int errorCode;
};

void checkstatus(int returnValue) {
    if(returnValue != 0) {
        throw RSA_Exception(returnValue);
    }
}

#define BLOCK_SIZE 16

void main() {
    B_ALGORITHM_METHOD *ENCRYPT_SAMPLE_CHOOSER[] = {
        &AM_AES_CBC_ENCRYPT,
        (B_ALGORITHM_METHOD *)NULL_PTR };

    //declare what we need for initialization
    B_KEY_OBJ myKey = (B_KEY_OBJ)NULL_PTR;
    B_ALGORITHM_OBJ aesEncrypt = (B_ALGORITHM_OBJ)NULL_PTR;

    try {
        int status = 0;
        //allocate the structures we need for encryption
        checkstatus(B_CreateAlgorithmObject(&aesEncrypt));
        checkstatus(B_CreateKeyObject(&myKey));

        //initialize the key and algorithm objects
        unsigned char IV[BLOCK_SIZE]; //IV is the same as the block
size
        memset(IV, 0x0, sizeof(IV)); //to demo, just use zeroes
        checkstatus(B_SetAlgorithmInfo(aesEncrypt, AI_AES_CBCPad,
IV));
        ITEM keyValue = {NULL_PTR, 0};
        keyValue.len = 16; //16 bytes = 128 bits
        keyValue.data = (POINTER)malloc(keyValue.len);
```

```
            char * theKeyData = "This is the Key Data";
            memcpy(keyValue.data, theKeyData, keyValue.len);
            checkstatus(B_SetKeyInfo(myKey, KI_Item,
(POINTER)&keyValue));

            //get ready to perform the cryptography
            checkstatus(B_EncryptInit(aesEncrypt, myKey,
                ENCRYPT_SAMPLE_CHOOSER, NULL));

            //things we need to encrypt
            char * toEncrypt = "This is what we are going to encrypt.";
            unsigned char * cipherText = 0;
            unsigned int outputSize = strlen(toEncrypt)+1+BLOCK_SIZE;
            cipherText = (unsigned char*)malloc(outputSize);
            unsigned int updatedSize = 0;
            unsigned int finalSize = 0;

            checkstatus(B_EncryptUpdate(aesEncrypt, cipherText,
                &updatedSize, outputSize, (unsigned char*)toEncrypt,
                strlen(toEncrypt), (B_ALGORITHM_OBJ)NULL, NULL));
            checkstatus(B_EncryptFinal(aesEncrypt,
cipherText+updatedSize,
                &finalSize, outputSize-updatedSize, NULL, NULL));

            //clean up
            free(keyValue.data);
            free(cipherText);
            B_DestroyKeyObject(&myKey);
            B_DestroyAlgorithmObject(&aesEncrypt);

        } catch (RSA_Exception error) {
            printf("An error has occurred.");
        }
    }
```

This code may look a bit daunting, but by walking through it, we'll see that it isn't that complicated.

10.8.1.8 Explanatory Code Walkthrough

In walking through the example code, trying to grasp the nuances of each of the calls all at once is difficult, but using some example code as a guide in creating new code is certainly a good starting point. Note that each of these calls is explained in depth in the BSAFE documentation, so developers can look there for more information on particular calls if they require it. We're going to go into a bit more detail in this walk-through than we have in other code listings, since it is important that the developer understands what is going on in each call, as the same sequences of calls are made over and over again throughout BSAFE. Although this might take some time, we only have to do it once, and the calls should make much more sense if explained with a high degree of detail.

Includes: The included files in this example are relatively straightforward. We are including `bsafe.h` for the definition of cryptographic types and for the declaration of cryptographic functions; the rest are included for memory management, printing to the console, etc.

Error handling: After the includes, the next few lines (including the rather small and uninteresting exception class and the small `checkstatus()` function), are provided to assist in the checking for and handling of BSAFE error conditions. The majority of the Crypto-C functions behave the same way with respect to error conditions: namely, they return zero (0) if they are successful, and an error condition (result code) if they are unsuccessful. RSA uses a do...while loop in its sample documentation (breaking from the loop in the event of an error condition), but some developers find this "do...while" loop confusing (or maybe just inelegant) and therefore prefer the use of exceptions in the event of failure of the RSA library functions. Of course, the particular methodology you have for handling errors would be appropriate in this context, and any other error-handling method can be used according to the preference of the developer, the capabilities of the compiler used, and the C/C++ language preference.

Algorithm and key initialization: Moving into the `main()` function of the sample, we see the creation of the chooser, the declaration of the key and algorithm objects, and then the allocation of these objects using `B_CreateAlgorithmObject()` and `B_CreateKeyObject()`. Once allocated, we can then use the "SetInfo" methods of both the algorithm and the key. The algorithm "SetInfo" function (`B_SetAlgorithmInfo()`) allows us to set the initialization vector and algorithm constant corresponding to the algorithm we wish to use. The key "SetInfo" function (`B_SetKeyInfo()`) allows us to specify the key data and the key constant corresponding to the key we wish to use. Note that the key value and the IV must be allocated and populated with the appropriate values prior to use. For our example, we've left out the details of filling the IV with random information for brevity; in a real-life scenario, however, we would want to make sure we use a strong value (either acquired from a random number source of cryptographic quality or another source according to our application needs).

Encryption: First, we initialize the encryption process by binding the key object and the chooser to the encryption object. Once this is done, we can begin to actually supply data to the encryption process using the update method. Both the update (`B_EncryptUpdate()`) and finalization functions (`B_EncryptFinal()`) take *two* algorithm objects. The second algorithm object (for which the examples specifies `NULL`) is a pseudo-random number generation algorithm (PRNG) that may be required for certain encryption algorithms; it is the responsibility of the caller to know if the algorithm requires a random number source for each algorithm that will be called. In this case, since we are using a "run of the mill" block cipher, a random number source is not required (the contexts under which a valid random number source are rare and outside the scope of this chapter—in short, for almost all usage, we won't have to worry about having a nonnull value here). During the calls to `B_EncryptUpdate()` and `B_EncryptFinal()`, we are supplying buffers for input and output data, integers for the size of the input and output buffers, and a pointer to an integer so the library can inform us about the size of the resulting output. The final parameter is the surrender function detailed earlier; note that we are not supplying a surrender function for this small (and therefore relatively quick) operation.

Freeing resources: The resources explicitly created by us for use in the BSAFE library in addition to those created implicitly by the BSAFE library should be freed at this time, as should any memory explicitly allocated by us outside of BSAFE calls (e.g., through `malloc` or `new`).

And that's it. Aside from the weak IV and hardcoded key associated with this sample code, these are all the steps required to symmetrically encrypting and decrypting data.

10.8.1.9 Troubleshooting

Perhaps the biggest boon to the developer when using the RSA Crypto-C toolkit is the one-time writing of an error-handling routine that translates the internal BSAFE error types to textual error messages. A sample of this has been included on the companion CD-ROM (/Examples/Chapter 10/Errors). A routine that does this does not take long to write and proves extraordinarily useful in the debugging of RSA Crypto-C applications.

Linking errors: Developers on the Microsoft platform may encounter linking errors (either of the type `__xxxx__xxx` is undefined, where `xxx` is a C function like `time()`, or multiple definitions for C functions) if they are using a C/C++ C runtime library that is incompatible with the version of the BSAFE lib they are using; for example, if a developer is using the "multithreaded statically linked" version of the BSAFE library in combination with the "multithreaded dynamically linked" runtime library (compiler switches `/MD` or `/MDd`). Should this occur, developers need merely to make sure the library version they are using maps to the appropriate version of the runtime library they're using.

Insufficient buffer sizes: Since the BSAFE library requires the developer to allocate memory that will be used by the library, developers are required to take into account additional padding that may be employed by the library to accommodate scenarios where padding is to be used. As such, developers must understand how padding will be performed during symmetric operations and account for that in their code—the most frequently occurring error of this type is `BE_OUTPUT_LEN`.

Functions out of order: If we attempt to use the library functions out of order (e.g., if we attempt to use `B_EncryptUpdate()` before we call `B_EncryptInit()`), we will obtain a variety of errors depending on the combination of which function we are calling and which function(s) are out of order. It is recommended that the functions be called in the order they are presented here and in the BSAFE documentation.

10.8.2 Asymmetric Encryption (Not Including Signing)

Again, for the purposes of backward compatibility, we may wish to perform a public-key encryption (for privacy) operation on some data (note that this does not including wrapping keys—key wrapping functionality is provided through an easier and safer to use mechanism). Note that this is not the recommended procedure for any context other than backward compatibility with existing applications. Should we wish to do so, we will need to follow the *exact* methodology described in the symmetric scenario, with the following differences:

- Include a compatible algorithm chooser: instead of `AM_AES_CBC_ENCRYPT`, an example would be `AM_RSA_ENCRYPT`.
- Substitute the RSA public key algorithm identifier (`AI_PKCS_RSAPublic`) for the AES AI during the call to `B_SetAlgorithmInfo()`.
- Create and specify an RSA public key rather than an arbitrary `KI_Item` in the calls to create and populate the key object.
- Specify data of the appropriate size for encryption. Note that the PKCS1.5 padding scheme requires at least 11 bytes, so data supplied to the algorithm must be of a size less than the public key modulus size minus 11. For example, if we were using a key size of 1024 bits, the maximum value would be (1024/8) – 11 bytes, or 117 bytes

ON THE CD

Although not reproduced textually inline to this text (given the length of the sample), sample code demonstrating this usage is included on the companion CD-ROM (/Examples/Chapter 10/Asym_Encrypt). Again, note that for most purposes, we will wish to avoid doing this directly, and instead look for other mechanisms (such as the key wrapping API) provided by the API in our application development.

10.8.3 Creating and Storing Keys

As we have seen time and time again, a large percentage of our development time will be spent in key creation, storage, transformation, and manipulation. The Crypto-C API does not provide a convenient mechanism for generating a random seed that we can use for seeding the random number generator. Therefore, it is of particular import when using the RSA library that we use robust strategies to get a good random seed for use in the RSA PRNGs. Given that harvesting "entropic" data from the machine on which our application is running is a difficult exercise, we will want to use some shortcut techniques where possible. We've outlined some of those shortcuts to spare the developers the pain of having to implement this type of non-portable and intricate code themselves. Following are some convenient shortcuts we can use depending on the platform we are writing to. In the event we are not in a position to use any of these shortcuts, we can implement a random seed gathering routine ourselves (which we'll endeavor to explain also), but it does streamline the development process to a great degree to take the "shortcut" route when available.

10.8.3.1 About Random Seed Data

Crypto-C provides a number of different random number generation techniques the developer can use. However, these techniques all require that the developer obtain a good seed for the initial value supplied to the random number generator. As we've already seen, polling the system for entropic information is slow, prone to failure, and time consuming. Therefore, most of the time, we'll find it advantageous to leverage the features of the platform we're running on to generate a seed for us. Following are a few shortcuts we can use on a few common platforms.

Unix Random Seed Shortcut

On most Unix platforms, we can use the same strategy used by OpenSSL and read random values from `/dev/random`. This is a very useful technique, as the random values read are usually robust and readily available. It should be noted that some platforms will have a limit to the amount of data that can be retrieved from these sources at any given time, so we don't want to use the source for anything more than the seed value. In situations in which we know ahead of time the details of the platform we're writing for, a bit of reading from the manual page is usually in order to vet the details of our usage beforehand. We can read from `/dev/random` the same way as we would read from any other file, by opening the file for reading and requesting that the number of bytes we desire be supplied. All in all, this is a very convenient strategy.

Windows Random Seed Shortcut

Although Windows does not have a structure akin to `/dev/random`, the CAPI call to generate randomness requires only three lines of code, so it can be a very useful shortcut. The CAPI randomness API seeds the generator for us using information gathered by the underlying library, so this can be a useful technique for us to use. The following code, for example, will generate random seed information using MS-CAPI:

```
HCRYPTPROV  ctx;
CryptAcquireContext(&ctx, NULL, NULL, PROV_RSA_FULL, 0);
unsigned char randSeed[64];
CryptGenRandom(ctx, sizeof(randSeed), randSeed);
CryptReleaseContext(ctx, 0);
```

A routine containing this code could be included in applications that use Crypto-C and called when initializing the random number generator.

Intel Hardware Shortcut

The BSAFE documentation includes sample code specifying techniques to use the built-in Intel hardware random number generator for operations that require random numbers; this example documentation is included in the RSA documentation file `intelrnd.c`. The example is provided in such a way as to allow cutting and pasting of the Intel hardware random-number seed-gathering function into our source code. This is a useful seed-generation shortcut on Intel platforms that include this random-number-generation hardware. We are not going to go into more detail here, because the "cut and paste"-able nature of the RSA supplied code is probably as easy to use as it's going to get. Therefore, to avoid supplying any superfluous information in this chapter, we've elected to leave it out. The companion CD-ROM (/Examples/Chapter 10/Intel_Rand) provides some alternative "cut and pasteable" code with explanatory comments should the developer not have ready access to the RSA documentation, but really either one will do.

No Shortcuts (The Hard Way)

In the event we cannot use any of the approaches described previously—for example, if we are running on an older Windows platform in which CAPI is not available or on a Unix platform without a usable /dev/random—we must then unfortunately obtain the random number information manually. This can be done according to the methodologies outlined earlier in this book (specifically, the discussion and usage examples in Chapter 6 detailing methods to obtain random number information from the system). Since the methodologies described are quite time consuming, we will not repeat that material here, but will instead refer the developer to those earlier sections and to the random-seed-generation examples included on the companion CD-ROM (/Examples/Chapter 10/Rand_Gen_Full).

10.8.3.2 Using the BSAFE PRNG Functions

As with most BSAFE calls, the PRNG functions in BSAFE require us to go through the sequence of create, set info, init, and update before we can get access to the random bytes. Additionally, once we are done with the random source, we will need to explicitly destroy the random source. The key generation examples later in this section will require a source of random information, so it is important that we trace through the steps required to create a random source of the type expected by BSAFE beforehand. The following steps will create a PRNG for our use, and we'll see this used in numerous subsequent examples in this chapter:

1. Declare an algorithm chooser that includes an `AM` of a type corresponding to the random algorithm we intend to use (e.g., `AM_SHA_RANDOM`).
2. Create an algorithm object to contain the state information associated with the PRNG algorithm; this should be done using a call to `B_CreateAlgorithmObject()`.
3. Set the algorithm information and set the algorithm type to `AI_SHA1Random` (or another desired random algorithm) using a call to `B_SetAlgorithmInfo()`.
4. Call `B_RandomInit()` to initialize the random number generation, specifying the random algorithm object and chooser created in the previous steps.
5. Obtain a random seed value to "prime" the PRNG; ideally, we'll want to use one of the easier shortcuts to do this rather than manually polling the system for entropic data.
6. Call `B_RandomUpdate()`, supplying the random seed information gathered in the previous step.

Once we have completed these steps, we can either make use of the random source directly by calling `B_GenerateRandomBytes()`, or by supplying the random source to a BSAFE call that requires a randomness source. When we are done obtaining the random data, we will need to free the resources associated with the algorithm object by calling `B_DestroyAlgorithmObject()`. Note that we should refrain from destroying the algorithm object in situations when we need to supply the random object to the library until we have made those API calls. Destroying the algorithm object frees the associated internal structures within the library, and the algorithm object is therefore useless once we've destroyed it.

10.8.3.3 Using PRNG Data for Symmetric IVs

Of particular utility is the use of BSAFE PRNG algorithms for symmetric IVs; as a matter of fact, this is something we will do quite often since the Crypto-C API does not perform any inherent IV handling for us. The IV should consist of random data exactly equal to the block size of our symmetric algorithm. For example, if we are using AES (16-byte blocks), we will want the IV data to be 16 bytes; if we are using Triple-DES (or regular DES for that matter), we'll want the IV to be 8 bytes in total length (corresponding to the 8-byte block size of DES and Triple-DES). We can store the IV in just about any data structure we like: in a dynamic (heap-based) buffer, a static (stack-based) array, a native BSAFE Item (i.e., Length/Value pair), and so forth. Any structure that will allow us to represent the IV as a contiguous buffer containing the IV will work and can be used according to our preference.

10.8.3.4 BSAFE PRNG Example Code

To initialize a PRNG using the BSAFE library, we would write code similar to the following:

```
  B_ALGORITHM_METHOD *RANDOM_CHOOSER[] = {
       &AM_SHA_RANDOM,
      (B_ALGORITHM_METHOD *)NULL_PTR };
int status = 0;
B_ALGORITHM_OBJ random = (B_ALGORITHM_OBJ)NULL_PTR;
status = B_CreateAlgorithmObject(&random);
status = B_SetAlgorithmInfo(random, AI_SHA1Random,  NULL_PTR);
status = B_RandomInit (random, RANDOM_CHOOSER,
                             (A_SURRENDER_CTX*)NULL_PTR);

//CAPI Shortcut
HCRYPTPROV  ctx;
CryptAcquireContext(&ctx, NULL, NULL, PROV_RSA_FULL, 0);
unsigned char randSeed[64];
CryptGenRandom(ctx, sizeof(randSeed), randSeed);
CryptReleaseContext(ctx, 0);

status = B_RandomUpdate(random, randSeed, sizeof(randSeed),
            (A_SURRENDER_CTX *)NULL_PTR);

    /* Here we use the random number generator, e.g. to generate an IV
*/

//clean up
B_DestroyAlgorithmObject(&random);
```

This code uses the CAPI shortcut we described earlier to assist in obtaining the random seed data. With the exception of this shortcut, the code would be portable to other platforms—the CAPI shortcut could be replaced with appropriate code to read from /dev/random if we should wish to port to a Unix platform, or we could substitute the Intel hardware random-number gathering technique as well.

10.8.3.5 Creating Session Keys and Other Random Symmetric Keys

The Crypto-C portion of BSAFE supports a few ways we can generate symmetric keys for use by our applications. Specifically, we can manipulate the key data directly, or we can request that a key be generated for us by the underlying implementation. Both ways are acceptable, but the latter is much more appropriate to a hardware HSM context. We'll go through both techniques here, but if we know that our application is not going to use a hardware device for key creation and/or storage, the first way is by far the less-development-effort scenario.

Random Key Generation (The Easy Way)

As we've seen in the previous section's example code, creation and initialization of a random algorithm object is a matter of only a few lines of code (provided we use a seeding shortcut). Since this is the case (and since we'll almost always have a seeded random number generator available for IV values), in most cases we'll want to make a call to `B_GenerateRandomBytes()` to populate the "data" portion of the `KI_Item` data structure with random data. Session keys are supplied to Crypto-C through the use of the `B_KEY_OBJ` struct and a corresponding `B_SetKeyInfo()` call. For most of the algorithms we would be interested in using (except for perhaps DES), we will supply the key to Crypto-C as a key of type `KI_Item`; in other words, we will be supplying the key in a structure that consists of a transparent data buffer and a corresponding length value. Since this structure is transparent, we can set the key data to whatever we want before we initialize the algorithm for use.

To do this, the callers will need to be aware of how the algorithms they will be calling work—or at least aware enough to know how big to make the keys. If, at any time, we are unsure about the appropriate key sizes to use, we can consult the BSAFE documentation apropos to the particular AI we wish to use—the requirements of key creation will be listed there, including size and the appropriate KI type expected by the library. As we've stated throughout this book, most of the time when we are working at an application layer (e.g., building business logic), we will be implementing one of a few algorithms that meet our security policy/requirements—so fortunately, there are only a few key lengths we have to remember. In the case of a cipher that takes a variable-length key, we have one of a few choices for key length when we're obtaining random data from a PRNG.

Using the example code from the symmetric encryption example, we could replace the line where we used a hardcoded key with the following lines to use a randomly generated key:

```
ITEM keyValue = {NULL_PTR, 0};
keyValue.len = 16; //16 bytes = 128 bits
keyValue.data = (POINTER)malloc(keyValue.len);
checkstatus(B_GenerateRandomBytes(random, keyValue.data,
        keyValue.len, NULL));
```

This code populates an ITEM with the appropriate randomly generated key material. Used in conjunction with the symmetric cryptographic API, this would be key data of type KI_ITEM just the same way as our hard coded key was.

Random Key Generation (The Hard Way)

The technique described previously works very well—for software keys. If we wish to use an HSM, creating the keys in software may not be desirable or even possible. If we wish to use an API that abstracts us one layer from the key (and hence works well with a hardware context where the key cannot be transparent), we'll want to turn to BSAFE's symmetric key generation API. This API is crystallized in the functions B_SymmetricKeyGenerateInit() and B_SymmetricKeyGenerate(). These two functions allow us to create a symmetric key while keeping the key data (and structure) opaque; while this API is more complicated to use in the case of software keys, it is useful in the case of hardware keys. The API is straightforward, but to use this API, we'll need to make sure we create a chooser that contains AM_SYMMETRIC_KEY_TOKEN_GEN.

10.8.3.6 Asymmetric Key Generation

Creation of an RSA or DSA key for use within Crypto-C is again similar to every other API call in the library with a few notable exceptions; the AM AM_RSA_KEY_GEN is included in at least one chooser that's in scope and can be supplied to the generation process, the identifier AI_RSAKeyGen is used during the call to B_SetAlgorithmInfo(), and the functions B_GenerateInit() and B_GenerateKeypair() are used to do the work of key generation. Filling in the details surrounding these functions, the following steps would be required to generate a key pair:

1. Create a chooser containing AM_RSA_KEY_GEN.
2. Instantiate the appropriate algorithm and key objects.
3. Call B_CreateAlgorithmObject() to contain the key generation state information.
4. Create a parameter struct of type A_RSA_KEY_GEN_PARAMS, and set the struct members to the appropriate values for our application.
5. Call B_SetAlgorithmInfo() to bind the parameters in the A_RSA_KEY_GEN_PARAMS to the algorithm object and specify type AI_RSAKeyGen.
6. Instantiate and initialize a pseudo-random number generator and seed it with random data for use in the key generation procedure.
7. Call B_GenerateInit() to bind the key generation chooser to the algorithm object.
8. Call B_GenerateKeypair, supplying structs for the private and public keys and supplying the random number source we are going to use for the key generation procedure.

9. Free the resources allocated in support of the above.

Again, to express this with more specificity, the following code will generate an asymmetric key pair for subsequent use in signing or asymmetric encryption operations:

```
B_ALGORITHM_METHOD *RSA_KEYGEN_CHOOSER[] = {
    &AM_RSA_KEY_GEN,
    (B_ALGORITHM_METHOD *)NULL_PTR
};

B_ALGORITHM_OBJ keygen = (B_ALGORITHM_OBJ)NULL_PTR;

B_KEY_OBJ publicKey = 0;
B_KEY_OBJ privateKey = 0;

//set up the params structure
unsigned char pubexp[] = {0x01, 0x00, 0x01}; //value 65537
A_RSA_KEY_GEN_PARAMS keygenParams;
keygenParams.modulusBits = 1024; //size of key
  //public exponent is usually one of a few small prime values
//here we're using 65537
keygenParams.publicExponent.data = pubexp;
keygenParams.publicExponent.len = sizeof(pubexp);

//create the objects we need
handleerror(B_CreateAlgorithmObject (&keygen));
handleerror(B_CreateKeyObject(&publicKey));
handleerror(B_CreateKeyObject(&privateKey));

handleerror(B_SetAlgorithmInfo (keygen, AI_RSAKeyGen,
                                  (POINTER)&keygenParams));

handleerror(B_GenerateInit (keygen, RSA_KEYGEN_CHOOSER,
                              (A_SURRENDER_CTX *)NULL_PTR));


handleerror(B_GenerateKeypair
                (keygen, publicKey, privateKey,
                 randomObj, NULL));

B_DestroyKeyObject (&publicKey);
B_DestroyKeyObject (&privateKey);
```

The handleerror function is similar in content to the function we used earlier for handling BSAFE error conditions, and the details of setting up the random number generator have been left out for portability; however, this code details the generation of an RSA key for use with BSAFE Crypto-C. This code is reproduced on the companion CD-ROM with the missing pieces filled in within the /Examples/ Chapter 10/Asym_Keygen directory.

ON THE CD

10.8.3.7 Exporting and Importing Keys (The Easy Way)

As we've see during the discussion of symmetric algorithms within Crypto-C, the most direct way to serialize key data (and to deserialize that same data) is to manipulate the data through the extremely transparent Crypto-C Key construct; in describing the method as "direct," note that this does not imply that the method is "easier." Specifically, manipulation of anything other than certain types of symmetric keys presupposes a familiarity of the algorithm in question by the developer (thereby limiting the degree with which the caller can be abstracted from the implementation details). Moreover, there are several situations in which direct control of the key is not possible (such as a hardware scenario: HSM, accelerators, etc.), and thereby precludes direct copying of the key.

To address the need for an abstract key manipulation-API, the RSA Crypto-C provides several useful pieces of functionality used for the manipulation of key data in an opaque way. With the exception of certain hardware contexts (which we will cover in more detail later in this section), the primary functionality used by BSAFE for this comes about via the API calls B_GetKeyInfo() and B_SetKeyInfo(). Most of the time, when we are working with Crypto-C, and we want to make sure we can export and import a key of a more complicated type than a contiguous buffer (e.g., an AES key), we will want to use these functions to render the key into a format we can print or store more easily than the default native format. For example, we could take a key of the RSA type KI_RSAPublic (which is not printable, serialized, or contiguous) and use GetKeyInfo() to turn it into type KI_RSAPublicBER (which will be BER encoded and therefore serialized and contiguous).

The following code illustrates how this is done with RSA:

```
ITEM keyBER;
//obtain the key info
int status = B_GetKeyInfo ((POINTER *)
      &keyBER, publicKey, KI_RSAPublicBER);
```

After this call is made, the data portion of the keyBER ITEM struct will contain a serialized representation of the public key that we can save for later use.

Note that when using DSA instead of RSA, we can merely substitute KI_DSAPublicBER in the call to B_GetKeyInfo()—everything else remains the same.

10.8.4 Wrapping Keys

Key wrapping is provided to the developer two ways within the BSAFE library; recalling our previous discussions of key wrapping, this is where we export the key to a serialized string and apply cryptography to it to ensure it is protected. Developers can undertake to implement the wrapping functionality directly (by manipulating the cryptographic primitives themselves to implement the functionality), or by using the key wrapping API. Note that the key wrapping API does not offer much of an advantage over and above our implementing the functionality ourselves in terms of code brevity, but it does provide a layer of standards compliance that would be difficult to implement ourselves. Additionally (and probably most importantly), the key wrapping API allows a key created and used within Crypto-C to be used within SSL-C (and vice versa). Therefore, those of us who will be using both SSL-C and Crypto-C would do well to familiarize ourselves with this functionality. Since there is an example within the Crypto-C documentation dedicated entirely to explicit demonstration of how to use the key wrapping API (specifically, `group__KEY__WRAP__SAMPLE.html` within the library documentation), we will provide only cursory usage examples within this section.

If we wish to wrap keys using the BSAFE API, we will need to follow these steps:

1. Instantiate the algorithm and key objects that are required.
2. Initialize the key object (`B_CreateKeyObject()`) and the algorithm object (`B_CreateAlgorithmObject()`).
3. Create an algorithm chooser that contains the encryption algorithm that will be used.
4. Create a key chooser that contains the type of key that is to be wrapped.
5. (Optionally) create a "params" struct that will hold any initialization information (such as IV). Note that since we will most often use the key wrapping functionality for compatibility with SSL-C, we will most often use the `AI_SSLC_KeyWrap` identifier (actually, given the fact that this option also encodes the key information, this is a useful choice in any context where key wrapping is required). Depending on the type of wrapping AI we select, other values must be manipulated within the params struct at this time. For our purposes, we will need to set IV, encryption algorithm identifier, and whether to PEM encode the key).
6. Call `B_SetAlgorithmInfo()`, specifying the params struct that we created and populated in the previous step, as well as the algorithm identifier (AI) corresponding to the type of wrapping function we wish to employ.
7. Call `B_SetKeyInfo()`, specifying the type of symmetric algorithm key we will be using, as well as the key data we wish to use.

8. Call `B_WrapKeyInit()`, specifying the symmetric key we will be using as well as the chooser that contains the encryption algorithm that will be used during the wrapping process.
9. If one is not already available for use, instantiate, initialize, and seed a random number source.
10. Call `B_WrapKey()`, providing a buffer for the key output, the input key to be wrapped, the key chooser (specifying key type), and the random algorithm.
11. Free all the resources created, destroying any objects we created along the way.

For example, the following sample code demonstrates how to wrap a key. Note that as mentioned, the BSAFE documentation contains a parallel example of how to implement this functionality:

```
B_KEY_METHOD *KEY_WRAP_CHOOSER[] = {
    &KM_PKCS_RSA_PRIVATE_BER_KEY,
        (B_KEY_METHOD *)NULL_PTR };

B_ALGORITHM_METHOD *WRAPPING_ALG_CHOOSER[] = {
    &AM_DES_EDE3_CBC_DECRYPT,
    &AM_DES_EDE3_CBC_ENCRYPT,
    (B_ALGORITHM_METHOD *)NULL_PTR };


B_SSLC_KEY_WRAP_PARAMS wrapParams;

//generate the wrapping key
B_KEY_OBJ wrappingKey;
checkstatus(B_CreateKeyObject(&wrappingKey));
//generate the wrapping algorithm
B_ALGORITHM_OBJ wrapper;
checkstatus(B_CreateAlgorithmObject(&wrapper));
//put key data into the wrapping key
checkstatus(B_SetKeyInfo(wrappingKey,
    KI_Item, symmetricData));

//we need to set all the wrapping key info
wrapParams.encryptAlgorithm = AI_AES_CBC;
    wrapParams.iv = (POINTER)malloc(16); //AES BLOCK SIZE
    wrapParams.pemEncode = 1;
    memcpy(wrapParams.iv, iv, 16);
checkstatus(B_SetAlgorithmInfo(wrapper, AI_SSLC_KeyWrap,
                                    (POINTER)&wrapParams));
```

```
//do the key wrapping
checkstatus(B_WrapKeyInit(wrapper, wrappingKey,
    WRAPPING_ALG_CHOOSER, (A_SURRENDER_CTX *)NULL_PTR));

//set up output buffer and length
checkstatus(B_WrapKey(wrapper, wrapOut, &wrapOutLen,
                         sizeof(wrapOut), privateKey,
                         KEY_WRAP_CHOOSER, rand,
                         (A_SURRENDER_CTX *)NULL_PTR)) ;
```

10.9 ENCRYPTION/DECRYPTION EXAMPLES

The following encryption examples are provided in (hopefully) a manner that can be cut and pasted by a developer into applications under development. Since the Crypto-C requires quite a bit of ancillary preparation prior to usage, it is the goal of these examples to provide classes that can be reused by application developers easily and quickly.

10.9.1 Sample Encryption and Decryption C++ Classes

The following example classes are provided that create a layer of abstraction from the API implementation details. They use the Crypto-C implementation internally, but perform the details of setting up the library, cleaning up data after use, and so on. It isn't necessary that a developer use these classes, but it is recommended that the developer centralize his or her calls into the API; doing so alleviates some of the complexities associated with multiple calls into the API and helps to cut down on the number of skills required for personnel to do maintenance programming.

The class that we've provided appears as follows:

```
class Buffer;

class AESCipher {
public:
    AESCipher();
    ~AESCipher();
    void Encrypt(const Buffer& plainText,
                 Buffer & cipherText,
                 Buffer & key);
    void Decrypt(const Buffer& cipherText,
                Buffer & plainText,
                Buffer & key);
```

```
private:
    void Init();
    void CreateStructures();
    char * bsafetypes;
};
```

At its bare minimum, this class hides much of the complexity from the developer. We can, of course, extend the functionality to perform other tasks such as by adding an "iterative" interface that allows a developer to send a large amount of data (the performance for this "first cut" would be terrible in such as situation). We'll go ahead and add more functionality to the class to allow that type of situation to take place; let's try to keep the interface as brief and simple to use as possible:

```
class Buffer;

class AESCipher {
public:
    AESCipher();
    ~AESCipher();
    void Encrypt(const Buffer& plainText,
                 Buffer & cipherText,
                 Buffer & key);
    void Decrypt(const Buffer& cipherText,
                Buffer & plainText,
                Buffer & key);

    //multi-part methods
    void SetKey(Buffer & key);
    void EncryptUpdate(const Buffer& plainText,
                       Buffer & cipherText);
    void DecryptUpdate(const Buffer& cipherText,
                       Buffer & plainText);
    void EncryptFinal(Buffer & cipherText);
    void DecryptFinal(Buffer & plainText);

private:
    void Init();
    void CreateStructures();
    char * bsafetypes;
};
```

Having added this, we can go ahead and iteratively call the class in a manner similar to the API added by the Java API. The implementation of this class is a bit painstaking, because we're going to handle much of the overhead associated with calling the RSA library internally, but with a bit of care, we can implement a robust class that is highly automated for all the developers on our team (and subsequent maintenance programmers) to use. This is the same approach used within the Framework demonstrated in the example Framework in Chapter 11 on the CD-ROM (/Examples/Chapter11/Framework). Here are some of the more important points:

Construction/Destruction: As you can probably guess, we're going to handle the details of creating the appropriate key, algorithm, and other artifacts required by BSAFE during the construction of the object, and we're going to handle the destruction of those artifacts during destruction of the object. We'll go ahead and use the member `bsafetypes` to hold this information; even though it claims to be of type `char*`, we'll actually cast this pointer to a new class type that we'll declare within our application. While this approach has some inherent type in-safety, which we will have to handle internally, it also servers as a convenience to callers so they do not have to include the BSAFE headers directly since we will be making use of those types within our new class. This could just as easily have been a struct, but the decision was made to use a class so we can self-initialize the memory and self-clear it and thus provide another layer of abstraction.

Encryption/Decryption: The encryption methodology is exactly what we would expect it to be. It's implemented using the symmetric functions we've outlined throughout this section, and performs the encryption on an as-needed basis. Additionally, we've set up the methods to report error conditions using a new exception type (mapping the BSAFE errors to textual descriptions for each of the possible error conditions).

And that's it! We've just taken a very complicated API and rendered it much simpler to use using automation. The callers of our new class do not need to know how to use any of the BSAFE structures (although they are currently responsible for their own key management). Abstracting the logic one step further, we could author a `Key` class and add a `GenerateKey()` method in the cipher class that would handle the details of key generation for us; let's go ahead and add that now:

```
void GenerateKey(Buffer & key) const;
```

In fact, there is quite a bit more we can add to these classes to round them out. That's what we've attempted to do on the companion CD-ROM within the framework code on the CD-ROM. Look for yourself and feel free to modify the samples as much as you'd like.

10.10 SIGNING AND VERIFYING DATA

The signing and verification API, as we shall see, is almost "call for call" identical with the encryption API. This is one of the strengths of BSAFE: the sequence of calls, once learned, is used over and over again to accomplish most anything that can be done within the library. Even though a developer is likely to be familiar with the calls that he or she needs to make, let's go through the specific calls in depth to make sure there is no ambiguity.

10.10.1 Signing Data

As with the encryption API, the sequence of events is fairly straightforward; the use of the API basically comes down to these steps: instantiation, construction, initialization, sign-specific API calls, and destruction. In more depth, let's look at the series of calls that we would make in a typical signing operation; these are the steps required for signing:

1. Instantiate an algorithm chooser containing the appropriate asymmetric (signing) algorithm we will use for our signing operation, the message digest function we will use to compute the digest (hash) of the message.
2. Declare the algorithm object for the sign/verify operation.
3. "Create" the algorithm object; in other words, prepare (preinitialize) the struct by calling `B_CreateAlgorithmObject()`.
4. Initialize the algorithm object by calling `B_SetAlgorithmInfo()`, specifying the appropriate algorithm identifier (`AI`) corresponding to the asymmetric cryptography function and hash algorithm we wish to use. For most purposes, we will want to use `AI_SHA1WithRSAEncryption`, although there may be situations (e.g., in the federal government) where we might wish to use another value here such as `AI_DSAWithSHA1`.
5. Create (or load) a private key for use in the signing operation (note that this description does not include any additionally required steps for initializing the key, such as calls to `B_CreateKeyObject()` or `B_SetKeyInfo()` and so forth).
6. Initialize the signing algorithm by calling `B_SignInit()` and specifying the private key, chooser containing the algorithms, and (optionally) a surrender context.
7. We now supply the data that is to be signed in "chunks" to the digest function by iteratively calling `B_SignUpdate()`. Note that we must call `B_SignUpdate()` at least once, since this call is the only mechanism available to use where we may specify the data to be signed (although we must call it at least once, there is no upper limit on the amount of times we can call it).

8. If we are using RSA, we do not require a random source. If we are using DSA or another algorithm that does require random numbers, we will need to instantiate, initialize, and seed a random source at this point (this can be done earlier depending on style and preference—we do not require it until the B_SignFinal() portion of the sequence).
9. At this point, we are ready to finalize the operation and "commit" the data that has been supplied into the signature process. We do this by calling `B_SignFinal()`. In addition to output buffer and output buffer length (for storing the created signature value), we may also require at this point a source of randomness (DSA will require a random source here—for RSA, we can supply a null-pointer). We also supply a surrender context in the event we wish to make use of this portion of the API.
10. We will wish to free any resources we have allocated; in addition to any resources allocated by the user, we will wish to make calls to `B_Destroy AlgorithmObject()` for any algorithms objects that we've created (e.g., the signing algorithm) and calls to `B_DestroyKeyObject()` for any keys that were created.

And that's all there is to it! The following sample code has been provided for the convenience of the reader (and to view these steps in context). The following code performs a signature operation on some test data:

```
    B_ALGORITHM_METHOD *SIGN_CHOOSER[] = {
      &AM_SHA,
      &AM_RSA_CRT_ENCRYPT,
      (B_ALGORITHM_METHOD *)NULL_PTR
    };

    B_ALGORITHM_OBJ sign;
    B_KEY_OBJ privateKey = GetPrivateKey();
    char * toSign = "data to sign";
    unsigned char signature[BIG_ENOUGH_BUFFER];
    unsigned int outputLen;

    checkstatus(B_CreateAlgorithmObject(&sign));
    checkstatus(B_SetAlgorithmInfo(sign, AI_SHA1WithRSAEncryption,
NULL));
    checkstatus(B_SignInit(sign, privateKey, SIGN_CHOOSER, NULL));
    checkstatus(B_SignUpdate(sign, (unsigned char*)toSign,
strlen(toSign),
                         NULL));
```

```
    checkstatus(B_SignFinal(sign, signature, &outputLen,
sizeof(signature),
                                NULL, NULL));
```

10.10.2 Verifying a Signature

In keeping with the rest of the RSA BSAFE Crypto-C API, the procedure to verify a digital signature is almost identical to the procedure used to create it. Instead of using the sequence of `B_SignInit()`, `B_SignUpdate()`, and `B_SignFinal()`, we'll substitute the sequence `B_VerifyInit()`, `B_VerifyUpdate()`, and `B_VerifyFinal()`. Otherwise, the steps are the same. To see that this is true, let's go through the specific steps that are required to verify a digital signature:

1. Instantiate an algorithm chooser containing the verification portion of the asymmetric algorithm (this will correspond to the algorithm that was used for the signing operation. For example, if we used DSA to sign, our chooser would contain `AM_DSA_VERIFY`, and if we used RSA, we would want to include `RSA_DECRYPT`) as well as the message digest function we will use to compute the digest (hash) of the message.
2. Declare the algorithm object for the verify operation.
3. "Create" the algorithm object; in other words, initialize the struct by calling `B_CreateAlgorithmObject()`.
4. Initialize the algorithm object by calling `B_SetAlgorithmInfo()`, specifying the appropriate algorithm identifier (`AI`) corresponding to the asymmetric cryptography function and hash algorithm we wish to use.
5. Create (or load) a public key for use in the verification operation (note that this description does not include any additionally required steps such as initializing the key such as calls to `B_CreateKeyObject()` or `B_SetKeyInfo()` and so forth).
6. Initialize the verification algorithm by calling `B_VerifyInit()` and specifying the public key, chooser containing the algorithms, and (optionally) a surrender context.
7. We now supply the data that is signed to the digest function by iteratively calling `B_VerifyUpdate()`. Note that, just as we must call `B_SignUpdate()` at least once, we also must call `B_VerifyUpdate` at least once (although we can call it as many times as we like with as much data as we like).
8. Now we are ready to "commit" the data that has been supplied to the verification process; we do this by calling `B_VerifyFinal()`. We will specify the signature value as input and the length of the signature; for all the algorithms we will make use of in this book, a random source is not required for the verification process. Therefore, we will supply a null pointer instead of a random source. Lastly, we may optionally supply a surrender context at this time.

9. The return value from `B_VerifyFinal()` should be retained or examined at this time, as it will indicate whether the signature was valid. In the case of a valid signature, 0 will be returned. In the case of an invalid signature, the usual return value is `BE_SIGNATURE` although note that other return/error values may also be generated depending on the algorithm in use.
10. At this point, we will free any resources allocated for what we have done so far; this includes calling `B_DestroyAlgorithmObject()` for any algorithms we have allocated, and `B_DestroyKeyObject()` for any keys we have allocated.

It is particularly important to note the penultimate step in the preceding list; in almost all other instances in our usage of the library, the return value communicates error status, and error status only. As such, we might be tempted to overlook the return value as the mechanism the library employs to impart information about the valid/invalid status of the signature. Therefore, special attention needs to be drawn to the fact that the return value communicates both error status and an invalid signature value in the case of signature verification.

The following sample code demonstrates this in practice:

```
B_ALGORITHM_METHOD *VERIFY_CHOOSER[] = {
  &AM_SHA,
  &AM_RSA_DECRYPT,
  (B_ALGORITHM_METHOD *)NULL_PTR
};

B_ALGORITHM_OBJ verify;
B_KEY_OBJ publicKey = GetPublicKey();
checkstatus(B_CreateAlgorithmObject(&verify));
checkstatus(B_SetAlgorithmInfo(verify, AI_SHA1WithRSAEncryption,
                        NULL));
checkstatus(B_VerifyInit(verify, publicKey, VERIFY_CHOOSER, NULL));
checkstatus(B_VerifyUpdate(verify, (unsigned char*)toSign,
                        strlen(toSign), NULL));
//note the significance of the return value here
int result = B_VerifyFinal(verify, signature, outputLen, NULL,
NULL);
bool verified = false;
if(result == 0) {
    verified = true;
} else if(result == BE_SIGNATURE) {
    verified = false;
} else {
    //some other problem occured such as format or internal error
    //turn over to the default error handling
```

```
        checkstatus(result);
    }
```

10.11 SIGNATURE EXAMPLES

As with the encryption examples, the goal of the examples provided in this chapter is to both provide a reusable framework for application developers, and to demonstrate the library functionality. We've gone ahead and created a few Signature/Verification classes that developers can use either as a frame of reference or directly in their applications.

10.11.1 Sample Signature and Verification Classes

In much the same way as we've tried to abstract the developer away from the details of encipherment through using a centralized class, we've tried to abstract the signature generation and verification process somewhat. Developers may find it easier to centralize the signature functionality in one place to make their software easier to debug and more "componentized." In so doing, we could create a class with a similar interface to the following:

```
class RSASignature {
public:
    RSASignature();
    ~RSASignature();

    void Sign(const Buffer& toSign,
            Buffer & signature,
            const Buffer& key);
    bool Verify(const Buffer& toVerify,
                const Buffer & signature,
                const Buffer& key);
private:
    void Init();
    void CreateStructures();
    char * bsafetypes;
};
```

However, we might want to supply large amounts of data (just as with encryption), so we could add a few extra methods to facilitate this. Doing so, we would now have a class design much like the following:

```
class RSASignature {
public:
    RSASignature();
    ~RSASignature();

    void Sign(const Buffer& toSign,
            Buffer & signature,
            const Buffer& key);
    bool Verify(const Buffer& toVerify,
                const Buffer & signature,
                const Buffer& key);

    //multipart interface
    void SetKey(const Buffer& key);
    void SignUpdate(const Buffer& toSign);
    void SignFinal(Buffer & signature);
    void VerifyUpdated(const Buffer& toVerify);
    bool VerifyFinal(const Buffer& signature);
private:
    void Init();
    void CreateStructures();
    char * bsafetypes;
};
```

This interface is much easier to use and centralized, which offers the same advantages we pointed out in creating the sample encryption classes.

10.11.2 Signing User-Supplied Text (Segregated Threading and the BSAFE Surrender Context)

The following example demonstrates how to use the surrender context to perform status update information during the key generation and signature process. We've also demonstrated how to use threads to segregate functionality (such as a UI) from the signature process—since threading is a very platform-specific endeavor, we've chosen the Microsoft Windows platform on which to demonstrate this approach in the CD-ROM example. Following is a code listing of the surrender context function in use; for the purposes of this code listing, note that this is not running in an isolated thread—to see that thread set up and started, the full application that uses this is located on the companion CD-ROM under the example material for this chapter (/Examples/Chapter 10/Threading).

ON THE CD

The following demonstration code sets up a surrender context and uses it. Note that since the `handle` value accepted by the callback function can be anything we like, it is helpful to supply a struct or class that we can use to govern the behavior of the function (much as we would do with a thread). The following listing demonstrates this:

```
class SurrenderInfo {
public:
    bool init;
    bool keepGoing;
};

int surrenderFunction(POINTER handle) {
    if(!((SurrenderInfo*)handle)->init) {
        //display any first time status info
        ((SurrenderInfo*)handle)->init = true;
    } else {
        //display progress bar
    }
    if(!((SurrenderInfo*)handle)->keepGoing) {
        return -1;
    }
    return 0;
}
void main() {
    A_SURRENDER_CTX surrender;
    SurrenderInfo handle;
    handle.init = false;
    handle.keepGoing = true;

    surrender.Surrender = surrenderFunction;
    surrender.handle = (POINTER)&handle;
    surrender.reserved = 0;
    //now we can use "surrender" in any function that accepts it
```

10.12 MESSAGE DIGESTS AND MESSAGE AUTHENTICATION CODES (MAC)

Crypto-C implements MAC and nonkeyed hashing (digests) in almost exactly the same way; this makes sense given that the two procedures make use of the same underlying cryptographic functions. Therefore, since the two procedures are almost identical from a usage perspective in this library, we can cover them both at this time in one unified section. First, we'll go through how to create a digest from arbitrary input data, and once we've gone through that, we'll talk about the additional steps required to create a MAC rather than a hash (there aren't many).

As we've seen with other Crypto-C routines, the core API calls (surrounded as they are by the numerous resource management and initialization calls) are the only portion of our usage that differs in any significant way. In the case of digests (both keyed and unkeyed), the API calls we need to note are `B_DigestInit()`, `B_DigestUpdate()`, and `B_DigestFinal()`. To "prime" these calls (i.e., to ready these functions to be called), we must follow the appropriate sequence for initialization, and then once we're done making these calls, we'll free the resources that are required for their operation.

Let's step through the sequence, calling particular attention to the "points of interest" along the way:

1. Instantiate an algorithm chooser containing the message digest function we wish to use (note that this is the same for both hashing and MAC functionality). Most of the time, we'll wish to create a chooser that contains at least `AM_SHA`.
2. Declare the algorithm object for the digest operation.
3. "Create" (preinitialize) the algorithm object by calling `B_CreateAlgorithmObject()`.
4. In the case of a simple hash, we'll immediately call `B_SetAlgorithmInfo()`, specifying the type of digest we'll be using (most of the time, we'll be using `AI_SHA1`).
5. We call `B_DigestInit()`. The inputs to this function are a key (which will be null since we're not performing a keyed hash), the digest chooser (the one we created that contains the `AM` mapping to this `AI`), and (optionally) a surrender context.
6. Call `B_DigestUpdate()`. This is our opportunity to iteratively supply the data of which we wish to create a hash; we will need to call the update function at least once, since this is our only opportunity to specify the input data.
7. Call `B_DigestFinal()` to complete the digest operation. This call will "finalize" the digest operation and create an output value. In calling this function, we will specify a buffer in which to place the digest value, an integer specifying the size of the buffer we've supplied, and a pointer to an integer that the library will populate with a value corresponding to the size of the hash placed in the output buffer.
8. Destroy the algorithm object created by calling `B_DestroyAlgorithmObject()`.

This is fairly simple to demonstrate; the following sample code demonstrates how these steps are implemented for hashing:

```
B_ALGORITHM_METHOD *MAC_HASH_CHOOSER[] = {
  &AM_SHA,
  (B_ALGORITHM_METHOD *)NULL_PTR
};

char * toHash = "to Hash";
unsigned char digest[BIG_ENOUGH_BUFFER];
unsigned int outputLen;

B_ALGORITHM_OBJ hash;
checkstatus(B_CreateAlgorithmObject(&hash));
checkstatus(B_SetAlgorithmInfo(hash, AI_SHA1, NULL));
checkstatus(B_DigestInit(hash, NULL, MAC_HASH_CHOOSER, NULL));
checkstatus(B_DigestUpdate(hash, (unsigned char*)toHash,
            strlen(toHash), NULL));
checkstatus(B_DigestFinal(hash, digest, &outputLen, sizeof(digest),
            NULL));
B_DestroyAlgorithmObject(&hash);
```

Creating an HMAC is not much more difficult; there are some additional steps, but all the calls that are used are the same. The differences are the following:

- We will need to create and initialize a key object. We'll set the value of the key explicitly.
- We will need to declare and populate a `B_DIGEST_SPECIFIER` struct. This struct should contain the type of digest we will use during the MAC operation.
- Rather than specifying a null pointer, we will include the key we created in our call to `B_DigestInit()`.

Therefore, putting these new steps in context, here are the steps for creating a MAC:

1. Instantiate an algorithm chooser. For our purposes, most of the time this will be `AM_SHA`.
2. Declare the algorithm object and key object for the MAC operation.
3. Declare the `B_DIGEST_SPECIFIER` struct, and initialize the internal state to zero.
4. Set the `B_DIGEST_SPECIFIER` struct's `digestInfoType` constant to reflect the algorithm we're using for our MAC. In most cases, we'll set it to `AI_SHA1`.
5. Preinitialize the key object by calling `B_CreateKeyObject()`.
6. Create an `ITEM` containing the key data we wish to use.

7. Initialize the key object to update the internal state of the object with the key data we wish to use; we'll do this by calling `B_SetKeyInfo()` and specifying the item we created in the previous step.
8. Preinitialize the algorithm object by calling `B_CreateAlgorithmObject()`.
9. Initialize the algorithm object by calling `B_SetAlgorithmInfo()` and specifying the AI type (`AI_HMAC`) and the `B_DIGEST_SPECIFIER` struct that we created and populated.
10. Initialize the digest process by calling `B_DigestInit()`. Inputs to this function consist of the MAC key we created, the chooser, and an optional surrender context.
11. Iteratively call the update function (`B_DigestUpdate()`), specifying the data that is to be MACed. As with the digest-only routine, we will want to call this at least once. The inputs to this function are unchanged from the unkeyed digest functionality.
12. Call `B_DigestFinal()` to finalize the MAC process and create the keyed hash value. The inputs and outputs to this function are also unchanged.
13. Free the key object using `B_DestroyKeyObject()`.
14. Free the algorithm object using `B_DestroyAlgorithmObject()`.

Following are these same steps in practice:

```
B_ALGORITHM_OBJ mac;
checkstatus(B_CreateAlgorithmObject(&mac));
B_DIGEST_SPECIFIER digestSpecifier;
digestSpecifier.digestInfoType = AI_SHA1;
digestSpecifier.digestInfoParams = 0;
checkstatus(B_SetAlgorithmInfo(mac, AI_HMAC,
            (POINTER)&digestSpecifier));
ITEM key;
key.data = keyData;
key.len = sizeof(keyData);
B_KEY_OBJ macKey;
checkstatus(B_CreateKeyObject(&macKey));
checkstatus(B_SetKeyInfo(macKey, KI_Item, keyData));
checkstatus(B_DigestInit(mac, macKey,
            MAC_HASH_CHOOSER, NULL));
//the rest of the operation is unchanged except for key cleanup
```

10.13 ADVANCED FUNCTIONALITY

The RSA library does provide some very advanced functionality to application developers; in fact, a large portion of the library will not be covered within this book (just as all the libraries, there is more than enough material for a whole book on just usage alone). Included in this section are some of the more advanced features of the library, including communications options, advanced key management functionality, and so forth.

10.13.1 SSL/TLS

Unlike the other libraries we've covered so far, BSAFE segregates its SSL functionality from the certificate processing and cryptographic functionality. In other words, within the context of BSAFE, SSL is self-contained within in its own separate "package" and must be dealt with separately. By "dealt with separately," we mean specifically that the developer must install a different package to use it, the developer will reference different include files, different library files, and will use a different, unrelated, API to make use of the functionality.

As developers, the news that we will need to learn a completely new API to make use of the SSL functionality isn't fantastic, but in this case, it's not terrible either—the API, as we will see, is "familiar" and easy to learn. The familiarity of the API comes about as it uses similar constructs as the OpenSSL library. This is not entirely surprising, as Eric Young (a primary author of SSLeay, which later became the foundation for OpenSSL) played an integral part in the development of the SSL-C library. In addition to finding the similarities to OpenSSL familiar, we can also see that the developers of SSL-C have further reduced the learning curve by electing to "mirror" the ubiquitous Berkeley sockets API. This is not to say that the SSL-C calls are identical to the Berkeley calls (they aren't) or that we can intuit what the names of calls will be ahead of time (we can't). However, there is enough similarity that we know the order in which calls need to be made on both the client and server sides.

Within this chapter, we are going to concentrate primarily on two very common scenarios: connecting to an SSL-enabled server, and implementing the server side of that same situation. Doing both of these tasks (i.e., making generic SSL socket connections) using SSL-C is a relatively straightforward process. It involves initializing the library, initializing the connection-specific structures we'll need, making our connection, and then freeing the resources we've allocated. Let's go through each of these phases in a bit more depth.

10.13.1.1 Initializing (and Freeing) the Library

The first thing we need to do when attempting to use SSL-C for SSL connections is to make sure we sandwich our code between the appropriate library management functions; we'll also need to make sure we seed the software PRNG before we use any of the SSL functionality. Specifically, here are the high-level steps we'll need to do before we can use the library:

1. Create a new library global context: We'll need to initialize the library (allowing the library to create and initialize any internal state tables that it will use) first before we use any library functionality, and we'll need to call a deinitialization routine when we're done using the library's functionality.
2. Seed the random number generator using a good random seed: We'll need to collect a random seed with which to seed the internal PRNG of the library.

10.13.1.2 Creating the Library Context

The process for meeting this first initialization step is fairly easy (or at least straightforward). The library's sample code uses the `PRODUCT_LIBRARY_NEW` macro for the initialization step. At first, this seems mildly confusing, since the library's example documentation uses this macro, but the library's documentation only makes reference of it in passing and does not include much detail on the usage of it. However, a bit of the confusion can be cleared up once we realize that the library's main header file (`sslc.h`) is merely doing a textual replace of `SSLC_library_new()` (fully documented in the docs) for `PRODUCT_LIBRARY_NEW`. Therefore, before we use any of the SSL functionality, we want to make sure we call this function once, specifying as we do so a *resource list* that will govern the operation of the product. Similar to the way in which algorithm choosers link in only the functionality required for particular cryptographic operations, resource lists in SSLC link in only those modules that are required for our particular usage. In almost every case, we'll be dealing with the default resources list—we can obtain the default resource list by using the `PRODUCT_DEFAULT_RESOURCE_LIST` macro (defined to `SSLC_get_default_resource_list()`). Putting this in context, we want to do the following before we make any further calls into the library:

```
returnVal = PRODUCT_LIBRARY_NEW(PRODUCT_DEFAULT_RESOUCE_LIST(),
            R_RES_FLAG_DEF, //default flag
            lctx); //context value
```

After making the call, we want to make sure no errors occurred; we do this by making sure the return value is equal to `R_ERROR_NONE` (no error). This will prepare the library for use and set up the internal structures that are required before we can proceed. The context value will be subsequently used by us during the actual connection to the server or for accepting connections from clients.

10.13.1.3 Loading Error Strings

This is an optional step that will map error strings to error numbers; by not including this step, we can reduce the image footprint (on disk and in memory) somewhat, but we will lose readable error information. The call `SSL_load_error_` strings() loads these error strings and maps them to the error codes. In context, the following code will load the library:

```
SSL_load_error_strings();
```

Despite the somewhat larger footprint, most of the time we will be loading the error strings, since the addition of human-readable text to a log or output file is a boon to debugging (and production support) situations. Unless there is a very good reason not to use this function, we highly recommend that this be called.

10.13.1.4 Initializing the PRNG

We need to find a secure source of randomness to seed the SSL-C software PRNG. Developers can "cheat" and use the output of their platform's RNG if available (such as /dev/random on Unix or the self-seeded CAPI generator), or they can implement a seed-gathering methodology themselves. The routine for seeding the PRNG is:

```
R_rand_seed(R_rand_get_default() //default RNG
        pSeedVal,     //seed value
        nSeedLen);  //seed len
```

This routine initializes the random number generator internal to the library, and is required before any connections can be attempted.

10.13.1.5 Connection Functions

To actually connect to a server, we will use almost exactly the same methodology we used in constructing a client socket connection in OpenSSL (remember, we said the APIs were historically related). In other words, if we're familiar with the OpenSSL connection methodology, implementation of SSLC sockets should be a "no brainer." While we won't reiterate all the functions involved here, since we've already covered their "cognates" in the discussion of OpenSSL, we will review some of the structures involved just to put into perspective the similarities. For example, if we wanted to create a connection to a new server, the first thing we will need to do is allocate and initialize an SSL structure; in fact, the mechanics of doing this are call-for-call identical with OpenSSL:

```
//create a new method allowing for all versions of the protocol
SSL_METHOD * method = SSLv23_client_method();
//bind method to context
SSL_CTX * ctx = SSL_CTX_new(method);
```

Moving along, we can optionally choose to set context behavior at this time (such as enabling or disabling vendor bug fixes, set supported ciphersuites, or other configuration values). A full list of the configuration values we can set is in the SSLC documentation, but these values are optional (*bsafe\sslc\sslc\doc\dev_guide\index.html*). Once we have initialized our context, we will create our SSL struct pointer the same way we did in OpenSSL; we will use `SSL_new()` and specify the current context we are working with. Once the SSL structure is created, and again in a manner similar to the OpenSSL API, we will bind the underlying transport to the SSL structure through a call to `SSL_set_fd()`. When using OpenSSL, we used the call `SSL_set_BIO()` instead of `SSL_set_fd()`, but the purpose is the same: bind a connected Berkeley (or Winsock) `SOCKET` structure to the SSL instance, and give the SSLC library control over the socket. At this point, we will need to inform the library that we're connected in "client mode" and that the socket is connected; this is done through the function `SSL_set_connect_state()`. Now, just as we did with OpenSSL, we can read on the socket (`SSL_read()`) or write on the socket (`SSL_write()`) to accomplish our application functionality. When done, we'll need to close the socket (`SSL_shutdown()`, disconnecting/freeing the underlying Berkeley socket), free all the resources we've allocated (`SSL_free()` and `SSL_CTX_free()`), and finally free the library (`PRODUCT_LIBRARY_FREE()`).

Since we've seen these routines before, we won't go into detailed usage at this time. However, one thing we should mention is that by default, certificate processing (verification) is turned off in the SSLC library; to enable it, we will need to insert a call in our software similar to:

```
SSL_CTX_set_verify_mode(ctx, SSL_VERIFY_PEER);
```

This will configure the context (ctx) to verify the peer (server) certificate on a client connection. We may wish to update the certificate verification callback function (`SSL_CTX_set_app_verify_cb()`) to perform application-specific verification routines such as certificate common-name checks or other checking (serial number, etc.). Basically, we would just add our verification code within our callback function and then call the default processing implemented by the library.

10.13.1.6 Server Functions

Again, the server-side routines are very similar to that of OpenSSL. We will set up the server connection in exactly the same way we did with a client connection; all our calls are the same: we load the library, specify a resource list, specify a method (this time using a server method like `SSLv2_server_method` rather than a client method), and create the SSL context structure. There are only a few differences after this. The first difference is that we will need to either specify a client certificate or use a ciphersuite that does not require one. Referring to the SSL demonstration code, a call like the following would set "temp key" mode, which does not require that we have access to a certificate:

```
SSL_CTX_set_tmp_key_mode(ssl_ctx, SSL_TMP_512_DH|SSL_TMP_1024_DH|
        SSL_TMP_512_RSA, SSL_TMP_GENERATE_LATER));
```

If we do have access to a certificate, we will need to load it before we actually start processing connections. Loading the certificate would take place using the `SSL_CTX_use_certificate()` function. We will also need to load the corresponding certificate private key using the `SSL_CTX_use_PrivateKey()` function. Once done, we can enter an `accept()` loop as we would in any socket server implementation, binding each SOCKET returned from `accept()` to an SSL instance using the `SSL_set_bio()` function (just like OpenSSL). We'll need to inform the SSL structure that we are in connect mode (`SSL_set_accept_state()`), and then proceed to read and write data from the socket normally. When done, we deallocate the SSLC and the SOCKET structures as normal. The SSLC user documentation describes in detail the functions listed in this usage. We're again assuming that typical usage will not involve implementing a Web server, or (if it does) that such an implementation will likely use one of the more accessible APIs described in this book (e.g., the .NET server socket implementation, JCE, etc.) rather than this lower level API.

10.14 SUMMARY

Within this chapter, we've gone through some of the BSAFE usage, particularly the SSL-C and Crypto-C libraries. By now, you probably noticed the incredible power and control the library provides with respect to how the cryptographic functionality is exposed. BSAFE is a very powerful tool, and while its usage may carry with it some extra code verbosity, the material covered in this book is only a fraction of that provided by the library. We did not, for example, go into any detail with respect to the certificate library contained within the toolkit. The BSAFE certificate library is powerful enough to build a commercial CA (in fact, it has been used for just that purpose). Some of the topics that were not discussed in the chapter due to space considerations are included for additional reference on the companion CD-ROM (e.g., /Examples/Chapter 10/Certs and /Examples/Chapter 10/FIPS). In most cases, your usage will probably not require that additional functionality, but we've put some samples of it in just in case in does.

ON THE CD

11 Example Applications

In This Chapter

- Chapter Notes
- Example Catalog
- Multilibrary Generic Cryptographic Interface, C++ Framework
- File Content Protection (C++)
- Three-Tier Data Protection (Java Servlets)
- Three-Tier Data Protection (ASP)

A good number of developers (ourselves included) find it easier to learn from example source than from manuals or usage documentation. Documentation may or may not be current, but if an application compiles, runs, and does what it's supposed to do, the application is as current as it needs to be. Additionally, it is also very helpful to learn by debugging a given sample versus just looking through the source. Stepping through an example line by line can be a great way to understand the order in which functions need to be called, how they should be used, how the arguments should be structured, and so forth. Within this chapter, we've tried to provide examples that satisfy those requirements: they are readable, they compile, and you can debug them to see what's going on.

ON THE CD

This chapter contains an example-by-example map of the applications provided on the companion CD-ROM (/Examples/Chapter 11/). These applications are constructed in such a way as to exercise a variety of different cryptographic functionalities, using a number of different libraries, and in a number of different contexts. In most of the applications that we write, cryptography or other security components will not be the centerpiece of the application. In other words, we'll be authoring these components to support other functionality, and it is that other functionality that is the centerpiece. In order to best do that, it is useful to see how security functions within a broader application context. That's what this chapter tries to do: present cryptography and cryptographic components in the context of a broader application such as we might come across as we perform our day-to-day jobs. Think of this chapter as an "index of samples"—a high-level overview that describes the thought process behind bringing security to our application—from requirements, to design, to implementation. These are by no means the only ways that this can be done, but they are hopefully some common ways that a developer is likely to see again and again.

ON THE CD

All of the applications contained in this chapter can be found in this section's CD-ROM material under the directory for Chapter 11, and draw significantly on material that was introduced throughout this book. These applications, in addition, draw on each other where possible. Specifically, the first example deals with the creation of a universal framework that will be used with other applications in the samples.

Since one of the goals is ease in compiling and debugging, the examples draw on libraries that are freely and ubiquitously available. Where noncore components are required (OpenSSL), a project file that includes the appropriate directories and libraries has been included.

11.1 CHAPTER NOTES

As this chapter is a map of sample applications, we have elected not to include code snippets from the actual cryptographic routines themselves. Doing so would be both verbose and somewhat inapplicable, since the applications themselves may make indirect calls into the cryptographic libraries (calling through the centralized framework instead) and may use additional support components (MFC/windowing APIs) that are ancillary to cryptographic functionality. Instead of concentrating on the source, we've tried to concentrate on the design, approaching the applications as we would any other application and attempting to apply a step-by-step design process to ensuring the application security goals are met. In general, we've favored UML with respect to laying out design methodologies, but that's just because that's what we're familiar with—any methodology will do just as well.

11.2 EXAMPLE CATALOG

There are four examples provided in this section, although there are variations of these located on the companion CD-ROM (/Examples/Chapter 11/). These all demonstrate generic cryptographic functionality that developers might need to implement in the context of doing their day-to-day job:

- Multilibrary generic cryptographic interface, C++ framework (with policy enforcement)
- File content protection, C++
- Three-tier data protection, Java servlet
- Three-tier data protection, ASP

11.3 MULTILIBRARY GENERIC CRYPTOGRAPHIC INTERFACE, C++ FRAMEWORK

As our first example, let's create a C++ framework the other subsequent examples can draw on for cryptographic functionality. We've seen in previous chapters some of the benefits of encapsulating this functionality into one place, so this framework will provide the low-level interface and centralized point of entry to the underlying libraries.

11.3.1 Overview

As stated earlier, this is to be a library used by our various other example applications for low-level cryptographic functionality. We are going to be developing it in C++, but it can be called in numerous ways: via dynamic link, COM, JNI, or any number of other methodologies. Since we are primarily interested in creating a layer of abstraction between our applications and the underlying libraries, we will not be incorporating any centralized policy enforcement at this time or any self-protecting structures. Instead, we are using conditional compilation and abstract classes to allow callers to control the specific library their application uses. We will ideally not want to increase the size of the resultant executable by statically linking against libraries we don't have to, so we've used the visual studio "target" functionality to allow us to build in only the library we want to support.

11.3.2 Requirements

Since this is an underlying toolkit, our requirements are fairly simple and straightforward. We want a flexible toolkit that supports all of the libraries we've discussed in this book. We want to be able to configure at compile time the libraries it links against so it meets the requirements of a wide variety of applications without excessive bloat (e.g., increased size from linking against libraries not used in the application itself). We need the following functionalities to be in place:

- Configurable support for different libraries
- Symmetric encryption functionality
- Asymmetric encryption functionality
- Signature and verification
- Message digests capability

We do not have a requirement for a simplified interface here, but we will go ahead and make the interface as simple as we can. Since we are not introducing policy enforcement until the next example, we don't need to introduce wrapper classes around artifacts such as keys. That will come in the next example.

11.3.3 Environment

This toolkit should be able to support a number of different platforms, such as Windows, Unix, OS X, and so forth. We will want to use conditional compilation to make sure we target only appropriate platforms for the libraries we select, such as not trying to compile in support for CAPI on Unix. To illustrate a few different environmental scenarios, Figure 11.1 represents a UML 2.0 deployment diagram illustrating how this module will operate on a Windows platform linked against CAPI, and Figure 11.2 is a UML 2.0 deployment diagram illustrating how it might operate on Unix linked against OpenSSL.

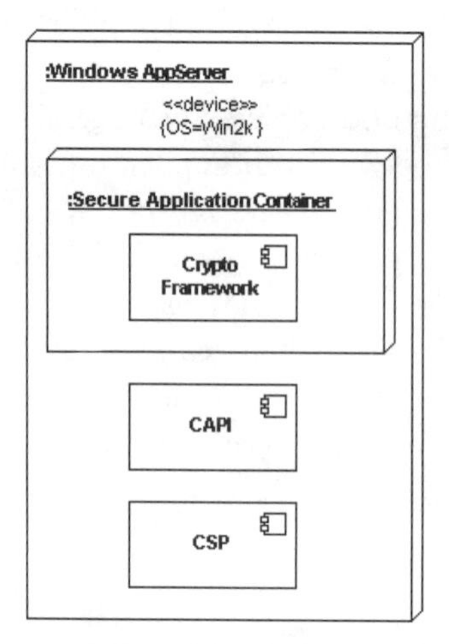

FIGURE 11.1 UML deployment diagram—Windows.

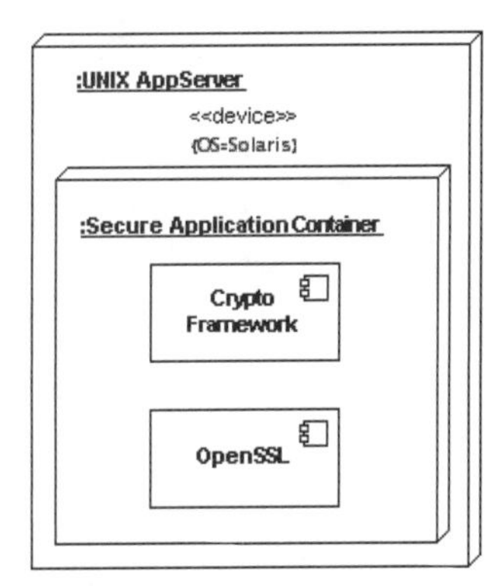

FIGURE 11.2 UML deployment diagram—Unix.

As you can see, the components behave very differently based on the environment in which they are located. They bring in different supporting components depending on which platform it is compiled for. However, we want to keep the logistics of this and any/all of the associated complexity invisible to the caller or user of the library.

11.3.4 Design

With respect to creating a functional design, we do not want to add too much complexity to the individual classes. We will not yet replace any of the types used by the cryptographic routines in creating this first lower level interface. Specifically, we will not be replacing any of the buffer types (buffers will be accepted as a pointer to a contiguous block of memory rather than an object), and we will not build in any safety with respect to how keys are handled. All of that functionality will be placed in the next example.

Since we are not building in policy enforcement at this time, our goal with this framework is the creation of a universal interface for each of the cryptographic operations we are going to support. Internal to the framework, we will translate requests to the native types required by the individual libraries themselves, and we will call the right routines within them. Figure 11.3 contains a UML 2.0 use-case diagram illustrating the various ways in which an application might call the framework.

As we can see, the interface is generic, and can be used in one call to encrypt a small piece of information, or can be used iteratively to encrypt a large volume of information serially.

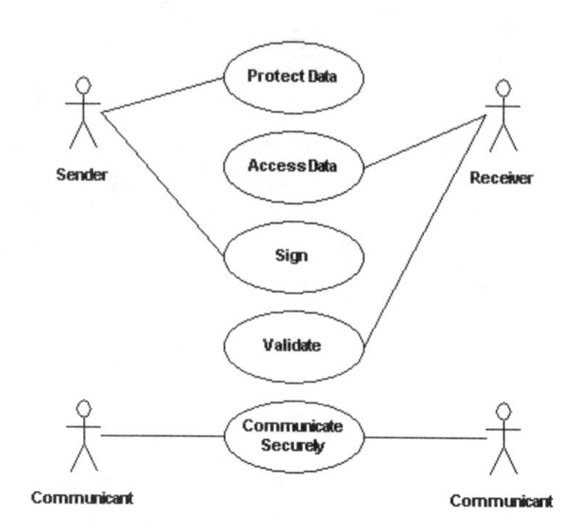

FIGURE 11.3 Framework use cases.

11.3.5 Implementation

There are a few ways this library could be improved with refinement of the implementation. Specifically, conditionally compiling in from one of three different libraries, while the most flexible approach, can present a few practical issues with respect to interoperability. In other words, depending on the application this library will support, we may need to make sure the cryptographic operations are interoperable with each other. For the most part, they are, but the mechanism that CAPI uses by default to store keys may present some interoperability difficulties if we need to exchange data with another instance of the library configured to use a different library. Specifically, CAPI's default methodology is to store signing and other asymmetric encryption keys in the context of a CSP associated with the user account context in which the application is running or (if specified) the machine on which we are running. To export that key, we need to use the appropriate exportation routines provided by CAPI. This is useful to note as we make use of the tool to build other applications; alternatively, we can eliminate this issue entirely by standardizing on one library ahead of time. The source code for this is located in /Examples/ Chapter 11/Framework on the companion CD-ROM.

ON THE CD

11.3.6 Maintenance Notes

Maintenance of this framework is straightforward. We will need to keep abreast of any changes in the underlying cryptographic libraries we have configured the tool to link against, and since some of the libraries (BSAFE) use static linkage, we may need to recompile and relink if a significant update occurs. Both CAPI and BSAFE are provided in such a way that some bug-fix releases will not require a recompile of the framework.

11.3.7 Adding Policy Enforcement

Building on the low-level interface we just created, we will now attempt to incorporate automated policy enforcement into the framework. In this iteration, in addition to having a universal interface, we are further implementing controls we can use to ensure the application is not misused accidentally and that we meet more stringent security requirements. We are still building a toolkit with the goal that our more-practical applications will make use of the functionality we've provided. We will be introducing the following additional features:

- Automated memory zeroization
- Key lifetime enforcement
- Algorithm selection enforcement
- Key quality enforcement
- Key locality enforcement

Note that these features are not always necessary, and could actually be a hindrance depending on the type of application we are authoring.

11.3.7.1 Requirements Additions

The functional requirements do not change in adding this new functionality. However, the security requirements have increased in scope. Specifically, we want our framework to be able to make sure that keys are protected as per the rules of enforcement we described in Chapter 6. We want to make sure that keys are expired after a period of time, are of a certain length and quality, and don't get moved between infrastructures (e.g., from development to QA or from QA to production). From a use-case perspective, the changes are subtle, but within the component itself, they are more drastic. Figure 11.4 contains a UML 2.0 use-case diagram illustrating the subtle changes to how the framework is used.

Note that the majority of changes relate to the caller's ability to interact with keys; specifically, an actor (caller) might now specify actions that can be performed on keys (such as determining when they expire). To illustrate what's going on under the hood, Figure 11.5 contains a UML object interaction diagram demonstrating some of the ramifications of the key-associated policy enforcement. For example, a caller might now be informed that a key is no longer useful for encryption because the useful lifetime has expired and a different key must now be used!

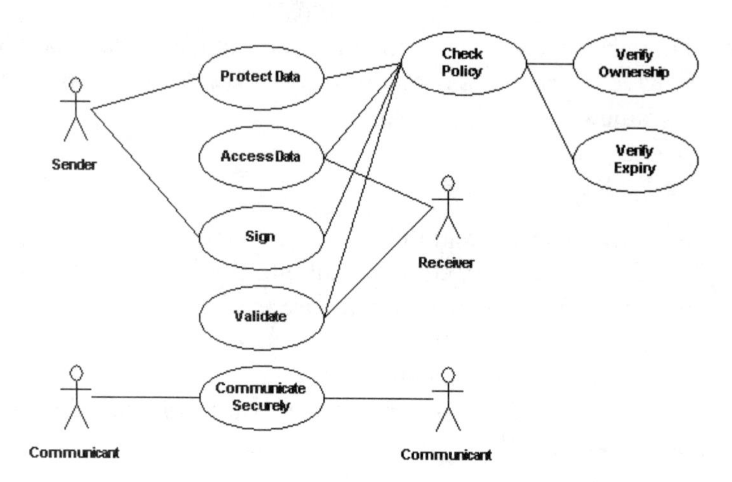

FIGURE 11.4 New framework requirements.

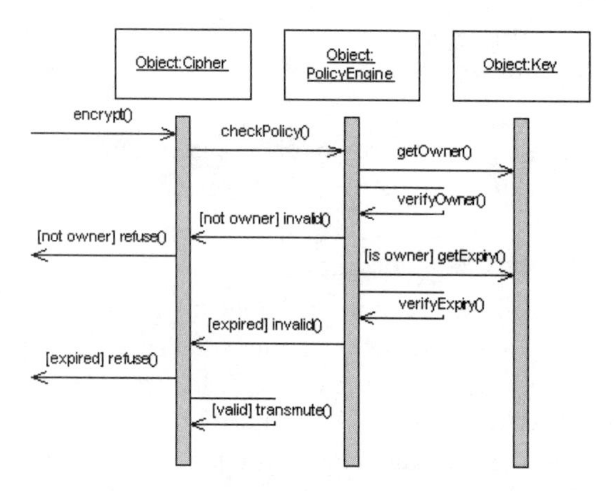

FIGURE 11.5 Object interaction updates for policy.

11.3.7.2 Implementation Additions

From a design and implementation perspective, we are implementing all of the concepts outlined in Chapter 6. We'll be making use of a serializable "interface" (implemented in C++ as a parent class) that will function in an almost identical way to Java's serializable interface. We'll use that for storing the key policy data. We'll be implementing an interface similar to Java's "SealedObject" that will allow us to apply protections (in this case, password-based key derivation) to the serialized data and allow us to require an "application password" when the data is loaded.

Implementation of this functionality consists of building additional support classes to process the additional key-related protections we've put in place and the creation of a more abstract interface that encompasses that functionality. We will use the interfaces provided in the previous example to implement these new interfaces, and by doing, so we won't waste any of the code base we've already developed.

11.4 FILE CONTENT PROTECTION (C++)

The goal of this example is to implement a level of security functionality for data we save in files. For example, in applications such as word processors, spreadsheet applications, compression utilities, and so forth, we might want to implement a feature whereby file contents are "protected" using features inside our program. By "protected," of course, we can mean a number of different things, such as locked for any user who does not know a password, signed by the user who originally created the data, and so forth. We can also modify this utility for a number of other purposes, such as to protect data in store-and-forward applications, or we can use the file as a security mechanism to ensure backups are protected. We'll describe fully how to use the framework we created in the previous example to get this functionality up and running.

11.4.1 Overview

Protecting file contents is probably the easiest way to apply cryptography to an application, which is why we're doing this example first. We'll be using the framework we created in the previous example as a prerequisite (the example on the companion CD-ROM, located in /Examples/Chapter 11/ContentProtection, is already configured to link in the framework). In addition, we'll be writing a simple command-line executable that allows us to perform these operations, and a Windows GUI that uses the same features. The command-line utility is provided as such for portability reasons with other non-Windows platforms only. In real-life applications, it would be assumed that if you were writing to a utility such as a word processor, you would call this functionality from the GUI rather than from the command line! This example illustrates, in perspective, how we would perform the following operations:

- File encryption/decryption
- File signature/verification

Password-based key derivation will be used to implement both sets of functionality and to ensure that the user's key is protected by a password that he or she knows.

11.4.2 Environment

In default configuration, the included example uses OpenSSL to perform the various operations on the data. It uses OpenSSL both on the Windows platform and on other platforms, although the GUI works only on Windows. Since we are using OpenSSL (which is highly portable), there are no immediately obvious environmental concerns we need to address prior to deployment. We just need to make sure OpenSSL compiles and runs on the platform we intend to use it on.

11.4.3 Design

The design of our example GUI is not complicated, and a word-processing or other client application that incorporates similar functionality also need not be complicated. From a high level, all we need do is call directly into the framework we created earlier and pass the data in to the appropriate operation. To illustrate this in the context of the sample, Figure 11.6 contains a UML 2.0 use-case diagram for our application. Note that we've deliberately used vague terminology for the user's actions to reinforce the notion that implementing a word processor or other software could proceed according to the same methodology.

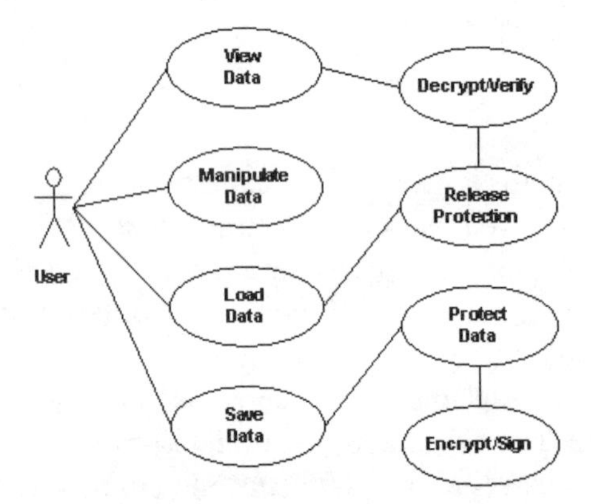

FIGURE 11.6 GUI use-case diagram.

Figure 11.7 demonstrates a UML object-interaction diagram detailing the implementation of this in software using the framework we developed in the previous example.

11.4.4 Implementation Notes

The implementation provided in this example could be further improved depending on the goals of our application. For example, we could implement a "stream"

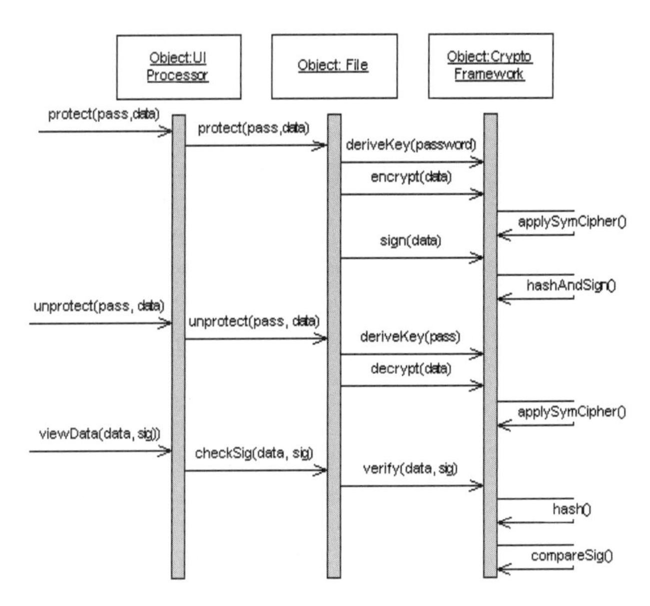

FIGURE 11.7 GUI object-interaction diagram.

concept that would prevent us from having to pass individual blocks of data to the encryption functionality and would allow us to point directly at a file instead. We could later expand this concept to handle network streams and file-based applications. We have incorporated some of this in the underlying framework, although it is not strictly necessary for this application.

11.5 THREE-TIER DATA PROTECTION (JAVA SERVLETS)

In the course of developing our applications, we will find that in the most cases, we will be developing *n* tier applications, by far the most common development being done today. This can be in the context of an enterprise application, an application service provider (ASP), Web development. Since developing this type of functionality is so common, we've included two examples of how this type of application can be written. The first is provided in Java, and the second uses Microsoft .NET technologies. In both cases, we will not be using the framework we've developed in the first example, but we will be using instead the cryptographic technologies available on each platform.

11.5.1 Overview

The application to which we wish to apply cryptography first is a three-tier system that receives data from a client application, performs minimal processing on that data, and returns a result. You can probably see how an example such as this would be apropos to almost any Web project you may be called upon to write in everyday development activities. To determine what our security requirements are, we will use the "data mapping" functionality we covered in the first few chapters of this book to determine where cryptography should be applied, and we will go ahead and add it in for the locations we determine are appropriate.

11.5.2 Environment

We will be working in Java for this example. Specifically, we are using the Tomcat application platform in combination with Java servlet technologies as our underlying platform. The Web server is IIS, and the client is a user's Web browser. Figure 11.8 contains a UML deployment diagram illustrating how these components will be deployed.

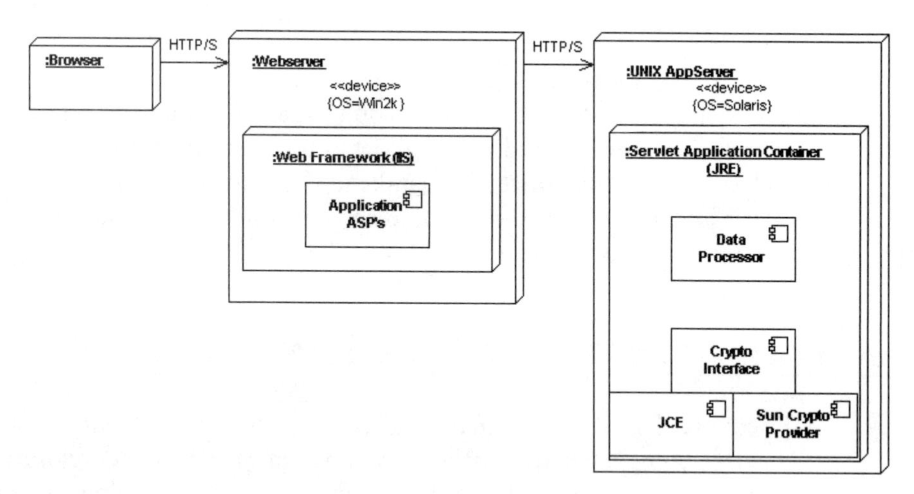

FIGURE 11.8 Three-tier deployment diagram—Java.

11.5.3 Requirements

To determine the security requirements we will need for our application, it is useful to follow the data mapping exercise we discussed early in this book. We have performed this exercise for both stored data and data in transit. Figure 11.9 represents the data map for both data at rest and transient storage; Figure 11.10 represents the map of data in transit.

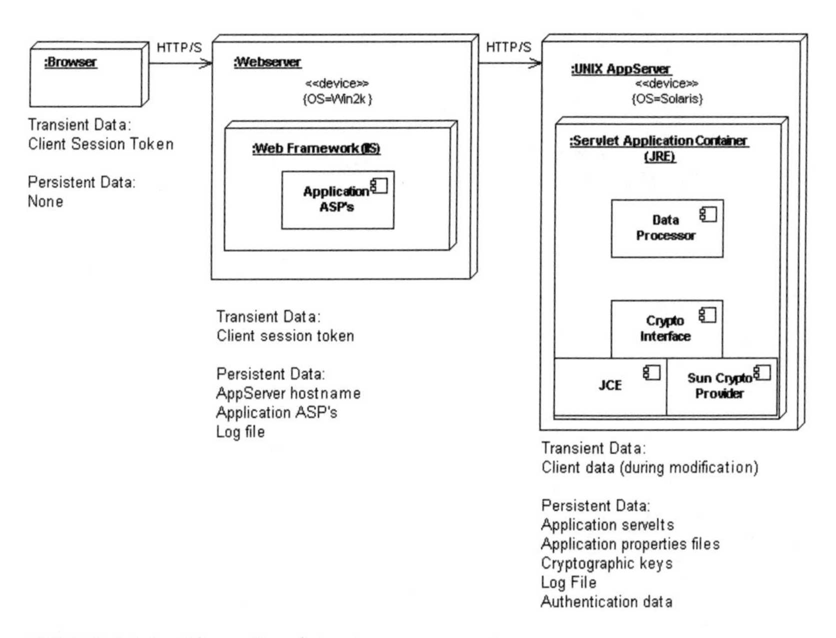

FIGURE 11.9 Three-tier data storage map—Java.

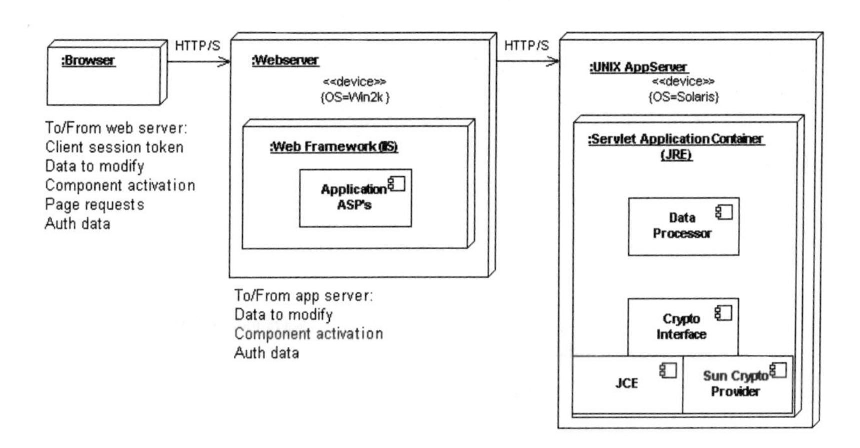

FIGURE 11.10 Three-tier data transfer map—Java.

You will note that there are quite a few security requirements we have to address. Observing these two diagrams in the context of the application business logic is helpful; Figure 11.11 contains a UML use-case diagram describing how the application operates.

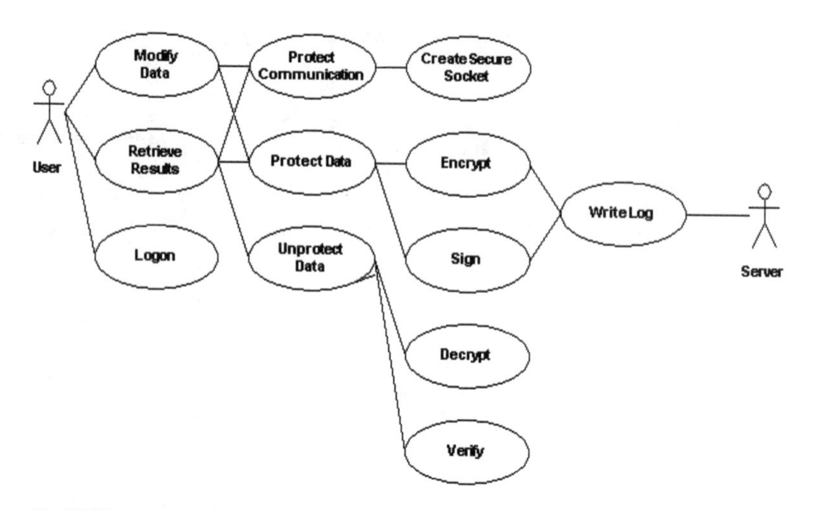

FIGURE 11.11 Three-tier use-case diagram—Java.

First and foremost, we will need to address the issue of user logon to the system. This does not have to be satisfied by functionality we write ourselves, but can be satisfied by mechanisms inherent to the application and Web server platforms. However, in this instance, we will assume the user information that is transferred requires privacy, and that the components will need to authenticate themselves to each other in some way.

11.5.4 Design

The design of this system is identical to most three-tier applications, with the following exceptions:

- We have added protection of the log file data (since user data may be stored in this file).
- We have added an application-level authentication component in between the Web and application tier. This can be done outside the application layer, but for the purposes of example, we have included it at this level.
- We have added a protection mechanism whereby we have shielded session information from the user by means of a cryptographically protected session cookie.

Note that there are some preparatory steps we will need to follow in ensuring that the various components can intercommunicate. The functionality in the context of the application design is easy to understand. To detail how this was effected, Figure 11.12 contains a UML object-interaction diagram that represents how the various components perform these functions.

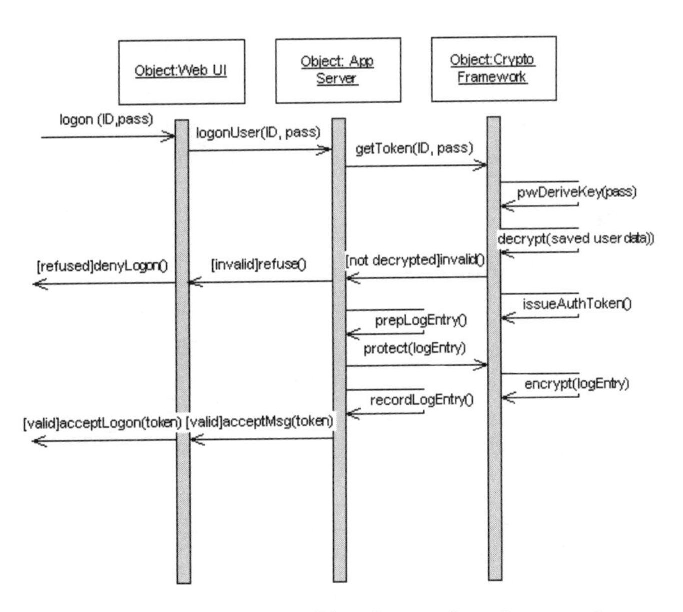

FIGURE 11.12 Three-tier object-interaction diagram—Java.

11.5.5 Implementation

All of this functionality has been implemented using the JCE. We have implemented the encryption of the log file contents using buffering in combination with a block cipher, and the intercomponent authentication scheme using digital signatures. We have implemented cryptographic protections of the session cookies using symmetric cryptography as well. Note that this application does not contain the underlying software upon which it runs.

11.6 THREE-TIER DATA PROTECTION (ASP)

The design of this application is very similar to the design of the servlet application discussed in the previous example. In this context, however, we have substituted an additional tier: a database. Again, this is a very recognizable application strategy we will almost certainly come across during our development activities.

11.6.1 Overview

This application showcases the .NET cryptographic components; we could very well have used a COM interface to use the framework we've developed earlier, but in this case, we thought it would be more instructive to use .NET classes directly.

The application itself is simple enough: we are receiving data from a client via a UI tier, and storing that data in a database. We could incorporate strategies from the previous example and build in an application tier as well, but the code in this example is complex enough without making it more so.

11.6.2 Environment

This entire application rests on Microsoft technologies: the Web server is IIS, and the database is SQL server. Our cryptographic logic is effected using a combination of scripting languages accessible from inside the context of IIS. We have not standardized on a particular language for this example. Figure 11.13 contains a UML deployment diagram, putting this application and its components in perspective of the platforms on which it will reside.

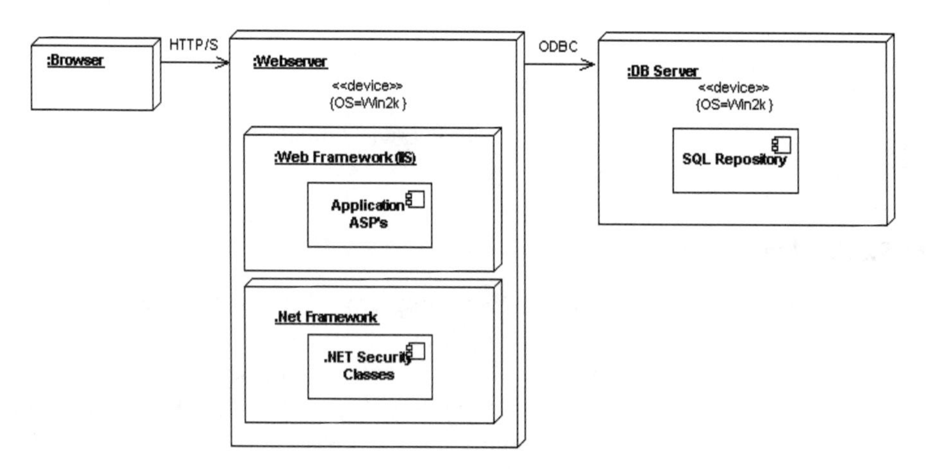

FIGURE 11.13 Three-tier deployment diagram—ASP.

11.6.3 Requirements

The functional requirements are encapsulated in Figure 11.14, which contains a UML 2.0 use-case diagram detailing the application functionality. Note that our application does very little processing of the data and almost immediately passes it back to the database tier.

To set our security requirements, we have completed the data mapping exercise just as we did with the previous example. Specifically, we have updated the deployment diagram to specify the location of sensitive information stored on the hosts according to the methodology for data mapping we covered in previous chapters. That stored data diagram is represented by Figure 11.15. The data transfer diagram is represented by Figure 11.16.

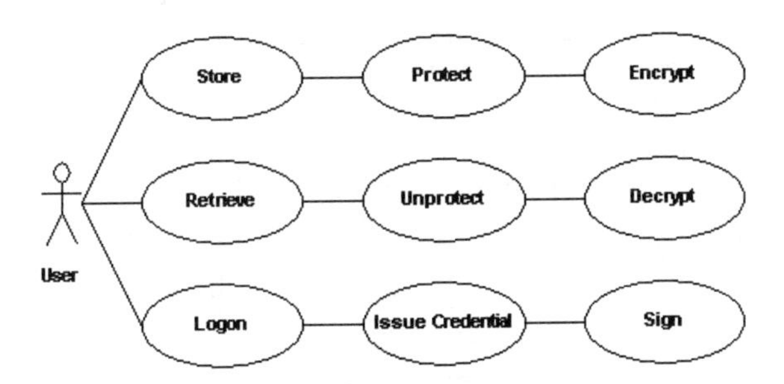

FIGURE 11.14 Three-tier use-case diagram—ASP.

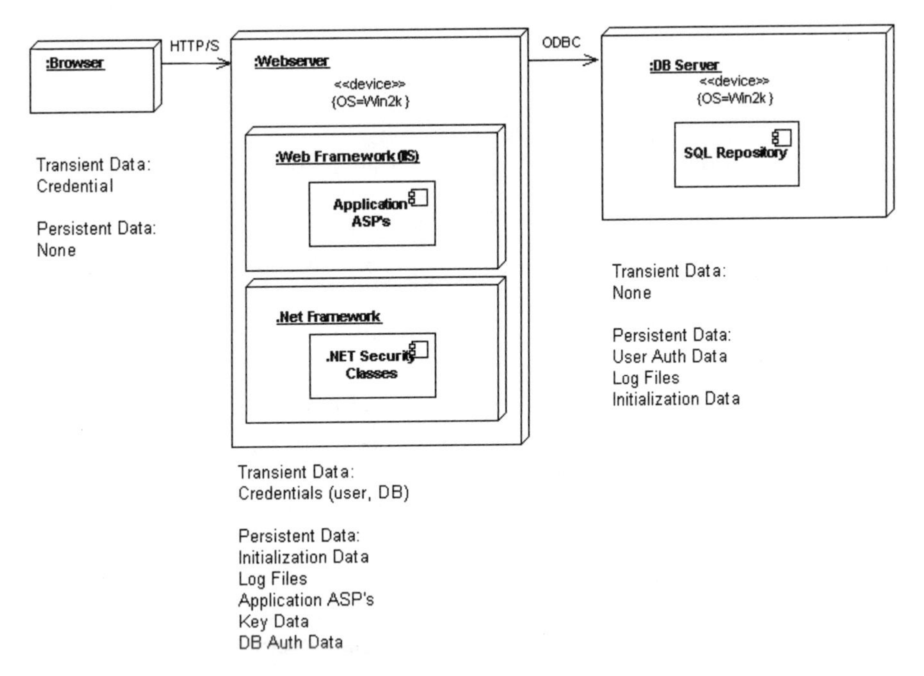

FIGURE 11.15 Three-tier data storage map—ASP.

Based on this diagram, we will want to make sure the user data is stored within the database in a manner that cannot be read or intercepted by other parties. We also want to make sure that we store database access information in a manner that does not represent a security vulnerability (e.g., we don't want it hardcoded in our application source or stored as cleartext on the filesystem). Since the database already has its own access control methodology, we can forego the intercomponent authentication measures we built in the previous example.

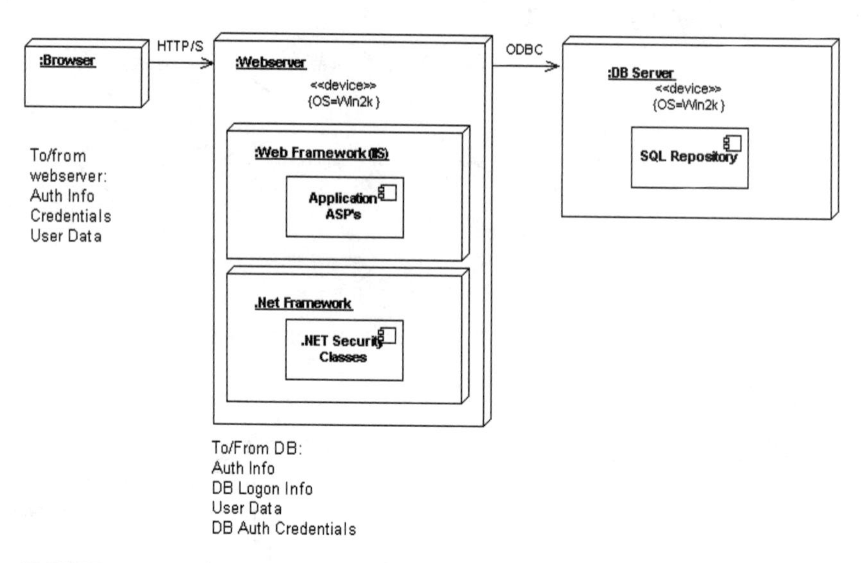

FIGURE 11.16 Three-tier data transfer map—ASP.

11.6.4 Design

We have added the following to the application based on the security requirements:

- Protection of information placed in the database via symmetric cryptography
- A secured data repository within which we will place database access information
- A protection mechanism whereby we have shielded session information from the user by means of a cryptographically protected session cookie

Note that as with the previous example, there are preparatory steps we have to take to ensure the system will be operational. For example, we have implemented a UI that will allow us to modify the information contained in the database access information. This is a requirement to ensure we can update that information later.

11.6.5 Implementation

These features are implemented using the .NET cryptography classes. The implementation uses the symmetric encryption functionality and password-based key derivation to store and retrieve the database access information. The application uses symmetric cryptography (AES) to encrypt data stored to the database and decrypt data retrieved from the database. Lastly, in keeping with the manner in the previous example, we have used symmetric cryptography to encrypt the user session cookie, only this time, we have substituted the .NET cryptographic operations for the Java operations.

About the CD-ROM

The CD-ROM included with *Cryptographic Libraries for Developers* includes the following categories of material:

Code Snippets: The snippets of example source code used throughout this book are included on this CD-ROM within their broader context.

Example Applications: Example frameworks and applications developed using the techniques, libraries, and strategies described within this book. Included as well are any and all design diagrams used in the preparation of the examples.

CD-ROM LAYOUT

To ensure cross-platform utility, the CD-ROM supports multiple methods of access to the examples materials. Specifically, the CD-ROM contains both an installer package for use on the Microsoft Windows family of operating systems, as well as a set of folders that include all of the samples. The following subsections describe the most common installation tasks.

INSTALLATION

Microsoft Windows

Prerequisites:

- Microsoft Windows NT 4.0 SP6, Microsoft Windows XP Professional or Home, or 2003 Server
- 256 MB RAM
- 20 MB Fixed Storage (required for compilation of samples)
- A compiler and/or development environment corresponding to the samples you wish to utilize. For example, Microsoft Visual Studio, Visual C++, Sun's Java 2 Platform Standard Edition (i.e. the JDK), etc.

Installation Instructions

To install the samples folders on a Windows system, double click on the installer executable located on the root directory of the included CD-ROM. When prompted, select the directory to which you wish to install the sample materials in the dialog box provided. The installer will create the appropriate directory structure and populate the folders with the sample material.

UNIX Operating System

- A POSIX-compliant operating system such as Solaris, Linux, BSD, HPUX, True-64, AIX, etc.
- 10 MB Fixed Storage (required for compilation of samples)
- A compiler and/or development environment corresponding to the samples you wish to utilize. For example, gcc/g++, Sun's Java 2 Platform Standard Edition (i.e. the JDK), etc.
- To compile C/C++ software, the "make" utility greatly increases the efficiency of the compilation process (optional)

Installation Instructions

To install the samples folders on a UNIX system, launch the installation script (installer.sh) located in the CD-ROM root directory. The install script will prompt for a location to install to, or the installer may optionally be run with a command line argument specifying the full path of the desired directory for installation (if this directory does not exist it will be created for you.)

Installation: Other OS

Should you wish to use another operating system other than those described in the previous sections, the "examples" folder off the root of the companion CD-ROM contains all the samples as well. Note that an installer executable or installer script is not provided in this case; however, the examples should be readable on these other platforms as well.

Glossary

Abstract Syntax Notation One (ASN.1): A methodology for representing self-describing logical structures.

access control: The process of ensuring that users have access only to functionality and/or data for which they have been approved and authorized.

Advanced Encryption Standard (AES): A symmetric block cipher chosen by the National Institute of Standards and Technology for the replacement of the *Data Encryption Standard (DES)* standard, which was demonstrated in recent years to be insufficient for the robust protection of data

asymmetric encryption: An encryption methodology that uses one *key* to *encrypt* data, and a different but related *key* to *decrypt* data.

attack vector: The vehicle by which *a threat agent* causes a *threat* to be realized.

authentication factor: One of three high-level categories of authentication vehicles: "what you have," "what you know," and "what you are."

authentication vehicle: A method such as password, PIN, dongle, etc. used to perform *authentication.*

authentication: The process of validating that users are who they claim to be.

authorization: The process of ensuring that users are who they claim to be, and enforcing that users access only the functionality and data for which they are approved.

availability: A property of data whereby the data is accessible to authorized parties.

Basic Encoding Rules (BER): A mechanism whereby *abstract syntax notation one* logical structures are represented concretely.

block ciphers: Encryption algorithms that operate on fixed-length "chunks" of data of a specific size.

brute force: The process of trying every possible key in an attempt to *decrypt* data without knowing the key.

CA SB-1386: Privacy regulation in the state of California requiring notification to users in the event of potential unauthorized access to information.

Certificate Authority (CA): A *trusted third party* responsible for issuing and revoking *public key certificates.*

certificate policy: The set of rules governing how a *Certificate Authority* will operate.

certificate revocation list (CRL): A list of *certificates* published by a *Certificate Authority* listing those *certificates* that have been invalidated.

certificate signing request (CSR): A formalized structure sent to a *Certificate Authority* to request issuance of a *certificate.*

certificate: An artifact used to formalize a *trusted third-party* model of *key distribution* whereby an *entity's public key* is placed in a formalized structure and **signed** by a *Certificate Authority.*

cipher block chaining (CBC) mode: A *block cipher mode of operation*, whereby each block of *ciphertext* is chained to the next block.

Cipher Feedback Mode (CFB): A block cipher mode of operation in which XOR is used to link ciphertext blocks; this method will allow units smaller than one block to be encrypted by the block cipher.

ciphertext: Data that has been *encrypted* by an *encryption algorithm.*

common name: One portion of an X.500 *distinguished name.* In some protocols such as SSL, the *common name* value may have particular significance.

confidentiality: A property of data whereby the data remains undivulged to unauthorized parties.

Counter Mode (CTR): A block cipher mode of operation whereby a counter is used to generate a keystream; this allows the encryption of data units smaller than the cipher block size.

countermeasures: Controls introduced to mitigate *threats.*

credential: An artifact issued subsequent to successful *authentication* validating that the user is who he or she claims to be.

cryptanalysis: The science of breaking *encryption.*

Cryptographic Service Provider (CSP): In Microsoft parlance, a library or set of libraries that implement cryptographic functionality in a manner usable by CAPI.

data at rest: Data that is stored by an application between sessions; data of a persistent rather than *transient* nature.

Data Encryption Standard (DES): A symmetric block cipher that was approved by the National Institute of Standards and Technology (NIST) as the standard for the encryption of data.

data in transit: Data communicated between two components or between two systems at the point in time when communication is underway.

decryption (decipherment): The process of transforming encrypted *ciphertext* into readable *plaintext* by using a *key* in combination with the decryption mode of an *encryption algorithm.*

denial of service: A category of attack whereby legitimate processing is unable to be conducted; particularly, attacks in which an application is unable to operate normally due to flooded transaction volume or deliberately induced malfunction.

DES weak keys: One of several few known keys that, when used with the DES algorithm, produce insecure encrypted values.

Digital Signature Algorithm (DSA): The asymmetric cryptographic algorithm approved by NIST as the standard for generation of digital signatures in *FIPS 186-2.*

Digital Signature Standard (DSS): The standard NIST-approved methodology for the creation of digital signatures; DSS specifies the use of *SHA-1, SHA-256, SHA-384,* and *SHA-512* for message digests in combination with the *Digital Signature Algorithm* (DSA) for signing.

digital signature: Creation of a cryptographic artifact that binds a message with the message originator.

Distinguished Encoding Rules (DER): A mechanism whereby *abstract syntax notation one* logical structures are represented concretely.

distinguished name: In X.500 parlance, the unique name assigned to an entity within a population.

eavesdropping: Gaining access to unauthorized data or messages via *interception* or monitoring.

electronic code book (ecb) mode: A *block cipher mode of operation* whereby each block of input text maps to exactly one unique block of output text.

Encrypted File System (EFS): A feature provided in recent versions of Microsoft Windows allowing for encrypted file storage.

encryption (encipherment): The process of transforming *plaintext* into unreadable *ciphertext* by using a *key* in combination with an *encryption algorithm.*

encryption algorithm (cipher): An algorithm that, in combination with a key, *encrypts* or *decrypts* data.

encumbered algorithms: Algorithms covered by patent.

entitlements: The collection of functionality and/or data for which a user has been *authorized.*

export grade cryptography: The deliberate use of reduced key values to satisfy U.S. cryptographic export restrictions under ITAR.

Extensible Access Control Markup Language (XACML): An OASIS standard allowing for the exchange of access control related information (such as entitlement information) between entities.

Federal Information Processing Standard (FIPS) 140-2: A standard used to certify cryptographic modules according to one of four levels of security.

Federal Information Processing Standard (FIPS) 186-2: The standards document outlining the *Digital Signature Standard* (DSS).

Federal Information Processing Standard (FIPS) 197: The standards document outlining the *Advanced Encryption Standard* (AES).

feedback register: A buffer used by *block cipher modes of operation* that require the maintenance of state from previous *encryption* or *decryption* operations.

forgery: The creation of a counterfeit ("spoofed") application artifact, particularly authentication credentials or application command messages.

Hardware Security Module (HSM): A device used to provide additional security for cryptographic operations.

hash function: A function that computes a hash within a data set.

hashing: Derivation of a representative hash ("index") value from a larger value or set of values.

impersonation: Fraudulently attempting to assume the identity of a user, process, system, or component.

Initialization Vector (IV): A value used to populate the *feedback register* in *block cipher modes of operation* that require state.

integrity: A property of data whereby it cannot be unknowingly modified or tampered with in an unauthorized manner.

interception: Eavesdropping between two communicating parties, particularly with the intent to modify messages exchanged between communicants.

key distribution: Ensuring that *keys* can be shared appropriately between parties.

key management: The logistical considerations involved in ensuring appropriate key handling procedures throughout the key lifecycle such as issuance, storage, expiration, etc.

key: A digital artifact that is used in combination with an *encryption algorithm* to *encrypt* or *decrypt* data.

keystream: A flow of bits combined with *plaintext* to produce *ciphertext* by drawing on the internal state of a *stream cipher*.

MD5: A commonly occurring message digest algorithm.

message digest: A collision-resistant (near-) unique value created as a result of *hashing* the data set that is every possible combination of characters.

mode of operation: One of a number of ways in which a *block cipher* may operate on input data. Examples are *CBC* (*Cipher Block Chaining*) and *ECB* (*Electronic Code Book*) modes.

Online Certificate Status Protocol (OCSP): A standard describing a method for querying *certificate* revocation status information from a *Certificate Authority.*

Output Feedback Mode (OFB): A block cipher mode of operation whereby blocks of ciphertext are obfuscated using XOR; this methodology allows for encryption of data smaller than the block size.

padding: A methodology used to encrypt data that does not fall cleanly along a cipher's block size boundary; in other words, data that is not a multiple of the block size.

password-based key derivation: The process of obtaining a robust cryptographic *key* from a password.

perfect hashing algorithm: A *hash function* that maps every possible input within a data set to a unique output index value.

PKCS5 padding: The most common symmetric block cipher padding methodology whereby padding is always present and the padding value is the number of padding bytes expressed as an 8-bit quantity.

plaintext: Data to which no cryptography has been applied.

Pretty Good Privacy (PGP): A suite of utilities providing (among other things) file encryption capability.

primitives: Atomic units of functionality upon which more complicated functionality can be built.

private key: One-half of a mathematically related *key pair* used in *asymmetric cryptography*; used for *decrypting* data or creating *digital signatures.* In most *public key cryptosystems*, the key owner keeps this value secret.

proof of possession: The process of ensuring that an artifact's originator has access to a private key known by the recipient.

Pseudo-Random Number Generator (PRNG): An algorithm used for the creation of semirandom ("unguessable") data; used in generating cryptographic keys.

public exponent: Sometimes called the *e* value, this is a prime number that is used as part of an RSA public key.

Public Key Cryptography Standards (PKCS): A set of documents describing low-level implementation details for implementers of *public key cryptosystems.*

public key cryptosystems: Implementations of *asymmetric cryptography*, including any underlying support infrastructure required to assist *key management* and *key distribution.*

Public Key Infrastructure (PKI): A formalized model of *key distribution* within a *public key cryptosystem.*

public key: One-half of a mathematically related *key pair* used in *asymmetric cryptography*; used for *encrypting* data or validating *digital signatures*. In most *public key cryptosystems*, this value is shared with others besides the key owner.

random seed: A (usually) small value required to initialize a *Pseudo-Random Number Generator* (PRNG) to a state indeterminable by an attacker or outside party.

RC4: A commonly occurring stream cipher invented and trademarked by RSA.

replay: Verbatim or near-verbatim reduplication of messages exchanged between communicants, particularly for the purposes of producing unexpected or undesired results (such as using a verbatim credential to log on to an application).

RSA Algorithm: An asymmetric encryption algorithm commonly used in public key cryptography. RSA has the property that it provides data confidentiality as well as digital signature.

Secure Copy (SCP): A mechanism for exchanging files securely; usage is similar to the `rcp` command.

Secure File Transfer Protocol (SFTP): A mechanism for exchanging files securely; usage is similar to the `ftp` command.

Secure Hash Algorithm (SHA-1, SHA-256, SHA-384, SHA-512): Message digest algorithms approved by NIST for use in the *Digital Signature Standard* (DSS).

Secure Shell (SSH): A common Unix secure remote shell utility and the associated protocol it uses.

Secure Sockets Layer (SSL): A standard protocol used to conduct secure communication over TCP.

Security Association Markup Language (SAML): An OASIS standard allowing for the exchange of authorization data between entities: most notably, authentication data and credentials.

server gated cryptography: Technology used by financial institutions to cause an *export grade* browser to use strong cryptography.

stream cipher: A *symmetric encryption algorithm* that operates on individual bits rather than on fixed-length blocks.

symmetric encryption: An *encryption* methodology whereby the same *key* is used to *encrypt* and *decrypt* data.

tamper evident: Built in such a manner as to detect unauthorized modification.

tamperproof: Built in such a manner as to prevent unauthorized modification.

target: The application, system, or network potentially impacted by a *threat*.

threat agent: A method or entity responsible for moving a *threat* from a potential event to actuality.

threat model: A formalized assessment of the threat potential in an application, system, or network.

threat: An event or condition that impacts the proper and reliable functioning of our application and/or that impedes the ability of authorized users to use our application.

transient storage: Caching or session-based data that is not stored persistently by an application.

Triple-DES (3DES): The use of *DES* in such a fashion that the same data is encrypted multiple times; this was used prior to the standardization of *AES* as a workaround for the unsuitability of *DES* as a secure block cipher.

trusted third party: An entity responsible for ensuring *key distribution* in a safe and reliable manner.

X.509 Digital Certificate: A *certificate* created according to ITU's X.509 standard.

Index

E

L

M